What Readers Are Saying About *Jython for Java*™ *Programmers:*

"This book is a straightforward and accessible approach to learning the Jython language and using it in your Java applications. The examples provided are easy to follow and illustrate everything you need to know to effectively use Jython."
—Kevin Dangoor, *Assistant Director of Development, Web Elite*

"Every programmer who seriously wants to use Jython will want/need this book because it brings together information not collected together anywhere else."
—Jeff Stearns, *Chief Architect, Savage Beast Technologies*

"This book is a must for anybody who wants a complete tutorial to Jython."
—Arno Schmidmeier, *Chief Scientist, Sirius Software GmbH*

"As a developer who uses Java on a variety of contracts, I'm extremely excited about Jython, as it has the potential to be very helpful in most aspects of my work. As the first book about the topic, this one is sure to be a success. Not only would I recommend it to others, I'll probably force it into their hands."
—Andrew Boyko, *Software Engineer/Architect, Fab Gear Interactive, Inc.*

"I would recommend this book to any new Jython developer as required material. It provides information that is either not available elsewhere or that is difficult to find. Many topics are covered and many questions answered that save Jython developers valuable time. The book is also valuable as a reference for experienced Jython developers, as it covers some difficult material without requiring you to dig the answers out of the source code or Jython user mailing lists."
—David Dunkle, *Director of Infrastructure, ePropose Inc.*

"This book is approachable by both beginner to intermediate level programmers as well as advanced programmers. Not only that, but it seems to be approachable by both Java and Python programmers."
—Anthony Eden, *CTO, Signature Domains, Inc.*

i

Jython for Java™ Programmers

Contents at a Glance

Jython for Java™ Programmers

Robert W. Bill

New Riders

www.newriders.com

201 West 103rd Street, Indianapolis, Indiana 46290
An Imprint of Pearson Education
Boston • Indianapolis • London • Munich • New York • San Francisco

Jython for Java™ Programmers

International Standard Book Number: 0-7357-1111-9

Library of Congress Catalog Card Number: 00-111656

06 05 04 03 02   7 6 5 4 3 2 1

Interpretation of the printing code: The rightmost double-digit number is the year of the book's printing; the right-most single-digit number is the number of the book's printing. For example, the printing code 02-1 shows that the first printing of the book occurred in 2002.

Composed in Quark and MCPdigital by New Riders Publishing.

Printed in the United States of America.

Trademarks

Warning and Disclaimer

Publisher
David Dwyer

Associate Publisher
Stephanie Wall

Production Manager
Gina Kanouse

Managing Editor
Kristy Knoop

Senior Development Editor
Lisa M. Thibault

Project Editor
Todd Zellers

Product Marketing Manager
Stephanie Layton

Publicity Manager
Susan Nixon

Copy Editor
Daryl Kessler

Indexer
Chris Morris

Manufacturing Coordinator
Jim Conway

Book Designer
Louisa Klucznik

Cover Designer
Brainstorm Design, Inc.

Cover Production
Aren Howell

Proofreader
Katherine Shull

Composition
Jeff Bredensteiner
Amy Parker

To my wife

Table of Contents

About the Author

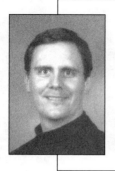

Robert W. Bill currently dedicates his time to software design and development in Python, Jython, and Java as an independent contractor. His experiences include a four-year tenure with the Minnesota Educational Computing Consortium, The Learning Company, and Mattel. Robert has studied at Baylor University, followed by various courses in music and sciences at the Eastman School of Music and the University of Wisconsin-Madison.

About the Technical Reviewers

These reviewers contributed their considerable hands-on expertise to the entire development process for *Jython for Java Programmers*. As the book was being written, these dedicated professionals reviewed all the material for technical content, organization, and flow. Their feedback was critical to ensuring that *Jython for Java Programmers* fits our reader's need for the highest quality technical information.

As member of the research staff at the California Institute of Technology, **Dr. Robert Brunner** focuses on Knowledge Discovery and Data-Mining in very large, heavily distributed databases. He also has been a Java and XML instructor at the Center for Advanced Computing Technology operated by the California State Polytechnic University at Pomona for the last two years. Recently, he has written a series for *Java Developers Journal,* reviewed numerous proposals for a variety of publishing houses, and has edited texts covering Linux, C++, Java, and XML. He is currently completing *Enterprise Java Database Programming* to be published by Addison Wesley, Inc.

John Ha is a support engineer and technical writer at NeTraverse, a software development firm in Morrisville, North Carolina. John is responsible for printed and online documentation for the firm's flagship product, Win4Lin. Win4Lin allows Microsoft Windows to be installed on a host Linux system. John also investigates distributed filesystem and remote display technologies for NeTraverse's server product currently under development. John earned his Bachelor of Arts degree in English Literature from the University of Connecticut in Storrs, Connecticut.

Acknowledgments

Those who work to refine and support Jython prove themselves invaluable day after day. Most notable is Finn Bock, the Jython project leader. His work currently propels Jython's rapid advance. Other valuable contributors to Jython and its online community who have helped me in one way or another include Samuele Pedroni, Brian Zimmer, Barry Warsaw, and many others.

Tell Us What You Think

As the reader of this book, you are the most important critic and commentator. We value your opinion and want to know what we're doing right, what we could do better, what areas you'd like to see us publish in, and any other words of wisdom you're willing to pass our way.

As the Associate Publisher for New Riders Publishing, I welcome your comments. You can fax, email, or write me directly to let me know what you did or didn't like about this book—as well as what we can do to make our books stronger.

Please note that I cannot help you with technical problems related to the topic of this book, and that due to the high volume of mail I receive, I might not be able to reply to every message.

When you write, please be sure to include this book's title and author as well as your name and phone or fax number. I will carefully review your comments and share them with the author and editors who worked on the book.

Fax: 317-581-4663
Email: nrfeedback@newriders.com
Mail: Stephanie Wall
            Associate Publisher
            New Riders Publishing
            201 West 103rd Street
            Indianapolis, IN 46290 USA

Introduction

Jython is the combination of two programming languages—Java and Python—that have achieved tremendous popularity separately. Java has tremendous acceptance, as evidenced by the number of organizations that deploy Java-specific applications. Additionally, Java has a huge library of classes to draw from and excellent documentation. However, Python provides such flexibility, speedy development, and a sense of ease. Choosing between two such languages would be difficult but, fortunately, is unnecessary thanks to Jython. With Jython, you may implement any class, algorithm, and pattern in Java or Python without regard for the other language, yet maintain near-seamless operation between the two languages.

The word *seamless* is of special significance and recurs throughout this book. Extending other languages, like Perl or Python, requires the use of a specific API, or annoying wrapper classes. Arbitrary C code will not work in Perl or Python without additional effort, but arbitrary Java code will work in Jython. Because of the seamless integration with Java, you can import, use, and even subclass any Java class in Jython. Not just those classes written to follow a specific API, or those wrapped with special tools, but any Java class. Furthermore, you can compile Jython into Java byte-code that runs in Java frameworks. You can even import, use, and subclass Python classes from within Java.

Any minor seams that do exist are required to negotiate the differences between Jython and Java, and understanding such differences helps in understanding Jython. Java is a type-rich language with static typing, whereas Jython uses dynamic types without explicit type declarations. Java has packages that contain classes, while Jython has packages, modules, classes, and functions. Java must be compiled, but Jython can run interactively, interpret an uncompiled script, or be compiled to byte-code. Java classes implement access modifiers such as `private` and `protected`; Jython has only minimal access restrictions and no explicit modifiers like `private`.

The interesting thing about the differences between Java and Jython is that rather than creating difficulties, these languages make for ideal complements. Jython's interactive mode is a quick way to test and explore Java classes, whereas Java's interfaces and abstract classes are a great way to specify protocols for Jython subclasses. Jython's dynamic typing helps in rapid prototyping and flexibility, while Java's static typing allows for increased runtime efficiency and type safety. This complement excels because it is seamless. Adding programming overhead to leverage each of these features would negate their power; fortunately, Jython makes leveraging them intuitive, easy, and free from detracting overhead.

What Is Jython?

Defining Jython begs the question "What is Python?" *Python* is a high-level, object-oriented, open-source programming language implemented in C. Guido Van Rossum was the original developer of Python and continues to guide a hoard of leading designers and programmers in Python's rapid evolution. The number of developers using Python has grown rapidly, and continues to do so. However, the advance of Sun's Java programming language is equally pervasive in the programming landscape. With the number of projects implemented in Java approaching those in C/C++, there became a need for a Java implementation of Python. *Jython*, originally called *JPython*, is just that: the Java implementation of the Python programming language. To eliminate confusion, this book uses *CPython* to signify the C implementation of Python, *Jython* to signify the Java implementation, and *Python* to represent the implementation neutral concepts and design features of the Python language specification.

Jython is a complete programming language—not a Java translator and not just a Python compiler, but a complete implementation of Python in Java. You can write complete complex applications with Jython itself. Jython also has a sizable library of modules inherited from CPython. The interesting thing is that Jython, unlike CPython and many other high-level languages, gives you access to everything it its implementation language, Java. So not only does Jython give you the Python libraries, it also gives you all available Java classes. This makes for a truly large library of resources.

Jython, and Python, emphasizes code clarity, simplicity, and legibility. Jython uses indentation to delimit code blocks to avoid the braces found in Java. Jython uses a newline to denote the beginning of a new statement, with a few important exceptions, allowing for the elimination of a semicolon at the end of each statement. Jython foregoes attribute access modifiers such as Java's `public`, `private`, and `protected`, giving the programmer the flexibility required for rapid development and to focus on program logic. And as mentioned earlier, Jython does not use explicit static typing, so there are no type declarations to distract from program logic.

Jython's history begins with Jim Hugunin, a colleague of Guido Van Rossum at the Center for National Research Incentives (CNRI), who recognized the need for a Java implementation of the Python programming language and implemented it under the original name JPython. Eventually, Jim Hugunin was unable to continue working on JPython because of an opportunity to develop aspectj (`http://aspectj.org/`). Therefore, Barry Warsaw, also at CNRI at that time, continued as the project leader during a time when Python developers were preparing to move away from CNRI.

The move away from CNRI was a transition toward the more open development model at Sourceforge where the Python and Jython projects currently reside. During this time, Finn Bock, a major contributor to Jython (JPython), took the reins of the Jython project. It is in a very large part due to Finn Bock's extremely prolific and quality additions to Jython that it has become such a valuable tool. Open-source projects like Jython excel only as much as those that develop and maintain them, and

Jython has proven to be most fortunate in this regard because of Finn Bock's contributions and guidance. Another more recent and valuable contributor to Jython is Samuele Pedroni. Recent advancements in Jython's classloading, import mechanisms, and more is thanks to Samuele's contributions. Finn and Samuele are currently the two primary developers of Jython.

Why Jython?

Jython is unique in that it inherits the desirable traits of both Java and Python. The sections that follow describe each of the traits and their benefits.

Seamless Access to Java Classes

Implementing Python in Java makes for an interesting look at the usefulness of Java's Reflection API. Reflection allows Jython to seamlessly use most any Java class. Jython inherits a number of advantages from CPython, but CPython has a bump between C and Python that restricts the usefulness of C libraries other than those specifically written for Python. Eliminating this bump in Jython truly has an impact of productivity and effectiveness.

Because of the seamless fit with Java, Jython can benefit any organization that deploys Java applications and frameworks without any additional work. Adopting another development language is a monumental and weighty decision for most organizations because of the implications for frameworks, servers, and peripheral tools. Jython, however, seamlessly masquerades as Java, making it but a seamless addition to an existing Java repertoire rather than a weighty decision. This is not the case for other high-level languages. A vast number of organizations have towering investments in Java that reduce the benefit, or at least the appeal, of CPython, Perl, Ruby, PHP, and other high-level languages that do not transparently leverage existing Java implementations. Jython, on the other hand, is a powerful complement to existing Java frameworks that blends in transparently.

Efficiency

A fair calculation of efficiency is a broad topic that must account for programmer time, total complexity, lines of code, reusability, maintainability, and runtime efficiency. Of course, many people disagree on the weight assigned to these variables, and more often than not the situation at hand dictates which is favored in the calculation; however, it is the premise of this book that Jython exceeds other languages in all areas but runtime efficiency. Jython's runtime speed compares well with other high-level languages, but speed is never the goal or advantage of a high-level language. The difference, however, is that when accelerating an application is required it is easier to translate Jython code into Java because of Jython's seamless integration with Java. Additionally, the direct access to all available Java classes increases the likelihood of leveraging existing classes.

Dynamic Types

You do not declare types in Jython as you would in Java because types are determined at runtime. Jython's list and mapping types are high-level, polymorphic objects that are instances of Java classes. *Polymorphic* means that an object works for differing types of data. Jython's `list` type, for example, can be a sequence of numbers, strings, characters, or a combination of types. Dynamic and polymorphic types are a dramatic contribution to programmer efficiency, reduced lines of code, and reduced complexity, as evidenced in numerous high-level languages that forgo explicit, static, and primitive types.

Introspection and Dynamic Execution

Jython has built-in functions that allow easy object introspections and dynamic execution of code. *Introspection* is the ability to discover information about an object, while *dynamic* execution is the ability to execute code that is generated at runtime. This functionality dramatically reduces lines of code and programmer efficiency while easing maintainability. This also allows a close integration of data and program structure or logic without affecting reusability because everything is determined at runtime.

First-Class Functions and Functional Programming

Jython, as does Python, has first-class functions. A *first-class function* is a callable object that can be passed around like any variable. First-class functions are valuable to event handling and many other situations, leading to Java's addition of inner classes. Although Java's inner classes are similar to first-class functions, they do not compare with the ease and flexibility of using Jython's first-class functions because of the reduced syntax overhead in Jython.

Jython also includes all the tools required for functional programming. This means that imperative, object-oriented, and functional programming approaches are supported in Jython. This is obviously an educational advantage, but it also allows a Jython programmer to choose the paradigm most appropriate to the situation rather than that imposed by the language. Functional tools such as list comprehension, lambda forms, `map`, `filter`, and `reduce`, also can have a dramatic affect on reducing lines of code, complexity, and the number of name rebindings (*name rebindings* increase risk of negative side effects, such as bugs).

Short Learning Curve

Any Java programmer can become proficient in Jython within days. As with many things, the art is in the details, but the ability to leverage the rapid development capabilities of Jython within only a few days is valuable. The ability to easily acquire Jython facility in testing and support groups that would not normally have time to study complex Java code can raise an organization's technical level and efficiency without incurring high training overhead.

Write Once, Run Anywhere

Because Jython is written in Java, and because it compiles into Java byte-code, Jython also benefits from Java's "write once, run anywhere" approach. Jython runs on any platform with a compliant Java 1.1 or greater Java Virtual Manager (JVM). Additionally, you can fully compile Jython applications into byte-code that is fully self-sufficient, and can run on any complaint JVM. Applications compiled on Linux will run on any other platform with a compliant JVM.

Java Security

Java's security is exceptional, and increasingly important. From sandbox to signatures, Jython has the potential to use Java's truly exceptional security framework.

Code Clarity

Code clarity is the Holy Grail of Python, and of course Jython. Unnecessary punctuation and line noise is avoided. Jython code should approach natural language in legibility and clarity. This begins with Python's commitment to whitespace delineation of code blocks and statements. Indentation marks code blocks and new lines mark new statements. Beyond that, the syntax is always chosen to favor clarity. Maintaining Jython code is easier because it is more clear.

Unicode and Internationalization

Jython uses Java's unicode implementation, allowing for easy implementation of international products.

Hotspot and Development Efficiency

Jython's speed is reasonable, but not as fast as pure Java. The major advantages to Jython are in development and maintenance time; however, multi-level language development has strong precedence, most notable in Java's Hotspot technology. Hotspot optimizes those sections of a program that are in most need of optimization. The theory is that only a small portion of a program incurs a large portion of its execution time. Only optimizing those portions of code that have a large effect on performance makes the most sense. Doing the same when developing the code is equally sensible. Using Jython to write an application and then converting processor-intensive classes to Java is the ideal combination of runtime performance and programmer efficiency. The Hotspot analogy makes multi-level language development with Jython and Java a convincing development model.

What You Can Expect from This Book

This book is designed for those who know Java or are learning Java. The Java-specific meaning of terms such as *classpath*, *garbage collection*, and *interface* appear without explanation, but no more than rudimentary Java knowledge is required. Specifically, Java developers desiring accelerated development, embedded interpreters, and increased flexibility will most appreciate this book. Although Jython is a complete programming language, it is unique in its ability to complement Java development rather than appear as an alternative to Java.

Chapter 1, "Jython Syntax, Statements, and Comments," introduces syntax and statements. Python's syntax is an essential part of what constitutes the coined word *pythonic*, an important descriptor of those details that make Python and Jython code clear, simple, and distinct. Python's use of indentation to delimit code blocks and newlines to delimit statements is new to most programmers, and Chapter 1 details the rules that apply to indentation, newlines, and statements. Additionally, Chapter 1 introduces the interactive interpreter, a Jython mode that immediately evaluates statements as you enter them. This chapter applies to Python in general with no references to material unique to Jython.

Chapter 2, "Operators, Types, and Built-In Functions," covers Jython's data object, operators, and built-in functions. Data objects, or types, are especially interesting because of Jython's ability to use both Python and Java objects. The Python language specification defines Python's, and therefore Jython's types, but types are where Jython-specific details emerge. One such detail is the conversion between Jython and Java types. Chapter 2 also defines Jython's built-in functions, which are those functions that are available without any import statements and that account for a sizable portion of Jython's functionality.

Jython's errors, exceptions, and warnings appear in Chapter 3, "Errors and Exceptions." Chapter 3 contains the definitions of Jython's built-in exceptions as well as a detailed look at the `try/except` and `try/finally` statements used to handle exceptions. Working with exceptions is of course important to Jython, but it is also an important step to working with Java classes and the exceptions they may raise.

Java does not have functions, but they are an important part of Jython. Chapter 4, "User-Defined Functions and Variable Scoping," shows how to define and use Jython functions and how to use Jython's functional programming tools. Functions are callable objects not defined within a class, but functional programming has a less succinct definition. Functional programming revolves around finding the results of an expression. Jython supplies all the tools required to learn and use functional programming, and these tools appear in Chapter 2.

Jython has modules, another unit that Java does not have, and Chapter 5, "Modules and Packages," describes Jython's modules. Jython also has packages, as does Java, but Jython packages differ from the Java counterpart as Chapter 5 explains. With Jython packages, modules, and classes as well as Java packages and classes, the details of the `import` statement quickly become important. Chapter 5 clarifies the `import` statement along with modules and packages.

Chapter 6, "Classes, Instances, and Inheritance," introduces the definition and use of Jython classes. This includes the subclassing of Java classes, the use of Java interfaces and Java abstract classes, and the implications of Java's access modifiers such as `public`, `private`, and `protected`. Jython classes do differ from Java classes, however, and Chapter 6 clarifies these differences.

Chapter 7, "Advanced Classes," extends the information on Jython classes to include Jython's special class attributes. Special attributes in Jython are those that follow a special naming convention and provide specific functionality. These special attributes let you customize a class's behavior and makes creating advanced classes relatively easy.

Chapter 8, "Compiling Jython with `jythonc`," details Jython's complicated `jythonc` tool. `jythonc` compiles Jython code to Java byte-code. `jythonc` lets you use classes written in Jython within Java frameworks, and even lets you create class files that you can import and use from within Java.

Chapter 9, "Embedding and Extending Jython in Java," describes how to embed a Jython interpreter. Compiling Jython to Java byte-code is extremely useful, but embedding a Jython interpreter within Java applications has many advantages. Embedding gives you total control over Jython's system state and allows you to use all of Jython's features and modules within a Java application. The amazing part is how simple it is to embed a Jython interpreter. A basic embedded interpreter requires only two lines of Java code, and adding additional configuration to an embedded interpreter is equally easy. An embedded interpreter allows you to write Jython modules to extend or implement features of Java applications without having to compile modules with `jythonc`. It is my impression that embedding Jython is the foremost advantage of Jython. It allows multi-level language development, leverages all that is good in Java and Python within a single application, and allows rapid development and extensibility. There is already a number of projects that embed Jython, and the trend to do so will likely continue.

Chapter 10, "GUI Development," describes how to develop graphical applications with Jython. The focus is on Java's Abstract Windowing Toolkit (AWT) and Swing application programmer's interface. Jython allows rapid development of graphical applications because of its addition of automatic bean properties and events. Chapter 10 covers the details of automatic bean properties and events, but the basic idea is that Jython automatically searches a component for these features and adds shortcuts to establishing properties and event handlers. The shortcuts leverage Jython syntax features to simplify and accelerate development. Chapter 10 also includes information on creating Java applets with Jython.

Java has become very prominent in database programming, and Jython is able to leverage all of Java's success in this area while adding its own advantages. Chapter 11, "Database Programming," introduces the use of Jython in database programming. Chapter 11 includes information on hashed database files as well as the MySQL and PostgreSQL relation database management systems (object-relation for PostgreSQL). Jython also has the advantage of being able to use Java's JDBC database connectivity or the Python database application programmer's interface implemented with zxJDBC. Chapter 11 discusses both of these APIs.

Chapter 12, "Server-Side Web Programming," describes web programming with Jython. For Jython, this means servlets, Java Server Pages (JSP), and taglibs. In other words, server-side web development with Jython coincides with the popular (standard) Java web development paradigm. Chapter 12 addresses using jythonc-compiled classes as servlets as well as an embedded Jython Servlet mapping and IBM's bean scripting framework (BSF).

Who This Book Is For

This book best fits those programmers already familiar with Java but who are interested Jython. This creates a wide range of potential readers, and further clarification follows to help narrow the field. Java programmers wishing to add a high-level language as a tool in their existing arsenal is the primary audience, but is equally applicable to those seeking an alternative to Java, yet bound to an organization dedicated to Java-based technology. A secondary audience is those beginning Python programmers wishing to extent their Python facility within Java frameworks. Because this book assumes some knowledge of Java basics, this secondary audience may require an additional source for Java fundamentals.

A distant tertiary audience would be those new to programming, but this requires careful qualification. This book alone is insufficient as an introduction to programming. At a minimum, an additional resource on the fundamentals of Java is required. The reason that this is a reasonable view is that Jython (and Python) is an ideal learning language. The Python language embodies clarity and simplicity while its interactive interpreter allows experimentation, immediate feedback, and rapid acquisition of language features. The fact that Jython supports functional programming as well as object-oriented programming is an educational advantage.

Who This Book Isn't For

If you have no interest in Java, then this book is not for you. Jython requires an understanding of Java, and those who do not know Java, or do not intent to pursue it in parallel with this book, will not benefit from this book. The advantage of Jython is its ability to masquerade as Java and to seamlessly use Java libraries. This means the absence of a basic conviction to Java-centric tools makes Jython, and this book, a poor choice for your needs.

If you are already an advanced Python programmer, this book may not be for you. A substantial portion of this book is Python syntax and usage. Java-specific examples and information do appear, but only within larger sections on syntax and usage that an experienced Python program may find too repetitious.

Additional Resources

Jython-related Internet resources, and the reason for their significance, are listed in this section.

- `http://www.jython.org/`   Jython's official home page.
- `http://www.python.org/`   Python's official home page. Python has a great collection of documentation available at this site that is also applicable to Jython.
- `http://www.digisprings.com/jython/`   The website associated with this book. You will find additional Jython information, as well as book errata, tips, and more at this site.
- `http://sourceforge.net/projects/zxjdbc`   This is the project page for the `zxJDBC` package. This package provides Python 2.0 database functionality for Jython.

Mailing lists specific to Jython are a valuable resource. It is best to subscribe to such lists from the links available on Jython's home page, and the lists available are `jython-users`, `jython-dev`, and `jython-announce`. The `jython-users` list is designed for general Jython questions and help, whereas the `jython-dev` list is for matters related to the development of Jython itself (as opposed to development with Jython). The `announce` list is a low-volume list designed to keep users posted about new releases. If you face problems that are not addressed in the book, at `http://www.newriders.com/`, or at the Jython website, it is best to consult the mailing lists.

I

Jython

1

Jython Syntax, Statements, and Comments

T HIS CHAPTER DESCRIBES JYTHON'S SYNTAX and statements. Jython has a simple, clean syntax that produces easy-to-read code, often considered the antithesis to the intricate appearances of Java, C, or Perl. Before addressing syntax, this chapter introduces Jython's interactive mode. This mode allows you to enter code one line at a time like common shell consoles, and it is the perfect venue for exploring Jython's syntax.

What's Not Included in this Chapter

This chapter assumes you have a working installation of Jython. The Jython section of the New Riders website (http:www.newriders.com) will have a thourough section on installation if help is needed. Additionally, "What is Jython?" and Jython's associated praises are not addressed here. The "what" and "why" appear in the introduction and throughout the book.

The Interactive Console

Programming is often a succession of little puzzles. These little puzzles need to be worked out, tested, and confirmed before they can be added to the larger whole. That's where the *interactive console* comes in—you can explore code interactively, test things immediately, and experiment until the little puzzles are solved. The use of the interactive console, also called the *interactive interpreter*, is similar to shell programming, where you can enter commands interactively until they work, then place them in a file to make a shell script. The similarity fades when you realize that Jython itself is a very full and rich object-oriented programming language with a clean, easy-to-understand syntax.

The interactive console is started by running jython without any parameters or by adding the -i command-line switch. After starting Jython you should see something that looks similar to this:

```
Jython 2.0 on java1.2.2 (JIT: symcjit)
Type "copyright", "credits" or "license" for more information.
>>>_
```

The first line printed after starting Jython should include version information about Jython and Java as well as information about the JIT you are using. If you set the JAVA_COMPILER environment variable to NONE, Jython would confirm the change in JIT:

```
Jython 2.0 on java1.2.2 (JIT: NONE)
Type "copyright", "credits" or "license" for more information.
>>>
```

The >>> in the third line is the prompt for the interactive interpreter. At this prompt you can type Jython code that is evaluated as each line is entered. There is also a second prompt, which is three periods, ... This is used when statements span multiple physical lines.

This testing, experimentation, and discovery within interactive mode is not limited to Jython. The interactive console is a powerful way of experimenting with and testing Java code. For this book, interactive mode is the primary means of learning Jython. Examples in the first part of this book are designed to be easy to experiment with, examine, and explore in interactive mode. The prompt symbols, >>> and ..., are used to designate the use of the interactive interpreter throughout this book.

Line Separators and Block Indentation Syntax

Simple Jython statements are contained in a logical line. What is a logical line? you might ask. Java and many other languages make this clear with punctuation. The semicolon is a line-separator in Java. A simple Java `print` would be

```
System.out.println("Hello world");
```

Notice the semicolon. Now look at the comparable simple Jython `print` statement:

```
print "Hello world"
```

There are no semicolons to mark the end of the logical line. The semicolon has been a standard for terminating lines in many languages, but in Jython, a newline is sufficient to denote the boundary between logical lines—with but a few exceptions. If a Jython `print` statement were entered into the interactive interpreter, pressing the Enter key would cause the interpreter to execute the contents of that logical line. The same goes for a Jython file. Separate lines of Jython code in a file are interpreted as separate logical lines, unless they fit one of the exceptions that follow.

There are cases in which the logical line for simple statements is not the same as the physical line. These cases are as follows:

- Semicolon
- Backslash
- Open groupings
- Triple-quotes

A Current Interactive Limitation

One disclaimer concerning the interactive interpreter: The current implementation of Jython produces an error when employing backslashes, open enclosures, and triple-quotes in interactive mode despite it being legal syntax. This syntax does work in Jython files as well as in the interactive interpreter for CPython (Jython's counterpart implemented in C). It could be working in interactive mode as well by the time you read this, but if not, those examples with extended logical lines should be placed in a file and run as an argument to the Jython interpreter (such as `jython example.py`).

Semicolon

The first case is the semicolon. This is the only case concerned with shortening the logical line. To place two or more logical lines on the same physical line, use the semicolon to separate statements. Even if there are not multiple statements on one line, the semicolon doesn't hurt anything. So, if Java programming habits lead to stray semicolons at the end of statements, no harm is done. Remember to be aware of code clarity when choosing this syntax to ensure that readability is not sacrificed for the sake of compactness.

Listing 1.1 has multiple `print` statements on one physical line. The semicolon acts as the logical-line separator between these two print statements. The second statement, however, does not have a semicolon, because the newline character after it functions as the separator.

Listing 1.1   **Use of the Semicolon**

```
>>># it's tradition, what can I say
>>>print "Hello "; print "world"
Hello
world
```

Notice that the print statement automatically inserted a newline. This is part of the behavior of Jython's `print` statement. If this is not desired, you can append a comma after the `print` statement which pre-pends a space to the second print statement instead:

```
>>>print "hello ",; print "world"
hello world
```

Backslash

The backslash (\) character is a line-continuation character. Multiple lines can be used to form one logical line with the \. An assignment is a simple Jython statement that binds a value to a variable, but what if you need to add so many values that they extended beyond the physical line? Listing 1.2 shows how the \ can be used to join multiple lines to do this. Listing 1.2 does not work interactively despite the legal syntax. To test Listing 1.2, place the code in a file (`backslash.py` used in example) and run it at the command line with `jython backslash.py`.

```
# file: backslash.py
var = 10 + 9 + 8 + 7 + 6 + \
5 + 4 + 3 + 2 + 1

print var
```

Results from running `jython backslash.py` at the command prompt:

```
55
```

Open Groupings

Open groupings—meaning paired brackets [ ], braces {}, and parentheses ()—
have their open (left) character on one line, and the closing character on a
subsequent line. The logical line is extended until the closing half of these
groupings appears. Listing 1.3 uses open groupings to spread a print statement
over multiple physical lines. Listing 1.3 also does not work interactively despite
being legal syntax (as of version 2.1a1).

```
# file: parens.py
print ("this, " +
       "that, " +
       "the other thing.")
```

Results from running `jython parens.py`:

```
this, that, the other thing
```

The indentations on the second and third lines of listing 1.3 are for appearances—this is unrelated to the continuation of the logical line. Indention matters in Jython, but in the case of joining lines with \ or open enclosures, the
indentation of the continued lines do not matter. It's the indentation of the
first line that does. Indention rules are addressed with compound statements
later.

Triple-Quotes

In Jython, you have the option to use three matching quotes to mark the start
and end of a string, matching either """ or '''. In a triple-quoted string, newlines and contained quotes are all preserved except for another triple-quote.
Listing 1.4 shows a triple-quoted string spanning multiple lines. Note how it
preserves internal quotes plus newline characters. Listing 1.4 is legal syntax, but
also does not work interactively.

Listing 1.4   **Triple-Quoted Strings**

```
# file: triplequote.py
print """This is a triple-quoted string.
Newlines and quotation marks such
as " and ' are preserved in the string."""
```

Results from running jython `triplequote.py`:
```
This is a triple-quoted string.
Newlines and quotation marks such
as " and ' are preserved in the string.
```

Code Blocks

With newline characters acting as the logical-line separators, it should be obvious that Jython already has much less punctuation than Java. What further reduces line noise is Jython's notation of code blocks in compound statements. These groupings, or "blocks" of code, are designated in Java by their enclosure in braces {}.

Here lies an important distinction—Jython does not use braces to group statements but rather uses a combination of the : character and indention whitespace. Java's braces handle multiple levels of groupings with multiple enclosures of braces, or braces within braces { {} }. Jython instead uses multiple levels of indention—one indention for first grouping, two indentions for the second, and so on. Listing 1.5 uses Jython's `if` statement to show how compound statements use the : and indention to denote groupings of code.

Listing 1.5   **Indention-Based Groupings**

```
>>>if 1:
...     print "Outer"
...     if 1:
...         print "Inner"
...     print "Outer- again"
...
Outer
Inner
Outer- again
```

Notice how the execution of the compound statement happens only after the newline is entered at the leftmost margin in line six. This entry at the leftmost level notifies the interpreter that the indented grouping is completed and thus, the compound statement is completed.

What Is an Indention Level?

An *indentation level* can be anything that is consistent. Most common is each indention level being a tab, or four spaces. This would mean the second indention level would be either two tabs or eight spaces. Mixing tabs and spaces works too, so you can have the first indention be four spaces, the second indention a tab, the third equal to a tab and four spaces, and so on. The priority is consistency. It is also good to know what whitespace your editor is using so you can eliminate potential confusion when switching editors. What is legal and what is recommended differ. The most sensible recommendation is use four spaces indents and never mix tabs and spaces.

Comments

Looking back at Listing 1.1 from earlier in this chapter, we see another important feature. The # sign. This designates a comment. All code between the # sign and the end of the physical line is ignored by the interpreter. Its appearance is not restricted to the beginning of a line; it can appear after a statement like this:

```
print "Hello world" # It's tradition, what can I do
```

The newline still terminates the logical line, but the space between # and the newline is treated as a comment and is ignored by the interpreter.

Another way to comment code is with anonymous string literals. If you do not assign a string to a variable, it is anonymous, and does not affect the namespace in which it appears. This makes strings useful as comments, especially triple-quoted strings because they allow comments to span multiple lines. Listing 1.6 shows different comments. Listing 1.6 does not currently work in the interactive interpreter as noted earlier.

Listing 1.6 **Comments**

```
# file: comments.py
# This is a comment
"This works for a comment"
"""This comment can span
multiple lines.  Code that you
do not want executed can go
in triple quotes, and it is safe
to use other quotation marks within
the triple quotes, such as:
print "hello" """
```

There is no output from running jython comments.py.

Documentation Strings

The exploration and discovery mentioned when introducing interactive mode depends on introspection, the ability to look under the hood. An important Jython tool that helps when looking inside objects is Jython's self-documentation convention called *doc strings*. These are anonymous string literals appearing in function, method, and class definitions.

Listing 1.7 defines a function called `foo`. The second line of this example is an anonymous string literal, and a doc string because of its location. Note that this string is one indention level in as it should be as part of `foo`'s code block. This doc string uses the triple-quote notation, but that is not required. Any legal string quoting works; triple-quotes just make it easier in case the documentation grows to more than one line.

Listing 1.7   **Documentation Strings, __*doc*__**

```
>>> def foo():
...       """This is an example doc string"""
...       pass
...
>>> dir(foo)
['__dict__', '__doc__', '__name__', 'func_closure', 'func_code',
'func_defaults', 'func_doc', 'func_globals', 'func_name']
>>> foo.__doc__
'This is an example doc string'
>>>
```

The function `dir()` is a built-in function that looks at name bindings within a namespace. Listing 1.7 uses `dir` to look at function `foo`, and returns a list of names defined inside `foo`. In this list it is `__doc__`. Looking at the contents of `foo.__doc__` show that it is the name bound to the doc string provided in the function definition. The actual results of calling `dir(foo)` differs between Jython 2.0 and Jython 2.1a1 (the current version as of this writing). Do not be concerned if your output differs slightly.

Statements

This section includes definitions and usage examples of Jython statements. Statements are categorized into *simple statements*, those with a single clause, and *compound statements*, those with multiple clauses or an associated code block.

Simple Statements

Simple statements are those Jython statements with a single clause, encompassing one logical line. These statements are often confused with built-in functions; however, there is a distinction. Statements are part of the syntax as opposed to functions or data objects defined within a namespace.

The following sections list Jython's simple statements and their syntax, and provides an example usage.

assert

The `assert` statement tests whether an expression is true and raises an exception if it is not true. If two expressions are supplied, the second expression will be used as the argument to the raised `AssertException`. Setting `__debug__`=0, and possibly the `-O` command-line switch in future releases, disables asserts.

Syntax:
```
"assert" expression [, expression]
```

Example:
```
>>>a=21
>>>assert a<10
Traceback (innermost last):
  File "<console>", line 1, in ?
AssertionError:
```

assignment

An assignment binds an object to an identifier. Jython has simple assignment (=) and augmented assignments (+=, -=, *=, /=, **=, %=, <<=, >>=, &=, |=, ^=).

Syntax:
```
variable  assignment-operator  value
```

Example:
```
>>>var=3
>>>print var
3
>>>var += 2
>>>print var
5
```

break

The `break` statement terminates execution of an enclosing loop and continues execution after the loop block. This means it does skip the `else` block if it exists.

Syntax:

```
break
```

Example:

```
>>>for x in (1,2,3,4):
...     if x==3:
...             break
...     print x
...
1
2
>>>
```

continue

The `continue` statement halts execution of the current loop block and start the enclosing loop again at its next iteration.

Syntax:

```
continue
```

Example:

```
>>>for x in (1,2,3,4):
...     if x==3:
...             continue
...     print x
...
1
2
4
>>>
```

del

The `del` statement removes a variable. The variable can be one within the namespace or a specific list or dictionary value.

Syntax:

```
"del"   identifier
```

Example:

```
>>>a="foo"
>>>print a
foo
>>>del a
>>>print a
Traceback (innermost last):
  File "<console>", line 1, in ?
```

```
NameError: a>>>
>>> a = [1,2,3]
>>> del a[1]
>>> print a
[1, 3]
```

exec

The exec statement executes Jython code. The exec statement requires an expression, which represents the code it needs to execute. A string, open file object, or code object can be supplied for this expression, which is the first parameter to exec(). If two parameters are provided, the second is used as the global dictionaries in which the code is executed. If three parameters are provided, the first is a dictionary used as the global namespace, and the second is the local namespace in which the code is executed.

Syntax:

```
"exec" expression ["in" expression ["," expression]]
```

Example:

```
>>>exec "print 'The exec method is used to print this'"
The exec method is used to print this
>>>
```

global

The global statement tells the parser to use global name bindings for listed identifiers throughout the current code block. Why? Because an assignment in a local code block identifies all references to that assigned variable as local. It's easier to see in the comparison of the following two code snippets:

```
>>>var = 10
>>>def test():
...     print var  # try and print the global identifier 'var'
...
>>>test()
10
>>>
```

We see that var is found and prints. So far, so good. Now, what happens if we assign something to var after the print statement?

```
>>>var = 10
>>>def test():
...     print var  # try and print the global identifier 'var'
...     var = 20   # assign to 'var' in local namespace
...
>>>test()
```

```
Traceback (innermost last):
  File "<console>", line 1, in ?
  File "<console>", line 2, in test
NameError: local: 'var'
>>>
```

The identifier var is designated as local because of the assignment within the code block, so the print statement is an error because var does not exist yet in the local namespace. This is the reason for global.

Syntax:

```
global identifier ["," identifier]*
```

Example:

```
>>>var = 10
>>>def test():
...    global var # must designate var global first.
...    print var  # try and print the global identifier 'var'
...    var = 20   # assign to 'var' in local namespace
...
>>>test()
10
>>>print var  # check global 'var'
20
>>>
```

import

The import statement locates and initializes what is imported and binds it to variables in the scope that import was called in. You can optionally change the name of the variables imports are bound to with an as new-name suffix to the import statement.

Syntax:

```
import module-name
     OR
from module-name import names
     OR
import module-name as new-name
     OR
from module-name import name as new-name
```

Example:

```
>>>import sys
>>>from java import util
>>>import os as myOS
>>>from sys import packageManager as pm
```

pass

The "do nothing" statement. This statement is a placeholder.

Syntax:

```
pass
```

Example:

```
>>>for x in (1,2,3,4):
...    pass
...
>>>
```

print

The `print` statement evaluates an expression, converts the result to a string if needed, and writes the string to `sys.stdout` or whatever file-like object it is directed to with the `>>` syntax. A file-like object is one with a `write` method defined.

Syntax:

```
print [expression]
      OR
print >> fileLikeObject, [expression]
```

Example:

```
>>>print "Hello world"
Hello world
```

raise

The `raise` statement evaluates any expressions provided with it and raises an exception accordingly.

Syntax:

```
raise [expression [, expression [, traceback]]]
```

Example:

```
>>>raise ValueError, "No value provided"
Traceback (innermost last):
  File "<console>", line 1, in ?
ValueError: No value provided
```

return

The `return` statement ends execution of the method or function it is called in after evaluating any provided expression for use as a return value. If no expression is provided, the value `None` is returned.

Syntax:

```
return [expression]
```

Example:

```
>>>def someFunction():
...    return "This string is the return value"
```

Compound Statements

Compound statements are those statements that have a grouping or "block" of code associated with them. Flow control statements such as `if`, `for`, and `while` are compound statements. These are difficult to introduce without mentioning Jython's block indentation syntax. A code block, or grouping of statements, in Java is contained in braces {}. Multiple levels of groupings are in nested braces { {} }. This is not so for Jython. Rather, Jython uses the colon, :, and indentation to identify blocks of code. With this knowledge, we can define Jython's compound statements. The following sections explain Jython's compound statements and their definitions.

class

The `class` statement is used to define a class. Evaluation of a `class` statement defines a class in that current scope. Calling a class calls its constructor if defined and returns an instance of that class.

Syntax:

```
"class" name[(base-class-name)]:
```

Example:

```
>>>class test:    # no base class
...    pass       # place holder
...
>>>t = test()     # Calls class statement to make an instance
```

def

The `def` statement is how functions and methods are defined.

Syntax:

```
"def" name([parameters]):
    statements
```

Example:

```
>>>def hello(person):
...  print "Hello ", person
...
```

```
>>>hello("world")  # calls the hello function
Hello world
```

for

The `for` statement is a flow-control statement that iterates through a loop once for each member of a sequence. The `for` statement can also include an optional `else` clause that is executed after the sequence has expired.

Syntax:
```
"for" variable "in" expression":"
    statements
["else:"]
    statements
```

The expression provided must evaluate to a list.

Example:
```
>>>for x in (1,2,3):
...     print x,
...else:
...     print "in else clause"
...
1 2 3 in else clause
>>>
```

if

The `if` statement executes a block of code conditionally when an expression evaluates to true.

Syntax:
```
if expression:
    statements
elif expression:
    statements
else:
    statements
```

If the first expression evaluates to false, the interpreter proceeds to evaluate the `elif` expression if provided. If all `elif` conditions are false, the `else` group of statements is executed.

Example:
```
>>>if a==b:
...     print "variable a equals variable b"
...elif a>b:
...     print "variable a is greater than b"
...else:
...     print "variable a is less than b"
```

try

The `try` statement executes a block of code until completion or until an error.

Syntax:
```
"try:"
    statements
"except" ["," expression ["," variable]]":"
    statements
["else:"
    statements]
   OR
["finally:"
    statements]
```

Only one of the `else` or `finally` clause can be used, not both. If the `try` block of code runs without error, it proceeds to execute the block of code in its `finally` block. If the `try` block has an error, it stops execution of that block and proceeds to the except clause.

Example:
```
>>>try:
...    1/0
...except ZeroDivisionError, e:
...    print "You cannot divide by zero:  ", e
...
You cannot divide by zero:  integer division or modulo
>>>
```

while

The `while` statement executes a block of code as long as a provided expression evaluates to true.

Syntax:
```
"while" expression ":"
```

Example:
```
>>>x = 10
>>>while x>0:
...    print x,
...    x -= 1
...
10 9 8 7 6 5 4 3 2 1
```

Comparing Jython and Java

Table 1.1 lists the statements used in Jython and compares them with Java's implementation.

Table 1.1   **Jython Statements Compared to Java's**

Statement	Comparison
assert	The `assert` does not have an immediate parallel in Java implementations previous to Java version 1.4
assignment	Jython and Java are similar in assignments despite there being some operator and scoping differences addressed later in this book.
break	Jython and Java `break` statements function the same.
continue	Jython and Java `continue` statements function the same.
del	The `del` statement in Jython does not have a Java counterpart.
exec	This has been confused with being a parallel to Java's `exec` method in the `Runtime` class. This is not the case, however. The Jython `exec` is for executing Jython code dynamically, whereas the Runtime `exec` in Java exists for running external system processes—not dynamically executing Java code.
global	Java does not have a direct parallel to Jython's `global`.

import	Java's `import` statement does not allow the binding of loaded classes to arbitrary names like Jython's `import module as newName` syntax. Nor does Java use the `from module import name` syntax. A simple comparison of similar Jython and Java `import` demonstrates these syntax differences:
	
	`Java:       import javax.servlet.*;`
	`Jython:     from javax.servlet import *`

pass	Java does not require a "do nothing" placeholder like `pass` because of the punctuation used in grouping code blocks. Java can have a code block do nothing by just having an empty set of braces—{ } or a semicolon-terminated null string. Jython's sparse punctuation creates situations where the placeholder `pass` is required to make sense of the syntax.
print	`Print` is a statement in Jython. In Java, however, `print` is always a method of another object.

continues

Table 1.1 **Continued**

Statement	Comparison
raise	Jython's `raise` statement is the parallel to Java's `throw` statement.
return	Jython and Java `return` statements function the same.
class	Jython and Java's `class` statements are similar in function but differ in syntax. A Jython class includes its base classes in parentheses after the class name, whereas Java uses the extends (`class this extends that`) syntax.
def	Method signatures in Java use a lot of information that Jython does not use. A signature like `public int getID(String name)` translates to `def getID(name)` in Jython. This brevity is because in Jython everything is public, and types are not explicitly declared.
for	The main difference is that Jython's `for` statement requires a sequence. It does not use the (variable, test, increment) used in Java. The first clause of a matching for loop in both Java and Jython would look like this: Java: `for (int x=10; x > 0; x++)` Jython: `for x in (10, 9, 8, 7, 6, 5, 4, 3, 2, 1):` Fortunately, Jython has the `range()` and `xrange()` functions to make sequences for Jython's `for` statement: Jython: `for x in range(10, 0, -1):` Java also lacks the optional `else` clause that exists in Jython's `for` statement.
if	Jython's `if` statement is similar to Java's, except that `else if`, as it is written in Java, is `elif` in Jython.
try	`try/except/else/finally` in Jython is the parallel to `try/catch/finally` in Java. They handle exceptions in their respective languages. In Jython, however, `try/except/else` and `try/finally` are two separate forms of the `try` statement that cannot be mixed.
while	Jython and Java `while` statements are similar, but Jython has an additional `else` clause that is executed when the condition evaluates to false.

2

Operators, Types, and Built-In Functions

THIS CHAPTER EXPLAINS JYTHON'S IDENTIFIERS, data objects, operators and built-in functions. Nearly all items discussed in this chapter are available without user-supplied syntax—just like Java programmers get the classes in the java.lang package without any import statement. The exception is Java objects. Jython uses Java objects within Jython's syntax, but interacting with Java objects requires an import statement. Before beginning with objects, it is important to know which names (identifiers) are legal to bind objects to—; therefore, this chapter begins with the definition of legal Jython identifiers.

Identifiers

User-specified identifiers consist of letters, numbers, and the underscore, but they must always begin with a letter or the underscore. Spaces are not allowed, and case *does* matter. The length of the identifier doesn't matter. Identifiers cannot be reserved words, and Jython's list of reserved words include the following:

and	def	finally	in	print
as	del	for	is	raise
assert	elif	from	lambda	return
break	else	global	not	try
class	except	if	or	while
continue	exec	import	pass	

Some examples of legal identifiers are as follows:

```
abcABC123

A1b2C3

_1a2

_a_1
```

Some examples of illegal identifiers and the reasons why are as follows:

```
1abc  # Identifiers cannot start with a number
this variable  # Spaces are not allowed
cost$basis  # Only letters, numbers and "_" are allowed
```

Legal identifiers are not necessarily good identifiers. Despite the numerous reasons people choose to use Jython, or Python, it really seems that clarity is primary. It only makes sense to complement this with thoughtful choices of identifiers, and comments that clarify them where needed.

Jython Data Objects

Jython's data objects are derived from the Python language description, just as Jython itself is. The names ascribed to Python's types are integer, long, float, complex, string, tuple, list, and dictionary, among miscellaneous others. Jython, however, has no types in the traditional sense. This paradox is really only semantics. Type primitives are data descriptors that are not classes or instances. In Jython, however, all data is represented by Java classes from the `org.python.core` package. Therefore, Jython has no primitive types.

The use of the word "type" in this book is only a convenient way to refer to Jython's data classes. The use of classes for every data object is unique to Jython considering CPython types are not all objects. The names of the Java classes that represent the corresponding Python types are prefixed with "Py" so that they are `PyInteger`, `PyLong`, `PyFloat`, `PyComplex`, `PyString`, `PyTuple`, `PyList`, `PyDictionary`, and so on. Each class name and its associated `Py*` classes is used interchangeably throughout the book (for example, `tuple` and `PyTuple`).

The introduction to the `Py*` class such as `PyFloat` and `PyList` is really an implementation detail that is premature technically at this point in the book, but the reason for their inclusion here is that these are the names you will get used to seeing when using the built-in function `type()`.

Jython's data classes are dynamic—they are determined at runtime. They are also implied in that the value assigned to an identifier at runtime determines which data class is used as opposed to explicit type declarations. Jython code that binds names to objects looks like this:

```
>>>aString = "I'm a string"
>>>aInteger = 5
>>>aLong = 2500000000L
```

This code binds the `PyString` object to the name `aString`, the `PyInteger` object to the name `aInteger`, and the `PyLong` object to `aLong`. The string type is implied by the quotation marks, the integer type by the numeric literal 5, and the long type is designated by an integral number suffixed with an `L`. None of these variables' classes are determined by prefixing them with `PyString` or `PyInteger`, as it is done in Java. Explicit notation, such as the `L` suffix for `PyLong` objects, is rare in Jython.

To confirm which type ("class") an objects is, you can use the built-in function `type()`:

```
>>>type("I'm a string")
<jclass org.python.core.PyString at 1777024>
>>>S = "Another string"
>>>type(S)
<jclass org.python.core.PyString at 177024>
>>>aInteger = 5
>>>type(aInteger)
<jclass org.python.core.PyInteger at 7033304>
>>>aLong = 2500000000L
>>>type(aLong)
<jclass org.python.core.PyLong at 871578>
```

Note that the representation of numbers may differ from how you originally entered them—not the value, just the representation (for example, .1 = 0.1).

There are a number of Py-prefixed classes in the org.python.core package. These classes have a plethora of public methods, but most of these methods are what is called *special class methods*, or they are methods for working with Py* classes from Java. An example of this is the toString() method. It is familiar and may be expected for Java programmers, but it is unique to the Java implementation of Python. Only those working in Java need to be aware of it. This section defines the basics of Jython's data objects, and leaves special class methods and Java specific methods for later chapters.

The classes discussed here are not all that is represented by the Py* classes. Of the classes discussed, there are four numeric objects, three sequence objects, two mapping objects, and Jython's None object.

Numeric Objects

PyInteger, PyLong, PyFloat, and PyComplex are the classes that represent Jython's numeric objects. Variables with numeric types result from assignment to a numeric value of matching type. This means that if you bind a variable to a complex number, the PyComplex object is used. To clarify this, look at the definitions and examples of numeric objects in Table 2.1.

Table 2.1   **Numeric Values**

Class	Definition	Examples
PyInteger	A whole number limited in size to what can be represented with a Java primitive int type (32 bits or +/−2147483647).	x = 28 x = -6
PyLong	A whole number followed by the letter "l" or "L". It is restricted in size only by available memory.	x = 2147483648L x = 6L
PyFloat	A floating-point number that is restricted in size to what can be represented with a Java primitive double type (64 bits).	x = 02.7182818284 x = 0.577216 x = 003.4E9
PyComplex	A complex number represented as the addition of two floating-point numbers. The first of which represents the real portion and the second is the imaginary. The letter "j" is appended to the second number to denote the imaginary portion.	x = 2.0+3.0 x = 9.32345+4j

Notice from Table 2.1 that values for the `PyInteger` class have a fixed range. An operation that causes a `PyInteger` object to exceed its maximum limit creates an overflow exception such as the following:

```
>>> int = 2147483647
>>> int += 1
Traceback (innermost last):
File "<console>", line 1, in ?
OverflowError: integer addition: 2147483647 + 1
```

If an integral numeric object risks exceeding this limit, it should be made a `PyLong` by adding the L suffix. Despite the fact that the `PyLong` can be designated with either a capital L or lowercase l, the lowercase option is discouraged because of its similarity to the number 1.

Out of the four numeric objects, only instances of the `PyComplex` class have a public instance method and instance variables that are commonly used from Jython. The instance variables are the real and imaginary portions of the complex number, accessed with `x.real`, and `x.imag` for the complex variable x. The instance method is `.conjugate`. The conjugate of a complex number is as follows:

```
conjugate(a + bi) = a - bi
```

Examples of accessing the real and imaginary portions of the complex object, or invoking the conjugate instance method, use the same dot-notations as Java objects (`instance.var`). Calling the conjugate method would look like this:

```
>>>z = 1.5+2.0j
>>>z.conjugate()
(1.5-2.0j)
>>>z + z.conjugate()
(3+0j)
```

Accessing the `.real` and `.imag` parts of a `PyComplex` instance would look like this:

```
>>>aComplexNumber = 1+4.5j
>>>aComplexNumber.real
1.0
>>>aComplexNumber.imag
4.5
>>># Note that .real and .imag are PyFloat types
>>>type(aComplexNumber.imag)
<jclass org.python.core.PyFloat at 3581654>
>>>type(aComplexNumber.real)
<jclass org.python.core.PyFloat at 3581654>
```

Another property of numerical objects is that they are all immutable—the value of a numeric object cannot be changed. Let's assume that you need to increment an integer object named x. To do so, you need to use an *assignment operator*, which instead of changing the value changes the object id. To look at an object's id, you can use the built-in function id().

```
>>>x = 10      # create our immutable variable
>>>id(x)       # get the id of x
2284055
>>>x = x + 1   # an assignment is required to add the 1
>>>id(x)       # check x's new id
4456558
```

The value of x appears incremented with the use of an assignment operator, but x is a different object because of the assignment, as noted by the difference in its id.

In Boolean (true/false) expressions, all numeric objects are false when their value is equivalent to zero. Otherwise, they are true. This is demonstrated using Jython's if-else statement:

```
>>>if (0 or 0L or 0.0 or 0.0+0.0j):
...    print "True"
...else:
...    print "False"
...
False
```

These four classes are Jython's numeric objects, but they are not all of the numeric objects that can be used in Jython. Java's numeric classes can be used without modification in Jython. To do this, start with import java, then instantiate the class you need.

```
>>>import java
>>>l = java.lang.Long(1000)
>>>print l
1000
>>>l.floatValue() # invoke Java instance method
1000.0
```

Sequence Objects

PyString, PyTuple, and PyList are the classes used for Jython sequences. These, being sequences, are ordered sets of data. The distinguishing features are the kind of data they hold, and their mutability. The PyString class holds only character data, whereas the PyTuple and PyList classes hold objects of any kind. Strings and tuples are immutable, meaning they cannot be changed, but lists are mutable. Unlike numeric objects, sequences have a length. The built–in function `len()` returns a sequence's length:

```
>>> len("This is a string sequence")
25
```

Sequences share some common syntax, namely index and slice syntax. Although there is different syntax for creating the different sequences, they all use square brackets to reference elements within the set. First, examine the creation of each of the sequences:

```
>>>S = "abc"              # This is a string
>>>T = ("a", "b", "c")    # This is a tuple
>>>L = ["a", "b", "c"]    # This is a list
```

You can see they all have unique enclosure tokens—quotation marks, parentheses, and square brackets. However, if you want to access the second element of each sequence (the "b"), they all use the same syntax:

```
>>>S[1]
'b'
>>>T[1]
'b'
>>>L[1]
'b'
```

The number within the square brackets is the *index number,* starting from 0, of an element within the sequence. Accessing a sequence element with an index like this returns the element at that index, counting from the start of the sequence (left). The index numbers can also be negative, which indicates the number of elements from the end of the sequence (right). This makes the index −1 the last element of a sequence, −2 the penultimate, and so on:

```
>>>S = "beadg"
>>>S[-1]
'g'
>>>S[-3]
'a'
```

Sequences also share the same slice notation. A *slice* returns a subset of the original sequence. The colon, :, within the square braces is used to designate a slice. Numbers appearing on either side of this colon designate the range of the slice. Positive numbers (counted from the left), negative numbers (counted from the right), and the absence of numbers (designating respective endpoints) can be used to represent the range. So, a slice notation that looks like S[3:6] should be read as, "A slice of sequence S beginning at index 3 and continuing up to, but not including, index 6." The code for this slice looks like this:

```
>>>S = [1, 2, 3, 4, 5, 6, 7, 8, 9]
>>>S[3:6] # slice from 3 up to, but not including 6
[4, 5, 6]
```

A slice such as S[3:] should be read as, "A slice of sequence S beginning at index 3 and continuing to its endpoint." The code for this slice looks like this:

```
>>>S = [1, 2, 3, 4, 5, 6, 7, 8, 9]
>>>S[3:]
[4, 5, 6, 7, 8, 9]
>>>
>>># if we invert the slice numbers...
>>>S[:3]
[1, 2, 3]
```

A slice such as S[4:-2] should be read as, "A slice of sequence S beginning at index 3 and continuing to, but not including, its second index from the end." The code for this slice looks like this:

```
>>>S = [1, 2, 3, 4, 5, 6, 7, 8, 9]
>>>S[4:-2]
[5, 6, 7]
>>>
>>># negative number can be on the left also...
>>>S[-4:-1]
[6, 7, 8]
```

Jython sequences also support a third integer in the slice syntax to represent step. This third integer is separated by a second colon within the square brackets, and it means a slice that looks like S[2:8:3] should be read as, "A slice of sequence S beginning at index 2 and including every third index until reaching index 8." Adding this third number lets you have slices like this:

```
>>> S = 'zahbexlwlvo2 fwzo4rslmd'
>>> S[2::2]  # this slices from index 2 to the endpoint, steping by 2
'hello world'
>>>
>>> L = [1,2,3,4,5,6,7,8,9]
>>> L[-1:3:-1]  # last index to third index, indexes step by -1
[9, 8, 7, 6, 5]
```

Of the sequence classes, two are immutable—PyString and PyTuple. Listing 2.1 demonstrates mutability and the exception that is raised when you try to change an immutable type (tuple or string). In addition, a PyList object is created and altered in Listing 2.1 to demonstrate its mutability.

Listing 2.1   **Examples of Sequence Objects**

```
>>> S = "This is a string"  # Make a PyString instance
>>> type(S)                 # Confirm object type
<jclass org.python.core.PyString at 8057966>
>>> S[2] = "u"              # Try to change the string
Traceback (innermost last):
File "<console>", line 1, in ?
TypeError: can't assign to immutable object
>>>
>>> T = (1, 2.1, "string") # make a PyTuple with varied data
>>> type(T)                # Confirm object type
<jclass org.python.core.PyTuple at 4573025>
>>> T[2] = "new string"    # Try to change the tuple
Traceback (innermost last):
File "<console>", line 1, in ?
TypeError: can't assign to immutable object
>>>
>>> L = [1, 2.1, "string"] # Make a List with varied data
>>> type(L)                # Confirm object type
<jclass org.python.core.PyList at 5117945>
>>> L[2] = "new string"    # Try to change the list
>>>L[2]
'new string'
```

In Boolean expressions, empty sequences evaluate to false. All other sequences evaluate to true.

Sequences are more involved than the numeric objects, and each require their own section. The following three sections detail the properties of Jython's sequences. Each section introduces the syntax of the object, properties of the object, and methods associated with it.

PyString—The *String* Object

Jython's string class inherits Java's string properties in that they are constructed with two-byte characters based on the Unicode 2.0 standard. This is the only string type in Jython, departing from CPython where there are 8-bit and 16-bit string types with Unicode 3.0 characters. The CPython implementation has a string syntax where the letter u prefixes a Unicode string. Jython supports this syntax for compatibility, but the only changes to the string is in the interpretation of the special characters \u and \N.

The string type, or instances of the PyString class, can be created by assigning a variable to a string literal. String literals are written with matching quotation marks. Either matching single-quotes ('), double-quotes ("), or the

Jython convention of triple-quotes (""" or ''') works. The different marks allow embedding of other quotations such as the following:

```
"single-quotes ' in double-quotes"
'double-quotes " in single-quotes'
"""Triple quotes let you use "anything" inside
except the matching triple quote, and
let you span multiple lines"""
'''This is also a triple quoted string
just in case you need """ inside.'''
```

Concatenation of string literals is an implied operation in Jython. Leaving white space between string literals concatenates them.

```
>>>print "Adding " 'strings ' 'together is ' "this simple."
Adding string together is this simple.
```

This is a convenient way to protect different quotation marks within a string, such as the following:

```
>>>print "I'm able to " 'mix "different" quotes this way.'
I'm able to mix "different" quotes this way.
```

Note that this only works with string *literals*. You cannot join a string literal with the value of an object. The concatenation operator + is required for that and is discussed later in this chapter. The following code demonstrates how attempting to use implied concatenation with non-string literals raises an exception:

```
>>>S = "String value held by object 's' "
>>>print "String literal " S
Traceback (innermost last):
(no code object) at line 0
File "<console>", line 1
"literal" S
              ^
SyntaxError: invalid syntax
```

There is an additional quotation convention designed to allow the string representation of data. This is reverse quotes. Results of expressions contained in reverse quotes are converted to a string representation of that data. The following code shows a `PyInteger` object and an integer literal within reverse quotes as an expression. Notice that the results of the expression is what is converted to a string, not the literal contents of the reverse quotes:

```
>>> n = 5
>>> s = `n + 2`
>>> s
'7'
>>> type(s)
<jclass org.python.core.PyString at 5471111>
```

Reverse quotes do the same as the `repr()` function. The `repr()` function returns a string representation of data that is useful in reconstructing that data. This differs from the built-in `str()` method, which returns a string description of an object. Often times `repr(object)==str(object)`, but there is no guarantee of this equality because these two functions have different objectives. This is revisited when discussing Jython objects and their special `__str__` and `__repr__` methods.

PyString instances are created when binding a literal string value to a name like this:

```
>>>S = "A string"
>>>type(S)
<jclass org.python.core.PyString at 177024>
```

Objects of type `PyString` support a number of methods. These methods are called with the Java-like dot notation `object.method`. The `split` method, for example, returns a list of sub-strings designated by a delimiter:

```
>>>S = "1,2,3,4,5"
>>>S.split(",")
["1", "2", "3", "4", "5"]
```

If no delimiter is specified, it splits on whitespace:

```
>>>S = "A string with spaces."
>>>S.split()  # notice, no delimiter specified
["A", "string", "with", "spaces."]
```

String processing is one of Jython's strengths as evidenced by how rich the `PyString` class is with methods. A list of `PyString` methods is given in Table 2.2. A very important characteristic of sting methods is that they always return a copy of the string and never modify the string in place.

Table 2.2   *PyString* **Methods**

Method	Description

capitalize	`s.capitalize()` returns string matching the value of s except that the first character is capitalized:
	
	`>>>s="monday"`
	`>>>s.capitalize()`
	`Monday`

continues

Table 2.2 **Continued**

Method	Description
center	s.center(width) returns the value of s centered within a string of specified width. The width represents a number of characters total desired in the returned string, and the value of s is padding with spaces to satisfy that width:

```
>>> s = "Title"
>>> s.center(40)
'                  Title                 '
``` |
| count | s.count(substring [,start [, end]]) returns an integer representing the number of times a substring was found in the string value of s. The start and end parameters are optional and define a slice of the string to search in:

```
>>> s = "BacBb is the music-cryptic spelling of Bach."
>>> s.count("c")
4
>>> s.count("c", 18)
3
>>> s.count("c", 18, 28)
2
``` |
| encode | s.encode([encoding] [, error-handling]) returns the string value of s as a string with the character encoding specified or the default character encoding if not specified. The error-handling parameter represents how the encoding conversion process should handle errors. Error-handling can be set to strict, ignore, or replace:

```
>>> s = "René Descartes"
>>> s.encode("iso8859_9", "replace")
'Ren? Descartes'  # note the replaced character "?".
``` |
| endswith | s.endswith(suffix[, start[, end]]) returns 1 if s ends with suffix, 0 otherwise. The optional start and end parameters represent the slice of the string to be considered when checking:

```
>>>s = "jython.jar"
>>>s.endswith(".jar")
1
>>>s.endswith("n", 5, 6)
1
``` |

Method	Description

expandtabs	`s.expandtabs([tabsize])` returns the string with tab characters replaced with the number of spaces designated in tabsize, or 8 if no tabsize is given. A tab character is represented in a string as `\t`.
	`>>>s = "\tA tab-indented line"`
	`>>>s.expandtabs(4)`
	`'    A tab-indented line'`

find	`s.find(substring [,start [,end]])` returns the index of the first occurance of substring in the string s. The start and end indexes are optional and restrict the search to within those bounds when supplied. A value of -1 is returned if the substring is not found.
	`>>>s = "abcdedcba"`
	`>>>s.find("c")`
	`2`
	`>>>s.find("c", 5)`
	`6`

index	`s.index(substring [,start [,end]])` is the same as `find`, except a `ValueError` exception is raised if the substring is not found.

isalnum	`s.isalnum()` returns 1 or 0 depending on whether the string value of s is all alphanumeric:
	`>>>s = "123abc"`
	`>>>s.isalnum()`
	`1`
	`>>>s = "1.2.3.a.b.c"`
	`>>>s.isalnum()`
	`0`

isalpha	`s.isalpha()` is the same as `isalnum` except that the string must be all characters before this method returns 1.
isdigit	`s.isdigit()` is the same as `isalnum` except that the string must be all numbers before this method returns 1.
islower	`s.islower()` returns 1 if there is at least one alpha character in the string and all the alpha characters are lowercased. If there are no alpha characters in the string or one of them is uppercased, it returns 0.

continues

Table 2.2   **Continued**

Method	Description
isspace	s.isspace() tests if the string is all whitespace and returns 1 if it is. If the string has non-whitespace characters, it returns 0.

istitle	"Title casing" is where the first letter of each word is capitalized and no non-first characters are capitalized. s.istitle() returns 1 if the string fits this convention.
	
	`>>>s = "Jython For Java Programmers"`
	`>>>s.istitle()`
	`1`

isupper	s.isupper() returns 1 if all characters in the string are upper-cased. It returns 0 if there is a lowercased character or if there are no alpha characters in the string.

join	s.join(sequence) joins a list, tuple, java.util.Vector, or any other sequence with the string value s as the separator.
	
	`>>>s = ", and "`
	`>>>s.join(["This", "that", "the other thing"])`
	`This, and that, and the other thing`

ljust	s.ljust(width) pads the right side of the string with spaces to make a string of the specified width.
lower	s.lower() returns a copy of the string with all alpha characters made lowercase.
lstrip	s.lstrip(width) pads the left side of the string with spaces to make a string of the specified width.
replace	s.replace(old, new [, maxsplits]) returns a copy of the string with each "old" string replaced with the "new" string. There is an optional parameter, maxsplits, that should be a numeric value designating the maximum number of times the old string should be replaced. So, s.replace("this", "that", 5) would return a string with only the first five instances of "this" being replaced with "that."
rfind	s.rfind(substing [, start [, end]]) is the same as find except that it returns the highest index in string s where the substring is found, or the rightmost occurrence of the substring.
rindex	s.rindex(substring [,start [,end]]) is the same as rfind except a ValueError exception is raised if the substring is not found.

Method	Description
rjust	`s.rjust(width)` pads the left side of the string with spaces to make a string of the specified width.
rstrip	`s.rstrip()` returns the string with all trailing whitespace removed.
split	`s.split([separator [, maxsplits]])` returns a list containing the string subdivisions of s divided by the provided separator, or by whitespace is no separator is provided. The `maxsplits` parameter, if provided, limits the number of splits performed, counting from the left, so that the last string in the list contains all that remains.
splitlines	`s.splitlines([keepends])` returns a list of strings created by dividing s at each newline character it contains. The newline characters are not preserved unless the optional `keepends` paramaeter evaluates to true.
startswith	`s.startswith(prefix [,start [,end]])` compares prefix to the beginning of the entire string, or to that portion of the string designated by the optional start and end parameters. If the prefix matches the beginning of the string it is compared against, it returns 1; otherwise it returns 0.
strip	`s.strip()` returns a copy of the string s with leading and trailing whitespace removed.
swapcase	`s.swapcase()` returns a copy of the string s with the capitalization of alpha characters inverted. Those that are lowercased are capitalized and vice-versa.
title	`s.title()` returns a titlecased copy of s. Titlecasing is where the first letter of each word is capitalized, whereas other letters are not.
translate	`s.translate(table [,deletechars])` returns a translated copy of s. A translation can involve two things: remapping of characters (denoted by `table`) and a list of characters to delete (denoted by `deletechars`). The characters you want deleted are included in a string as an optional parameter, so to delete a, b, and C, use the following: `>>>s.translate(table, "abC")`

continues

Table 2.2   *Continued*

Method	Description
	The translation table is a 256-character string usually made with the string module's `maketrans` method. Importing and using modules is a bit premature here, but this is fairly intuitive:
	`>>>import string # this loads the string module`
	`>>>table = string.maketrans("abc", "def")`
	`>>>s = "abcdefg"`
	`>>>s.translate(table, "g") # translate "abc" and delete "g"`
	`'defdef'`
upper	`s.upper()` returns a copy of string s with all alpha characters uppercased.

The variable s *is used to represent the* PyString *instance.*

PyTuple

The PyTuple class is an immutable sequence that can contain references to any type of object. There can sometimes be confusion over the fact that a tuple is immutable but can contain references to mutable objects. If its contents change, how can a tuple be immutable? This works because tuples contain references to objects—the id of the object. When a mutable object's value is changed, its id remains constant; thus, the tuple itself remains immutable.

The syntax for a tuple is odd in that a comma-separated list evaluates to a tuple, but a tuple is represented by parentheses (). This means you can create a tuple with a comma-separated list within parentheses, or with a comma-separated list, or with empty parentheses for an empty tuple.

```
>>>t = (1,2,3)
>>>type(t)
<jclass org.python.core.PyTuple at 6879429>
>>>t = 1,2,3
>>>type(t)
<jclass org.python.core.PyTuple at 6879429>
>>> type((1,2,3))
<jclass org.python.core.PyTuple at 6879329>
>>>myTuple = (1, "string", 11.5)  # tuples can contain any object type
```

Constructing a single-element tuple still requires a comma:

```
>>> t1 = ("element one",)
>>> t2 = "element one",
>>> type(t1)
```

```
<jclass org.python.core.PyTuple at 4229391>
>>> type(t2)
<jclass org.python.core.PyTuple at 4229391>
>>> print t1
('element one',)
>>> print t2
('element one',)
```

Now, try to change the `tuple` to confirm it is immutable:

```
>>> T = ("string", 1, 2.4)
>>> T[0]="another string"
Traceback (innermost last):
File "<console>", line 1, in ?
TypeError: can't assign to immutable object
```

In contrast to the PyString object, the PyTuple object has no associated methods.

PyList

PyList is similar to PyTuple, but it is mutable. The values can be changed. This makes PyList unique among the sequence classes.

A list is denoted by enclosing comma-separated objects in square brackets [1,2,3], or just the square brackets to create an empty list []. The objects contained in a list can be any objects. Making a list that contained various objects, such as an integer, string, float, and complex, would look like the following:

```
>>>myList = [1,"a string", 2.4 , 3.0+4j]
>>>type(myList)
<jclass org.python.core.PyList at 250438>
```

Objects of type PyList have nine associated methods. These methods are described in Table 2.3

Table 2.3 *PyList* **Methods**

Method	Description
append	L.append(object) adds the object to the end of the list L.
count	L.count(value) returns an integer representing the number of times "value" occurs in the list.
extend	L.extend(list) adds the elements of "list" to the end of L.
index	L.index(value) returns an integer that represents the index of the first occurrence of value in the list.

continues

Table 2.3   **Continued**

Method	Description
insert	L.insert(index, object) inserts object into the list L at the specified index and shifts all elements of the list at that index and greater up one.
pop	L.pop([index]) removes an object from the list and returns it. If no index is provided, the last element of the list is used.
remove	L.remove(value) removes the first occurrence of the specified value from the list L.
reverse	L.reverse() reverses the order of the list in place. There is no return value as this operation is done on the list in place.
sort	L.sort([cmpfunc]) sorts the list in place. If a cmpfunc is provided, it should compare two values (x, y) such that it returns a negative number if x is less than y, 0 if x equals y, and a positive number if x is greater than y.

The letter L is used to represent the PyList *instance.*

As with numeric classes, Jython can use all of Java's sequences without modification. PyString, PyTuple, and PyList are Jython-specific objects, but you can just as easily use a java.util.Vector. Note that slice notation and other Jython specific list attribute may not work on the Java sequence object you are using.

Mapping Objects

Jython has two *mapping classes*, or hash types, that are referred to as *dictionaries*. The "mapping" is the connection between an immutable key and another object—the value. The difference in Jython's two mapping classes is the type of key that is used.

The values within a dictionary are accessed by supplying the key in square brackets, or by using one of the PyDictionary methods. The key notation appears as D[key], and an example usage looks like this:

```
>>>D = {"a":"alpha", "b":"beta"}
>>>D["a"]
'alpha'
>>>D["b"]
'beta'
```

Mappings also have a length—a number that represents how many key:value pairs the mapping contains. The built-in function `len()` retrieves this value:

```
>>> D = {1:"a", 2:"b", 3:"c"}
>>> len(D)
3
```

PyDictionary

The `PyDictionary` class represents user-created dictionaries and is the parallel to the single dictionary type found in CPython. Curly braces are used to create a dictionary, and a colon is used to separate the key-value pair. Creating a `PyDictionary` bound to the name "D" looks like:

```
>>>D = {"String type key": "String", 1:"int", 2.0:"float"}
>>>type(D)
<jclass org.python.core.PyDictionary at 1272917>
```

The keys in the preceding dictionary are different types, but all of the types are immutable. A mutable type that compares by value cannot be a `PyDictionary` key as noted by the exception it creates:

```
>>> L = [1,2,3,4] # create a list (mutable sequence)
>>> D = {L:"My key is a list"}  #Try to make L the key
Traceback (innermost last):
File "<console>", line 1, in ?
TypeError: unhashable type
```

Another important note on keys is that numerical values used as keys are hashed according to how their values compare. The `PyInteger` 1 is a different object than the `PyFloat` 1.0, but they compare as equal and thus function as the same key in a dictionary.

```
>>> A = 1
>>> B = 1.0
>>> C = 1+0j
>>> eval("A==B==C") # Note: the integer 1 means true
1
```

The three preceding numeric values evaluate to being equal. In this case it also means that they hash to the same value:

```
>>> hash(A)==hash(B)==hash(C)
1   # This means true
```

This means using those values as dictionary keys would be interpreted as the same key.

```
>>>D = {1: "integer key", 1.0: "float key", 1+0j: "complex key"}
>>>D  # dump the value of D to prove that there was really only one key
{1: 'complex key"}
```

Objects of type `PyDictionary` have nine methods associated with them. They are described in Table 2.4.

Table 2.4   **PyDictionary Methods**

Method	Description
clear	D.clear()removes all the key:value pairs from the dictionary D.
copy	D.copy() returns a shallow copy of the dictionary D.
get	D.get(key [,defaultVal]) returns the value associated with the specified key if it exists. If the dictionary does not have the specified key, it can return an optional default value instead.
has_key	D.has_key(key) returns 1 if the dictionary D does in fact have the specified key. If not, it returns 0.
items	D.items() returns a copy of all the key:value pairs in dictionary D.
keys	D.keys() returns a list of all the keys in dictionary D. The list is a copy of D's keys, so changes to this list do not affect the keys in the original dictionary.
setdefault	D.setdefault(key [, defaultVal]) returns the value associated with the specified key. If that key does not exist, and the optional defaultVal is provided, the specified key is added with defaultVal as its associated value and defaultVal is returned.
update	D.update(dict) updates all the key:value pairs in dictionary D with all the key:value pairs found in the dict parameter. Keys that did not exist in D are added and keys that did exist in D are updated with the values from the dict parameter.
values	D.values() returns a list of all the values in dictionary D. The list is a copy of D's values, so changes to this list do not affect the values in the original dictionary.

The variable D is used to represent the PyDictionary instance.

PyStringMap

Jython's `PyStringMap` class is a dictionary that uses only strings for keys. This is in contrast to the `PyDictionary` that can use any immutable object for a key. This is not an object normally created by the Jython programmer, but is the object returned by a number of built-in functions. It exists for the performance advantage such restricted keys provides.

The PyStringMap is mostly used for namespaces where it makes sense for the keys to be strings. Therefore, the built-in functions that return namespace information return a PyStringMap object. These functions are locals(), globals(), and vars(). Additionally, Jython objects maintain object attributes in a PyStringMap named __dict__. Examine these in the interactive interpreter to see the PyStringMap usage:

```
>>># Fill up namespace so there's something to look at
>>>functional = ['Erlang', 'Haskell']
>>>imperative = ['C++', 'Java']
>>>
>>>globalStringMap = globals()
>>>type(globalStringMap)
<jclass org.python.core.PyStringMap at 6965863>
>>> # Now let's look at the global namespace contents with a "print"
>>> # Your global namespace may differ significantly if you have
>>> # been doing other exercises in the same interpreter session.
>>>print globalStringMap
{'globalStringMap': {...}, '__name__': '__main__', '__doc__': None,
'imperative': ['C++', 'Java'], 'functional': ['Erlang', 'Haskell']}
>>>
>>>class test:
...     pass
...
>>>testNames = vars(test)
>>>type(testNames)
<jclass org.python.core.PyStringMap at 6965863>
>>>print testNames
{'__module__': '__main__', '__doc__': None}
>>>
>>>type(test.__dict__)
<jclass org.python.core.PyStringMap at 6965863>
```

PyStringMap and PyDictionary are Jython-specific mapping classes. However, all of Java's mapping classes are also available in Jython.

PyNone

The lack of a value is represented by the built-in object None. None is used in Jython as null is used in Java. The PyNone class is the object that represents this type. PyNone is a subclass of an internal object called PySingleton. This means that there is only one, single object of type PyNone. A PyNone instance evaluates to false in conditional statements and has no length:

```
>>>type(None)
<jclass org.python.core.PyNone at 3482695>
>>>a = None
>>>len(a)
Traceback (innermost last):
```

```
File "<console>", line 1, in ?
TypeError: len() of unsized object
>>>if a:
...     print "This will not print because a evaluates to false."
...
>>>
```

Operators

Operators are divided into five categories: arithmetic operators, shift operators, comparison operators, Boolean operators, and sequence operators. The type of object that an operator can be used with is included in its description by including the specific classes it works with or categories of types, such as "numeric" for PyInteger, PyLong, PyFloat, and PyComplex, "sequence" for PyList, PyTuple, and PyString, and "dictionary" for, of course, PyDictionary.

Arithmetic Operators

The first three of the numeric operators are unary so their descriptions are based on the assumption they prefix a single variable, x. The last six operators are binary and are described according to what the expression "x operator y" yields. The arithmetic operators are listed in Table 2.5.

Table 2.5   **Arithmetic Operators**

Operator	Description
- (-x)	The unary minus operator produces the negative of the numeric object it prefixes and applies only to numeric objects.
+ (+x)	The unary plus operator leaves the numeric object x unchanged and also applies to numeric objects only.
~ (~x)	The unary inversion operator yields the bit-inversion of x (algebraic equivalent $-(x+1)$). This may be used on PyInteger and PyLong objects only.
+ (x+y)	The addition operator yields the sum of two numeric objects. Note that addition applies to numeric objects, but the + sign is also used to join sequence objects as noted in the section on sequence operators.
- (x-y)	The subtraction operator yields the difference between two numeric objects.
* (x*y)	The multiplication operator yields the product of x times y. This applies to numeric objects, but the * operator is also used with sequences as noted in that section.

Operator	Description
** (x**y)	The power-of operator yields the value of x to the power of y and applies to all numeric objects.
/ (x/y)	The division operator yields the quotient of x divided by y. The division operator works for all numeric objects except for y=0, of course, which raises a `ZeroDivisionError` exception.
% (x%y)	The modulo operator yields the remainder for x divided by y. Modulo works for all numeric objects except for y=0, which raises a `ZeroDivisionError` exception.

The variable D is used to represent the `PyDictionary` instance.

Shift Operators

The shift operators apply to numeric objects. Table 2.6 lists the shift operators.

Table 2.6 **Shift Operators**

Operator	Description
x<<y	The left shift operator, which yields the binary result of shifting all bits y values to the left.
x>>y	The right shift operatory, which yields the binary result of shifting all bits y spaces to the right.
x&y	The bitwise AND operator, which yields the bitwise AND of x and y.
x|y	The bitwise OR operator, which yields the bitwise OR of x and y.
x^y	The bitwise exclusive OR operator, which yields the XOR of x and y.

Comparison Operators

Comparison operators require an understanding of what is true and false. In Jython, false is the numeric 0, `None`, an empty list, empty `tuple` or an empty dictionary. Anything else is true. The comparison operators (see Table 2.7) themselves yield the integer 1 for true and 0 for false, and they can be used on any type of Jython object—numeric, sequence, or dictionary.

Table 2.7   **Comparison Operators**

Operator	Description
<	Less than
>	Greater than
==	Equal
>=	Greater than or equal
<=	Less than or equal
!=	Not equal
<>	Another spelling for not equal. This spelling is considered obsolete so its use is discouraged.
is object identity match.	"x is y" yields 1 if the object x is the same as the object y. "id" is a built-in function that returns the id of an object, so "is" is a shortcut for id(x)==id(y).
is not object identity mismatch.	"x is not y" yields 1 (true) if the object identity for x is not the same as the object identity for y.
in sequence membership.	"x in L" returns 1 (true) if x is a member of the sequence L.
not in sequence exclusion.	"x not in L" returns 1 (true) if x is not a member of the sequence L.

Boolean Operators

These Boolean operators (see Table 2.8) add conditions for truth evaluation.

Table 2.8   **Boolean Operators**

Operator	Description
not	A Boolean operator that returns 1 if the argument is false.
or	A Boolean operator that returns the value of the first argument if it evaluates to true. If not, the value of the second argument is returned.
and	A Boolean operator that returns the value of the first argument if it evaluates to false, but returns the value of the second argument if the first evaluates to true.

Sequence Operators

Table 2.9 shows the operators for sequence objects. Listing 2.2 shows how to concantentate the sequences.

Table 2.9   **Sequence Operators**

Operator	Description
+	Used to concatenate sequences. Listing 2.2 shows concatenation used with each of Jython's sequence objects.

*	The repeat operator when used with sequences. The syntax is: sequence * multiplier. The multiplier is the number of times the sequence should be repeated, so it must be a whole number. This means it can only be a `PyInteger` or `PyLong` object. Example usage is as follows:
	
	`>>> L = [1] * 3`
	`>>> L`
	`[1, 1, 1]`

Listing 2.2   **Concatenating Sequences**

```
>>>var1 = "This, "
>>>var2 = 'that, '
>>>var1 + var2 + "and the other thing."
"This, that, and the other thing.
>>>
>>>L = ["b", "e", "a"]
>>>L + ["d", "g"]
['b', 'e', 'a', 'd', 'g']
>>>
>>>T1 = (1, 1.1, 1.0+1.1j)
>>>T2 = (1L, "one", ["o", "n", "e"]) #notice list within the tuple
>>> T1 + T2
(1, 1.1, (1+1.1j), 1L, 'one', ['o', 'n', 'e'])
```

Despite not being operators, string format characters are important to Jython's string processing ability and are included here. Jython also supports string format characters of the type used in C's `printf` function. These are placeholders appearing within a string, which consist of a % sign and a letter. For example, `%s` is a placeholder that can be supplanted by a string value external to the string itself. These characters are replaced with values when the string is followed by a % and a `tuple` or dictionary containing the required values. Table 2.10 shows a list of the format characters available and the data type they support.

Table 2.10   **String Format Characters**

Character	Jython type
%c	Character.
%d	Integer (originally signed decimal integer in C's `printf`).
%e	Floating-point number in scientific notation using the lowercase "e".
%f	Floating point number.
%g	Floating point number formatted like %e or %f depending on which is shorter.
%i	Integer.
%o	Unsigned octal integer.
%r	The string representation of the object provided. The representation is determined from the use of the built-in function `repr()`.
%s	String.
%u	Unsigned integer (originally unsigned decimal integer in C's `printf`).
%x	Unsigned hexadecimal integer with letters in lowercase.
%E	Floating point number, `PyFloat`, converted to scientific notation using the uppercase "E".
%G	Floating point number formatted like %E or %f depending on which is shorter.
%X	Unsigned hexadecimal integer with letters in uppercase.
%%	A literal %.

Values supplied to formatted strings at conversion time can be within a dictionary or a `tuple`. If a `tuple` is used, the format characters are interpolated in the order they occur with the values from the `tuple` in the order they occur. This syntax looks like this:

```
>>>"Meet the %s at %i o'clock" % ("train", 1)
"Meet the train at 1 o'clock"
```

As format strings become larger, the sequential conversion get a bit unwieldy. To handle that, Jython allows dictionaries to supply the values to format strings. The dictionaries key, however, must be supplied within parentheses in the string. An example of this syntax appears as follows:

```
>>>D = {"what":"train", "when":1}
>>>"Meet the %(what)s at %(when)i o'clock" % D
"Meet the train at 1 o'clock"
```

The key name becomes a useful clue when you run into errors or confusion in longer strings.

Built-Ins

Jython's *built-ins*, as the name implies, are the exceptions, functions, and variables available in Jython without any user-defined objects. This section includes the functions and variables only, while exceptions are reserved for Chapter 3, "Errors and Exceptions."

Jython's built-in functions are a rich set of tools that streamline introspection, type manipulation, and dynamic execution. These abilities are also the organization of this section.

Introspection Functions

Introspection is the information a language provides about itself. Java has the reflection API for this. Jython provides its introspection through built-in functions. A rough categorization of the introspective functions is those that inspect objects, and those that show what objects are defined.

Each object in Jython has a type and id that can be retrieved from the built-in functions `type()` and `id()`, respectively. These functions are defined as shown in Table 2.11.

Table 2.11   **Object Inspection Functions**

Function	Description
`type(object)`	Returns the type of the specified object as a name of one of the classes from the `org.python.core` package.
`id(object)`	Returns an integer representing the unique identification of the specified object.

Suppose you have a string object called S. Retrieving the type and id of S looks like this:

```
>>>S = "String object"
>>>type(S)
<jclass org.python.core.PyString at 1272917>
>>>id(S)
2703160
>>>S2 = S
>>>id(S2) # to prove S2 is a reference to the same object
2703160
```

Examining a built-in function, rather than a string, works the same way. Take a look at the built-in function `type`.

```
>>>type(type)
<jclass org.python.core.PyReflectedFunction at 2530155>
>>>id(type)
2804756
```

`PyReflectedFunction` is one of the `Py*` classes from `org.python.core` not discussed in this chapter. It is obviously a function type, considering `function` is part of the type name, and should be callable. After all, the example called it to retrieve its own type. Knowing an object is callable is not always the case though. Fortunately Jython has the built-in function `callable(object)`. `callable(object)` returns 1 or 0 (true or false) as to whether the object in question is a callable object.

```
>>>callable(type)  # Is the built-in function "type" callable?
1
>>>callable(S)  # Is the string "S" callable?
0
```

The built-in function `callable()` does not always tell the truth about Java objects however, and cannot always be trusted.

The `type`, `id`, and `callable` functions examine object attributes. However, you do not always know which objects are defined. There are built-in functions that examine just that—what names bindings exist. These functions are `dir()`, `vars()`, `globals()`, and `locals()`. Fully understanding these requires a better understanding of Jython's namespaces than is offered in this chapter. Chapter 4, "User-Defined Functions and Variable Scoping," contains the details about Jython's namespaces.

`dir([object])`	Returns a list of names defined in the object specified, or names in the current scope if no object is specified.
`vars([object])`	Returns a dictionary of bound names within the specified object. This is actually the objects own internal __dict__ object that will be discussed with Jython class definitions later on. The `vars` function only works on objects with a __dict__ attribute. If no object is specified, it does the same as `locals()`.
`globals()`	Returns a dictionary like object representing the variables defined in the global namespace.
`locals()`	Returns a dictionary like object representing the variables defined in the local namespace.

Listing 2.3 includes a function definition and a class definition so we can make use of `locals()` and `vars()`. The `def` is what creates a function and the `class` keyword creates a class. Note that the exact output you get when trying Listing 2.3 may differ. Variations in output may result from previous interactive experimentation or other inconsequential reasons.

Listing 2.3   **Exploring Namespaces**

```
>>>def test1():
...     "A function that prints its own local namespace"
...     avariable = "Inside test function"
...     print locals()
...
>>> class test2:
...     "An empty class"
...     pass
...
>>> dir()       # look at list of global names
['__doc__', '__name__', 'test1', 'test2']
>>>
>>> globals()   # look at global names and values
{'test2': <class __main__.test2 at 5150801>, '__name__': '__main__',
'__doc__': None, 'test1': <function test1 at 7469777>}
>>>
>>> dir(test1)  # look at names in the test function
['__doc__', '__name__', 'func_code', 'func_defaults', 'func_doc',
'func_globals', 'func_name']
>>>
>>> dir(test2)  # look at list of names in the class
['__doc__', '__module__']
>>>
>>> test1()     # invoke method that prints locals()
{'avariable': 'Something to populate the local namespace'}
>>>
>>> vars(test2) # user-defined classes have a __dict__, so vars works
{'__module__': '__main__', '__doc__': None}
```

This attribute inspection is not limited to Jython-only objects. The greatness of Jython is that it equally applies to Java objects. The statement `import java` makes the root java package available in Jython. Then all that is Java can be inspected in the same manner. Listing 2.4 inspects `java.util.ListIterator`. This is a familiar interface, but lets assume it is a newly downloaded package you wish to explore. You can traverse contents of each level of the package with `dir(package)` to see what is in them. All this can be done interactively in Jython as demonstrated in Listing 2.4. The actual output from Listing 2.4 will differ depending on your version of Java.

Listing 2.4 **Exploring Java Packages**

```
>>> import java
>>> dir(java)
['__name__', 'applet', 'awt', 'beans', 'io', 'lang', 'math', 'net', 'rmi',
'security', 'sql', 'text', 'util']
>>> dir(java.util)
['AbstractCollection', 'AbstractList', 'AbstractMap',
'AbstractSequentialList', 'AbstractSet', 'ArrayList', 'Arrays', 'BitSet',
'Calendar', 'Collection', 'Collections', 'Comparator',
'ConcurrentModificationException', 'Date', 'Dictionary',
'EmptyStackException', 'Enumeration', 'EventListener', 'EventObject',
'Gregorian Calendar', 'HashMap', 'HashSet', 'Hashtable', 'Iterator',
'LinkedList', 'List', 'ListIterator', 'ListResourceBundle', 'Locale', 'Map',
'MissingResourceException ', 'NoSuchElementException', 'Observable',
'Observer', 'Properties', 'PropertyPermission', 'PropertyResourceBundle',
'Random', 'ResourceBundle', 'Set',
'SimpleTimeZone', 'SortedMap', 'SortedSet', 'Stack', 'StringTokenizer',
'TimeZone', 'Timer', 'TimerTask', 'TooManyListenersException', 'TreeMap',
'TreeSet', 'Vector', 'WeakHashMap', '__name__', 'jar', 'zip']
>>> dir(java.util.ListIterator)
['', 'add', 'hasPrevious', 'nextIndex', 'previous', 'previousIndex', 'set']
>>> test = java.util.ListIterator() # try calling it anyway
Traceback (innermost last):
File "<console>", line 1, in ?
TypeError: can't instantiate interface (java.util.ListIterator)
```

Numeric Functions

The built-in numeric functions are convenience functions for common math operations. These six functions are shown in Table 2.12.

Table 2.12 **Built-In Numeric Functions**

Function	Description
abs(x)	Returns the absolute value of the number x.
divmod(x, y)	Returns both the division and modulus of x divided by y (for example, 2/3, 2%3).
hex(x)	Returns the hexadecimal representation of the integer x as a string.
oct(x)	Returns the octal representation of the integer x as a string.
pow(x, y [,z])	Returns x**y. If z is provided, it returns x**y % z.

Function	Description
`round(x [, ndigits])`	Returns `PyFloat` number representing the number x rounded to 0 decimal places. If the optional `ndigits` is provided, x is rounded to the `ndigits` from the decimal. Negative `ndigits` numbers mean left of the decimal; positive mean right of the decimal. Currently, in Jython 2.0, the `ndigits` argument must be an integer. This differs slightly from the CPython implementation where it can be any number that can be converted to an `int`.

Type Conversion Functions

Conversion of Java types requires type casts—something that is usually pervasive in Java programs. In Jython, such type conversions are handled with built-in functions. These functions are named according to the object returned. This simplicity makes definition unnecessary—an example of this is sufficient to clarify their usage. Listing 2.5 shows each of the type conversion functions: `int`, `long`, `float`, `complex`, `tuple`, and `list`.

Listing 2.5   **Type Conversions**

```
>>>int(3.5)
3
>>>long(22)
22L
>>>float(8)
8.0
>>>complex(2.321)
(2.321+0j)
>>>tuple("abcdefg")
('a', 'b', 'c', 'd', 'e', 'f', 'g')
>>>list("abcdefg")
['a', 'b', 'c', 'd', 'e', 'f', 'g']
```

`coerce(object1, object2)` is also a built-in function. The `coerce` function takes two objects as parameters, tests if the values of these objects can be represented in a common object, and returns the two values in a `tuple` of same-type objects. If it is not possible to represent the values as a common type, `coerce` returns the object `None`. A float and integer value can both be represented by a float:

```
>>>coerce(3.1415, 6)
(3.1415, 6.0)
```

However, a string and float cannot be represented as the same type:

```
>>>results = coerce("a", 2.3)
Traceback (most recent call last):
File "<stdin>", line 1, in ?
TypeError: number coercion failed
```

The Built-in File Function

There is only one built-in file function. That function is `open`. The `open` function returns a file object that can be read from or written to. The syntax for the open functions is as follows:

```
open(filepath [, mode [, buffer]])
```

`filepath` is the platform specific path and filename to the file that is being opened.

The `mode` symbol supplied to the `open` function determines whether the file is open for reading, writing, appending, or both reading and writing. This mode option also specifies if this is a text or a binary file. Text mode implies the platform specific new-line translations. Binary mode implies just binary data, so no newline translations and only the low-order byte of Unicode characters are used. Binary mode must be explicitly specified to write binary data in Jython, otherwise Unicode characters will pass through the default java codec to and from the file. Note that the mode setting is optional in the open function, and when not specified, the default mode of reading text is used. The symbols used in the mode argument are as follows:

r = reading
w = writing

a = appending

+ = designates both reading and writing when added to "r", "w" or "a" (e.g. "r+", "w+" or "a+")

b = binary mode

The optional `buffer` argument to the `open` function is currently ignored.

Sequence Functions

These built-in functions either require a list type as a parameter or return a list except for the string specific functions.

The functions specific to the `PyString` sequence are `intern`, `chr`, `unichr`, and `unicode`, and are described in Table 2.13.

Table 2.13   *PyString*-**Specific Functions**

Function	Description
intern(string)	This places the specified string in a PyStringMap of long-lived strings. The reason being it should provide performance advantages in dictionary lookups.
chr(integer)	For integers <= 65535, chr returns the character (PyString of length 1) that has the specified integer value.
ord(character)	This function is the opposite to chr(integer) (see preceding list item). For character c, chr(ord(c))==c.
unichr(integer)	This does the same as chr. These two methods, chr and unichr, exist for compatibility with CPython.
unicode(string [, encoding[, errors]])	This function creates a new PyString object using the encoding specified. The available encodings are found in Jython Lib directory within the encodings folder. The optional errors argument can be either strict, ignore, or replace.

The functions that work on any Jython sequence object are described in Table 2.14.

Table 2.14   **Built-In Sequence Functions**

Function	Description
max(sequence)	Returns the greatest value within the sequence.
min(sequence)	Returns the least value within the sequence.
slice([start,] stop[, step])	The slice function is a synonym for sequence slice syntax. It is used by extensions, mainly.
range([start,] stop [,step]) *and* xrange([start,]stop [,step])	The range and xrange functions are used to generate lists. The of these functions are the same; however, their implementation differs. The range function builds and returns a list of integers, while the xrange function returns an xrange object that supplies integers as needed. The idea is that xrange is an advantage for very large ranges. All arguments for range must be integers (PyInteger or PyLong).

continues

Table 2.14   **Continued**

Function	Description
	Counting starts at the designated start number, or 0. Counting continues to, but not including, the designated stop integer. If the optional step argument is provided, it is used as the increment number. Examples best clarify range and xrange:

```
>>>range(4)
[0, 1, 2, 3]
>>>range(3, 6)
[3, 4, 5]
>>>range(2, 10, 2)
[2, 4, 6, 8]
>>>xrange(4)
(0, 1, 2, 3)
>>>type(xrange(4))   # check the type returned
from xrange
<jclass org.python.core.PyXRange at 7991538>
>>>type(range(4))    # check the type returned
from range
>>> type(range(4))
<jclass org.python.core.PyList at 7837392>
>>>range(10, 0, -1) # use range to count
backwards
[10, 9, 8, 7, 6, 5, 4, 3, 2, 1]
```

Dynamic Language Functions

Jython's dynamic language functions allow dynamic code generation, compilation and execution with functions like compile, apply, execfile, and eval. They are not addressed here because the brevity with which they would be treated at this point in the book would only provide confusion.

Attribute Tools

Jython has a rich set of built-in functions for working with Jython classes and their attributes. For attributes specifically, there are the hasattr, delattr, getattr, and setattr functions. Parameters for hasattr, delattr, and getattr are all object, attribute (such as hasattr(object, attribute)). setattr requires an additional (third) parameter which is the value the specified attribute should be set to.

Jython class attributes are normally accessed with dot notation much like
Java's. If object A contains attribute b, the syntax for accessing attribute b is A.b:

```
>>> class A:
...     b = 10
...
>>> A.b
10
```

Jython's attribute tools exist as an alternative way of working with object
attributes, but they are definitely less common that the traditional dot notation. This section walks through the usage of these built-in functions on two
objects. The first of these objects is an empty Jython class, but the second is a
Java class that has nothing but a public instance variable—var1. The catch
with Java classes is that they are not as flexible as a Jython class. Arbitrary
attributes cannot be added or deleted from Java classes.

Start by creating and empty Jython class:

```
>>>class JythonClass:
...     pass
```

Next, make an instance of the new class so we have an object to use hasattr,
setattr, and getattr on:

```
>>>jyInstance = JythonClass()
```

The hasattr function checks whether an object contains an attribute. The
object and attribute name are also the hasattr function's parameters. To check
for the attribute var1 in our instance named jyInstance, use this:

```
>>>hasattr(jyInstance, "var1")
0
```

The result you get is zero, or false. var1 is not currently defined.

Now let's assume we want to define, or "set" it. While an assignment would
work to do this, there is also the setattr function. setattr requires three parameters: the object, the attribute name, and the value to bind to the attribute
name. Setting a jyInstance attribute named var1 to a string value looks
like this:

```
>>>setattr(jyInstance, "var1", "A new value for var1")
```

Now use hasattr to check again for "var1" within jyInstance:

```
>>>hasattr(jyInstance, "var1")
1
```

The result of 1, or true, confirms var1 is there.

Now that `jyInstance` has an attribute, we can use `getattr` to retrieve its value. The `getattr` function requires the object and attribute name as parameters:

```
>>>getattr(jyInstance, "var1")
'A new value for var1'
```

The `getattr()` function also works for accessing members in classes and objects in modules:

```
>>> import os
>>> getattr(os, "pathsep") # get a variable from a module
';'
>>> getattr(os, "getcwd")() # call a function within a module
'C:\\WINDOWS\\Desktop'
```

And finally, the attribute may be deleted with `delattr`:

```
>>>delattr(jyInstance, "var1")
>>>hassattr(jyInstance, "var1")
0
```

Java classes differ from Jython classes, however. Forget the preceding Jython example and continue anew with a Java class. Assume the java class definition is as follows:

```
public class JavaClass {
    public String var1;
    public void JavaClass() {}
}
```

Also assume that `JavaClass` is compiled with `javac` and that it is in the current directory from which you start Jython.

You can use `JavaClass` to show how Jython's built-in attribute functions also work on Java objects. Start by importing `JavaClass` and creating an instance of it:

```
>>>import JavaClass
>>>javaInstance = JavaClass()
```

Now use `hasattr` to test for the existence of the attribute `var1` in `JavaClass`:

```
>>>hasattr(javaInstance, "var1")
1
```

Now that the existence of `var1` is confirmed, change it a few times with `setattr` and test the new value with `getattr`:

```
>>>setattr(javaInstance, "var1", "A new value for var1")
>>>getattr(javaInstance, "var1") # check out the new value
'A new value for var1'
>>>setattr(javaInstance, "var1", "Yet another value")
>>>getattr(javaInstance, "var1")
'Yet another value'
```

So far the Java object works the same as the Jython object. The difference appears when you try to delete an attribute, or when you try to add an arbitrary attribute. First, can you delete var1?

```
>>>delattr(javaInstance, "var1")
Traceback (innermost last):
File "<console>", line 1, in ?
TypeError: can't delete attr from java instance: var1
```

That's a no. Can you add an arbitrary attribute?

```
>>># Can we add another arbitrary attribute
>>>setattr(ja, "var2", "Value for var2")
Traceback (innermost last):
File "<console>", line 1, in ?
TypeError: can't set arbitrary attribute in java instance: var2
```

No, yet again.

Continue object inspection with a different Java class: java.util.Vector. First, import and create an instance of Vector like this:

```
>>>import java
>>>v = java.util.Vector()  # import a well-known java class
```

Inspect the Vector instance for the attribute toString:

```
>>>hasattr(v, "toString")  # in case you forgot
1
```

Object inspection includes testing whether an instance is part of a specific class. The built-in isinstance function determines this for the instance and class supplied as arguments:

```
>>>isinstance(v, java.util.Vector)
1
```

If the result had instead been zero, it would mean that v is not an instance of java.util.Vector.

Note from Listing 2.6 that the built-in function isinstance returns 1 or 0 (true or false) for whether the instance is in fact an instance of the supplied class. Syntax is isinstance(instance, class).

Functional Tools

Elements from functional programming show up in Jython's built-in functions. These functions work with lists and are filter, map, reduce, and zip. All of these built-in functions require another function as their first parameter, so discussion of these is reserved until the chapter on Jython functions.

Miscellaneous Functions

Some built-in functions, while equally useful, are less easily categorized than others. As these have no special relationship, it is best to provide just a list of functions and their definitions, including examples where it benefits clarity. Table 2.15 provides these miscellaneous functions.

Table 2.15   **Miscellaneous Functions**

Function	Description
cmp(x, y)	The compare function, cmp, requires two parameters to compare. A value of −1, 0, or 1 is returned based on whether x<y, x==y, or x>y, respectively.
len(object)	len returns the length of a sequence or mapping object. It would have been included with the sequence functions if it didn't also work on mapping objects.

repr(object)	repr returns a string representation of an object that is useful in reconstructing that object. Suppose you need a string representation of a java.lang.Vector object. The repr function provides this as noted in this brief example:
	
	``
	>>>>>> import java
	>>> v = java.util.Vector()
	>>> repr(v)
	'[]'
	>>> v.add("A string")
	1
	>>> v.add(4)
	1
	>>> v.add([1,2,3,4,5])
	1
	>>> repr(v)
	'[A string, 4, [1, 2, 3, 4, 5]]'
	``

str(object)	str returns a string that describes the specified object. This differs from repr in that this string can be a description or label rather than the more strict representation of data expected from repr().
reload(module)	This function is self-evident, but its usefulness isn't immediately evident. This function allows you to work something out in interactive mode, switch to an editor to change a module as needed, then return to interactive mode to reload the altered module.

Function	Description
raw_input([prompt])	The raw_input function reads a string from standard input with the trailing newline removed:

	``
	>>>>>> name = raw_input("Enter your name: ")
	Enter your name: Robert
	>>> print name
	Robert
	``

input([prompt])	This is the same as raw_input except that what is entered at the prompt is evaluated.

	``
	>>> input("Enter a Jython expression: ")
	Enter a Jython expression: 2+3
	5 <-- the evaluated result of 2+3
	``

hash(object)	Two objects with the same value have the same hash value. This hash value is retrieved with the built-in hash function.

Comparison of Jython Data Types and Java Data Types

What is the difference between Java's data types and Jython's? Java is a strictly typed language where data values are stored in objects that have an explicitly specified type. The following Java statement clearly creates an object bound to the name myString of type java.lang.String with the self-aware value I'm a string:

```
String myString = "I'm a string";
```

Jython is also a strongly typed language in which data is represented by objects of a specific type. The big difference is that Jython is dynamically typed. Unlike the preceding little Java snippet, Jython does not use explicit type information in its code. Therefore, that information is not available at compile time. Instead, Jython eagerly determines types based on assigned values at runtime.

What does this difference in typing mean? It's good to be wary of oversimplifications of type systems, but with that said—Java explicit typing means that Java compilers can make certain assumptions about a variable at compile time. This allows for many optimizations and compile-time type-safety checks. For Jython's dynamic types, it means flexible, high-level data objects that allow for compact code, increased clarity of program logic, and often increased programmer productivity. In short, Jython data objects help provide great flexibility at the expense of compile-time optimizations.

Java Types

The primary advantage of Jython is the ability to use Java classes without modification. This creates problems with converting types from Java's types to Jython's. Java is type-rich. Methods, constructors, and variables use types. Jython, on the other hand, is free of primitive types, has data objects that are not native in Java, and determines types dynamically. This means Jython's types require translation to Java types for method arguments, and translation from Java types for method return values. Jython automatically translates types according to Table 2.16.

Table 2.16 **Type Translations Between Java and Jython**

Java	Jython
Char	PyString of length 1
Byte	PyInteger
Short	PyInteger
Int	PyInteger
Long	PyInteger
Float	PyFloat
Double	PyFloat
java.lang.String	PyString
byte[]	PyString
char[]	PyString
PyObject	PyObject
A java class	PyJavaClass, which represents the given Java class.

An instance of a Java class	PyInstance of the Java class identified in instance.__class__. For example:
	
	`>>> from java.lang import Double`
	`>>> d = Double(2.0)`
	`>>> d.__class__`
	`<jclass java.lang.Double at 3291150>`

Boolean	PyInteger (When translating from a Jython PyInteger to a Java Boolean, 0==false and nonzero==true. When translating from a Java Boolean to a Jython type, true==1 and false==0.)
java.lang.Object	java.lang.Object

These types translate consistently. The specified Jython object works when its corresponding Java type appears in a method signature, and a returned Java type converts to its corresponding Jython class.

Java method parameters or return values may also be an instance of a Java class or an array of a Java class. If a method specifies the Java class A as a parameter type, you can instantiate and supply an instance of A, an instance of a Java subclass of A, or a Jython subclass of A to meet the requirement. If an instance of A is the return type of a Java method, Jython turns that into a PyInstance of A or whatever subclass of A was returned.

If an array of a Java objects is expected in a Java method signature, you must supply an array containing objects created from the class or subclass of the specified object. To create a Java array, you must use the jarray module. The jarray module contains two functions: array and zeros. The array function requires two arguments: the first is a sequence, and the second is a code letter that designates the type of the array. The length of the array equals the length of the supplied sequence. Note that the sequence must contain objects of the same type. A sequence can be a string, list, or tuple as appropriate. To create a character array (char[] in Java), first import the jarray module, then supply a sequence of characters as the first parameter, and the type code c as the second parameter like this:

```
>>> import jarray
>>> myJavaArray = jarray.array("abcdefg", "c")
>>> myJavaArray
array(['a', 'b', 'c', 'd', 'e', 'f', 'g'], char)
>>> myJavaArray = jarray.array(['a','b','c','d'], "c")
>>> myJavaArray
array(['a', 'b', 'c', 'd'], char)
```

The Java "class" of an array type may also be used to designated the array's type in the second argument to the jarray.array function. For Java primitive data types, this means the java.lang class that wraps the primitive type. To make an int[] array from a Jython PyList, you could use the following:

```
>>> import jarray
>>> import java  # Required to see the java.lang.Integer class
>>> myIntArray = jarray.array([1,2,3,4,5,6,7,8,9], java.lang.Integer)
array([1, 2, 3, 4, 5, 6, 7, 8, 9], java.lang.Integer)
>>> i = java.lang.Integer(1)
```

To create an array of a specific length and type, but only 0, or null, values, use the function jarray.zeros. The jarray.zeros function also requires two arguments: the first is the length of the array, and the second the type code or class which designates the array type. An example of using jarray.zeros to create a java byte[] of length ten looks like this:

```
>>> import jarray
>>> byteArray = jarray.zeros(10, "b")
>>> byteArray
array([0, 0, 0, 0, 0, 0, 0, 0, 0, 0], byte)
```

The list of all the type codes, their associated Java types, and classes from the java.lang package for those types appear in Table 2.17.

Table 2.17   **Array Typecodes, Types, and Classes**

Typecode	Java Type	Type Wrapper Class
z	Boolean	java.lang.Boolean
c	char	java.lang.Character
b	byte	java.lang.Byte
h	short	java.lang.Short
i	int	java.lang.Integer
l	long	java.lang.Long
f	float	java.lang.Float
d	double	java.lang.Double

For arrays of classes without a typecode, use the class to designate the array type. For example, a Data[] for the class java.util.Data can be created with the following:

```
>>> import java
>>> import jarray
>>> myDateArray = jarray.zeros(5, java.util.Data)
>>> myDateArray
array([None, None, None, None, None], java.util.Date)
```

When you encounter difficulty in calling a specific Java method signature due to limitations on type translations and overloaded methods, the best solution is to create an instance of the Java type's object wrapper. If a PyInteger doesn't convert properly to call a method signature requiring an short type, force proper recognition by first creating an instance of the short type's object wrapper java.lang.Short. Assume method A is overloaded with one signature A(short s) and another A(int i) and calling the short signature is not working. The following example demostrates how to correct this:

```
>>> import java
>>> myPyInt = 5
>>> myJavaShort = java.lang.Short(myPyInt)
>>> ## Here you could call the hypothetical method "A(myJavaShort)"
```

3

Errors and Exceptions

THIS CHAPTER DETAILS JYTHON'S BUILT-IN EXCEPTIONS and related mechanisms. The topic of exception objects also invites a closer study of the `try`/`except` statement, `raise` statement, `traceback` object, `assert` statement, `__debug__` variable, and the recently added warnings framework.

Jython Exceptions

Jython's exceptions are defined in the class `org.python.core.exceptions`. The source for this class contains a hierarchy of the exceptions that is shown in Figure 3.1. Each exception's corresponding message string is included following the class name in this image.

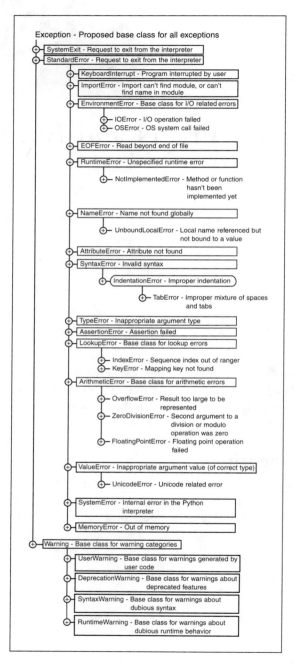

Figure 3.1   Jython's exception hierarchy.

You cannot divide a number by zero. You cannot access a name that does not exist, and you cannot use more memory than your machine has. The Jython interpreter enforces such edicts by raising an exception whenever something tries to break these rules. Jython version 2.1 infuses some gray into this black-and-white world with the addition of warnings. The warnings you see in Figure 3.1 are exceptions, but they introduce something unique because of the warnings framework, discussed later in this chapter.

The simplest way to study Jython's exceptions is to try to create an exceptional situation in Jython's interactive interpreter. Below is an example of some errors and the exceptions raised because of the error.

You cannot access a variable that is not defined:

```
>>> print x
Traceback (innermost last):
  File "<console>", line 1, in ?
NameError: x
```

You cannot access a list index beyond the range of the list:

```
>>> L = []
>>> print L[1]
Traceback (innermost last):
  File "<console>", line 1, in ?
IndexError: index out of range: 1
```

You cannot call a non-existent method:

```
>>> L.somemethod()  # Calling a non-existent method name is an error
Traceback (innermost last):
  File "<console>", line 1, in ?
AttributeError: 'list' object has no attribute 'somemethod'
```

Indention matters in Jython, as seen in this loop:

```
>>>for x in range(10):
...     i = x      # This line is indented one tab
...       print i  # This line is indented 5 spaces
Traceback (innermost last):
  (no code object) at line 0
  File "<console>", line 3
              print i
              ^
SyntaxError: inconsistent dedent
```

Java exceptions can also be raised in Jython. This occurs when an imported Java class throws an exception within the Java code. This exception is reported in Jython as the Java exception. Listing 3.1 shows a simple example of this.

Listing 3.1   **A Java Exception Within Jython**

```
//file:  Except.java
public class Except {
    public Except() {}
    public void test() throws IllegalAccessException {
        throw new IllegalAccessException("Just testing");
    }
}

>>>#Using the above Java class in Jython
>>> import Except
>>> e = Except()
>>> e.test()
Traceback (innermost last):
  File "<console>", line 1, in ?
java.lang.IllegalAccessException: just testing
        at Except.test(Except.java:4)
    ...
java.lang.IllegalAccessException: java.lang.IllegalAccessException:
Just testing
```

Exception Handling

In Java terminology, an exception is *thrown* when an error occurs. This thrown exception propagates until something "catches" it. In Jython lingo, exceptions are "raised" instead of thrown. When a Jython exception is raised, the flow of the program changes to a search for exception handlers. This searching not only includes the scope in which the exception occurred, but propagates through the stack levels looking for an appropriate except clause. If an appropriate except clause does not exist, it halts the program and displays the exception with traceback information.

> **Jython 2.1 and** sys.excepthook
> New in Python 2.1 is sys.excepthook, which you can set to a callable object. although this feature is not in Jython at the time of this writing, it is likely that it will exist by the time you read this. What this means is that when an exception finds no appropriate except clause to handle it, it is passed to sys.excepthook before halting the program. That way, whatever you assign to sys.excepthook can do anything you want with the exception before program termination. This is valuable for closing and flushing resources before program termination.

The try statement in Jython has two formats. The first is the try/except/else, which has the following syntax:

```
"try:" code-block
"except" [expression ["," target]] ":" code-block
["else:" code-block]
```

Listing 3.2 shows an example usage of this syntax.

Listing 3.2   **The *try/except/else* Syntax**

```
>>> try:
...     print a  # a is not defined, so is a NameError
... except SyntaxError:
...     print "I caught a SyntaxError"
... except NameError:
...     print "I caught a NameError"
... except:
...     print "A plain except catches ANY type of exception"
... else:
...     print "no exception was raised in the try block
...
I caught a NameError
```

The flow of execution in Listing 3.2 starts with the block of code within the try. If an exception is raised, except blocks are searched for the first one to handle the specific type of exception raised or an except without a specified exception type (it is generic and handles any exception). If no exception is raised within the try block, execution continues with the else block. The except half of the try/except can have two optional elements before its code block. The first is the class of exception that the associated block of code is to handles. Listing 3.2 specifies an exception class for all but the last except clause. Listing 3.2 does not make use of the second optional element—the target element. The target receives the exception's parameter value if provided. A brief, pre-emptive look at the raise statement shows what is meant by the exception's "parameter value":

```
>>> try:
...     raise SyntaxError, "Bad Syntax"
... except SyntaxError, target:
...     print target
...
Bad Syntax
```

The string Bad Syntax is the parameter given the SyntaxError class when raising the exception. Therefore, this would also be what the variable target is bound to in the except clause.

Figure 3.1 not only shows Jython's exceptions and their message strings, it also shows the hierarchy of exceptions. To handle an OverflowError, ZeroDivisionError, or FloatingPointError, you only need to handle their super class—ArithmeticError. Handling the StandardError exception would cover most errors, and handling the base class Exception should handle all exceptions except user-defined ones that do not inherit from `Exception` as is recommended. Listing 3.3 shows how the class hierarchy of exceptions allows you to handle a group of exceptions by handling their common base class.

Listing 3.3   **Base Classes in the *Except* Clause**

```
>>> try:
...     1/0
... except ArithmeticError, e:
...     print "Handled ArithmeticError- ", e
...
Handled ArithmeticError-  integer division or modulo
>>>
>>> L = [1,2,3]
>>> try:
...     print L[10]  # this index does not exist
... except LookupError, e:
...     print "Handling LookupError- ", e
...
Handling LookupError-  index out of range: 10
```

The second format is the `try/finally`. This executes the `try` block of code, and whether an exception is raised or not, the `finally` block of code is executed. The syntax for this is as follows:

```
"try:" code-block
"finally:" code-block
```

Listing 3.4 shows an example of `try/finally` that uses the `finally` block to close a file object regardless of what happens in the `try` block.

Listing 3.4   **Using *try/finally* to Ensure that a File Is Closed**

```
>>> fileA = open("datafile", "w")
>>> try:
...     fileB = open("olddata", "r")
...     print >>fileA, fileB.read()
... finally:
...     fileA.close()
...     if "fileB" in vars():
...         fileB.close()
...
```

Another valuable trick in Listing 3.4 is testing if the file is in `vars()` before trying to close it. If the `open()` function failed, there is no `fileB` to close, so the testing for existing in `vars()` prevents a second exception from being raised within the `finally` block by trying to close a non-existing file object.

Listing 3.5 demonstrates nesting `try`/`except` statements. In this listing, only the outermost `try` statement has an appropriate except expression, so this outer level is what handles the exception. Another interesting note about Listing 3.5 is the use of the `sys.exit()` function. You must first import the `sys` module before using this function, and what this actually does is raise the `SystemExit` exception. This means if you catch the `SystemExit` exception in the `except` clause, the system does not exit.

Listing 3.5   **Nested *try* Statements**

```
>>> import sys
>>>
>>> try:
...     try:
...         try:
...             sys.exit() # This raises the "SystemExit" exception
...         except ValueError:
...             pass
...     except SyntaxError:
...         pass
... except SystemExit:
...     print "SystemExit exception caught- not exiting."
...
SystemExit exception caught- not exiting.
```

Listing 3.1 showed a Java program that throws a `java.lang.IllegalAccessException`. This raises the issue of how Java specific exceptions are handled (caught) in Jython. Listing 3.6 has a revised version of the Jython code that appeared in Listing 3.1. A `try`/`except` has been added with an `except` clause that specifically handles the `java.lang.IllegalAccessException` thrown in the java class. To handle a Java exception you can either use an empty `except` clause so that it is generic and handles any exception, or you can use `import java` before the exception and provide the specific exception's package and class in the `except` clause that is designed to handle the exception or its subclasses.

Listing 3.6   **A Java Exception Handled in Jython**

```
//file: Except.java
public class Except {
    public Except() {}
    public void test() throws IllegalAccessException {
        throw new IllegalAccessException("Just testing");
    }
}
```

continues

Listing 3.6 **Continued**

```
>>> #Using the above Java class in Jython
>>> import Except  # import the exception-throwing Java class
>>> import java
>>> try:
...     e = Except()
...     e.test()
... except java.lang.IllegalAccessException:
...     print "Caught IllegalAccessException"
...
Caught IllegalAccessException
```

The *raise* Statement

Explicitly raising an exception where one would not normally occur may be desirable at times in Jython. To do this, use the `raise` statement. An example situation where this is useful is checking parameter types. Jython does not have compile-time checking for this in the 2.1 or earlier versions. This means that if a parameter must be a certain type, the code must test it at runtime and use the `raise` statement for inappropriate types. Listing 3.7 does exactly that. The function `listComplement` requires two lists or `tuples` for parameters. The parameters' types are tested before any other processing, and a `TypeError` exception is raised if either parameter is not a list or `tuple`.

Interfaces and Jython

Jython 2.1 and earlier does not have parameter, protocol, interface, or type checking. Python's "types" special interest group is churning with proposals related to these topics. Substantial thought, research, and hard work have resulting in a few Python enhancement proposals that could likely change this in future releases. Check for this on Jython's website or the website associated with this book.

Listing 3.7 determines the set complement of two lists. The complement of list 1 (`L1`) relative to list 2 (`L2`) is all elements in `L2` that are not in `L1`. An optimization note is that list 1 (`L1`) is converted into dictionary keys so that the fast `has_key` can be used instead of the sequence member test, `in`. The types module is imported in Listing 3.7 to compare parameter types with the types that are required by the `listComplement` function (`TupleType` and `ListType`).

Listing 3.7 **Jython's *raise* Statement**

```
# file sets.py

# import cononical types to compare with parameter types
from types import ListType, TupleType

def listComplement(S1, S2):
    if not (type(S1) == ListType or type(S1) == TupleType and
            type(S2) == ListType or type(S2) == TupleType):
        raise TypeError, "Only lists and tuples are supported."
    D = {}
    for x in S1:
        D[x] = 1  # Convert S1 to dictionary keys.
    complement = []            # An empty list to hold results.
    for item in S2:
        if not D.has_key(item):
            complement.append(item)
    return complement

# Test the function with lists
list1 = range(0, 100, 3)
list2 = range(0, 100, 7)

resultSet = listComplement(list1, list2)
print "Complement of list1 relative to list2: ", resultSet

# Now Test the function with a list and a numeric type
notalist = 5

resultSet = listComplement(notalist, list2)
```

Results from running jython sets.py at a command line:

```
Complement of list1 relative to list2:  [7, 14, 28, 35, 49, 56, 70, 77, 91,
98]
Traceback (innermost last):
  File "sets.py", line 26, in ?
  File "sets.py", line 8, in listComplement
TypeError: Only lists and tuples are supported.
```

Listing 3.7 is longer than the average interactive example, and it is better to place its contents in a file that can be ran with the command-line jython sets.py. The results from running the sets.py script show how the listComplement function raises a TypeError for inappropriate parameters.

The raise statement in Listing 3.7 uses two expressions, but there are actually three optional expressions in the raise statement's syntax. The syntax for the raise statement is as follows:

```
"raise" [expression ["," expression ["," expression]]]
```

Substituting names of what the expressions represent makes it read like this:

```
"raise" [type ["," value ["," traceback]]]
```

The type can be the actual class of the exception, a string, or an instance of the exception class raised. Listing 3.7 uses the actual TypeError class to raise the error. However, it could have used an instance of TypeError to raise the same exception as demonstrated in Listing 3.8. Using a string for the type in a raise statement raises a string-based exception. String-based exceptions are legal, but are discouraged in favor of class or instance exceptions instead.

Listing 3.8   **Different Ways to Specify the *type* of a Raised Exception**

```
>>> # The first way is the actual class.
>>> # Use the built-in function "type()" to confirm it is a class.
>>> type(TypeError)
<jclass org.python.core.PyClass at 7907289>
>>> raise TypeError
Traceback (innermost last):
  File "<console>", line 1, in ?
TypeError:
>>>
>>> # The second way is a string.
>>> raise "A String-based exception"
Traceback (innermost last):
  File "<console>", line 1, in ?
A String-based exception
>>>
>>> # The third way is an instance.
>>> Err = TypeError()   # Create the instance.
>>> type(Err)           # Confirm it is an instance.
<jclass org.python.core.PyInstance at 2735779>
>>> raise Err           # Raise the instance
Traceback (innermost last):
  File "<console>", line 1, in ?
TypeError:
```

The value, or second expression of the raise statement, is a constructor parameter for the exception class. Looking back at Listing 3.7, we see the class TypeError is instantiated with the value Only lists and tuples are supported. This means the following line:

```
>>>Err = TypeError("Only lists and tuples are supported")
>>>raise Err
```

is the same as is the same as this line:

```
>>>raise TypeError, "Only lists and tuples are supported"
```

It is a special case when the `type`, first expression in the `raise` statement, is an instance. The `value` expression is a constructor parameter, but if the class is already constructed (an instance), there is nothing to do with the value. The rule in this case (which may already be obvious) is that if the type of exception is an instance, the value expression must be `None`.

The number of parameters the exception's constructor gets depends on whether the `value` expression is a `tuple`. A list, dictionary, number, or anything except a `tuple` is passed as only one parameter. A `tuple`, on the other hand, is passed as a parameter list. This means there are `len(T)` parameters for a value of tuple `T`. Listing 3.9 imports a class called `MyException` that does nothing except print out the number of parameters passed to its constructor. Listing 3.9 includes a new import statement: `from MyException import exceptionA`. This imports the `exceptionA` class from the module `MyException`. With this import syntax, `exceptionA` becomes the name bound in the namespace, and it is the exception class used in Listing 3.9.

Listing 3.9   **Exception Parameters**

```
>>> from MyException import exceptionA
>>> raise exceptionA, (1,2,3,4,5,6,7,8,9)
Number of parameters = 9     <-- 9 parameters, all PyInteger objects.
Traceback (innermost last):
  File "<console>", line 1, in ?
exceptionA: <MyException.exceptionA instance at 1669053>
>>>
>>> # Now try a list instead of a tuple
>>> raise exceptionA, [1,2,3,4,5,6,7,8,9]
Number of parameters = 1     <-- Only one parameter, a PyList object.
Traceback (innermost last):
  File "<console>", line 1, in ?
exceptionA: <MyException.exceptionA instance at 1075173>


# MyException.py source

class exceptionA(Exception):
    """An exception class for testing contstructor parameters"""

    def __init__(self, args): #'*args' catches all remaining arguments
        print "Number of parameters =", len(args)
```

The `__init__` method in Listing 3.9 contains a tricky parameter: `*args`. The asterisk allows this to catch all remaining arguments, which is the mechanism that allows the number of parameters test to work properly. More detailed discussion of the * parameter sytnax appears in Chapter 4, "User-Defined Functions and Variable Scoping."

If the optional third expression exists in the raise statement, it must be a traceback object. See the next section concerning tracebacks for more information.

What if there are no expressions provided to the raise statement? This re-raises the exception last raised within the same scope, and is demonstrated in Listing 3.10.

Listing 3.10 *raise* **Without any Expressions**

```
>>> # First, define a function so the two exception can
>>> # be within the same local scope
>>> def test():
...     try:
...         raise SyntaxError, "Bad Syntax"
...     except:
...         pass
...     print "passed first raise"
...     raise
...
>>> # Call the function to see how the second "raise" works
>>> test()
passed first raise
Traceback (innermost last):
  File "<console>", line 1, in ?
  File "<console>", line 3, in test
SyntaxError: Bad Syntax
```

Tracebacks

When an exception occurs, the message you see begins with a traceback. Also, when you raise an exception, the optional third expressions must evaluate to a traceback object. The traceback object helps unravel the steps taken to the point where an exception was raised. The traceback object is accessible with sys.exc_info() when you are within an exception handler (the except or finally after a try). Three items are returned from sys.exc_info(), and they can be paraphrased as type, value, and traceback. This is similar to the order of expressions after the raise statement. A traceback module also exists and is helpful in working with tracebacks.

Listing 3.11 ties these items together by raising a exception, using the sys.exc_info() method to get the traceback information, and then uses the exc_lineno and extract_tb functions within the traceback module to print the line number where the exception was raised, and to print the entire traceback.

The function `sys.exc_info` actually returns a `tuple` of length three. Jython allows you to unpack `tuples` on assignment, so this line supplies three identifiers that catch each of the `tuple` elements.

Listing 3.11   **Working with *traceback***

```
# file: raise.py
import sys
import traceback

try:
    raise SyntaxError, "Bad syntax"
except:
    exc_type, exc_value, exc_tb = sys.exc_info()
    print "The type of exception is:", exc_type
    print "The value supplied to the exception was", exc_value
    print "The type of exc_tb is:", type(exc_tb)
    print "The line where the exceptions was raised is",
    print traceback.tb_lineno(exc_tb)
    print "The (filename, line number, function, statement, value) is:"
    print traceback.extract_tb(exc_tb)


The results from running "jython raise.py" are:
The type of exception is: exceptions.SyntaxError
The value supplied to the exception was Bad syntax
The type of exc_tb is: org.python.core.PyTraceback
The line where the exceptions was raised is 6
The (filename, line number, function, statement, value) is:
[('raise.py', 6, '?', 'raise SyntaxError, "Bad syntax"')]
```

The *assert* Statement and the __*debug*__ Variable

Another way to raise an exception is with the `assert` statement. Jython's `assert` statement assists in debugging programs by testing for certain user-specified conditions and raising an `AssertionError` exception accordingly. The syntax for the assert statement is as follows:

```
"assert" expression ["," expression]
```

If the first expression evaluates to true, nothing is done; if false, an `AssertionError` is raised. The optional second expression is the value passed to the `AssertionError` exception. Listing 3.12 requests user input then uses the `assert` statement to ensure that the user actually entered data.

Listing 3.12 **Testing User Input with** *assert*

```
>>> def getName():
...     name = raw_input("Enter your name: ")
...     assert len(name), "No name entered! program halted"
...     print "You entered the name %s" % name
...
>>> getName()
Enter your name: Robert
You entered the name Robert
>>> getName()
Enter your name:
Traceback (innermost last):
  File "<console>", line 1, in ?
  File "<console>", line 3, in getName
AssertionError: No name entered! program halted
>>>
>>> # assert's behavior changes when __debug__ = 0
>>> __debug__ = 0
>>> # With __debug__ off, the AssertionError is never raised
>>> getName()
Enter your name:
You entered the name
>>>
```

Because the `assert` statement is designed as a debugging tool, `assert` statements are only evaluated when the internal variable `__debug__` is equal to 1. In
the current release of Jython, this `__debug__` variable is a bit of a quandary. It
should be a read-only variable that is set at Jython's startup, and Jython should
have a `-0` switch, meaning optimize, which sets the `__debug__` variable equal to
0. Current releases, however, do not have a `-0` switch, and to disable `assert`
statements in fully debugged code, you must assign 0 to the `__debug__` variable
(which isn't read-only either). This may have changed by this book's release
date, and if it has, information regarding this will be found at the website associated with this book. Listing 3.12 demonstrates assigning to the `__debug__`
variable and how the `assert` statement is no longer evaluated when `__debug__`
`== 0`.

The Warnings Framework

Warnings allow Python to gently evolve. Instead of suddenly facing an exception in old code as soon as you upgrade to a newer version of Jython, a warning is issued for at least a year's worth of releases to ensure that any
deprecation or altered behavior is never a surprise. The warnings framework is
new in Jython 2.1.

What is the difference between an exception and a warning? Warnings are not fatal. You could receive innumerable warnings without the process being terminated. Built-in functions or statements specific to warnings do not exist as they do for exceptions. To work with warnings, you must import the `warnings` module. Warnings do not "propagate" or require handling like exception, although there is a warning filter within the warnings module that lets you turn warnings into exceptions.

Within the `warnings` module, there is a `warn` function. This is to warnings what `raise` is to exceptions. The `warnings.warn` function is what issues a warning. Listing 3.13 defines a function called `oldFunction` that we will assume is deprecated. To notify the user of this change, `oldFunction` issues a warning.

Listing 3.13   A Function that Warns of its Own Deprecation

```
# file "warn.py"
def oldFunction():
    import warnings
    warnings.warn('"oldFunction" is deprecated. Use "newFunction"')
```

The Jython code in Listing 3.13 is the contents of a file called `warn.py`. Listing 3.14 uses this file as well. To test the warning in `warn.py`, start the Jython interpreter from the same directory that contains the file `warn.py`, and type:

```
>>> import warn
>>> warn.oldFunction()
/home/rbill/warn.py:3: UserWarning: "oldFunction" is deprecated. Use
"new Function"
  warnings.warn('"oldFunction" is deprecated. Use "newFunction"')
```

With warnings like this, the warning is displayed but the execution of the file would continue without interruption.

Listing 3.13 provides one parameter to the `warn` function—the message to displayed. There is also an optional second parameter that is the type of warning (often called the warning *category*). This category should be a subclass of the exception class `Warning`, and there are four built-in choices for this optional "category" parameter. The generic category is, of course, `Warning`—the superclass of the other warnings. The others are `UserWarning`, `SyntaxWarning`, and `RuntimeWarning`. The default category when there is no category parameter supplied is `UserWarning`.

There is also an optional third parameter to the `warnings.warn` function, which is `stacklevel`. The `stacklevel` is like a row of dominoes that all successively topple after the first one is pushed. To continue with this analogy, suppose the last domino to fall is the equivalent of the module that issues the warning—warn in our case. A `stacklevel` of 1 means the warning reports its occurrence inside of the module `warn` (the last domino). Maybe a different module actually called the deprecated `oldFunction`. This different module is like the second-to-last domino to fall. If you wanted the warning to report this second-to-last module, use a `stacklevel` of 2. A third-from-last module would be a `stacklevel` of 3. Remember that if no `third-from-last` object exists, the use of a `stacklevel` equal to 3 creates an error reported as `KeyError: __name__`.

What if you want, or need, to disable warnings? The warnings module contains the `warnings.filterwarning` function that allows you to modify the behavior of warnings including disabling their display. Listing 3.14 demonstrates using the `warnings.filterwarnings` function to disable `warning` messages issued from the module `warn`.

Listing 3.14   **Filtering a Warning**

```
# file: warntest.py
import warnings

warnings.filterwarnings(action = 'ignore',
                        module = 'warn')

import warn
warn.oldFunction()
```

Running `jython warntest.py` creates no output.

No warning occurs in Listing 3.14 because of the filter. There are actually six parameters for `warnings.filter` (action, message, category, module, lineno, and append), but only the `action` parameter is required. The `action` parameter can be `ignore`, `error`, `always`, `default`, `module`, or `once`. The `message` parameter must be a string that matches the warning message you are trying to filter. The `category` parameter must be a class that is a subclass of `warning`. The `module` parameter limits the filter to warnings coming from that specific module, and it must be a string. There is also a `lineno` and `append` parameter. If provided, `lineno` must be a positive integer and restricts the filter to only warnings coming from that specific line. The `append` parameter designates whether the filter you are creating should be appended to the end of existing filters or inserted to front of the list of filters.

The Python language description includes a `-W` command-line option for specifying certain behaviors for warnings. This is not implemented in Jython at the time of this writing, so check the Jython website or the website associated with this book for more information on this.

Comparing Jython and Java

The subtle differences between Jython's and Java's error handling might be a source of confusion as you switch back and forth between languages. I often find myself confusing `throw` with `raise`, and `catch` with `except`. Beyond the obvious difference in statement names, Java allows a full `try/catch/finally` as in the following:

```
try {
    throw new IllegalAccessException("Illegal access message");
} catch (IllegalAccessException e) {
    e.print
} finally {
    //Add some cleanup code here that is always executed
}
```

Jython only has the `try/finally` or `try/except/else`, and `try/except/finally` is a syntax error in Jython.

The simple assertion facility supplied with Jython's `assert` statement is available in Java since version 1.4, but not in earlier versions of Java.

The warnings framework is also unique to Jython. There isn't a comparable facility in Java for library developers to use in the deprecation and evolution of their libraries. Yes, there are documentation and compile-time errors, but nothing that supplies forewarning as the code evolves. This framework seemed to evolve as a means of enabling the evolution of Python itself—the core language, but it is valuable for any module and could be very useful especially for internal tools where changes can occur rapidly.

Java also has compile-time checks to ensure that whatever could be thrown is either declared thrown or caught. If method A calls method B, and B throws an exception, A must catch it or also declare it as thrown. This requirement is absent from Jython.

4

User-Defined Functions and Variable Scoping

FUNCTIONS ARE THOSE CALLABLE OBJECTS THAT can exist outside of a class. Functions also appear in class definitions, where they are made into methods by object attribute lookup. This chapter, however, focuses on function definition outside of classes. Java does not allow such classless entities; Jython, on the other hand, does. In Jython, functions are first-class objects, meaning the language allows for their dynamic creation and the ability to pass them around as parameters or return values. Jython functions are instances of the `org.python.core.PyFunction` class (`PyReflectedFunction` for built-in functions). Inspecting a Jython function with the built-in function `type()` reports that it is an instance of the `org.python.core.PyFunction` class:

```
>>> def myFunction():
...     pass
...
>>> type(myFunction)
<jclass org.python.core.PyFunction at 6879429>
```

This chapter describes how to define a function—its syntax, documentation, and parameters. Understanding Jython's namespaces is essential to writing functions so also warrants inclusion here. The latter portion of this chapter addresses the tools available within Jython that are normally associated with functional programming. The detour through functional programming is included to balance the arduous language description with some clues as to what the language can do. Within this chapter's rubric, Jython can do first class functions and efficient functional programming.

> **Note from Author**
>
> This chapter would have been more profound before the addition of inner classes to Java 1.1, which serves the first-class function need, but the conciseness and efficiency of functional programming in Jython is still intriguing. Note that the reference to functional programming does not mean examples throughout the chapter exemplify the functional programming style found in the strictly functional languages Erlang, Haskell, and Clean (as opposed to the imperative style of Ada, C/C++, Java, and Pascal). Examples are very much imperative through most of the chapter, while functional programming examples occur at the end and otherwise where noted.

Defining Functions

The syntax for a Jython function is as follows:

```
"def" function_name([parameter_list])":"
     code block
```

The function name, like all identifiers, can be any alphanumeric strings without spaces as long as the first character is an alpha character or the underscore _. Names are case sensitive, and the use of the underscore has special meaning, which Chapter 5, "Modules and Packages," explains in detail. The only caution associated with function names is to be wary of accidentally rebinding to the same name of another function, such as one of the built-in functions. If you were to define a function named type as demonstrated in Listing 4.1, it would make the built-in type function inaccessible.

Listing 4.1   **Defining a Function that Replaces the Built-In** *type()*

```
>>> S = "A test string"
>>> type(S)               # test the built-in type()
<jclass org.python.core.PyString at 6879429>
>>> def type(arg):
...     print "Not the built-in type() function"
...     print "Local variables: ", vars() # look for 'arg'
...
>>> type(S)
Not the built-in type() function
Local variables: {'arg': 'A test string'}
>>>
>>> # to restore the builtin "type()" function, do the following:
>>> from org.python.core import __builtin__
>>> type = __builtin__.type
```

The parameter list is an optional list of names that occur in parentheses following the function name. Variables passed to a function are bound to the supplied parameter names within the local namespace. The function defined in Listing 4.1 accepts one parameter, which is bound to the local name `arg`.

A colon, :, ends the function declaration and designates the beginning of the associated code block.

Indentation

Indentation delimits blocks of code in Jython. A function's associated block of code must start one indention level in from its `def` statement. Because indention is the only delimiter for code blocks, you cannot have an empty code block—there must be some kind of placeholder within a function. Use the `pass` statement if you need a placeholder. Listing 4.2 has functions that demonstrate Jython's relative indention levels.

Listing 4.2 determines which numbers are prime numbers out of a list provided as a parameter. The testing for prime is grossly inefficient, but is a good demonstration of a function's syntax and structure. The `isPrime` function is a function that simply returns 1, meaning true, for those numbers that are prime, 0 otherwise. Because generating primes occurs throughout this chapter, elements of a more efficient prime search should be discussed. Above the number 2, all primes are odd. All non-prime numbers can be created by multiplying prime numbers. Knowing these things makes it esy to disqualify many candidates and reduce loop iterations when testing for prime. Listing 4.2 is inefficient because it ignores the later principle and only restricts the divisor search to odd numbers. Other prime number generators in this chapter will contain similar weaknesses due to the preference for simple, clear examples of Jython principles rather than algorithms.

Listing 4.2   **Finding Primes with Nested Functions**

```
#file primes.py
def isPrime(num):
    """Accepts a number and returns true if it's a prime"""
    for base in [2] + range(3, num, 2):
        if (num%base==0):
            return 0
    return 1

def primes(S1):
    """Accepts a list of numbers and returns a
        list of those numbers that are prime numbers"""
    primes = []
```

continues

Listing 4.2 **Continued**

```
    for i in S1:
        if isPrime(i):
            primes.append(i)
    return primes

list1 = range(20000, 20100)
print "primes are:", primes(list1)
```

Results from running jython primes.py:

primes are: [20011, 20021, 20023, 20029, 20047, 20051, 20063, 20071, 20089]

Because the isPrime function in Listing 4.2 returns values that are Jython's understanding of true and false (for numbric objects, 0=false, non-zero=true), the function can be the conditional portion of an if statement. The if statement in this case discards values for which the isPrime function returns 0.

Return Values

Listing 4.2 uses the return statement to designate the function's return value. A function returns the results of the expression following the return statement. If no return is supplied, the function returns None. If return occurs with no value following it, None is returned. If more than one value is returned, the values are returned as a tuple. It is worth mentioning that a function exits when a return is called. The call-return style of programming assumes that a return statement does just that—returns the value and program flow to the calling statement.

Listing 4.3 defines a function that determines the relationship of a point to a circle with specified center and radius. The bounds function in this listing explicitly returns 1, 0, or −1 depending on whether the point is inside, on, or outside the circle. The final return statement in Listing 4.3 is reached only when the first if statement evaluates to false. Because of the absence of an expression following that return, it returns the value None. This final return statement could have been left out because without an explicit return, a function returns None anyway.

Listing 4.3 **A Circle Inclusion Function**

```
# file: bounds.py
def bounds(p, c, r):
    """Determine a points "p" relationship to a circle of
    designated center "c" and radius "r".
    1 = within circle, 0 = on circle, -1 = outside circle"""
```

```
        ## Ensure args are not empty nor 0
        if p and c and r:
            ## Find distance from center "dfc"
            dfc = ((p[0]-c[0])**2 + (p[1]-c[1])**2)**.5

            return cmp(r, dfc)
    print bounds((1,2), (3,1), 3)
    print bounds((-3, 1), (1, 1), 4)
    print bounds((4,3), (5,-2), 1)
    print bounds((), (2,2), 4)
```

Output from running `jython bounds.py`:

```
1
0
-1
None
```

Documentation Strings

Listing 4.2 has a documentation string for each of the two functions. This string begins in the first line of the code block so must be one indention level in from the `def` statement. The content of this string becomes the value of the function's __doc__ attribute (two prefixing and trailing underscores). If we look at a simple function in the interactive interpreters, as is done in Listing 4.4, we see that exploring objects interactively is much more valuable when documentation strings are available.

Listing 4.4   **Function Documentation Strings**

```
>>> def getfile(fn):
...     """getfile(fn), Accepts a filename, fn, as a parameter and quietly
returns the resulting file object, or None if the file doesn't exist."""
...     try:
...         f = open(fn)
...         return f
...     except:
...         return None
...
>>> print getfile.__doc__
getfile(fn), Accepts a filename, fn, as a parameter and quietly returns the
resulting file object or None if the file doesn't exist.
```

Numerous modules are thoroughly documented in their __doc__ strings, and it's worth looking for an associated __doc__ string first when encountering troubles with a function, module, or class.

Function Attributes

As of Jython version 2.1, functions can also have arbitrary attributes. These are attributes assigned with `function.attribute` syntax, and this assignment can be within the function block, or outside of the function. Here's an example of a function with attributes:

```
>>> def func():
...      func.a = 1
...      func.b = 10
...      print func.a, func.b, func.c
...
>>> func.c = 100
>>> func()
1 10 100
```

Parameters

Jython's parameter scheme is very flexible. In Jython, a function's parameters can be an ordered list, the parameters can have default values, and you can even allow for unknown numbers of arguments. Additionally, you can use key-value pairs when calling functions and even allow for unknown numbers of these key-value pairs.

Positional Parameters

Function examples so far have used the simplest form of parameters: a list of names, or *positional* parameters. In this case, arguments passed to the function are bound to the local names designated in the parameter list in the order they occur. Examining this in the interpreter with the `vars()` function clarifies this. The `vars()` function returns a dictionary object, and dictionary objects do not preserve order. This means that the results you see may be unordered but remain correct as long as all the keys and values appear:

```
>>> def myFunction(param1, param2, param3):
...      print vars()
...
>>> myFunction("a", "b", "c")
{'param1': 'a', 'param2': 'b', 'param3': 'c'}
```

Default Values

You can assign default values to parameters. To do so, simply assign a value to the parameter in the function definition. If we define a function with three parameters, and two have default values, then the function requires only one argument when called but can be called with one, two, or all three supplied. When using default values, a parameter without a default value may not follow a parameter with a default value.

Here is an example of a function with two default parameters preceded by a third parameter. This creates flexibility in calling the function:

```
>>> def myFunction(param1, param2="b", param3="c"):
...     print vars()
...
>>> myFunction("a")       # call with the 1, required parameter
{'param1': 'a', 'param2': 'b', 'param3': 'c'}
>>> myFunction("a", "j")  # call with 2 parameters
{'param1': 'a', 'param2': 'j', 'param3': 'c'}
>>> myFunction("a", "j", "k")  # call with 3 parameters
{'param1': 'a', 'param2': 'j', 'param3': 'k'}
```

Here is another example, but the function has a non-default parameter following a default parameter. This is not allowed, as evidenced by the SyntaxError exception:

```
>>> # let's test a non-default arg following a default arg
>>> def myFunction(param1, param2="b", param3):
...     print vars()
...
Traceback (innermost last):
  (no code object) at line 0
  File "<console>", line 0
SyntaxError: non-default argument follows default argument
```

params and Handling an Unknown Number of Positional Parameters

If you need to allow for an unknown number of arguments, you can prefix a parameter name with an asterisk *. The asterisk designates a wild card that holds all extra arguments as a tuple. This should appear after other parameters in the function definition. The asterisk is the essential syntax; the name used after it is arbitrary:

```
>>> def myFunction(param1, param2, *params):
...     print vars()
...
>>> myFunction('a','b','c','d','e','f','g')
{'param1': 'a', 'param2': 'b', 'params': ('c', 'd', 'e', 'f', 'g')}
```

Keyword Pairs as Parameters

When calling a function, you can also use key-value pairs to designate parameters, also called keyword parameters. The key must be the actual parameter name used in the function's definition. When using keys-value pairs the order is no longer significant, but when mixing key-value pairs with plain, positional arguments, order matters until the right-most positional argument:

```
>>> def myFunction(param1, param2, param3="d"):
...     print vars()
...
>>> myFunction(param2="b", param3="c", param1="a")
{'param1': 'a', 'param2': 'b', 'param3': 'c'}
>>> # next let's mix key-value pairs with positional parameters
>>> myFunction("a", param3="c", param2="b")
{'param1': 'a', 'param2': 'b', 'param3': 'c'}
```

**kw params and Handling Unknown Key-Value Pairs

Just as the asterisk handles an unknown number of plain arguments, the double-asterisk, **, handles unknown numbers of key-value pairs. The name you choose to prefix with the double-asterisk becomes a PyDictionary type containing the unused key-value pairs.

```
>>> def myFunction(param1, param2, param3, **kw):
...     print vars()
...
>>> myFunction("a", "b", "c", param4="d", param5="e")
{'param1': 'a', 'param2': 'b', 'param3': 'c', 'kw': {'param5': 'e', 'param4':
'd'}}
```

Note that all types of parameters can occur in the same function definition:

```
>>> def myFunction(param1, param2="b", param3="c", *params, **kw):
...     print vars()
...
>>> myFunction("a", "b", "j", "k", "z", key1="t", key2="r")
{'param1': 'a', 'params': ('k', 'z'), 'param3': 'j', 'kw': {'key2': 'r',
'key1': 't'}, 'param2': 'b'}
```

Namespaces

Jython has static and statically nested scoping. The bridge between these two occurs in Jython 2.1. Jython version 2.1 and version 2.0 have static scoping; however, you can optionally use static nested scopes, also called *lexical scoping*, in version 2.1. Future versions of Jython will use the statically nested scoping (lexical scoping) exclusively. The reason Jython 2.1 bridges both types of scoping rules is that Python developers needed a safe way to introduce new scoping rules while providing time to amend adversely affected legacy code.

Two Static Scopes

Jython's static scoping entails two specific namespaces: *globals* and *locals* (three if you include the built-in namespace). When a name binding action occurs, the name appears in either a global or local namespace. Actions that result in a name binding are assignment operations, an import statement, the definition of a function or a class, and assignments derived from statement behavior (such as `for x in list`). The location of a name binding action determines which namespace will contain that name. For functions, anything bound within the function's code block and all of the function's parameters are local with but one exception—the explicit use of the `global` statement within the code block.

Listing 4.5 contains a function that makes a few assignments and prints its local namespace for confirmation. Listing 4.5 also prints global names to show how global variables are unique and separate from the local variables in `function()`.

Listing 4.5   **Global and Local Namespaces**

```
>>> a = "This is the global variable a"
>>> def function(localvar1, localvar2):
...     a = 1
...     b = 2
...     print locals()
...
>>> function(3, 4)
{'b': 2, 'localvar1': 3, 'localvar2': 4, 'a': 1}
>>>
>>> globals()
{'a': 'This is the global variable a', '__doc__': None, 'function1':
<function function1 at 5135994>, '__name__': '__main__'}
```

Because Listing 4.5 uses a local name for the variable a within `function()`, the global variable a is unaffected.

A function can use variables from the global namespace, however. This happens if the name binding action occurs outside of the function, or if the `global` statement is used. If a name occurs within a function, but the name binding occurred in the global namespace, the name lookup continues beyond the locals and into the global namespace. Here is an example of this use of a global name:

```
>>> var1 = [100, 200, 300]    # This is global
>>> def function():
...     print var1
...     var1[1] += 50
...
```

```
>>> function()
[100, 200, 300]
>>> function()
[100, 250, 300]
>>> print var1    #Look at the global var1
[100, 300, 300]
```

If you try to use a `global` variable within a function that later binds to the same name, it is an error. The reason is that the name binding designates a variable as local for the entire code block, no matter where that name binding sequentially occurs in the block:

```
>>> var = 100    # This is global
>>> def function():
...      print var
...      var = 10  # this assignment makes ALL occurrences of var local
...
>>> function()
Traceback (innermost last):
  File "<console>", line 1, in ?
  File "<console>", line 2, in function
UnboundLocalError: local: 'var'
```

The second way to use a global variable within a function is to declare the variable global with the statement `global`. Explicitly declaring intentions with the `global` statement looks like this:

```
>>> var = 100    # This is global
>>> def function():
...      global var
...      print var
...      var = 10
...
>>> print var    # Peak at global var
100
>>> function()
100
>>> print var    # Confirm function acted on global var
10
>>>
```

Statically Nested Scopes

Why change to statically nested scopes? After all, what is wrong with the static scoping that Jython, and Python, have historically used? The problem manifests itself with nested functions and the lambda form (lambda forms are discussed later in this chapter). These two are non-intuitive within the two-namespace, static scoping model. Defining simple nested functions in the interactive console sheds light on this:

```
>>> a = "BacBb"
>>>
>>> def decode():
...     b = "h"
...     def inner_decode():
...         print a.replace("Bb", b)
...     inner_decode()
...
<console>:1: SyntaxWarning: local name 'b' in 'decode' shadows use as
global in nested scopes
>>> decode()Traceback (innermost last):
  File "<console>", line 1, in ?
  File "<console>", line 5, in decode
  File "<console>", line 4, in inner_decode
NameError: b
```

Jython version 2.1 is kind enough to give you the console warning about the invisibility of variable b in the inner function. With only local and global namespaces, inner_decode() cannot see variables in its containing function. Overcoming this usually means supplying the inner function with parameters. However, beginning with Jython version 2.1, you can also choose to use statically nested scopes to overcome this.

Using statically nested scopes in Jython 2.1 requires the use of the recently added __future__. Python, and thus Jython, have recently added __future__ as a means of migrating to functionality that may be standard in subsequent releases. To import nested scopes from __future__, use the following:

```
>>> from __future__ import nested_scopes
```

Currently, nested_scopes is the only futuristic behavior that users can import, but when done, the interpreter obeys the rules of statically nested scopes. If we revisit the decode example with the futuristic nested_scopes imported, we receive a different result:

```
>>> from __future__ import nested_scopes
>>>
>>> a = "BacBb"
>>>
>>> def decode():
...     b = "h"
...     def inner_decode():
...         print a.replace("Bb", b)
...     inner_decode()
...
>>> decode()
Bach
```

With lexical scoping, an inner function can hold some additional, non-global information. Suppose you wanted to hide a built-in function under a different name while you used its old name: You could use an inner function as somewhat of a proxy like that in Listing 4.6

Listing 4.6   **Using *nested-scopes* to Create a Proxy**

```
# file: typeproxy.py
from __future__ import nested_scopes

def typeProxy():
    _type = type
    def oldtype(object):
        return _type(object)
    return oldtype

f = typeProxy()
type = 10 # rebind name "type"
print f(4)
```

Results from running `jython typeproxy.py`:

```
org.python.core.PyInteger
```

Because lexical scoping allows nested functions to use variables from their containing function, nested functions can carry non-global data around as baggage. This creates an object of combined data and procedure, much like a class. This is similar to what functional languages call *closures*.

Listing 4.7 uses nested functions, and the closure-like behavior of the returned inner function, to generate a stream of fibonacci numbers. The `xfib` function `accepts` one argument: the iteration the sequence should begin with. Two `assert` statements provide some runtime parameter checking to add some robustness, and after the inner function `fibgen` is defined, it is used to set the data to the designated iteration before it is returned. The ability to return this function is part of the first-class object requirement and is also an important ingredient in functional programming. The script uses the returned function to print the first 20 numbers of the fibonacci sequence.

Listing 4.7   **Nested Functions with Lexical Scoping**

```
# file: fibonacci.py
from __future__ import nested_scopes

def xfib(n=1):
    """Returns a function that generates a stream of fibonacci numbers
        Accepts 1 arg- an integer representing the iteration number of
        the sequence that the stream is to start with."""
```

```
        assert n > 0, "The start number must be greater than zero"
        from types import IntType, LongType
        assert type(n)==IntType or type(n)==LongType, \
                "Argument must be an integral number."

        # make cache for penultimate, current and next fib numbers
        fibs = [0L, 1L, 0L]

        # Define the inner function
        def fibgen():
            fibs[2] = fibs[1] + fibs[0]
            fibs[0] = fibs[1]
            fibs[1] = fibs[2]
            return fibs[1]

        # Set state to the iteration designated in parameter n
        for x in range(1, n ):
            fibgen()

        # return the primed inner function
        return fibgen

    fibIterator = xfib()
    for x in range(20):
        print fibIterator(),
    print # Print an empty newline for tidyness after execution
```

Results from running `jython fibonacci.py`:

   1 2 3 5 8 13 21 34 55 89 144 233 377 610 987 1597 2584 4181 6765 10946

Passing the `fibIterator` object in Listing 4.7 to other functions or classes is also a likely scenario. The fact that it is the combination of data and procedure makes it useful in many situations much like class instances are useful for their combined methods and data.

Special Variables in User-Defined Functions

"Special" variables in Jython are usually those with two preceding and trailing underscores, such as `__doc__`. However, Jython functions have function-specific special variables that are prefixed with `func_`. One such special function variable is `func_doc` which is a pseudonym for `__doc__`. As you explore functions with `dir()` or `vars()` you will encounter these variables, so they are listed here for reference even though examples within this chapter do not directly use them.

Special function variables are as follows:

- `func_doc` is the same as `__doc__`.
- `func_name` (also `__name__`) is the name of the function.

- `func_defaults` lists default parameter values.
- `func_code` contains the compiled version of the function.
- `func_globals` is the function's global namespace.
- `func_dict` (also `__dict__`) is the functions local namespace.
- `func_closure` is a `tuple` binding for the variables used from a containing function in `nested-scopes`. It is always `None` if not using `nested-scopes`.

Recursion

Recursion occurs when a procedure calls itself. Recursion is a powerful control structure that is similar to other loop constructs and is an essential ingredient in functional programming. Recursion occurs with repeating math operations like those found in sequences and graphs. Another common example of recursion is evaluating a factorial. A simplified description of a *factorial* is the product of all integers between a designated number and 1. This means 5 factorial (written as 5!) is 5 * 4 * 3 * 2 * 1 (if details of the gamma function are ignored). Implementing a recursive function to do this calculation is shown in Listing 4.8.

Listing 4.8   **Implementing a Recursive Function**

```
>>> def factorial(number):
...     number = long(number)
...     if number == 0:
...         return 1 # It just is by mathmatician's decree
...     return number * factorial(long(number - 1))
...
>>> print factorial(4)
24
>>> print factorial(7)
5040
```

Recursion has its limits. A function can call itself only so many times before a `StackOverflowError` occurs. If we extend our interactive example from above, we can try larger and larger numbers to see what this limit is. Note that the actual number will depend on your available memory.

```
>>> bignum = factorial(1000)
>>> biggernum = factorial(1500)
>>> hugenum = factorial(1452) # The breaking point on my machine
traceback (innermost last):
...
java.lang.StackOverflowError: java.lang.StackOverflowError
```

Built-In Functional Programming Tools

Examples up to this point have mostly been imperative in style. However, many important ingredients of functional programming exist in Jython. Those already noted are first-class functions, recursion, and closures. Additional tools in Jython that aid in functional programming are lambda forms, which provide anonymous functions, built-in functions for list processing, the list generation tool `zip()`, and list comprehension. This section looks at Jython's functional tools including `lambda` forms, `map`, `filter`, `reduce`, `zip`, and list comprehension.

lambda

Creating anonymous functions requires the use of `lambda`. Functions defined with `lambda` are `lambda` forms or `lambda` expressions. The term `lambda` expression may be most instructive as what this type of function does is return the results of an expression. `Lambda` expressions cannot contain statements. The syntax of a `lambda` expression is as follows:

```
"lambda" parameters: expression
```

The problem of determining if a number is odd or even creates this `lambda` form:

```
>>> odd_or_even = lambda num: num%2 and "odd" or "even"
>>> odd_or_even(5)
'odd'
>>> odd_or_even(6)
'even'
```

You can see that this is functionally the same as the following:

```
>>> def odd_or_even(num):
...     return num%2 and "odd" or "even"
```

A `lambda` form's parameters are no different than a named function's parameters. They can be positional parameters, have default values, and can use the wild card parameters `*` and `**`.

Because `lambda` forms cannot contain statements like `if/else`, they usually leverage the `and/or` operators to provide the logic of execution. In functional programming, the evaluation of expressions is preferred over statements. Using expressions in `lambda` forms is not only required, it is valuable practice in functional programming.

Another example of a `lambda` expression is a rewrite of an earlier factorial evaluator. The control structure employed in this example is recursion: The `lambda` form calls itself to determine each successive value:

```
>>> factorial = lambda num: num==1 or num * factorial(num - 1)
>>> factorial(5)
```

120

The `lambda` expression is especially susceptible to the side effects of Jython's scoping rules. In static scoping, it is all too frequent that default parameter values obscure the `lambda` code. Just a few variables that require default values become unwieldy. Listing 4.9 figures the volume of a cylinder of static height, but variable radius and shows default arguments in a `lambda` expression.

Listing 4.9   **Using Default Arguments in a *lambda* Form**

```
# file: staticpi.py
# Note "nested_scopes" is not imported
from math import pi

def cylindervolume(height):
    return lambda r, pi=pi, height=height: pi * r**2 * height

vrc = cylindervolume(2)  # vrc = variable radius cylinder
print vrc(5)
```

Results from running `jython staticpi.py`:

```
157.07963267948966
```

Compare this with the missing default parameter values in a lexically scoped `lambda` form. `Lambda` forms are much more intuitive with lexical scoping as demonstrated in Listing 4.10.

Listing 4.10   ***lambda* Forms in Lexical Scoping**

```
# file: lexicalpi.py
from __future__ import nested_scopes
from math import pi

def cylindervolume(height):
    return lambda r: pi * r**2 * height

vrc = cylindervolume(2)  # vrc = variable radius cylinder
print vrc(5)
```

Results from running `jython lexicalpi.py`:

```
157.07963267948966
```

map( )

The `map` function is a list-processing tool. The syntax for `map` is as follows:

```
map(function, sequence[, sequence, ...])
```

The first argument must be a function or None. Map calls the function for each member of the designated sequence with that respective sequence member as an argument. The returned list is the results of each call of the function. To create a list of the squares of integers, you apply map like so:

```
>>> def square(x):
...     return x**2
...
>>> map(square, range(10))
[0, 1, 4, 9, 16, 25, 36, 49, 64, 81]
```

A lambda form satisfies the function requirement as well:

```
>>> map(lambda x: x**2, range(10))
[0, 1, 4, 9, 16, 25, 36, 49, 64, 81]
```

If a map function is called with multiple sequences, the function receives the same number of parameters as there are sequences. If we assume map was called with a function (or None) and three sequences, each call to the function would include three parameters:

```
>>> map(None, range(10), range(2,12), range(5,15))
[(0, 2, 5), (1, 3, 6), (2, 4, 7), (3, 5, 8), (4, 6, 9), (5, 7, 10), (6,
8, 11), (7, 9, 12), (8, 10, 13), (9, 11, 14)]
```

For multiple sequences of differing lengths, map iterates through the longest of the sequences and fills in missing values with None:

```
>>> map(None, range(5), range(6,20), range(3))
[(0, 6, 0), (1, 7, 1), (2, 8, 2), (3, 9, None), (4, 10, None), (None, 11,
None), (None, 12, None), (None, 13, None), (None, 14, None), (None, 15,
None), (None, 16, None), (None, 17, None), (None, 18, None), (None, 19,
None)]
```

To compensate for the numeric focus so far, take a look at an example of using map to process a string. This example assumes there is a need to replace all tabs in a string with four spaces. An empty string is used to allow use of the join function, and the lambda expression makes use of Boolean evaluation to return four spaces when a tab is found.

```
>>> s = 'a\tb\tc\td\te'
>>> "".join(map(lambda char: char=="\t" and "    " or char, s))
'a    b    c    d    e'
```

filter( )

The filter function is similar to the map function in that it requires a function or None as the first parameter and a list as the second. The differences are that filter can only accept one sequence, filter's function is used to determine a true/false value, and the result of `filter` is a list that contains the original sequence members for which the function evaluated to true. The function filters out those sequence members for which the function returns false—thus the name. The syntax for `filter` is as follows:

```
filter(function, sequence)
```

An example that clarifies `filter`'s behavior is testing for even numbers. The `range` function has the optional step parameter, so this functionality is trivial, but it makes for a clear example of `filter`'s behavior. The results contain the original sequence's members, unaltered except for the exclusion of those for which the function disapproves:

```
>>> filter(lambda x: x%2==0, range(10))
[0, 2, 4, 6, 8]
```

The `filter` function can also compact code used to search for set intersections. This example iterates through the members of `set1` and uses a `lambda` form to return 1 or 0 depending on that element's inclusion in `set2`:

```
>>> set1 = range(0, 200, 7)
>>> set2 = range(0, 200, 3)
>>> filter(lambda x: x in set2, set1)
[0, 21, 42, 63, 84, 105, 126, 147, 168, 189]
```

If you revisit Listing 4.2 from very early in this chapter, you will notice that it is a very verbose and inefficient primes search. The `filter` function can decrease the verbosity, and does in Listing 4.11. The efficiency, however, is not improved. Listing 4.11 is likely less efficient because the use of the `filter` function is not lazy. *Lazy* means a process only evaluates what it needs to. The `isPrime` function in Listing 4.11 successively tests each potential divisor. To be lazy, the `isPrime` function would have to test only those divisors up to the first contradiction of prime. This detrimental effect is burdensome as numbers get larger.

Listing 4.11   **A Functional Search for Primes**

```
# file: functionalprimes.py
from __future__ import nested_scopes

def primes(S):
    isDiv = lambda num, x: num<3 or num%x==0
    isPrime = lambda num: filter(lambda x, num=num: isDiv(num, x),
                                 [2] + range(3,num,2))==[]
    return filter(isPrime, S)

print primes(range(4, 18))
```

Results from running `jython functionalprimes.py`

```
[5, 7,  11, 13, 17]
```

reduce( )

The `reduce` function requires a function and sequence like `map` and `filter`. The function supplied to `reduce`, however, must accept two arguments and cannot be `None` as it can be in `map` and `filter`. The syntax for `reduce` is as follows:

```
reduce(function, sequence[, initial])
```

The result returned from `reduce` is a single value that represents the cumulative application of the specified function to the supplied sequence. The first two values from the list, or the optional initial value and first list value, become the function's first pair of arguments. The results from that operation and the next list item are the subsequently arguments to the function, and so on until the list is exhausted. An example follows:

```
>>> reduce(lambda x, y: x+y, range(5, 0, -1))
```

The result of this expression is $((((5+4)+3)+2)+1)$, or 15. Suppose the optional initial value is supplied:

```
>>> reduce(lambda x, y: x+y, range(5, 0, -1), 10)
```

The results would be $(((((10+5)+4)+3)+2)+1)$, or 25.

zip( )

The `zip` function combines respective elements of multiple lists as a `tuple` and returns a list of `tuples`. The length of the returned list is the same as the shortest sequence supplied. The syntax for `zip` is as follows:

```
zip(seq1 [, seq2 [...]])
```

An example usage looks like this:

```
>>> zip([1,2,3], [4,5,6])
[(1, 4), (2, 5), (3, 6)]
```

Another example is using `zip` to supply key-value pairs in constructing a dictionary. Because `zip` produces a list of `tuples`, the `lambda` form has only one parameter for the single `tuple` argument:

```
>>> d = {}
>>> map(lambda b: d.setdefault(b[0],b[1]), zip(range(4), range(4,8)))
[4, 5, 6, 7]
>>> d
{3: 7, 2: 6, 1: 5, 0: 4}
```

List Comprehension

List comprehension is a way of generating lists according to a set of rules. List comprehension syntax is really a short cut. What it does is possible with other Jython syntax, but list comprehension provides more clarity. The basic syntax is as follows:

```
[ expression for expr in sequence1
                for expr2 in sequence2 ...
                for exprN in sequenceN
                if condition]
```

Evaluation of the list comprehension form is equivalent to nested `for` statements such as the following:

```
for expr1 in sequence1:
        for expr2 in sequence2:
            for exprN in sequenceN:
                if (condition):
                    expression(expr1, expr2, exprN)
```

The list comprehension used here produces a list of only the elements that evaluate to true:

```
>>> L = [1, "a", [], 0, "b"]
>>> [ x for x in L if x ]
[1, 'a', 'b']
```

This could be rewritten without the list comprehension as follows:

```
>>> L = [1, "a", [], 0, "b"]
>>> results = []
>>> for x in L:
...      if x:
...              results.append(x)
...
>>> results
[1, 'a', 'b']
```

The advantage of the list comprehension is obviously its clarity. This advantage increases as the number of `for` statements increases. The list comprehension in Listing 4.12 may look a bit confusing at first, but that is only because the surrounding `lambda` expression. The actual list comprehension in Listing 4.12 has only four expressions equal to the following nested form:

```
for x in [num]:
    for y in ([2] + range(3, num, 2)):
        if x%y==0:
            returnlist.append(x)
```

The result of this list comprehension is a list of successful divisors of the variable num. The `lambda` form merely tests to see if this list of divisors is empty, meaning the number must be a prime.

Listing 4.12 **Primes Through List Comprehension**

```
# file: primelist.py
def primes(S):
    isPrime = lambda num: [x for x in [num]
                             for y in [2] + range(3,num,2)
                             if x%y==0]==[]
    return filter(isPrime, S)

print primes(range(2,20))
print primes(range(200, 300))
```

Output from running, `jython primelist.py`:

```
[3, 5, 7, 11, 13, 17, 19]
[211, 223, 227, 229, 233, 239, 241, 251, 257, 263, 269, 271, 277, 281,
283, 293]
```

Jython file objects have a `readlines()` method that returns a list of strings representing each line of the file. For another list comprehension example, assume
that the file `config.cfg` is a configuration file with commented lines starting
with # and all other non-blank lines are important directives. It is more likely
that you would want the parsed results of such a file in a dictionary, but
because we are focused on functional programming here, the `realines()` and
list comprehension are used to parse this file into a list of lists.

Another important point about this list comprehension is that the first
expression invokes a method. Limiting this first expression to just declaring
which value to return seems to be the common usage, but this is certainly not
a restriction. It can also invoke an object's methods or can be a function.

```
# file: configtool.py
def parseConfig(file):
    return [ x.strip().replace(" ", "").split("=")
             for x in open(file).readlines()
             if not x.lstrip().startswith("#") and len(x.strip())]

print parseConfig("config.cfg")
```

The content of the config.cfg file used is:

```
    a    = b
c =    d
   # comment

dog = jack

cat = fritz
```

Results from running `jython configtoo.py`:

```
[['a', 'b'], ['c', 'd'], ['dog', 'jack'], ['cat', 'fritz']]
```

The preceding list comprehension makes for clean and compact syntax as well as helping make the example more of a functional style program.

The Functional Programming Idiom

Defining and using functions does not qualify as functional programming. Functional programming is much more. It emphasizes list processing such as map, filter, and reduce do. It also requires functions that are first class objects, employs closures, and uses expressions like list comprehension. Other important features of functional programming are the discouragement of rebinding names and the emphasis on expressions instead of typical compound statement control structures. Most Jython programming is imperative and object oriented, but we can see from the description of functional programming that Jython is capable of a functional style as well.

What is the advantage of functional programming in Jython? There is the potential for increased robustness and there may be situations where this style increases code clarity. If you go to the effort to eliminate rebinding of variables, you've eliminated the opportunity for a certain variable to end up with an unexpected value. If everything is evaluated as an expression, there is little opportunity for a misplaced statement. Take a look at some imperative code:

```
>>> def odd_or_even(num):
...     var = 9        # potential side effect
...     if num%2:      # statement instead of expression
...         return "odd"
...     return "even"
...
>>> odd_or_even(10)
'even'
>>> odd_or_even(7)
'odd'
```

This uses the compound if/else statement. Functional programming discourages statements and encourages expressions. So, to convert the above code into something more functional, use the and and or operators:

```
>>> def odd_or_even(num):
...     return num%2 and "odd" or "even"
...
>>> odd_or_even(20)
'even'
>>> odd_or_even(33)
'odd'
```

In addition to avoiding statements, minimizing rebinding of names is important in functional programming. Rebinding is what is normally done in imperative programming, there are even shortcut operators such as += to make it more convenient. Functional programming considers such rebinding to increase the risk of side effects. Those who have suffered at the hands of Perl's debugger before learning the value of my know better than most about unexpected and deleterious side effects from variable rebinding. If you look back at Listing 4.12, you will see that list comprehension enabled the elimination of many name bindings in that function so side effects would be unlikely. The same is true for Listing 4.11; names are bound to lambda forms and the parameter, but no extraneous name rebindings exist.

What is exciting is that all of Jython's list-processing tools work on any sequence. Not just Jython sequences, but Java sequences as well. To iterate through a `java.util.Vector` object, designate it as the sequence in a map function:

```
>>> import java
>>> v = java.util.Vector()
>>> map(v.add, range(10)) # fill the vector with PyIntegers
[1, 1, 1, 1, 1, 1, 1, 1, 1, 1]
>>> filter(lambda x: x%2==0, v)
[0, 2, 4, 6, 8]
```

Java objects were not emphasized in this chapter for fear of their impact on example clarity, but an instructive next step is to experiment with incorporating Java objects into some functional style scripts. Purely functional code is uncommon once Java is included, but the extent to which you can use Java objects in list processing and lambda forms is impressive.

Synchronization

Java and Jython allow programs with multiple threads of execution. Python's `thread` and `threading` module is the means of create multithreaded programs in Jython and CPython. What is unique to Jython is the `synchronize` module, which simplifies synchronization much like Java's `synchronized` keyword.

This chapter on functions introduces synchronization because Jython functions are callable objects. Multiple threads of control often require synchronization of callable objects. Java programmers are accustomed to synchronized methods, but there is no such keyword in the Python language specification. This raises the question of how you actually synchronize functions or methods in Jython. You could use tools from the threading module to acquire and release locks when entering and leaving callable objects, but Jython makes it much easier than that. Jython includes a `synchronize` module that has two functions that allow users to synchronize callable objects. These two functions are `make_synchronized` and `apply_synchronized`.

Listing 4.13 defines a `count` method that is started in two separate threads. The `count` method merely prints a sequential count along side the thread responsible for producing the number. This makes for a clear example because output is interleaved without synchronization, but sequential when synchronized.

Listing 4.13 **Synchronizing a Function**

```
# file: sync.py
import thread
import synchronize
import sys

threadID = 0

def count(out):
    global threadID
    thisid = threadID
    threadID += 1
    threadnames = ["first thread", "second thread"]
    for i in range(5):
        print threadnames[thisid], "counted to", i

count = synchronize.make_synchronized(count)

thread.start_new_thread(count, (sys.stdout,))
thread.start_new_thread(count, (sys.stdout,))
```

The function `thread.start_new_thread()` starts two threads in Listing 4.13, and it has the following syntax:

```
thread.start_new_thread(callable_object, args[, kwargs])
```

The first parameter is the name of the callable object that is to run in the thread. The second parameter is a `tuple` of the arguments to pass to the callable object designated in the first parameter. The optional third parameter consists of keyword arguments also passed to the callable object.

Listing 4.13 implements synchronization with the `make_synchronized` function. `make_synchronized` accepts a callable object and returns a new callable object. This new object is synchronized on the first argument supplied when the object is called. The syntax is as follows:

```
make_synchronized(callableObject) -> callableObject
```

The fact that the object is synchronized on the first argument means that the callable object used must accept at least one argument. Listing 4.13 uses `sys.stdout` as that object to ensure that output is sequential. Even though

Jython methods have not been discussed yet, it is valuable to note that they are similar to Jython functions; however, they receive an instance reference called `self` as their first argument. Therefore, when `make_synchronized` is used on a method, that method becomes synchronized on the object `self`.

If you execute the `sync.py` file from Listing 4.13, you should see output like the following:

```
prompt>jython sync.py
first thread counted to 0
first thread counted to 1
first thread counted to 2
first thread counted to 3
first thread counted to 4
second thread counted to 0
second thread counted to 1
second thread counted to 2
second thread counted to 3
second thread counted to 4
```

For comparison's sake, try commenting out the synchronization line like so:

```
# count = synchronize.make_synchronized(count)
```

Next, run the `sync.py` file again to see how the output is interleaved without the synchronization. A sample of the non-synchronized output appears as follows:

```
prompt>jython sync.py
second thread counted to 0
second thread counted tofirst thread 1
 counted tosecond thread 0
 counted tofirst thread 2
 counted tosecond thread 1
 counted tofirst thread 3
second thread counted to 4
 counted to 2
first thread counted to 3
first thread counted to 4
```

You could alternatively use the `synchronize.apply_synchronized` function to synchronize callable objects. The `synchronize.apply_synchronized` function reproduces the functionality of the built-in apply function with an additional argument that specifies an object to synchronize on. Syntax for this statement is as follows:

```
apply_synchronized(syncObject, callableObject, args, keywords={})
```

The operation performed in the `apply_synchronized` method is synchronized on the first argument (`syncObject`).

5

Modules and Packages

I N JYTHON, ONE MUST MANAGE JYTHON modules and packages, as well as Java packages and classes. Jython imports and uses all such items, but imports from where? Java uses the `classpath` to locate Java packages and classes while Python has the `sys.path` to locate and load its modules. Jython's appeal is that it uses both. This becomes an interesting quagmire when implementing both such mechanisms, but what appears to be hairy behind the scenes, merely creates choices for the Jython user.

The study of these choices begins with the `import` statement, followed by a quick comparison of Java and Python conventions. The middle section of this chapter is in two parts: Python packages and modules, and Java packages and classes. Working interactively or maybe even working with dynamically generated code means modules can change after being imported. Jython's "reload" facility assists in these situations and is discussed at the end of this chapter.

The *import* Statement

The `import` statement appears in four permutations. If the variables X, Y, and Z replace module and package names, these four permutations look like this:

```
import X
import X as Y
from X import Y
from X import Y as Z
```

import X

This is the first of the basic forms of the `import` statement. This is similar to Java's `import` statement in appearance, but it binds the leftmost name. This is opposite of Java's `import` which binds the rightmost name in the dotted `pack-age.class` hierarchy. An example Java `import` could be:

```
import java.awt.TextComponent;
```

This Java `import` statement allows you to directly use the name `TextComponent`, or the rightmost name, without any package names qualifying it. In Jython, however, a similar `import` binds the name `java` within the namespace in which the `import` occurred so that all following references to `TextComponent` must be qualified with `java.awt`. Inspecting the namespace with the `dir()` function shows how the name binding works in Jython:

```
>>> import java.awt.TextComponent
>>> dir()
['__doc__', '__name__', 'java']
```

If a module named `b` existed within package `A`, its `import` statement could be as follows:

```
import A.b
```

The name bound, however, is the name `A`. The use of module `b` would require the package name `A` to qualify `b`. This means function `c` within module `b` is referenced as follows:

```
import A.b
A.b.c()  # call function c
```

The module `sys` is a Jython module that is not part of a package, so it does not require any dot notation during import:

```
>>> import sys
```

After the module `sys` is imported, you access contents with dot notation. This means accessing the variable `path` requires the following:

```
>>> import sys
>>> sys.path
['', '.', '/jython/Lib']
```

The sys.path variable is the Python version of Java's classpath. This example also serves as an opportunity to check your sys.path variable. The sys.path does depend on your installation directory and is most likely different from the results above.

This form of the import statement also accepts a comma-separated list of modules or packages to import. The modules os and sys are Jython modules, while java is the root package of Java proper. To import these on one line, use a comma-separated list like the following:

```
>>> import os, sys, java
```

import X *as* Y

Adding the word "as" to the simple import statement allows you to specify the name used to reference the imported item, and allows a direct binding to the rightmost element of the import. Specifying the name is an advantage in that you can avoid naming conflicts. Binding to the rightmost element eliminates the dot-notation required to qualify name.

Let's look at importing the sys module again, only this time as bound to the name sys_module to avoid naming conflicts with a previously defined variable:

```
>>> sys = "A variable that creates a name conflict with module sys"
>>> import sys as sys_module
>>> dir()
['__doc__', '__name__', 'sys_module', 'sys']
>>> sys
'A variable that creates a name conflict with module sys'
>>> s
sys module
```

Let's revisit the A.b.c scenario stated earlier, where function c is within module b, which resides in package A. To bind module b to a new name, use the import X as Y syntax. This syntax binds the rightmost element of X to the name Y, so binding module b to a new name looks like this:

```
>>> import A.b as mod_b
>>> dir(mod_b)
['__doc__', '__file__', '__name__', 'c']
>>>mod_b.c()  # call function c
```

from X import Y

To extend control beyond packages and modules to actually control selective imports of module contents, you can use the `from x import y` syntax. This is not restricted to importing only module content—it works equally well with packages, modules, and classes. This syntax allows the import of sub-elements similar to the rightmost binding used with the `as` modifier, but in addition to sub-elements like sub-packages and sub-modules, it also allows importing selective contents of modules themselves.

Revisiting the `A.b.c` scenario yet again, you can bind module `b` by using the following:

```
from A import b
b.c()  # call function c
```

To selectively import variables, functions, or classes from within a module using the `from X import Y` syntax, add the module name to `X` and include the desired module contents to `Y`. This means importing function `c` from module `b`, which resides in package `A`, uses the following:

```
from A.b import c
c()  # call function c
```

As with the simple `import` statement, a comma-separated list is allowed. You can import multiple sub-elements with the following:

```
from A.b import c, d, e, f, etc
```

Importing module-internal names such as the `path` variable within the `sys` module looks like this:

```
>>> from sys import path
```

To import two names from the sys module, use the following:

```
>>> from sys import path, prefix
```

The `from X import Y` syntax also allows an asterisk in the `Y` location. The asterisk designates the import of all available items (the definition of `all` is pliant and is described later). The use of the asterisk in imports is strongly discouraged in Jython—it has historically created numerous problems (such as when using `import *` with Java packages), so it is best to assume this option doesn't really exist.

from X import Y as Z

The syntax of the last form of import is as follows:

```
from X import Y as Z
```

Where X is a fully qualified package or module, Y is a package, module, or module-global name, and Z is an arbitrary, user-specified name that Y is bound to. Importing function c as myFunc from module b in package A, looks like this:

```
from A.b import c as myFunc
```

A Comparison of Jython and Java

Java has packages, which can contain other packages or classes. Java packages are associated with directories containing files whereas classes are the results of compiling such files. Jython has packages, which can contain other packages or modules, but not classes. Class definitions occur only within Python modules. Both languages, however, use the same dot notation to traverse their hierarchy. In Java, if you wish to import class B from package A you would use an import statement that looks like this:

```
import A.B;
```

This package.class hierarchy translates as a package.module hierarchy for Jython modules. A similar import statement in Jython would look like this:

```
import A.B
```

This import statement results in the import of package A, followed by the import of module, or package B. This is an important distinction between Jython and Java. Jython imports each parent package as part of the import process. Additionally, Jython packages are functionally similar to modules after being imported.

Python's *package.module* Hierarchy

This section reviews the Python convention for making, locating and loading Python packages and modules. This entails a study of the sys.path variable as well as descriptions of modules and packages. The Python language is rich with special variables. These are the variables beginning and ending with two underscores. Packages and modules contain special variables and, therefore, these variables are also described in this section.

The *sys.path* Variable

Locating Python modules depends on the sys.path variable. The directories within the sys.path list tell Jython where to search for modules. Trying to import a *.py file that does not reside anywhere in the sys.path raises an

ImportError exception. Within this `sys.path` list is Jython's `Lib` directory. This is where Jython's installed module library resides. To inspect the `sys.path` variable for your Jython installation, use the following:

```
>>> import sys
>>> print sys.path
['', 'C:\\WINDOWS\\Desktop\\.', 'C:\\jython 2.1\\Lib', 'C:\\jython 2.1']
```

To add a path to the `sys.path` list, import the `sys module` and append the required path. To load modules located in the directory `/usr/local/jython_work` (on *nix), you must add this directory to the `sys.path` like:

```
>>> import sys
>>> sys.path.append("/usr/local/jython_work")
```

For the Windows directory `c:\jython_work`, use this code:

```
>>> import sys
>>> sys.path.append("c:\\jython_work")  # notice the double-backslash
['', 'C:\\WINDOWS\\Desktop\\.', 'C:\\jython 2.1a1\\Lib', 'C:\\jython
2.1a1', 'c:\\jython 2.1a1\\Lib\\site-python', 'c:\\jython_work']
```

Again note that `sys.path` is installation specific, so the contents of your `sys.path` may appear different than those in the book.

The backslash designates special characters like tab (`\t`) and newline (`\n`), as well as literal characters such as quotations (`"\""`) or a literal backslash (`\\`). It is safest to use the double-backslash in windows paths to ensure the backslash is interpreted as a literal backslash rather than the start of a special character. However, in most cases the front slash, `/`, can be used as a directory separator on Windows within Jython code.

There are other ways to add to the `sys.path` variable. Jython has a file named `registry` that is located in Jython's installation directory. The `registry` file contains a number of variables, including `python.path` and `python.prepath`, which both affect the contents of Jython's `sys.path` list. To add the path `/usr/local/jython_work` to the `sys.path` without having to explicitly append this path in each module that uses it, just add it to the `python.path` or `python.prepath` variable. The difference between these two variables is that `python.path` appends the path at the end of `sys.path`, whereas `python.prepath` pre-pends the designated path before the rest of items in `sys.path`. The respective *nix and Windows registry entries look like this:

```
# for windows, use the double-backslash, and the semi-colon
# path separator.
python.path = c:\\first_directory;d:\\another_directory

# For *nix, use the forward-slash, and the colon path separator
python.path = /first/directory/to/add:/usr/local/secondDir/
```

Jython and Python also use a file called `site.py` to help with system paths. The `site.py` file is a module in Jython's lib directory that is automatically loaded at Jython's startup. One important feature of the `site.py` module is that it automatically looks for and imports the file `sitecustomize.py`. The `sitecustomize.py` module is not installed as part of Jython; it is a file that you author and is usually placed in Jython's `Lib` directory. The automatic execution of `sitecustomize.py` at startup makes it useful for site-specific information such as extra library paths. Suppose you have Jython installed in the directory `/usr/local/jython-2.1` on a Solaris machine, and you wish to organize user-defined modules in the directory `/usr/local/jython-2.1/Lib/site-python`. To add this extra directory to `sys.path`, you can create a `sitecustomize.py` file in the directory `/usr/local/jython-2.1/Lib` that includes the following code:

```
# file sitecustomize.py
import sys
sys.path.append(sys.prefix + "/Lib/site-python")
```

The `sys.prefix` variable is a string representing the path to Jython's installation directory. Actually, it's the value of the `python.home` variable, which can be any arbitrary path and is discussed later, but for now it is most practically thought of as the path in which Jython is installed. Jython's `Lib` directory is determined as `sys.prefix` + `Lib`. When import problems occur, it is often most instructive to print `sys.prefix` and `sys.path` to confirm their accuracy.

What Is a Module?

A *module* is a file that contains Jython code and has a `.py` extension. There are no other special syntax or directives required to make it a module. During any previous examples where you placed Jython code within a `*.py` file, you were actually creating a module. Modules also appear as `.class` files, or files containing Java bytecode, with names like `modulename$py.class`. These are the compiled version of modules that have been imported. Subsequent imports use these byte-compile files as an optimization if their associated `.py` has not changed. Modules are byte-compiled when they are imported or by using Jython's compiler, `jythonc`, or by running the module `compileall.py` (found in Jython's `Lib` directory).

Numerous modules are included with the Jython distribution, and they are located in Jython's `Lib` directory. These modules are mostly Python modules originally included in the CPython distribution and a part of CPython's documentation set. Not all of CPython's modules work with Jython, however. Some of the modules in CPython rely on code written in C. Jython currently cannot make use of modules written in languages other than Java or Python, so these C-dependant modules will not work. Documentation for most of Jython's modules is in the Python Library Reference currently located at `http://www.python.org/doc/current/lib/lib.html`, and available in the book *Python Essential Reference* by David Beazley (New Riders Publishing). Those modules that are unique or missing in Jython have descriptions in Appendix C of that book.

User-defined modules are those `*.py` files that you or others have written, and are not included in the distribution. These files could be placed in Jython's `Lib` directory in order for them to be found and loaded; however, that usually makes it frustrating to upgrade Jython versions. A separate location for these files is more desirable, and a separate location requires an additional item in `sys.path`. For the remainder of this chapter, it is assumed that newly written modules are placed in a location in the `sys.path` list. The easiest would be the current working directory, which is automatically in the `sys.path`. Otherwise, in the directory `sys.prefix + /Lib/site-python`, which would require that you have added this to the `sys.path` list as described earlier.

Special Module Variables

Modules have special variables or "magic" variables. *Magic* is a colloquial term often ascribed to variables in Jython, and Python, that have two leading and trailing underscores. The magic variables in a module are `__doc__`, `__file__`, `__name__`, and `__all__`.

The `__doc__` variable in a module is similar to the `__doc__` string of functions. If a module begins with a string literal, that string literal becomes the module's `__doc__` attribute. This is part of Jython's self-documentation mechanism. Suppose you need to create a directory-syncing tool. You would likely start out by documenting your intentions in a module's `__doc__` attribute:

```
# file: dirsync.py
"""This module provides tools to sync a slave directory to a master
directory."""
```

After placing the `dirsync.py` file in somewhere in the `sys.path`, you can look at the results of this string in the interactive interpreter:

```
>>> import dirsync
>>> print dirsync.__doc__
This module provides tools to sync a slave directory to a master
directory.
```

The `__name__` attribute of a module is the module name. The exception to this is the `__main__` module. When Jython starts with a module name supplied as a command-line argument, such as `jython test.py`, the module supplied on the command line is considered the `__main__` module. This introduces an important and useful convention in Jython modules.

Listing 5.1 shows a more complete version of the `dirsync.py` file. It doesn't actually sync files, but Listing 5.1 calculates the work required to do so. The final `if` statement in Listing 5.1 is the useful module convention. First, examine Listing 5.1, beginning with explaining a couple of functions used:

- **`os.path.join`**: Adds multiple path elements into a legal path.
- **`os.path.isfile`**: Returns 1 if a path points to a file, 0 otherwise.
- **`os.path.isdir`**: Returns 1 if a path points to a directory, 0 otherwise.
- **`os.listdir`**: Returns a list of the contents of a designated directory.
- **`os.stat`**: Returns a ten-element list of file info.
- **`stat.ST_MTIME`**: Is a number that designates which element of a stat list is the modification time.

Listing 5.1   **A Module for Syncing Directories**

```
# file:  dirsync.py
"""This module provides tools to sync a slave directory to a master
directory."""

from __future__ import nested_scopes
import os
from stat import ST_MTIME

def __getRequiredUpdates(master, slave):
    """getRequiredUpdates(master, slave) -> list of files that are old or
        missing from the slave directory"""

    needUpdate = []   # holds results
    def walk(mpath):  # recursive function that does the work
        if os.path.isfile(mpath):
            spath = mpath.replace(master, slave)
            if (not os.path.exists(spath) or
                (os.stat(mpath)[ST_MTIME] > os.stat(spath)[ST_MTIME]):
                    needUpdate.append(mpath.replace(master, ""))
        if os.path.isdir(mpath):
            for item in os.listdir(mpath):
                walk(os.path.join(mpath, item))
    walk(master)
    return needUpdate

def __getExtraneousFiles(master, slave):
    """getExtraneousFiles(master, slave) -> list of files in the slave
        directory which do not exist in the master directory"""

    extraneous = []   # holds results
    def walk(spath):  # recursive function that does the work
```

continues

Listing 5.1 **Continued**

```
        mpath = spath.replace(slave, master)
        if not os.path.exists(mpath):
            extraneous.append(spath)
        if os.path.isdir(spath):
            for item in os.listdir(spath):
                walk(os.path.join(spath, item))
    walk(slave)
    return extraneous

def sync(master, slave):
    updates = __getRequiredUpdates(master, slave)
    extras = __getExtraneousFiles(master, slave)
    for item in updates:
        # copy those files needing updated
        print os.path.join(master, item), "need copied to slave dir."
    for item in extras:
        # delete those files that are extras
        print item, "should be deleted."

if __name__ == '__main__':
    from time import time
    import sys
    t1 = time()
    sync(sys.argv[1], sys.argv[2])
    print "Directory sync completed in %f seconds." % (time()-t1)
```

The last if statement in Listing 5.1 tests if the name of the module is __main__.
If this is true, it means the module was run with the command jython
dirsync.py and is expected to act lake the main script, or similar to what you
would expect from methods with the public static void main(String args)
signature in a Java program. However, if another script imports this module,
__name__ is not __main__ and the associated code is not executed. Many Jython
modules make use of this convention, either so that they can function as
stand-alone scripts as well as modules, or so that they self-test when they are
run as a stand-alone script. In the case of Listing 5.1, the script dirsync.py can
be run as a standalone script to determine the work required to sync a master
and slave directory that are supplied in the command-line with a command
like the following:

```
jython dirsync.py "c:\path\to\master\dir" "c:\path\to\slave\dir"
```

The variable sys.argv is a list that contains all the command-line parameters
used when starting Jython. The actual script running as the main script is
always sys.argv[0], so in Listing 5.1, sys.argv[0] is dirsync.py, and sys.argv[1]

and `sys.argv[2]` would be the master and slave directories, respectively. The shell command to run `dirsync.py` and the respective `sys.argv` assignments would be as follows:

```
jython dirsync.py c:\mywork c:\mybackups
        argv[0]      argv[1]      argv[2]
```

Listing 5.1 introduces another special naming convention: functions that begin with two underscores. Identifiers that begin with two underscores are special in that they are not imported when the `from X import *` syntax is used. Actually, in Jython 2.1, this should apply to those identifiers starting with one or two underscores, but those with one underscore didn't work properly at the time this was written, so Listing 5.1 uses two underscores. To test this with the `dirsync.py` module in Listing 5.1, first ensure that it is in the `sys.path`, then type:

```
>>> from dirsync import *
>>> dir()  # look to see which names where imported
['ST_MTIME', '__doc__', '__name__', 'nested_scopes', 'os', 'sync']
```

The results of the `dir()` function confirm that no names that begin with two underscores were imported.

The magic variable `__all__` further controls the list of names imported from a module. The variable `__all__` is a list that contains which names a module exports. If Listing 5.1 had a line like the following, the only name appearing after a `from dirsync import *` statement would be the name sync.:

```
__all__ = ['sync']
```

What Are Packages?

A Python *package* is a hierarchy of modules contained in a directory tree. The concept is the same as Java packages, except the contents of Python packages are modules, not classes. An excellent example of the package system is Jython's `pawt` package found in Jython's `Lib` directory.

Figure 5.1 is the directory listing of a Jython installation on a Windows machine. Note that depending on your version of Jython and whether or not you created the `site-python` directory discussed earlier, your directory, contents could differ. The `Lib` directory within `c:\jython-2.1\` is where modules and packages distributed with Jython are stored. Within this directory, you'll find the directory called `pawt`. It is not just another directory however—it is a Jython package. What makes it a package? It contains a file that initializes it as a package. This file is `__init__.py`.

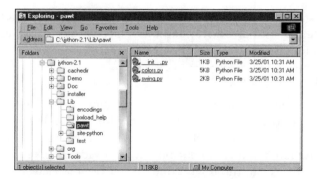

Figure 5.1 The *pawt* Package.

When a package is imported, its __init__.py file is executed. Because pawt is a package, you can import its contents with any of the following statements:

```
>>> import pawt.colors
```

```
>>> import pawt.swing
```

```
>>> from pawt import colors, swing
```

```
>>> from pawt import *
```

You can also import the package itself with this statement:

```
>>> import pawt
```

The unique thing about Python packages is that an import statement actually initializes all parent packages. This means if you have a hierarchy such that package A contains package B, which contains module C, the actual import of module C runs A.__init__.py, then runs B.__init__.py, and then imports module C. Listing 5.2 shows the implementation of this scenario. Three files, A.__init__.py, B.__init__.py, and moduleC, each merely print a message to announce the point of their evaluation. Listing 5.2 continues this example in the interactive interpreter by importing moduleC. The messages printed to the screen confirms the initialization of parent packages.

Listing 5.2 **Package Initialization**

```
# file sys.prefix/site-python/A/__init__.py
"""Root package in a nested package demonstration"""
print "Initializing package A"


# file sys.prefix/site-python/A/B/__init__.py
```

```
        print "Initializing package B"


        # file sys.prefix/site-python/A/B/moduleC.py
        print "Executing module 'moduleC'"
        import moduleD

        # file sys.prefix/site-python/A/B/moduleD.py
        print "Executing module 'moduleD'"


        >>> # examine packages A, B, and moduleC interactively
        >>> import A.B.moduleC
        Initializing package A
        Initializing package B
        Executing module 'moduleC'
        Executing 'moduleD'
```

Listing 5.2 also includes a moduleD.py file to demonstrate how a module can import package-sibling modules without the fully qualified name, meaning moduleC can import moduleD with just its name. Modules in different packages must be qualified, however.

Jython's self documentation conventions extend to packages in that if a package's __init__.py file begins with a string literal, the package's __doc__ attribute is assigned that string as a value. Notice that the file sys.prefix/site-python/A/__init__.py in Listing 5.2 has a string literal. If we revisit this package, we can see how the __doc__ attribute is assigned in this package. Note that you have to restart the interpreter between Listing 5.2 and the following in order for the package initialization to work as shown:

```
        >>> import A
        Initializing package A
        >>> A.__doc__
        'Root package in a nested package demonstration'
```

A package's __init__.py file can also contain the magic variable __all__, which designates the names that package exports when the from package import * statement is used.

An imported package is similar to a module except that a package has one additional special variable: __path__. The __path__ variable is just as you might guess: the system path to the specified package. Examining the pawt package demonstrates the __path__ variable:

```
        >>> import pawt
        >>> pawt.__path__
        ['C:\\jython 2.1a1\\Lib\\pawt']
```

Java's *package.class* Hierarchy

The loading of Java packages and classes uses the same syntax as importing Python modules, but there is some extra information required to fully understand Java loading. Java uses the classpath to locate and load packages and classes. Jython's import mechanism does inspect the Java classpath. When running Jython, the classpath is taken from the classpath environment variable. To add the jar file zxJDBC.jar to the classpath that Jython uses, you can set the classpath environment variable before starting Jython with shell commands like these:

```
# for Windows users at a dos prompt, or within a *.bat file
>set CLASSPATH=c:\path\to\zxJDBC.jar
>jython

# for *nix users at the bash prompt
>export CLASSPATH=/path/to/zxJDBC.jar
>jython
```

On either platform, make sure that the paths in the classpath follow the platform-specific guidelines for paths: \ and ; for Windows, and / and : for *nix.

All four permutations of Jython's import statement work with Java classes and packages and even class contents. Name binding rules remain the same for imports when importing Java items. This means that import java.util.Vector still binds the leftmost name, java, instead of the Java behavior of binding the rightmost name. This also means that the from X import Y syntax can import contents of X that are not classes or packages.

Listing 5.3 shows a number of import statements that import Java classes, and even class contents to demonstrate how the import behavior works with Java elements. Note that Listing 5.3 requires Java 1.2 (only tested with Sun JDK).

Listing 5.3 **Importing and Using Java Items**

```
>>> import java.applet
>>> # inspect name with dir() to show leftmost binding
>>> dir()
['__doc__', '__name__', 'java']
>>>
>>> import java as j
>>> dir()
['__doc__', '__name__', 'j', 'java']
>>>
>>> # 'from X import y' even works on class contents such as...
>>> from java.security.AlgorithmParameters import getInstance
>>> from java.applet.Applet import newAudioClip as nac
>>> dir()
['__doc__c', '__name__', 'getInstance', 'j', 'java', 'nac']
```

You can see that not only does Jython's import flexibility apply to Java classes and packages, but it also allows selective importing of class contents.

The `classpath` is not the only path used to locate and load Java classes and packages. They can also be located and loaded from the `sys.path`. In Jython, the `sys.path` acts as an extension of Java's `classpath`. This creates some problems in determining which items are Java and which are Python, and in that packages spread across the `classpath` and `sys.path` do not see themselves as package siblings.

Listing 5.4 shows a minimal Java class. The focus of this example is to show how a Java class loads from the Python `sys.path`. The first half of Listing 5.4 is the Java class `mjc` (for minimal Java class). To try the example in Listing 5.4, save the Java `mjc` class to the file `mjc.java` and compile it with javac. Then place the compiled `mjc.class` file in the user-defined module directory this chapter has been using (`sys.prefix/Lib/site-python`). The interactive interpreter section of Listing 15.4 prints Java's `classpath` to confirm `mjc.class` is not within it, then prints `sys.path` followed by importing `mjc`. In this case, the Java class is located and loaded from the `sys.path`.

Listing 5.4 **Loading Java Classes from *sys.path***

```
// file mjc.java
public class mjc {
    String message = "This is all I do- return a string.";
    public mjc() {}

    public String doSomething() {
        return message;
    }
}
```

```
>>> from java.lang import System
>>> System.getProperty("java.class.path")
'C:\\jython 2.1a1\\jython.jar;c:\\windows\\desktop'
>>> import sys
>>> print sys.path
['', 'C:\\WINDOWS\\Desktop\\.', 'C:\\jython 2.1a1\\Lib', 'C:\\jython 2.1a1',
'c:\\jython 2.1a1\\Lib\\site-python']
>>> import mjc
>>> m = mjc()
>>> m.doSomething()
'This is all I do- return a string.'
```

Things are not always that simple, though. `*.jar` and `*.zip` files do not load from the `sys.path` at the time of this writing. There are also cases where Java packages are not recognized properly. One instance of misrecognition is when a `jar` or `zip` file's extension is not all lowercased. This will be corrected at some point, but for Jython versions 2.1a1 and earlier, those files should be renamed with lowercased extensions. The loading of `*.jar` and `*.zip` files from the `sys.path` will eventually be added as well.

Listing 5.5 makes use of the Java loading facility to play a network audio resource. Note that some firewall setups create problems for Listing 5.4.

Listing 5.5   **Using Java Classes Within Jython to Play a Sound**

```
>>> from java import net
>>> from java.applet.Applet import newAudioClip
>>>
>>> url = net.URL("http://www.digisprings.com/test.wav")
>>> audio = newAudioClip(url)
>>> audio.play()
```

Java manages dynamic loading with the `Class.forName` method. This is still available in Jython, and the only catch is that most people forget that the content of `java.lang` is not imported by default in Jython. With the explicit import of `Class`, or even the static method `forName`, this dynamic loading functions the same. Here is an example that imports the `java.util.Hashtable` class:

```
>>> from java.lang.Class import forName
>>> forName("java.util.Hashtable")
<jclass java.util.Hashtable at 2105495>
>>>
>>> # OR
>>> from java.lang import Class
>>> Class.forName("java.util.Hashtable")
<jclass java.utilc.Hashtable at 2105495>
```

Reloading

If you imported a module, but that module has since changed, you can reload that module with the built-in reload function. This is most useful when working within the interactive interpreter and editing a module at the same time. The syntax for the reload function is as follows:

```
reload(modulename)
```

Whereas the `import` statement allows the import of module-global entities with the `from x import Y` syntax, the `reload` function does not. `Reload` only works for modules and packages. Here are a few example `reload` lines to demonstrate:

```
>>> from pawt import colors
>>> reload(colors)
<module pawt.colors at 860800>
>>> import dumbdbm
>>> reload(dumbdbm)
<module dumbdbm at 5654181>
```

Reloading Java packages and classes is trickier. Samuele Pedroni is a programmer and Jython project member who has contributed an experimental package to the Jython project that allows the reloading of Java entities. Samuele's `jreload` module is what enables Java reloading. Java packages and classes imported as part of a `jreload` `load` `set` are the only ones that are re-loadable. This is very different than other imports because all package and class access is via the load set instance.

To make a load set you must use the `jreload.makeLoadSet` function. This function requires two arguments: The first is a `name`, which is any arbitrary string you want assigned to the load set. The second argument must be a `PyList`, which contains a list of strings representing `classpath` entries of items you wish to include in the load set. Suppose you have the `jar` file for the `javax.servlet` packages located in `C:\web\tomcat\lib\servlet.jar` (this jar does not come with the JDK; it must be downloaded separately—usually as part of the Tomcat web server located at `http://jakarta.apache.org`). Creating a load set for the packages contained within the `servlet.jar` file looks like this:

```
>>> import jreload
>>> ls = jreload.makeLoadSet("servlet classes",
                             ["c:\\web\\tomcat\\lib\\servlet.jar"])
>>> dir(ls.javax)
['__name__', 'servlet']
```

If you want to reload packages and classes from this load set, possibly because you have re-created the `servlet.jar` file with newer files, use the following:

```
>>> ls = reload(ls)
```

While this example is specific to the packages within the `servlet.jar` file, `jreload` works with any class or package not already on the `classpath` or `sys.path`. To try another package or class with `jreload`, you must change the second argument to the `makeLoadSet` method to include the location of the package you intend to import. Changing the first argument to `makeLoadSet` is also a good idea, but it is just an arbitrary name for the set and doesn't affect its functionality. The `classpath`-like list in the second argument of `makeLoadSet` is the essential part of the `jreload` mechanism.

There are some caveats to `jreload`. First, the list of `classpath`-like entries supplied to the `makeLoadSet` function (the second argument) should not be entries already found in `sys.path` or the `classpath`. Second, Java inner classes produce unexpected results.

6

Classes, Instances, and Inheritance

THIS BOOK ASSUMES ITS AUDIENCE HAS previous Java knowledge, or that the reader is acquiring Java knowledge from additional sources. What this means is that object-oriented programming (OOP) requires no introduction. If you know Java, you know objects. The terms class, instance, encapsulation, polymorphism, and inheritance all permeate Java discussions so there is only need for brief mention here. This chapter begins with an overview of encapsulation, abstraction, and information hiding followed by the definition of Jython classes. This quick start due to previous OOP knowledge does not mean that Jython classes and instances are the same as Java's. Differences do exist, and using both Jython and Java classes within Jython creates a duality that you should keep in mind while reading on. This duality means references to a class's properties may be unique to Java or Jython so always consider the context in which the class occurs. Fortunately Jython does not alter the nature or behavior of Java classes, so confusion concerning context is unlikely.

After describing how to define Jython classes and discussing Jython class attributes, the details concerning Jython's inheritance, method overloading, constructors, and destructors appear. To complete the introduction to Jython classes, this chapter concludes with a plethora of example Jython classes.

Encapsulation, Abstraction, and Information Hiding

This section is really about name mangling and electric fences, but let's start with a review of more traditional object terms. Encapsulation is the combining, or aggregation, of multiple entities to produce a new, often higher-order entity such as a class. A class encapsulates data and related functionality into a single object. A class also provides abstraction by organizing functionality in a way that simplifies the interface and hides the details of the implementation. The battle against complexity continues with information hiding—showing users only what they need to see in the name of simplicity. Java, among other languages, takes an additional step to enforce abstraction with attribute permissions modifiers like private and protected—the *electric fence* approach. Despite the immediate appeal electric fences have when facing software complexity, others contend that such strictness is unnecessary, that the electric fence should merely be warning signs that the adventurous continue past at their own risk. This analogy serves to contrast Java's strict approach with Jython's privacy mechanisms, which are quite open and contrary to those in Java.

Programmers can see and change most everything in Jython classes. A Jython convention for method and variable names implies privacy, though. An attribute that begins with one underscore is internal to the class. This is only by convention, not *de jure*. You can call attributes beginning with an underscore with impunity, but convention dictates you do so at your own risk. Jython variables that begin with two underscores are one step closer to enforced privacy, but it is only privacy through obscurity. The obscurity referred to is *name mangling*. Jython mangles the names of Jython class and instance attributes that begin with two underscores to encourage programmers to respect their privacy. The actual mangling is the addition of an underscore and the class name to the beginning of the attribute's name. The variable __var within the class A becomes _A__var. Mangling is the end of the protection—there is no further enforcement. Attributes are accessible using this mangled name, as can be seen in this example:

```
>>> class A:
...     __classVar = "A class variable designated as private"
...     def __init__(self):
...         self.__instVar = "An instance variable designated as private"
...     def __privateMethod(self):
...         print "This method is designated as private."
...
>>> inst = A()
```

```
>>> inst._A__classVar
'A class variable designated as private'
>>> inst._A__instVar
'An instance variable designated as private'
>>> inst._A__privateMethod()
This method is designated as private.
```

Jython, in other words, doesn't work so hard to protect programmers from themselves. The complete digest of Jython's privacy mechanisms amounts to one underscore for "don't use unless you're sure of what your are doing" and two underscores for "don't use unless you're really sure of what you are doing."

Another naming convention is two preceding and trailing underscores. This convention designates special or magic attributes that have special meaning in Jython, such as the __doc__ attribute. Therefore, the use of variables with two leading and trailing underscores is unwise unless implementing predefined special attributes. More details of Jython's special class attributes appear in the following chapter.

Defining Jython Classes

Jython class definitions occur within modules, in the interactive interpreter, or in dynamically generated code. The syntax of a class definition follows:

```
"class" class_name[(bases)]:
    code block
```

The name class is the statement that begins the definition. The class name is any legal Jython identifier. Following the class name is an optional list of base classes, within parenthesis. A colon designates the end of the class statement and the beginning of the associated code block. A near-empty Jython class looks like this:

```
>>> class emptyClass:
...     """This is a near-empty Jython class"""
...
```

Dissecting this empty class reinforces the essential parts of a class definition. The word class starts the class definition. The identifier for the class is emptyClass. This class is not a subclass of any other classes because there is no parenthesis and list after its identifier. As is always the rule in Jython, the code block obeys indention delimiting, beginning with the code block being one indention level in from the class statement. We also see that the class is not quite empty because it has a documentation string. Just like functions and modules, a literal string at the beginning of a class code block becomes that class's __doc__ attribute, or docstring in Python lingo.

A class is a callable object, and calling a class returns an instance object. To call our example class, emptyClass, add empty parenthesis after its name; emptyClass does not have a constructor that requires a certain number of arguments, so an empty argument list suffices. To confirm the distinction between the class emptyClass and the instance object it returns, use the built-in function type() as is done here:

```
>>> c = emptyClass()
>>> type(emptyClass)
<jclass org.python.core.PyClass at 3838683>
>>> type(c)
<jclass org.python.core.PyInstance at 7833967>
```

What good is an empty class? Not much in Java, but Jython allows arbitrary changes to a Jython class. The emptyClass example lacks attributes except for __doc__. However, dynamically assigning attributes to emptyClass or an instance of emptyClass is possible because of Jython's dynamic nature. This example demonstrates:

```
>>> emptyClass.z = 30
>>> c = emptyClass()
>>> c.x = 10
>>> c.y = -20
>>> c.__doc__ = "This was a near-empty Jython class"
>>> c.x
10
>>> c.y
-20
>>> c.z
30
>>> c.__doc__
'This was a near-empty Jython class'
```

Such arbitrary additions to Java classes do not work:

```
>>> from java.applet import Applet
>>> a = Applet()
>>> dir(a)
[]
>>> a.a=10
Traceback (innermost last):
  File "<console>", line 1, in ?
TypeError: can't set arbitrary attribute in java instance: a
```

Jython Class and Instance Attributes

Although it is clear that calling a class returns an instance of that class, the clarity of Jython's class-instance relationship from then on is wanting. Both the class and the instance have attributes unique from the other (Python literature uses attributes like Java literature uses members.) An instance attribute is unique and separate from a class attribute of the same name. Java designates class members with the use of the `static` keyword, but Jython has no such keyword. Because Jython lacks explicit modifiers that designate whether an attribute is class specific or unique to an instance, the guidelines that determine this require delineation. The following lists pertain only to Jython classes. Using Java classes and instances within Jython does not change the behavior of Java's class and instance members. The guidelines to creating Jython class and instance attributes are as follows:

- All methods are instance methods.
- Defining a data objects within the class, but not within a method, makes it a class attribute.

    ```
    class A:
        x = "This is a class attribute"
    ```

- Assigning to a data object qualified, or prefixed, with the class name makes it a class attribute.

    ```
    >>> class A:
    ...     def aMethod(self):
    ...         A.x = "This is a class attribute"
    ```

- Assigning to an identifier qualified, or prefixed, with the instance reference, or name, makes it an instance attribute.

    ```
    >>> class A:
    ...     def aMethod(self):
    ...         "Hint: 'self' is the instance ref- more on this later."
    ...         self.x = "This is an instance attribute"
    ```

The guidelines to accessing class and instance attributes are as follows:

- An identifier qualified with a class's name references a class attribute.

    ```
    >>> class A:
    ...     x = "Class attribute"
    ...     def aMethod(self):
    ...         self.x = "Instance attribute"
    ...         print A.x
    ...
    >>> test = A()
    >>> test.aMethod()
    Class attribute
    ```

- An identifier qualified with an instance's name may reference an instance attribute or a class attribute. If the instance attribute exists, it is used. An instance attribute shadows, or hides from accessibility, any class attribute of the same name. If no instance attribute of that name exists, the identifier references a class attribute. This requires two examples to clarify: the first prints the class attribute, but the second example adds an instance attribute of the same name to show how it precedes the class attribute in the lookup order.

```
>>> # Example 1- Only a class attribute "x" exists
>>> class A:
...     x = "Class attribute"
...     def aMethod(self):
...         print self.x
...
>>> test = A()
>>> test.aMethod()
Class attribute
>>>
>>> # Example 2- Both a class and instance attribute "x" exist
>>> class A:
...     x = "Class attribute"
...     def aMethod(self):
...         self.x = "Instance attribute"
...         print self.x
...
>>> test = A()
>>> test.aMethod()
Instance attribute
```

The only tricky portion to remember is that `self.x` references a class attribute, but assigning to `self.x` creates a new instance attribute of that name that shadows the class attribute. One advantage of this is that immutable class attributes can serve as initial default values for instance attributes of the same name.

After reviewing the list, what seems to be missing? A Python programmer is tempted to answer "Nothing." A Java programmer, however, will inevitably answer "Class static methods." While numerous mechanisms to add this functionality have floated around, there is no standard, built-in support for class static methods in Jython classes. Despite recurrence of the idea, there is also no clamoring to add such support because module-level functions suffice.

All instances of a class share class attributes. On the other hand, instance attributes are unique to each instance of a class. Consider the class `myFiles`, which contains a class attribute definition like this:

```
>>> class myFiles:
...     path = "/home/rbill"
```

Because the `path` is a class attribute, all instances of the class `myFiles` share this same `path` object. However, if an instance creates an instance attribute named `path`, it is not only unique from the class attribute of the same name, but is also unique from all other instances of the `myFiles` class. To confirm `path` is class static requires creating two instances, changing the path, and then checking the value of `path` in each instance:

```
>>> c1 = myFiles()
>>> c2 = myFiles()
>>> myFiles.path = "c:\\windows\\desktop"
>>> c1.path
'c:\\windows\\desktop'
>>> c2.path
'c:\\windows\\desktop'
```

Confirming the uniqueness of instance variables requires three instances. Remember that assignment to an identifier that is qualified, or prefixed, with the instance name, creates an instance attribute. This is equally true outside of the class definition and is used here to example instance variables:

```
>>> class myFiles:
...     path = "/home/rbill"
...
>>> c1 = myFiles()
>>> c2 = myFiles()
>>> c3 = myFiles()
>>> c2.path = "c:\\windows\\desktop"  # creates a new instance attrib
>>> c3.path = "/export/home/solaris"  # creates a new instance attrib
>>>
>>> c1.path  # class attrib
'/home/rbill'
>>> c2.path  # instance attrib unique to c2
'c:\\windows\\desktop'
>>> c3.path  # instance attrib unique to c3
'/export/home/solaris'
```

Defining instance methods in a Jython class is similar to writing a Jython function. Jython methods use the very flexible parameter scheme already described for Jython functions. Jython methods can use ordered arguments and keyword arguments, parameters can have default values, and you can allow for unknown numbers of parameters with the * and ** designations in the method signature. The difference centers on the instance reference. In Java, the variable `this` references the specific instance in which it is contained. `this` is assumed, or implicit in Java, but Jython does no such implicit name binding for the instance object. Instead, every method in a Jython class must specify an identifier for the instance object in the first slot of the method's parameter list. While this first slot is an arbitrary identifier, the word `self` has become standard practice. An instance method that creates and prints an instance variable looks like the following:

```
>>> class test:
...     def imethod(self):
...         self.message = "This is an instance variable"
...         print self.message
...
>>> t1 = test()  # create the instance
>>> t2 = test()  # create a second instance for comparison
>>> t1.imethod()
This is an instance variable
>>>
>>> # To prove the "message" data is unique to only instance "t1"...
>>> t1.message
'This is an instance variable'
>>> t2.message  # imethod not called- so t2.message is not defined
Traceback (innermost last):
  File "<console>", line 1, in ?
AttributeError: instance of 'test' has no attribute 'message'
```

You'll notice that the method definition of `imethod` is the same as a function definition except that the added `self` parameter (or other suitable identifier) is required to meet the instance obligation. Within the class's code block, references to instance attributes must be qualified with `self`, there is no implied understanding of other attributes contained within the object as is the case in Java. Consider a class with two methods called `methodA` and `methodB`. Because `self` must be explicit in attribute lookups, any reference to `methodA` from within `methodB` must use `self.methodA`. The `Calendar` class below serves to demonstrate the `self` prefix in instance references:

```
>>> class Calendar:
...     def setDay(self, day):
...         self.day = day
...     def setMonth(self, month):
...         self.month = month
...     def getDay(self):
...         return self.day
...     def getMonth(self):
...         return self.month
...     def getDayandMonth(self):
...         return self.getDay() + " " + self.getMonth()
...
```

Setting and retrieving the instance variables day and month both use the self prefix in the Calendar class. Note that the use of other instance methods, as is done in getDayandMonth, also requires the self prefix to qualify other instance methods.

Methods have their own local namespace, just like functions, so only variables within the instance and outside the method's local namespace require the self prefix. An example follows:

```
>>> class test:
...     def methA(self):
...         data = 10 # This is local to methA
...         self.data = 20 # this is a separate instance variable
```

Class and instance attributes are stored in the object's dictionary, or __dict__ variable. This means that attribute B in class A is available through A.__dict__[B]. The built-in function vars() is designed to return the __dict__ attribute of objects and is useful in exploring objects.

Constructors

A *constructor* is a method that initializes an instance of a class. A constructor in Jython is a method named __init__ defined within a Jython class. This __init__ method's parameters look similar to any other method's parameters in that the first slot belongs to the instance object usually called self. A constructor may not return a value other than None. The return statement is allowed in a constructor and is useful in cases where a certain condition should return control before completing the entire __init__ block. If return appears, it must be simply return or return None. A Jython class with a constructor that creates some instance variables looks like this:

```
>>> class contact:
...     def __init__(self):
...         self.name = ""
...         self.phone = ""
...
```

The number of parameters defined in a constructor determines how many arguments appear when calling a class. If a constructor requires two parameters plus the self slot, two arguments must appear when calling that class. If a contact class required a name and phone number as constructor parameters, it would look like this:

```
>>> class contact:
...     def __init__(self, name, phone):
...         self.name = name
...         self.phone = phone
...
```

This `contact` class uses the constructor to initialize the name and phone variables to the name and phone constructor parameters. Creating an instance of this new contact class now requires two parameters and looks like this:

```
>>> c = contact("Someone's name", "555-555-1234")
>>> # Or with keyword arguments
>>> c = contact(phone="555-555-1234", name="Someone's name")
```

Supplying default values makes constructor parameters optional. Java can have multiple constructors to implement differing parameters. Jython cannot, but it does allow for great flexibility with parameters, including default values in methods like the constructor. Optional constructor parameters look like this:

```
>>> class contact:
...     def __init__(self, name="", phone=""):
...         self.name = name
...         self.phone = phone
...
```

Now calling the `contact` class can take any one of the following forms:

```
>>> c = contact()
>>> c = contact("Someone's name")
>>> c = contact("Someone's name", "555-555-1234")
>>> c = contact(name = "Someone's name")
>>> c = contact(phone = "555-555-1234")
>>> c = contact(name="Someone's name", phone="555-555-1234")
```

A common use for a constructor is establishing a database connection that stays connected for the life of the object. The following example contains a constructor that demonstrates establishing a database connection at the object's instantiation. Note that this example depends on the MySQL database and its associated Java driver, both of which are available from `http://www.mysql.org/`.

```
>>> import java
>>> import org.gjt.mm.mysql.Driver
>>> from java.sql import DriverManager

>>> class DBAdapter:
...     def __init__(self, dbname):
...         conString = "jdbc:mysql://localhost/%s" % dbname
...         self.db = DriverManager.getConnection(conString, "", "")
...         print "DB connection established"
```

After the `DBAdapter` class is instantiated, any instance method can access the database connection through the instance variable `self.db`. The time-consuming connection process is therefore only incurred once per instance.

Constructors often need to call superclass constructors. To do so, use the `classname`, followed by the __init__ method, and no matter what the parameters are, make the first parameter `self`. The syntax looks like this in Jython:

```
Superclass.__init__(self, otherArgs)
```

A more specific example is sub-classing the `java.net.Socket` class. The `Socket` class in Java has no such method as __init__, but the same syntax still applies. Jython internals handle which constructor to call. The following example demonstrates sub-classing the Socket class. Note that this example assumes you have an active Internet connection.

```
>>> from java.net import Socket
>>> class SocketWrapper(Socket):
...     def __init__(self, host, port):
...         Socket.__init__(self, host, port)
...
>>> s = SocketWrapper("www.digisprings.com", 80)
```

The syntax used to initialize a superclass is not restricted to just Java superclasses. Initializing a Jython superclass works the same way, and even makes more sense considering its constructor really is __init__.

Finalizer or Destructor

A finalizer or destructor is a method that if defined, is called when the object is collected by garbage collection. Jython uses Java's garbage collection (gc), so when a Jython object becomes unreachable, and memory needs trimming, the JVM gc thread may reclaim that object. There are two things to remember when using finalizers in Jython: First, they incur a performance penalty, and secondly, there is no way to tell when, or if, an object will be finalized.

A Jython finalizer is an instance method named __del__. This method looks like this:

```
>>> class test:
...     def __del__(self):
...         pass # close something, or clean up something here
...
```

The "Constructors" section demonstrated the creation of a database connection in a constructor, but to truly make the class complete, that connection should be closed in a finalizer or in some other method that is explicitly called. The following example demonstrates closing a database connection in the object finalizer, but there are some caveats in doing this that are described following the example:

```
>>> import java
>>> import org.gjt.mm.mysql.Driver
>>> from java.sql import DriverManager
```

```
>>> class DBAdapter:
...     def __init__(self, dbname):
...         conString = "jdbc:mysql://192.168.1.77/%s" % dbname
...         self.db = DriverManager.getConnection(conString, "", "")
...         print "DB connection established"
...     def __del__(self):
...         if not self.db.isClosed():
...             self.db.close()
...
```

Java's garbage collection, the nature of database resources and database licenses often conflict with the above approach. Because the Java virtual machine, and thus Jython, provides no guarantees as to when, or even if, garbage collection collects an unused object, relying on finalizers is dangerous. If an application creates numerous objects with database connections that are closed in finalizers, any delays in collecting such objects waste limited database resources. This is most evident where database licenses restrict the number of connections, but it is always a concern. The preceding example clarifies finalizers, but is not a prudent example of managing database connections. More on databases, including more clever resource management appears in Chapter 12, "Server-Side Web Programming."

Inheritance

We've seen that the ability to set an arbitrary attribute is one difference between Java and Jython classes. The explicit use of the self variable is another difference between Jython and Java. Clues pointing to a third difference between Jython and Java appeared early in the section Defining Jython Classes. Note that the definition of a Jython class allows a list of base classes. The use of the word "list" should pique interest for those accustomed to Java's enforcement of single-inheritance. Single-inheritance means that a Java class can only inherit from a single base class. A Java class can implement multiple interfaces, but can only subclass a single Java class. Jython, on the other hand, allows multiple-inheritance but still must comply with Java's restrictions. This again introduces the Java-Python duality found in Jython.

Jython's inheritance capacity depends on the type of superclass. Because Java enforces single inheritance, Jython may only inherit from a single Java class; however, because Python allows multiple inheritance, Jython may inherit from multiple Python (Jython) classes. This duality makes Jython unique. It is not fully like Python, C++, and other languages that allow multiple inheritance because the number of Java superclasses is restricted. Additionally, it is not fully like Java because it may inherit from multiple Jython classes. Despite being restricted to a single Java base class, a Jython class may multiply-inherit from a single Java class along with multiple Jython classes (and Java interfaces). What follows are details concerning inheriting from Jython classes, Java interfaces and Java classes.

Subclassing Jython Classes

A Jython class need not inherit from any but can inherit from one, two, or many Jython base classes. Defining base, or super, classes occurs in the parentheses following the class identifier in a class definition. If you wish to inherit from the `Thread` class within the threading module and inherit from the `scheduler` class within the `sched` module, you can use:

```
>>> from sched import scheduler
>>> from threading import Thread
>>> class threadedScheduler(scheduler, Thread):
...     pass
...
```

Inheriting from multiple classes allows you to use methods from either base class or override methods from either base class. There are two ways to use, or call, a method defined in a base class from within a descendant. One is using the base class name and method name in dotted notation with the `self` instance object as the first argument.

```
>>> class parentClass:
...     def parentMethod(self):
...         print "Parent method called"
...
>>> class child(parentClass):
...     def callSuper(self):
...         parentClass.parentMethod(self)
...
>>> c = child()
>>> c.callSuper()
Parent method called
```

Explicitly calling a superclass with the current instance object as the first parameter as demonstrated just above has two purposes. First, this is how you initialize superclasses in Jython. Second, this allows you to call a superclass's method even if it is overridden in the current class. The following example demonstrate the latter with a revised child class:

```
>>> class parentClass:
...     def parentMethod(self):
...         print "Parent method called"
...
>>> class child(parentClass):
```

```
...       def parentMethod(self):
...           print "Overridden parent method"
...       def callSuper(self):
...           parentClass.parentMethod(self)
...
>>> c = child()
>>> c.callSuper()
Parent method called
```

The other way to call a method in a superclass is using the `self` prefix. To call method B in the superclass, use `self.B()` then allow the object attribute lookup mechanisms to locate the method. This assumes that method B does not exist in the child instance:

```
>>> class Super:
...     def B(self):
...         print "B found in superclass"
...
>>> class A(Super):
...     def callSuper(self):
...         self.B()
...
>>> test = A()
>>> test.callSuper()
B found in superclass
```

Attribute lookup for those identifiers qualified with the `self` prefix begins in the current instance, then proceeds through superclasses according to the order they are listed in the class definition. Therefore, changing the order of superclasses may change which attribute is found (assuming multiple super-classes define the same attribute). An example of this follows:

```
>>> class SuperA:
...     def A(self):
...         print "Test method from SuperA"
...
>>> class SuperB:
...     def A(self):
...         print "Test method from SuperB"
...
>>> class C(SuperA, SuperB):
...     def callSuper(self):
...         self.A()
...
>>> test = C()
>>> test.callSuper()
Test method from SuperA
>>>
>>> class C(SuperB, SuperA):
...     def callSuper(self):
```

```
...          self.A()
...
>>> test = C()
>>> test.callSuper()
Test method from SuperB
```

Subclassing Java Interfaces

In Java, you implement an interface rather than subclass it. However, there currently is no explicit interface equivalent in Jython, or Python, versions 2.1 and earlier. Interfaces, or protocols, are currently only implied in Jython and Python. This means that to implement a Java interface in Jython, you use the same syntax as if the interface were a base class. Just as Java can implement multiple interfaces, you can inherit from multiple Java interfaces. The combination of multiple Jython classes and multiple Java interfaces is also acceptable:

```
>>> from java.text import CharacterIterator
>>> from java.io import Serializable
>>> from java.io import DataInput
>>> from threading import Thread
>>> class test(CharacterIterator, Serializable, DataInput, Thread):
...      pass
...
>>> t = test()
```

What Is a PEP?

A PEP is a Python Enhancement Proposal. PEPs document the design and development of Python, and thus Jython. Requests for new features appear in PEPs, and there are currently two interesting PEPs concerning interfaces. PEP number 245 describes an interface syntax for Python so that defining an interface similar to Java's interfaces would be native in Jython. More information on PEP 245 is available at http://www.python.org/peps/pep-0245.html. Another PEP concerns an "object adaptation" proposal and it assumes an object does not necessarily know which protocols it supports when written, but can reply to the question, "Do you support this protocol (interface)?" This would require the introduction of a new adapt function, __adapt__ method, and __conform__ method. The "adaptation" proposal is PEP number 246 and is located at http://www.python.org/peps/pep-0246.html.

Either of these proposals could affect the way Jython uses Java interfaces in the future; however, neither is accepted at this point. Look for information concerning this in Jython's, and Python's 2.2 releases.

More information on all of Python's PEPs is at http://python.sourceforge.net/peps/.

Subclassing a Java Class

Because Java enforces single-inheritance, Jython classes are also restricted to at most one Java class as a base class. An attempt to inherit from more that one Java class raises an exception:

```
>>> from java.applet import Applet
>>> from java.util import Vector
>>> class a(Applet, Vector):
...     pass
...
Traceback (innermost last):
  File "<console>", line 1, in ?
TypeError: no multiple inheritance for Java classes: java.util.Vector and
java.applet.Applet
```

A Jython class that inherits from a Java class can also inherit from interfaces and Jython classes however. A sneaky few will try to fake multiple inheritance by using a Java class and another Java class wrapped in a Jython class, but this does not work:

```
>>> from java.awt import Checkbox
>>> from java.awt import Label
>>> class labelWrapper(Label):
...     pass
...
>>> class labelCheckbox(Checkbox, labelWrapper):
...     pass
...
Traceback (innermost last):
  File "<console>", line 1, in ?
TypeError: no multiple inheritance for Java classes:
org.python.proxies.__main__$labelWrapper$0 and java.awt.Checkbox
```

Multiple inheritance from a Java class and a Jython class works, but only applies if the Jython class does not inherit from a Java class as is the case with Jython's `Thread` class:

```
>>> from threading import Thread
>>> from java.awt import Label
>>> class threadedLabel(Label, Thread):
...     pass
...
>>> tl = threadedLabel()
```

Listing 6.1 is a module that contains an example of a class that inherits from a Java class. A full dissection of this follows starting with imports, then the class definition and the two instance methods within the `FileFilter` class. This example is a Jython module that should be placed somewhere on the `sys.path` so that the discussion can continue by importing the `filefilter` module.

The `filefilter` module imports the following items:

- `from java import io`—The `Filter` class inherits from the Java class `java.io.FilenameFilter`, and this inheritance requires that the base class first be imported.

- `from os import path`—This enables the use of the `path.join` function. This function joins path elements, adding platform specific separators where appropriate. The `Filter` class applies regular expressions to entire paths, so this necessitates joining the path and filename elements.

- `import re`—This imports Jython's regular expression module. The `FileFilter` class approves only those files that match a list of specified regular expressions. Remember that a regular expression is different that glob wildcards. The asterisk (*) is a repeating operator in regular expressions, and the period (.) matches any character.

The `FileFilter` class in Listing 6.1 inherits from the Java class `java.io.FilenameFilter` so that a `java.io.File` class can use it to retrieve a filtered directory listing. The list is filtered according to which files return `1` when applied to the `accept` instance method.

Of the two instance methods in Listing 6.1, `addFilter` allows the loading of regular expressions into an instance variable, but `accept` is the method required to satisfy the role as a `FilenameFilter`. The instance variable `self.ffilter` is a `PyList` that holds the compiled regular expressions. This instance variable is created when the first filter is added, and that is the reason for the `if 'ffilter' not in vars(self).keys()` condition. A similar condition appears in the `accept` method as part of an `assert` statement that ensures at least one regular expression is added before using the filter.

Listing 6.1   **A File-Filtering Class that Uses a Java Base Class**

```
# file: filefilter.py

from java import io
from os import path
import re

class FileFilter(io.FilenameFilter):
    def addFilter(self, ffilter):
        if 'ffilter' not in vars(self).keys():
            self.ffilter = []
        self.ffilter.append(re.compile(ffilter))

    def accept(self, dir, name):
        assert 'ffilter' in vars(self).keys(),'No filters added'
```

continues

Listing 6.1 **Continued**

```
        for p in self.ffilter:
            if not p.search(path.join(str(dir), name)):
                return 0
        return 1
```

To use this new Jython module and class in the interactive interpreter, ensure that it is in the `sys.path`, and then type:

```
>>> import filefilter
>>> from java import io
>>> ff = filefilter.FileFilter()
>>> ff.addFilter(".*\.tar\.gz")
>>> ff.addFilter("eiei")
>>> # Change the following line to use a path specific to your platform
>>> L = io.File("c:\\windows\\desktop").list(ff)
>>>
>>> # print the list of files found
>>> for item in L:
...     print item
...
eieio-0_16.tar.gz
```

Working with Java classes requires extra care. First, Java types require translation into Jython classes, and vice-versa, for method parameters and return values. Information about how Jython and Java types translate is available in Chapter 2, "Operators, Types and Built-In Functions." Calling members of a Java superclass requires careful explanation. There are two syntaxes for calling an attribute in a base class. The first is the class name plus method in dotted syntax with `self` supplied as the first argument, as in the following:

```
>>> from java import util
>>> class test(util.Vector):
...     def addToSuper(self, objectToAdd):
...         "Calling a java superclass looks like this:"
...         util.Vector.addElement(self, objectToAdd)
...
>>> t = test()
>>> t.addToSuper("a string")
>>> t.toString()
'[a string]'
```

The problem with this first syntax is that the Java superclass does not see the call as originating from a subclass. This syntax does work for any public method, and it is required when explicitly initializing Java superclasses, but it does not work for protected instance methods—use the second syntax for that.

The second syntax is `self.method`. This `self` prefixed syntax ensures Java sees the call as originating in a subclass, which is required to access protected instance methods. Listing 6.2 demonstrates accessing members of a Java superclass using both syntaxes.

Listing 6.2   **Calling Methods in a Java Superclass**

```python
# file: javabase.py
import sys
from java import util

class cal(util.GregorianCalendar):
    def __init__(self):
        # This uses the "classname.method(self)" syntax
        # to initialize the superclass
        util.GregorianCalendar.__init__(self)

    def max(self):
        # This uses the "classname.method(self)" syntax
        return util.GregorianCalendar.getActualMaximum(self, 1)

    def min(self):
        # Another example of "classname.method(self)" syntax
        return util.GregorianCalendar.getActualMinimum(self, 1)

    def compute1(self):
        # This tries the "classname.method(self)" syntax.
        # This will not work because the method called is protected.
        try:
            util.GregorianCalendar.computeTime(self)
            return "Success"
        except AttributeError, e:
            print "compute1 failed.\n", e

    def compute2(self):
        # This uses the "self.method()" syntax so that the call appears
        # to originate from the base class.
        try:
            self.computeTime()
            return "success"
        except AttributeError, e:
            print "compute2 failed.", e
```

Assuming that the above module is in the sys.path, you can test it with this:

```
>>> import javabase
>>> c = javabase.cal()
>>> print "Trying max: ", c.max()
Trying max:  292278994
>>> print "Trying min: ", c.min()
```

```
Trying min:  1
>>> print "Trying compute1: ", c.compute1()
Trying compute1:  compute1 failed.
class 'java.util.GregorianCalendar' has no attribute 'computeTime'
None
>>> print "Trying method compute2: ", c.compute2()
Trying method compute2:  success
```

Java's `protected` and `static` modifiers are of special concern to Jython sub-classes. Explaining this requires a quick peek under the hood of Jython. How does Jython access Java superclass class members? Some of the access is through a proxy object, which is the real subclass of the Java object, but some access is not through the proxy. Using `self.add` in a subclass of `java.util.Vector` (that does not override `add`) actually asks the proxy object to call the `superclass` method. The proxy, being the `real` subclass, has access to protected instance methods. However, the current implementation does not create proxy entries for class fields, or static members. What does this mean? It means that when a Jython subclass tries to access static methods or class fields, it does not occur from a real Java subclass. This makes protected fields, and protected static members the equivalent of private as far as the Jython subclass is concerned.

Here's a quick list of what a Jython subclass does have access to:

- Public class (static) methods and fields
- Public instance methods and fields
- Protected instance methods (only with the `self.method` notation.)

Here is a list of what a normal Java subclass has access to, but a Jython sub-class does not:

- Protected class (static) methods and fields
- Protected instance fields
- Package-protected members

Such limitations are normally handled one of two ways. First, you can write Java classes to mediate access to required protected fields and protected static methods that you need. A section on trees at the end of this chapter demonstrates a Java class written to mediate inaccessible members. Second, there is the Jython registry setting `python.security.respectJavaAccessibility`. The Jython registry file is a file called `registry` in Jython's installation directory, or a file called `.jython` in a user's directory. The `respectJavaAccessibility` setting within this file can be true or false. If false, Jython gains access to protected and private members of Java classes (not just superclasses). As you might expect, there are additional implications for security and stability when circumventing accessibility restrictions this way. Also, requiring subsequent users of your work to also set `respectJavaAccessibility` to false might be troublesome. These issues require consideration when deciding to change the `respectJavaAccessibility` property.

A final note on using Java superclasses involves superclass constructors. Explicitly calling a Java superclass constructor uses the `classname.__init__(self)` syntax. Without an explicit call, an empty superclass constructor is called after completion of the subclass's __init__ method.

Method Overloading

Java uses method overloading extensively. Method overloading allows, or requires, multiple methods with the same name for differing parameter lists. The differences in the parameter lists are the number of parameters and the parameter types. For example, the java implementation of Jython's `xrange` function requires three methods to implement:

```
public static PyObject xrange(int n) {
    return xrange(0,n,1);
}

public static PyObject xrange(int start, int stop) {
    return xrange(start,stop,1);
}

public static PyObject xrange(int start, int stop, int step) {
    return new PyXRange(start, stop, step);
}
```

While this is pervasive in Java, Jython does not provide for method overloading. The lack of method overloading certainly does not diminish Jython's expressiveness, but it does become an issue when working with Java classes. What happens when Jython code calls an overloaded Java method? It generally works as expected. Despite Jython's lack of method overloading, it does do a good job of using overloaded methods in Java classes. An example is this usage of the class `java.lang.StringBuffer`:

```
>>> import java
>>> sb = java.lang.StringBuffer()
>>> sb = java.lang.StringBuffer(10)
>>> sb = java.lang.StringBuffer("Jython ")
>>> sb.append(2.1)
Jython 2.1
```

```
>>> sb.append("b")
Jython 2.1b
>>> sb.append("1")
Jython 2.1b1
```

The `StringBuffer` class has three different constructors, and the append method is also overloaded, but Jython employs all methods without trouble. Internally Jython identifies which Java method to call first by the number of parameters, then by types. Implementing overloaded Java methods does not mean overloading is possible in Jython classes, however. Because users can invoke overloaded Java methods from Jython, they assume overriding only a certain Java method in a Jython subclass should work. This is not true. When a Jython subclass overrides an overloaded Java method, it must handle all overloaded cases of that method. Jython does not employ method overloading by type signatures at all in this case. Even if it appears that the number of parameters should explicitly select a particular method, Jython remains non-selective. It's all or nothing when overriding an overloaded method.

Listing 6.3 examines subclassing the `java.awt.Dimension` class. Listing 6.3 extends the Dimension class to make a similar class with boundaries. The interesting methods in Listing 6.3 are the constructor and `setSize`. The constructor establishes maximum sizes with optional parameter values, or a default of `100`. The constructor also must initialize the superclass, which actually has three constructors. The subclass allows for each of the `java.awt.Dimension` constructors depending on what arguments it receives. Additionally, the `setSize` method of `BoundaryBox` overrides the superclass's methods of the same name. The superclass, `Dimension`, overloads the `setSize` method with these two type signatures:

```
void  setSize(Dimension d)

void  setSize(double width, double height)
```

Remember that overriding an overloaded method shadows all superclass methods of the same name. While specific usage of a class may mean some of these methods are insignificant to the situation, it is often the case that a new method within the subclass must handle multiple, or all superclass method signatures of the same name. In this case, it should allow for width, height values, or a Dimension instance in the `setSize` method. Listing 6.3 does allow for either of these arguments, but because of the limit testing, Listing 6.3 only need use one of the superclass's `setSize` methods.

Listing 6.3 **Overriding Overloaded Java Methods**

```python
# file: boundarybox.py
from java import awt
import types
import warnings as wrn # to shorten some lines

class BoundaryBox(awt.Dimension):
    """BoundaryBox is a java.awt.Dimension  subclass with max limits.
       The constructor accepts optional width and height values
       or a java.awt.Dimension instance, which provide max values"""

    def __init__(self, *args):
        if len(args)==2: # assume this is width, height
            self.maxWidth = args[0]
            self.maxHeight = args[1]
            awt.Dimension.__init__(self, args[0], args[1])
        elif len(args)==1: # assume this is a Dimension instance
            self.maxWidth = args[0].getWidth()
            self.maxHeight = args[0].getHeight()
            awt.Dimension.__init__(self, args[0])
        elif len(args)==0:
            self.maxWidth = 100
            self.maxHeight = 100
            awt.Dimension.__init__(self)

    def setSize(self, *dim):
        if len(dim) == 2:  # args must be width, height
            w = self._testWidth(dim[0])
            h = self._testHeight(dim[1])
        elif len(dim) == 1 and isinstance(dim, awt.Dimension):
            # in case arg is a Dimension instance
            w = self._testWidth(dim.getWidth())
            h = self._testheight(dim.getHeight())
        else:
            assert 0, "'setSize accepts w, h or a Dimenstion inst"
        awt.Dimension.setSize(self, w, h)

    def _testWidth(self, w):
        if w > self.maxWidth:
            msg = "Width, %s, exceeds bounds. Changed to %s"
            print msg % (w, self.maxWidth)
            return self.maxWidth
        return w # width within bounds

    def _testHeight(self, h):
        if h > self.maxHeight:
            msg = "Height, %s, exceeds bounds. Changed to %s"
            print msg % (h, self.maxHeight)
            return self.maxHeight
        return h  # height within bounds
```

To test the `BoundaryBox` class, place the `boundarybox.py` file in the `sys.path`, and use the following:

```
>>> import boundarybox
>>> bb = boundarybox.BoundaryBox(100, 200)
>>> bb.setSize(50, 201)
Height, 201, exceeds bounds. Changed to 200
>>> bb.setSize(101, 100)
Width, 101, exceeds bounds. Changed to 100
>>> bb.width
100
>>> bb.height
100
```

Sample Classes

To better understand Jython classes, it is best to examine demonstrations. This section provides demonstrations of not only Jython classes, but how they relate to similar Java classes.

Singletons

This example compares a Java implementation with similar functionality in Jython. The differences noted in the comparison helps clarify usage of Jython classes.

When an application requires a single point of interaction with some specific object, Java programmers often create a class that restricts creation of more than one instance of itself. While there are different implementations of this, the most frequent seems to be combining a class field and class method to return the instance. Listing 6.4 shows a Java class containing an instance of itself in a class field. This class also has a class method, `getInstance`, which determines if an instance already exists before returning one. In this case, the class method returns a pre-existing instance if it already exists, but it is also common to raise an exception, or just return nothing.

Listing 6.4   **Java Singleton**

```
# file: Singleton.java

public class Singleton {
    private static Singleton single=null;

    private Singleton() {}

    public static Singleton getInstance() {
```

```
        if (single==null) single = new Singleton();
        return single;
    }

    //The methods which required a single point of access
    //go here.
}
```

This makes for an interesting comparison due to the lack of class methods and the inability to make a constructor private in Jython. How do you implement this in Jython? Using a non-constructor to return an instance is little value without a private modifier to restrict the actual constructor. A constructor cannot return a value, so it cannot choose a pre-existing instance to return. However, static class data attributes exist, and this can help test for an existing sequence. This only allows for a test, so this is most useful in an assertion or other expression that raises an exception when trying to create a second instance. This could look something like this:

```
# file: SimpleSingleton.py
class Singleton:
    single = None
    def __init__(self):
        assert Singleton.single==None, "Only one instance allowed"
        Singleton.single = self

    def __del__(self):
        Singleton.single = None
```

The usage would raise an AssertionError at the creation of a second instance:

```
>>> from SimpleSingleton import Singleton
>>> s1 = Singleton()
>>> s2 = Singleton()
Traceback (innermost last):
  File "SimpleSingleton.py", line 11, in ?
  File "SimpleSingleton.py", line 4, in __init__
AssertionError: Only one instance allowed
```

While raising an exception is sufficient in many situations, you may want the pre-existing instance. To more closely mimic the Java class in Listing 6.4, you need a substitute for class methods. Java's class-centric programming can dissuade some from module-level encapsulation and the use of functions, but you should be careful to not discount them. Combining a class and factory function within a module is often a solution, as it is here. Listing 6.5 shows this combination.

Listing 6.5   **Function + Class = Singleton**

```
# file: singleton.py

class _Singleton:
    single = None
    def __init__(self):
        pass
    # put required methods here

    def __del__(self):
        _Singleton.single = None

def Singleton():
    if _Singleton.single == None:
        _Singleton.single = _Singleton()
    return _Singleton.single

#add testing code to the module
if __name__=='__main__':
    s1 = Singleton()
    s2 = Singleton()

    # set an instance data attribute in s1
    s1.data = 4
    # s2 should point to the same data value if it is really
    # the same instance
    print s2.data
```

The result from running jython singleton.py is merely the integer 4, which confirms the same instance is shared by both the s1 and s2 identifiers in the preceding example.

File *grep* Utility

Listing 6.6 is a simple class that searches lines or files for a specified pattern. The constructor only caches a list of files in the specified directory. The findFiles method compares a pattern against this cached list (self.files) and returns a filtered list. The findLines reads each file line-by-line to return a list of lines containing the specified pattern. The two methods are most sensible used together by first limiting the file list with findFiles, then searching those files with findLines.

Listing 6.6   **Searching Files with a Jython Class**

```python
# file: grep.py
import os
from os.path import isfile

class directoryGrep:
    def __init__(self, directory):
        self.files = filter(isfile, [os.path.join(directory, x)
                                for x in os.listdir(directory)])

    def findLines(self, pattern, filelist=None):
        """Accepts pattern, returns lines that contain pattern
        Optional second argument a filelist to search"""

        if not filelist:
            filelist = self.files

        results = []
        for file in filelist:
            fo = open(file)
            results += [x for x in fo.readlines()
                            if x.find(pattern) != -1]
            fo.close() # explicit close of file object
        return results

    def findFiles(self, pattern):
        "Accepts pattern, returns filenames that contain pattern"
        return [x for x in self.files if x.find(pattern) != -1]

# test
if __name__=='__main__':
    g = directoryGrep("c:\\windows\\desktop")
    files = g.findFiles(".py")
    print g.findLines("java", files)
```

The result from running jython grep.py on my machine is as follows:

```
['from java.lang import System\n', 'from java.lang import Runtime\n', 'from
java.io import IOException\n', 'import java\n', 'from java.sql import
DriverManager\n']
```

When reading files, Listing 6.6 explicitly closes the file objects it opens. Python programmers very frequently use the following phrase:

```
open(file).readlines()
```

This creates and reads from an anonymous file object. This assumes that closing the file and releasing the resource occurs when garbage collection sees a need to collect it. Remember, Jython relies on Java garbage collection, so the actually closing of the file and releasing of the resource is delayed an unknown extent of time. The explicit closing of the object in Listing 6.6 avoids potential problems due to this latency.

HTTP Headers

HTTP headers consist of an actual request followed by a series of key-value pairs called headers and a blank line (\r\n\r\n), which terminates the request header. Listing 6.7 eases the manipulation of request data by parsing strings into data fields, and back to a string.

Classes often help by mere containment and representation, meaning they group related data and can present that data in a useful way when needed. The containment in Listing 6.7 consists of two dictionaries, one containing request data, and the other containing headers. The interesting thing is that the dictionary containing the request data (method, URL, and HTTP version) is the instance dictionary, or self.__dict__. Listing 6.7 sets entries in this instance mapping as if it were a normal dictionary with self.__dict__.setdefault, and by using the instance attribute notation self.attribute = x syntax. Both approaches update self.__dict__.

Representation, normally the toString method in a Java class, is the special method __repr__ in a Jython class. This method must return a string representation of an object if it exists, and when there is a need for a string representation of the object (like a print statement), this is the method called to provide it. Constructors, finalizers, and this representation method are all the special class methods discussed so far, but numerous special methods for customizing an objects behavior exist. Consider __repr__ just foreshadowing of a much larger set of special methods discussed in Chapter 7, "Advanced Classes."

Listing 6.7   **Parsing HTTP Request Headers**

```
# file: request.py

import string
import re

class Request:
    """Class for working with request strings:
    The constructor optionally takes an http request string.
    e.g., req = Request("GET http://localhost/index.html HTTP/1.0")"""
```

```python
    def __init__(self, request=None):
        "Parses a raw request string, if supplied.
        self.headers = {}
        if not request:
            request = "GET None HTTP/1.0"
        self.method, self.url, self.version = request.split())
        self.host = self.path = self.file = ""
        match = re.match("http://(\S*?)(/.*)", self.url)
        if (match != None):
            self.host, self.path = match.groups()

    def setHeader(self, stringHdr):
        try:
            x,y = [x.strip() for x in stringHdr.split(":")]
            self.headers[x] = y
        except ValueError:
            raise SyntaxError("A header string must be "
                            "in the format key : value")

    def __repr__(self):
        d = self.__dict__ # make a local copy for convenience
        request = " ".join([d['method'], d['url'], d['version']])
        request += "\r\n"
        for key in self.headers.keys():
            request += (key + ": " + self.headers[key] + "\r\n")
        request += "\r\n"
        return request

# module testing code
if (__name__=='__main__'):
    # Creating the instance can be without arguments...
    a = Request()
    # or with a raw request string like...
    a = Request("GET HTTP://freshmeat.net/index.html HTTP/1.0")

    # Headers are added/altered with "setHeader".
    # setHeader works with a header string as an argument...
    a.setHeader("Accept: image/jpeg, image/pjpeg, image/png, */*")
    a.setHeader("Proxy-Connection: Keep-Alive")
    a.setHeader("Accept-Encoding : gzip")

    #put it all together
    print a
```

Output from running Jython `request.py` is:

```
GET HTTP://freshmeat.net/index.html HTTP/1.0
Accept: image/jpeg, image/pjpeg, image/png, */*
Accept-Encoding: gzip
Proxy-Connection: Keep-Alive
```

Trees

Trees are common data structures that are excellent examples for demonstrating classes. *Trees* are collections of nodes and leaves, where a node contains other nodes and leaves, and a leaf terminates the branch (does not contain other nodes). The analogy more closely relates to family trees than the arborous alternative because of their top-down representation, and because the inter-relationship of nodes and leaves is often referred to as a parent-child relationship. Listing 6.8 defines two classes: `leaf` and `node`. The great thing about using trees is that nodes and leaves can have the same methods, so the interface for using a `node` or a `leaf` remains the same. This, combined with their inherent recursive structure makes for a clean, consistent, and widely applicable pattern. Hierarchical data such as taxonomies, company personnel, and filesystems are only a few examples of tree-like data. It's possible to apply the generic `leaf` and `node` classes in Listing 6.8 to a great number of similar tree-like structures. You only need to know three things about trees to create appropriate classes.

1. A tree consists of nodes.
2. Some nodes can have children.
3. Leaves are nodes, but they are special because they cannot have children.

What does this mean for classes? It means there are specific expectations about what a class knows about itself and what functionality it provides. Questions a node object should be able to answer about itself are, Am I a leaf? Who's my parent? and Who are my children? The behavior expected from a non-leaf node object is the ability to add and remove children. The `leaf` class, despite not having children, also includes methods for adding and removing children, as well as answering, Who are my children? This ensures a consistent interface. These methods raise an exception, except in the case of the `getChildren` method, which returns a `tuple` so that it better matches node behavior. One additional requirement that is an implementation detail is that each object has a `setParent` method, which is required when adding objects to a node.

Because a leaf node is just a node minus children, the `leaf` class subclasses `node` and overrides only those methods related to children.

Listing 6.8   **Making Trees with Jython Classes**

```
# file: trees.py

class node:
    def __init__(self, name, value=None):
```

```
            self._children = []
            self.name = name
            self.value = value
            self._leaf = 0 # Means this node can have children

        # These methods answer question the object must know about itself.
        def isLeaf(self):
            """returns answer to, "Am I a leaf?" """
            return self._leaf

        def getParent(self):
            """returns answer to, "Who is my parent?" """
            return self._parent

        def getChildren(self):
            """returns answer to, "Who are my children?" """
            return tuple(self._children)

        # These methods supply required functionality of the object
        def addChild(self, node):
            node.setParent(self)
            self._children.append(node)

        def removeChild(self, node):
            try:
                self._children.remove(node)
                return 1
            except ValueError:  # in case that child doesn't exist
                return 0

        # implementation detail
        def setParent(self, parent):
            self._parent = parent

        # A quick way to view the tree
        def dump(self, level=0):
            print "%s%s %s" % ("   "*level, self.name, self.value or "")
            for child in self.getChildren():
                child.dump(level+1)

        def __repr__(self):
            return self.name

class leaf(node):
    def __init__(self, name, value=None):
        node.__init__(self, name, value)
        self._leaf = 1

    def addChild(self, node):
        raise ValueError, "Cannot add children to a leafNode"
```

continues

Listing 6.8   **Continued**

```python
    def removeChild(self, node):
        raise ValueError, "A leaf node has no children to delete."

    def getChildren(self):
        return () # returns empty tuple


# Code to test these two classes
if __name__ == '__main__':
    root = node("root", "trees")
    evergreens = node("evergreens")
    evergreens.addChild(node("Picea", "Spruce"))
    deciduous = node("deciduous")
    deciduous.addChild(node("Acer", "Maple"))
    quercus = node("Quercus", "Oak")
    quercus.addChild(leaf("Alba", "White Oak"))
    quercus.addChild(leaf("Palustris", "Pin Oak"))
    quercus.addChild(leaf("Rubra", "Red Oak"))
    deciduous.addChild(quercus)
    root.addChild(evergreens)
    root.addChild(deciduous)
    children = root.getChildren()
    print children
    print quercus.getParent()
    print # add blank line
    print "Here is a dump of the entire tree structure:"
    root.dump()
```

The results from running jython trees.py should look like:

```
(evergreens, deciduous)
deciduous

Here is a dump of the entire tree structure:
root trees
  evergreens
    Picea Spruce
  deciduous
    Acer Maple
    Quercus Oak
      Alba White Oak
      Palustris Pin Oak
      Rubra Red Oak
```

The Java implementation of a similar tree would no doubt be different, but how it would be different is interesting to look at. A Java tree would likely have an abstract class to ensure a consistent minimum for a legitimate node. Additionally, some instance variables would use the protected modifier. A potential abstract class in Java would look something like Listing 6.9.

Listing 6.9   **An *abstract* Java Node Class**

```java
// file: Node.java
import java.util.Vector;

public abstract class Node {
    protected String name;
    protected Node parent = null;
    protected boolean leaf = false;

    public abstract Vector getChildren();
    public abstract boolean addChild(Node n);
    public abstract boolean removeChild(Node n);

    public boolean isLeaf() {
        return leaf;
    }
    public String toString() {
        return name;
    }
}
```

This introduces some problems for the Jython tree classes. Namely, the protected fields `leaf`, `parent`, and `name`. A Jython subclass cannot access a protected Java field unless Jython's `respectJavaAccessibility` registry setting equals false. Let's assume that sidestepping access modifiers with the registry setting is unacceptable for whatever reason. The alternative is to write a Java class to mediate Jython's access to the abstract `Node` class. Listing 6.10 shows just such a Java `adapter` class.

Listing 6.10   **A Java-to-Jython *adapter* Class**

```java
// file: JyNodeAdapter.java
import Node;
import java.util.*;

public abstract class JyNodeAdapter extends Node {
    protected void setLeaf(boolean leaf) {
        this.leaf = leaf;
    }
    protected void setName(String nodeName) {
        name = nodeName;
    }
    public String getName() {
        return name;
    }
    public Node getParent() {
        return parent;
```

continues

Listing 6.10 **Continued**

```
    }
    public void setParent(Node p) {
        parent = p;
    }
    public void dump() {
        this.dump(0);
    }
    public void dump(int level) {
        for (int i = 0; i < level; i++) {
            System.out.print("  ");
        }
        System.out.println(name + "  " + this.value);
        Vector v = getChildren();
        for (Enumeration e = v.elements(); e.hasMoreElements();) {
            JyNodeAdapter node = (JyNodeAdapter)e.nextElement();
            node.dump(level + 1);
        }
    }
}
```

The only revisions required to make the Jython tree classes is to add
`JyNodeAdapter` as a superclass and alter attribute fetching and setting to use
the appropriate `set` and `get` methods as designated in the Java superclasses.
One additional change is altering the return value of `getChildren` to always
be a Vector (empty Vector for the leaf) to comply with the protocol specified
in the abstract `Node` class. Listing 6.11 shows the modified version of the
Jython tree implementation with the appropriate modifications to use the
`Node` and `JyNodeAdapter` base classes.

Listing 6.11 **Jython Subclass of the *JyNodeAdapter***

```
# file: SubclassedTree.py

import JyNodeAdapter
from java.util import Vector

class JyNode(JyNodeAdapter):
    def __init__(self, name, value=None):
        self.setName(name)
        self.value = value
        self._children = Vector()

    def getChildren(self):
        return self._children
```

```
        def addChild(self, c):
            c.setParent(self)
            self._children.add(c)
            return 1

        def removeChild(self, c):
            self._children.removeElement(c)
            return 1

        def __repr__(self):
            return self.toString()


class leaf(JyNodeAdapter):
    def __init__(self, name, value=None):
        self.setName(name)
        self.value = value
        self.setLeaf(1)

    def addChild(self, node):
        raise ValueError, "Cannot add children to a leafNode"

    def removeChild(self, node):
        raise ValueError, "A leaf node has no children to delete."

    def getChildren(self):
        return Vector() # returns empty Vector

    def __repr__(self):
        return self.toString()

if __name__=='__main__':
    root = JyNode("root", "trees")
    evergreens = JyNode("evergreens")
    evergreens.addChild(JyNode("Picea", "Spruce"))
    deciduous = JyNode("deciduous")
    deciduous.addChild(JyNode("Acer", "Maple"))
    quercus = JyNode("Quercus", "Oak")
    quercus.addChild(leaf("Alba", "White Oak"))
    quercus.addChild(leaf("Palustris", "Pin Oak"))
    quercus.addChild(leaf("Rubra", "Red Oak"))
    deciduous.addChild(quercus)
    root.addChild(evergreens)
    root.addChild(deciduous)
    children = root.getChildren()
    print children
    print quercus.getParent()
    print # add blank line
    print "Here is a dump of the entire tree structure:"
    root.dump()
```

The results from running jython `SubclassedTree.py` should look like:

```
(evergreens, deciduous)
deciduous

Here is a dump of the entire tree structure:
root trees
  evergreens
    Picea Spruce
  deciduous
    Acer Maple
    Quercus Oak
      Alba White Oak
      Palustris Pin Oak
      Rubra Red Oak
```

7

Advanced Classes

SPECIAL ATTRIBUTES, THOSE IDENTIFIERS with two leading and trailing under-scores, are abundant in Jython classes. They are the primary means of creating highly customized objects with complex behaviors. This chapter considers advanced Jython classes as those that leverage these special attributes. Describing these objects as advanced might be misconstrued to mean difficult or reserved for those more studied in Python, but that is not the case. Adding special attributes to classes is part of the ongoing battle against complexity. The ability to tune an object's behavior to act like a list or the ability to intercept attribute access only costs a few special methods while potential gains in design, reusability and flexibility are great.

Pre-Existing Class Attributes

Classes and instances implicitly have certain special attributes—those that auto-matically appear when a class definition executes or an instance is created. Jython wraps Java classes and instances so that they also have special attributes. Jython classes have five special attributes, whereas Java classes have three of the same five. Note that while all of these attributes are readable, only some allow assignment to them.

To further examine these special attributes, let's first define a minimal Jython class suitable for exploring. Listing 7.1 is a Jython module that contains an `import` statement and a single class definition: `LineDatum`. The `LineDatum` class merely defines a line expression (datum) based on the slope and intercept supplied to the constructor. The instance then may add points that lie on the line with the `addPoint` method.

Listing 7.1   **A Jython Class Tracking Points on a Line**

```
# file: datum.py
import java

class LineDatum(java.util.Hashtable):
    """Collects points that lie on a line.
    Instantiate with line slope and intercept: e.g. LineDatum(.5, 3)"""

    def __init__(self, slope, incpt):
        self.slope = slope
        self.incpt = incpt

    def addPoint(self, x, y):
        """addPoint(x, y) —> 1 or 0
        Accepts coordinates for a cartesian point (x,y). If point is
        on the line, it adds the point to the instance."""

        if y == self.slope * x + self.incpt:
            self.put((self.slope, self.incpt), (x, y))
            return 1
        return 0
```

Using the `LineDatum` class from within the interactive interpreter looks like this:

```
>>> import datum
>>> ld = datum.LineDatum(.5, 3)
>>> ld.addPoint(0, 3)
1
>>> ld.addPoint(2, 3)
0
>>> ld.addPoint(2, 4)
1
```

The special class variables are described in the next few sections.

__name__

This read-only attribute contains the name of the class. The name of the
LineDatum class in Listing 7.1 is LineDatum. Even if the import as syntax is used,
the __name__ is LineDatum. An example of this follows:

```
>>> from datum import LineDatum
>>> LineDatum.__name__
'LineDatum'
>>> from datum import LineDatum as ld
>>> ld.__name__
'LineDatum'
```

Java classes used within Jython also have the __name__ attribute as
demonstrated here:

```
>>> import java
>>> java.util.Hashtable.__name__
'java.util.Hashtable'
```

__doc__

This attribute contains the class documentation string, or None if it is not
provided. You can assign to __doc__.

```
>>> from datum import LineDatum
>>> print LineDatum.__doc__
Collects points that lie on a line.
    Instantiate with line slope and intercept: LineDatum(.5, 3)
```

Java classes used within Jython do not have a __doc__ attribute.

__module__

This attribute contains the name of the module in which the class is defined.
You can assign to __module__. For the LineDatum class in Listing 7.1, it is defined
in the module datum and is confirmed with this example:

```
>>> from datum import LineDatum
>>> LineDatum.__module__
'datum'
```

Java classes used within Jython do not have a __module__ attribute. Java doesn't
have modules, so this makes sense.

___dict___

This attribute is a `PyStringMap` object containing all the class attributes. We can guess from looking at the `LineDatum` class definition in Listing 7.1 what keys should be found in `LineDatum.__dict__`: There must be an `__init__` and an `addPoint` because those are the two methods defined. There should also be `__doc__` and `__module__` keys as described previously. The `__name__` key is a good guess, but it actually doesn't appear in the `class.__dict__` in Jython. The `LineDatum` class in Listing 7.1 is more complex than a normal class because it actually subclasses a Java class. The implementation of this requires additional attributes as seen in this example:

```
>>> from datum import LineDatum
>>> LineDatum.__dict__
{'__doc__': 'Collects points that lie on a line.\n        Instantiate with
line slope and intercept: LineDatum(.5, 3)\n    ', 'rehash': <java function
rehash at 1298249>, '__init__': <function __init__ at 913493>, 'addPoint':
<function addPoint at 1939121>, 'finalize': <java function finalize at
1068455>, '__module__': 'datum'}
```

Attributes defined in a class appear in the class's `__dict__`. The conventional notation for accessing attribute `b` in class `A` is `A.b`; however, the class `__dict__` allows an alternate notation of `A.__dict__['b']`. Here's an example of the differing syntaxes for attribute access:

```
>>> from datum import LineDatum
>>> LineDatum.__module__
'datum'
>>> LineDatum.__dict__['__module__']  # same as "LineDatum.__module__"
'datum'
```

You can even call methods with this alternate naming. A bit of a trick is required for the `addPoint` method of Listing 7.1 because it is an instance method. An instance must be the first parameter. Fortunately, Jython isn't fussy about which instance, so you can just create an instance before testing the syntax and pass it as the first argument:

```
>>> from datum import LineDatum
>>> inst = LineDatum(.5, 3)  # get a surrogate instance
>>> LineDatum.addPoint(inst, 5, 4)
1
>>> LineDatum.__dict__['addPoint'](inst, 5, 4)  # does same as above
1
```

This indirect way of accessing class and instance attributes is part of some popular Python patterns. Directly using a class `__dict__` is something many flexible Jython object designs employ, and is sometime required when certain special methods are defined such as the `__setattr__` method described later.

Even more interesting is that Java classes used within Jython also have a
__dict__, which contains their members. Looking at the `java.io.File` class's
__dict__ in Jython requires the following:

```
>>> import java
>>> java.io.File.__dict__
{'createNewFile': <java function createNewFile at 4294600>, 'lastModified':
<java function lastModified at 3759986>, ... }
```

The full results of looking at the `java.io.File.__dict__` is left to the reader to
discover due to its length. If you just want to look at the member names use
the following:

```
>>> java.io.File.__dict__.keys()
['mkdirs', 'exists', ...]
```

Additionally, you can call a method such as `listRoots` by using its key in
`java.io.File.__dict__`. What would traditionally be called with
`java.io.File.listRoots()` works with `java.io.File.__dict__['listRoots']()` as
demonstrated in this example:

```
>>> java.io.File.__dict__['listRoots']()
array([A:\, C:\, D:\, G:\], java.io.File)
```

Currently, you can also assign to a Java class's __dict__. While this is likely bad
practice for beginners, it clarifies the nature of __dict__. If you wish to alter
the lookup of a Java class member, you can change the value of that key in its
__dict__. Suppose you wanted a different method called for
`java.io.File.listRoots()`; you can alter it this way:

```
>>> import java
>>> def newListRoots():
...     return (['c:\\'])
...
>>> java.io.File.__dict__['listRoots'] = newListRoots
>>> java.io.File.listRoots()  # try the circumvented method
['c:\\']
```

__bases__

This is a `tuple` of bases, or super classes. In Jython version 2.0 and the first
alpha versions of Jython 2.1 designate this variable as read-only; however, versions after 2.1a1 allow assignments to this variable. The implementation at the
time of this writing differs slightly from CPython because you can alter
CPython's __bases__. In Listing 7.1, the superclass of `LineDatum` is
`java.util.Hashtable`. The special variable __bases__ confirms this:

```
>>> from datum import LineDatum
>>> LineDatum.__bases__
(<jclass java.util.Hashtable at 5012120>,)
```

Java classes used within Jython also have the special `__bases__` variable, which includes base classes and interfaces implemented:

```
>>> import java
>>> java.io.File.__bases__
(<jclass java.lang.Object at 7290061>, <jclass java.io.Serializable at
62789>, <jclass java.lang.Comparable at 6728374>)
```

Pre-Existing Instance Attributes

Jython instances have two special variables that are implicitly defined, while Java instances used within Jython have one. These attributes are readable and assignable.

__class__

The `__class__` variable denotes the class that the current object is an instance of. If we continue abusing Listing 7.1, we can demonstrate how an instance of `LineDatum` knows its class.

```
>>> from datum import LineDatum
>>> ld = LineDatum(.66, -2)
>>> ld.__class__
<class datum.LineDatum at 867682>
```

You can see that the `__class__` variable is not just a string representing the class, but an actual reference to the class. If you know the required parameters, you can create an instance of an instance's class. Continuing the previous example to do so looks like this:

```
>>> ld2 = ld.__class__(1.2, 6)
>>> ld2.__class__
<class datum.LineDatum at 867682>
```

You can examine all class properties of `instance.__class__` just as you can with the actual class. This is especially advantageous when examining Java instances. The `dir()` of a Java instances isn't very informative about its instance members because of the nature of the proxy used to access them. That means being able to examine a Java instance's `__class__` dictionary aids in exploring a Java instance in the interactive interpreter. If you forget methods available in a `Java.io.File` instance, you can examine the instance's class for attributes.

```
>>> import java
>>> f = java.io.File("c:\\jython")
>>> dir(f)
[]
>>> dir(f.__class__)
['__init__', 'absolute', 'absoluteFile', 'absolutePath', 'canRead',
'canWrite','canonicalFile', 'canonicalPath', 'compareTo', 'createNewFile',
```

```
'createTempFile', 'delete', 'deleteOnExit', 'directory', 'exists', 'file',
'getAbsoluteFile', 'getAbsolutePath', 'getCanonicalFile', 'getCanonicalPath',
'getName', 'getParent', 'getParentFile', 'getPath', 'hidden', 'isAbsolute',
'isDirectory', 'isFile', 'isHidden', 'lastModified', 'length', 'list',
'listFiles', 'listRoots', 'mkdir', 'mkdirs', 'name', 'parent', 'parentFile',
'path', 'pathSeparator', 'pathSeparatorChar', 'renameTo', 'separator',
'separatorChar', 'setLastModified', 'setReadOnly', 'toURL']
```

___dict___

This represents the instance's name space. It is the same idea as the class
__dict__, except that it instead contains instance attributes. You can read and
alter the contents of an instance's __dict__ just like a class __dict__.

Special Methods for General Customization

Although three of the four general customization methods for objects were
introduced in Chapter 6, "Classes, Instances, and Inheritance," they are reiter-
ated here to make this chapter a more complete reference of special attributes.

___init___

The __init__ method is a Jython object's constructor; it gets called for instance
creation. Jython superclasses requiring explicit initialization should be initialized in a constructor with baseclass.__init__(self, [args...]). The same syntax works for explicitly initializing a Java superclasses. If a Java superclass is not
explicitly initialized, its empty constructor is called at the completion of a
Jython subclass's __init__ method. See Chapter 6 for more on constructors.

___del___

The __del__ method is a Jython object's destructor or finalizer. It accepts no
arguments so it's parameter list should only contain self. There is no guarantee
as to when garbage collection will collect an object and thus call the __del__
method. Java does not even guarantee it will be called at all. Because of this, it
is best to plan objects so that contents of the __del__ method are minimal or
so that a finalizer is unnecessary. Also note that Jython classes that do define
__del__ incur a performance penalty. Finalizing methods of Java superclasses are
automatically called along with the __del__ method of a Jython instance, but
Jython superclass destructors must be explicitly called when their execution is
required. Syntax for calling a parent class's destructor is demonstrated here:

```
>>> class superclass:
...     def __del__(self):
...         print "superclass destroyed"
...
```

```
>>> class subclass(superclass):
...     def __del__(self):
...         superclass.__del__(self)
...         print "subclass destroyed"
...
>>> s = subclass()
>>> del s
>>>
>>> # wait for a while and hit enter a few time until GC comes around
superclass destroyed
subclass destroyed
```

Exceptions that either Java or Jython finalizing methods raise are all ignored. The only effect a raised exception has is that the finalizing method returns at the point of the exception rather than running to normal completion.

__repr__

The __repr__ method provides an object with string conversion behavior. The use of reverse-quotes or the repr() built-in method calls an object's __repr__ method. Also, if no __str__ attribute exists in the object, the object's __repr__ method is called when it is printed. The __repr__ method should return a valid Python expression as a string that represents the formal data structure of the object. If an appropriate expression is not possible, convention suggests a technical description within angle brackets (<>). Assume that you have an object that is supposed to act like a list. The __repr__ method of this object should return a string that looks like a list (for example, '[1, 2, 3, 4]').

__str__

The __str__ method provides an informal representation of an object called when the object is printed, or when the built-in str() method is used on the object. This differs from __repr__. The __repr__ method returns an expression or data-full representation of an object while the __str__ method usually returns a brief description or characterization of the object.

Listing 7.2 demonstrates the implementation of both the special methods __str__ and __repr__. The class in Listing 7.2 implements both these methods so there may be a canonical data object representation (the __repr__ results) and an HTML characterization (the __str__ results).

Listing 7.2 **Implementing __str__ and __repr__**

```
# file: html.py
class HtmlMetaTag:
    """Constructor requires "name" field of metatag.
    Use the intance's "append" method to add to the list"""

    def __init__(self, name):
        self.name = name
        self.list = []

    def append(self, item):
        self.list.append(item)

    def __repr__(self):
        return `{'name':self.name, 'list':self.list}`

    def __str__(self):
        S = '<meta name="%s" content="%s">'
        return S % (self.name, ", ".join(self.list))


if __name__=='__main__':
    mt = HtmlMetaTag("keywords")
    map(mt.append, ['Jython', 'Python', 'programming'])
    print "The __str__ results are:\n  ", mt
    print
    print "The __repr__ results are:\n  ", repr(mt)
```

The results from running jython html.py:

```
The __str__ results are:
  <meta name="keywords" content="Jython, Python, programming">

The __repr__ results are:
  {'name': 'keywords', 'list': ['Jython', 'Python', 'programming']}
```

Dynamic Attribute Access

Jython allows programmers to customize the access, setting and deletion of instance attributes with the corresponding special methods __getattr__, __setattr__, and __delattr__. There is an implied interrelationship between these methods, but there is no requirement to define certain ones. If you want dynamic access, define __getattr__. If you want dynamic attribute assignments, define __setattr__, and if you want dynamic attribute deletion, define __delattr__. What makes these different than using normal attribute access is that they are dynamic: They evaluate at the time the attribute is requested during runtime.

__getattr__

In a class that lacks dynamic attribute lookups, accessing a non-existing attribute is an `AttributeError`:

```
>>> class test:
...     pass
...
>>> t = test()
>>> t.a
Traceback (innermost last):
  File "<console>", line 1, in ?
AttributeError: instance of 'test' has no attribute 'a'
```

A minimal example of dynamic attribute access is the ability to avoid such `AttributeErrors` as is done in Listing 7.3. Adding dynamic attribute access to an instance requires defining the __getattr__ method. This method must have two parameter slots, the first for `self` and second for the attribute name. Once __getattr__ is defined, instance attribute lookups that fail in traditional means continue to call the __getattr__ method to fulfill the request. Listing 7.3 is a module containing a class that merely avoids the `AttributeError` by supplying a default __getattr__ value of `None`.

Listing 7.3 **Adding Dynamic Attribute Access to a Class**

```
# file: getattr.py
class test:
    a = 10
    def __getattr__(self, name):
        return None


if __name__ == "__main__":
    t = test()
    print "The value of t.a is:", t.a
    print "The value of t.b is:", t.b
```

Results from running `jython getattr.py`:

```
The value of t.a is: 10
The value of t.b is: None
```

The __getattr__ in Listing 7.3 provides a default value of `None` for missing attributes. It is a succinct example of using __getattr__, but I should mention that it is somewhat suspect in design. An implementation of __getattr__ normally returns a useful value or raises an `AttributeError` if it's unable to compute a useful value. Default values are certainly appropriate at times, but they can also hide design flaws. Listing 7.4 more closely resembles common implementations of __getattr__. The valuable principle exploited in Listing 7.4 is the use of an object separate from the class and instance for locating object attributes. Why this is valuable is related to an asymmetry between __getattr__ and __setattr__, which is explained later. In Listing 7.4 the data object used to hold instance attributes is a module-level dictionary, but it could just as easily be a list, an instance of another class, or a network resource. It all depends on what you do in the __getattr__ method (and __setattr__).

Listing 7.4   **Attributes Supplied from a Separate Object**

```
# file extern.py
data = {"a":1, "b":2}

class test:
    def __getattr__(self, attr):
        if data.has_key(attr):  # lookup attribute in module-global "data"
            return data[attr]
        else:
            raise AttributeError


if __name__=="__main__":
    t = test()
    print "attribute a =", t.a
    print "attribute b =", t.b
    print "attribute c =", t.c # doesn't exist in "data"- is error
```

Results from running jython extern.py

```
attribute a = 1
attribute b = 2
attribute c =Traceback (innermost last):
  File "extern.py", line 15, in ?
AttributeError: instance of 'test' has no attribute 'c'
```

As noted earlier, calling the __getattr__ method occurs only after traditional attribute lookup fails. What is the traditional lookup? Listing 7.3 proves that it must obviously include class variables; otherwise, the output would not include 10. The typical scenario is that attribute lookup begins with the instance dictionary, then the instance dictionary of initialized base classes, then the class dictionary, and finally base class dictionaries. Only after those fail does Jython call the __getattr__ method. In Listing 7.3, looking up the attribute a does not go through __getattr__ because a is found in the class __dict__.

One catch in instance initialization is that if you define an __init__ method in a subclass, you need to explicitly call the __init__ in Jython superclasses to ensure proper instance lookup. If you do not define an __init__ method, the superclass constructor is automatically called, as demonstrated here:

```
>>> class A:
...     def __init__(self):
...         self.val = "'val' found in instance of superclass"
...
>>> class B(A):
...     pass
...
>>> c = B()
>>> c.val
"'val' found in instance of superclass"
```

If you do define an __init__ in a subclass, but fail to call the constructor of the Jython superclass, attributes cannot be resolved in the instance of the superclass:

```
>>> class B(A):   # assume class A is the same as the previous example
...     def __init__(self):
...         pass
...
>>> c = B()
>>> c.val
Traceback (innermost last):
  File "<console>", line 1, in ?
AttributeError: instance of 'B' has no attribute 'val'
```

This initialization catch does not apply to Java superclasses. If a Java superclass is not explicitly initialized, its empty constructor is called upon completion of the subclasses __init__ method, and instance attribute lookup proceeds as normal.

__setattr__

Adding dynamic attribute assignment to an instance requires a __setattr__ method. This method must have three parameter slots, the first for self, the second for the attribute name, and the third is the value assigned to the attribute. Once defined, the __setattr__ method intercepts all assignments to instance attributes except the implicitly defined __class__ and __dict__. Because of this, you cannot directly set an instance attribute in the __setattr__ method without creating a circular lookup and overflow exception. You can however rebind the instance __dict__ without such errors because of its exemption from the __setattr__ hook, and you can access __dict__ directly because of its exemption from __getattr__.

Listing 7.5 demonstrates using the __setattr__ method to restrict field types to integers. Additionally, the use of both __getattr__ and __setattr__ methods allows storage of instance attributes in a data object other than the instances __dict__. Listing 7.5 instead uses a Hashtable called _data to store any instance fields assigned.

The assignment of _data in the class constructor does not use self._data=..., but instead uses the instance __dict__ directly. Why? Instance assignments, including those in the constructor, now all go through __setattr__; however, __setattr__ is expecting a _data key in the instance __dict__. This paradox is avoided by adding _data directly to the instance dictionary with the self.__dict__[key]=value syntax, and thus avoids the __setattr__ hook.

Another valuable quality of Listing 7.5 is that the __setattr__ method ensures instance variables are not stored in the instance's __dict__. Why is this good? To understand the value, we must first look at the asymmetry between __setattr__ and __getattr__. The __setattr__ always intercepts instance attribute assignments, but __getattr__ is called only when normal attribute lookup fails. This is bad if you want each get and set to perform some symmetrical action such as always accessing and storing values from an external database. Keeping instance values outside the instance __dict__ ensures they are not found and __getattr__ is called. Instance variables in superclasses, and class variables short-circuit this control, so careful planning in subclasses is due. Also note that there is a bit of a performance hit for each __getattr__ call considering the normal lookup must complete unsuccessfully before calling the __getattr__ method.

Listing 7.5 **Using __setattr__ and __getattr__**

```
# file: setter.py
from types import IntType, LongType
import java

class IntsOnly:
    def __init__(self):
        self.__dict__['_data'] = java.util.Hashtable()

    def __getattr__(self, name):
        if self._data.containsKey(name):
            return self._data.get(name)
        else:
            raise AttributeError, name

    def __setattr__(self, name, value):
```

continues

Listing 7.5 **Continued**

```
            test = lambda x: type(x)==IntType or type(x)==LongType
            assert test(value), "All fields in this class must be integers"
            self._data.put(name, value)

if __name__ == '__main__':
    c = IntsOnly()
    c.a = 1
    print "c.a=", c.a
    c.a = 200L
    print "c.a=", c.a
    c.a = "string"
    print "c.a=", c.a   # Shouldn't get here
```

Results from running `jython setter.py`:

```
c.a= 1
c.a= 200
Traceback (innermost last):
  File "setter.py", line 25, in ?
  File "setter.py", line 17, in __setattr__
AssertionError: All fields in this class must be integers
```

__delattr__

Adding dynamic attribute deletion requires defining the __delattr__ method. This method must have two parameter slots, the first for `self`, and the second for the attribute name. The __delattr__ method is called when using `del object.attribute`. The attribute could be a resource requiring flushing/closing before deletion. The attribute could also be part of a persistent resource requiring deletion from a database or file system, or could be an attribute you don't want users of your class to delete. It could also be that attributes are stored in a data object other than the instance __dict__ and require special handling for deletion, as would be required for Listing 7.5. The __delattr__ hook allows the programmer to properly handle these types of situations. Listing 7.6 examples using the __delattr__ hook to prevent deletion of an attribute:

Listing 7.6 **Using __delattr__ to Protect an Attribute from Deletion**

```
# file: immortal.py

class A:
    def __init__(self, var):
        self.immortalVar = var
    def __delattr__(self, name):
        assert name!="immortalVar", "Cannot delete- it's immortal"
```

```
        del self.__dict__[name]

c = A("some value")print "The immortalVar=", c.immortalVar
del c.immortalVar
```

Results from running `jython immortal.py`

```
The immortalVar= some value
Traceback (innermost last):
  File "immortal.py", line 12, in ?
  File "immortal.py", line 7, in __delattr__
AssertionError: Cannot delete- it's immortal
```

The Callable Hook—*__call__*

The special method `__call__` makes an instance callable. The number of parameters of the call method is not restricted in any way. On a basic level, this makes an instance act like a function. Creating a function-like instance that prints a simple message looks like this:

```
>>> class hello:
...     def __call__(self):
...         print "Hello"
...
>>> h = hello()
>>> h()  # call the instance as if it were a function
Hello
```

The `hello` example is a bit misleading in that it disguises the real potential of the `__call__` method. Listing 7.7 is a slightly more interesting example that fakes static methods with an inner class that implements the `__call__` method. The inner class in Listing 7.7 gets a `java.lang.Runtime` instance and defines a `__call__` method for running a system command and returning its output. The inner class in Listing 7.7 is named `_static_runcommand`. What a user would call is the instance of the inner class. Remember, the instance is what is callable because of `__call__`, and is what becomes the static method. A user of the class would instantiate the outer class `commands`. Let's call this instance `A`, and then would call the `runcommand` instance with `A.runcommand(command)`. The `runcommand` instance looks and acts like a method. Despite numerous instances of the outer `commands` class, only a single instance of `_static_runcommand`, and thus a single instance of `java.lang.Runtime`, is required (this assumes no synchronization requirements).

Listing 7.7   **Faking Static Methods with** __*call*__ **and Inner Classes**

```
# file: staticmeth.py
from java import lang, io

class commands:
    class _static_runcommand:
        "inner class whose instance is used to fake a static method"
        rt = lang.Runtime.getRuntime()
        def __call__(self, cmd):
            stream = self.rt.exec(cmd).getInputStream()
            isr = io.InputStreamReader(stream)
            results = []
            ch = isr.read()
            while (ch > -1):
                results.append(chr(ch))
                ch = isr.read()
            return "".join(results)

    runcommand = _static_runcommand() # create instance in class scope


if __name__ == '__main__':
    inst1 = commands()
    inst2 = commands()

    # now make sure runcommand is static (is shared by both instances)
    assert inst1.runcommand is inst2.runcommand, "Not class static"

    # now call the "faked" static method from either instance
    print inst1.runcommand("mem") # for windows users
    #print inst1.runcommand("cat /proc/meminfo") # for linux users
```

The results from running `jython staticmeth.py` on Windows 2000 is:

```
 655360 bytes total conventional memory
 655360 bytes available to MS-DOS
 633024 largest executable program size

1048576 bytes total contiguous extended memory
      0 bytes available contiguous extended memory
 941056 bytes available XMS memory
        MS-DOS resident in High Memory Area
```

Special Comparison Methods

Comparison is the use of operators ==, !=, <, <=, >, and >=. This is simple for many objects like integers (5 > 4), but what about user-defined classes. Jython allows the definition of methods that implement such comparisons, but Jython version 2.1 (and Python 2.1) introduced some changes in implementing class comparisons methods. This new feature is rich comparisons. For the sake of contrast, the old comparison method is dubbed *poor comparisons*.

Three-Way, or Poor, Comparisons

Three-way, or poor comparisons entail a single special comparison method called __cmp__, which returns -1, 0, or 1 depending on whether self evaluates as less, equal, or more than another object. The __cmp__ method must have two parameter slots, the first of which for self and the second for the other object. The verbose version of what compare should do is this:

```
def __cmp__(self, other):
    if (self < other):
        return -1
    if (self == other):
        return 0
    if (self > other):
        return 1
```

Listing 7.8 uses the __cmp__ method and a class attribute, role, to determine sort order for a list of members of a family circle. The built-in cmp() function is used on the appropriate class value as determined by the role the class is set to. If the other class is not an instance of the family class, it always compares as less (note that 'eldest' inverts things so less is really more). Note that setting a class instance flag, role in this case, is not the preferred way to control sort behavior in more complex classes.

Listing 7.8 **Comparison by Role**

```
#file: poorcompare.py
class family:
    role = "familyMember" # default value

    def __init__(self, name, age, relation, communicationSkills):
        self.name = name
        self.age = age
        self.relation = relation
        self.communicationSkills = communicationSkills
        self._roles = {1:"familyMember",
                       2:"communicator",
                       3:"eldest"}
```

continues

Listing 7.8 **Continued**

```
    def __cmp__(self, other):
        if other.__class__ != self.__class__:
            return -1 # non-family classes are always less
        if self.role=="familyMember":
            relations = {"mother":1, "father":1, "aunt":2, "uncle":2,
                         "cousin":3, "unrelated":4}
            return cmp(relations[self.relation],
                       relations[other.relation])
        elif self.role=="communicator":
            return cmp(self.communicationSkills,
                       other.communicationSkills)
        elif self.role=="eldest":
            return cmp(other.age, self.age) #, other.age)

    def __repr__(self):
        # This is an abuse of __repr__- "canonical" data not returned.
        # Included only for sake of example.
        return self.name

if __name__ == '__main__':
    L = []
    # add ppl to list
    L.append(family("Fester", 80, "uncle", 2))
    L.append(family("Gomez", 50, "father", 1))
    L.append(family("Lurch", 75, "unrelated", 3))
    L.append(family("Cousin It", 113, "cousin", 4))
    L.append("other data-type")

    # print list sorted by default role
    L.sort()
    print "by relation:", L

    # print list sorted by communication skills:
    family.role = "communicator"
    L.sort()
    print "by communication skills:", L

    # print list eldest to youngest
    family.role = "eldest"
    L.sort()
    print "eldest to youngest:", L
```

Output from running jython poorcompare.py is:

```
by relation: [Gomez, Fester, Cousin It, Lurch, 'other data-type']
by communication skills: [Gomez, Fester, Lurch, Cousin It, 'other data-type']
eldest to youngest: [Cousin It, Fester, Lurch, Gomez, 'other data-type']
```

Rich Comparisons

Rich comparisons appear in Jython's 2.1 versions and are not restricted to the -1, 0, 1 return values that __cmp__ is. If comparing two lists or two matrices, you can return a list or matrix containing the element-wise comparisons, another object, None, NotImplemented, a Boolean or raise an exception. The special rich comparison methods are a set of six special methods representing the six comparison operators. Each method requires two parameters: the first for self and the second for other. Table 7.1 lists the operator and associated special, rich-comparison method.

Table 7.1   **Rich Comparison Methods**

Operator	Method
<	__lt__(self, other)
<=	__le__(self, other)
==	__eq__(self, other)
!=	__ne__(self, other)
>	__gt__(self, other)
>=	__ge__(self, other)

For objects A and B, the rich comparison of A < B becomes A.__lt__(B). If the comparison is B > A, the method B.__gt__(A) is evaluated. Each operator has a natural compliment, but there is no enforcement of an invariant such as A.__lt__(B) == B.__gt__(A). The left-hand object is first searched for an appropriate rich comparison method. If one is not defined, the right-hand object is searched for the compliment method. If both halves define an appropriate method, the left hand object's method is used.

Listing 7.9 defines two classes: A and B. Class A defines all six rich comparison methods such that they compare self's class name with the name of the other class. Class B defines only one comparison method: greater-than (__gt__). Note that the means of comparison in class B's __gt__ method is by an instance creation timestamp: something incongruous with class A's definition of comparability. Such divergent definitions are troublesome and are cautioned against without strong cause. The remainder of Listing 7.9 goes through testing the comparison combinations using one instance of each class. You can see from the output how appropriate comparison methods are resolved.

Listing 7.9 **Rich Comparison Methods**

```python
# file: rich.py
import time

class A:
    def __init__(self):
        self.timestamp = time.time()

    def __lt__(self, other):
        print "...Using A's __lt__ method...",
        return self.__class__.__name__ < other.__class__.__name__

    def __le__(self, other):
        print "...Using A's __le__ method...",
        return self.__class__.__name__ <= other.__class__.__name__

    def __ne__(self, other):
        print "...using A's __ne__ method...",
        return self.__class__.__name__ != other.__class__.__name__

    def __gt__(self, other):
        print "...Using A's __gt__ method...",
        return self.__class__.__name__ > other.__class__.__name__

    def __ge__(self, other):
        print "...Using A's __ge__ method...",
        return self.__class__.__name__ >= other.__class__.__name__

    def __eq__(self, other):
        print "...Using A's __eq__ method...",
        return self.__class__.__name__ == other.__class__.__name__

class B:
    def __init__(self):
        self.timestamp = time.time()

    def __gt__(self, other):
        print "...Using B's __gt__ method...",
        return self.timestamp > other.timestamp


if __name__ == '__main__':
    inst_b = B()

    inst_a = A()
    print "Is a < b?", inst_a < inst_b
    print "Is b < a?", inst_b < inst_a
    print "Is a <= b?", inst_a <= inst_b
    print "Is b <= a?", inst_b <= inst_a
    print "Is a == b?", inst_a == inst_b
```

```
      print "Is b == a?", inst_b == inst_a
      print "Is a != b?", inst_a != inst_b
      print "Is b != a?", inst_b != inst_a
      print "Is a > b?", inst_a > inst_b
      print "Is b > a?", inst_b > inst_a
      print "Is a >= b?", inst_a >= inst_b
      print "Is b >= a?", inst_b >= inst_a
```

The output from running `jython rich.py` is:

```
   Is a < b? ...Using A's __lt__ method... 1
   Is b < a? ...Using A's __gt__ method... 0
   Is a <= b? ...Using A's __le__ method... 1
   Is b <= a? ...Using A's __ge__ method... 0
   Is a == b? ...Using A's __eq__ method... 0
   Is b == a? ...Using A's __eq__ method... 0
   Is a != b? ...using A's __ne__ method... 1
   Is b != a? ...using A's __ne__ method... 1
   Is a > b? ...Using A's __gt__ method... 0
   Is b > a? ...Using B's __gt__ method... 0
   Is a >= b? ...Using A's __ge__ method... 0
   Is b >= a? ...Using A's __le__ method... 1
```

Listing 7.9 clarifies the rich comparison methods but is pointless with regard to practical applications. A more plausible usage is the element-wise comparison of list objects. Listing 7.10 defines a class called `listemulator`, which includes an `__lt__` method definition. The `listemulator` class behaves like a list thanks to the help of the `UserList` class imported at the beginning of the listing. The details of emulating other types occurs later in this chapter, but for now, let's assume an instance of the `listemulator` class acts exactly like a normal Jython list except for the `__lt__` comparison. The `__lt__` method in Listing 7.10 does two things. First, it compares the length of itself and `other` to ensure the element-wise comparison is legitimate (they are the same length). Then, the `__lt__` method compares each element of `self` and `other` and returns the list of comparison results.

Listing 7.10   **Element-Wise Rich Comparison**

```
# file: richlist.py
from UserList import UserList

class listemulator(UserList):
    def __init__(self, list):
        self.data = list
        UserList.__init__(self, self.data)

    def __lt__(self, other):
```

continues

Listing 7.10 **Continued**

```
        if len(self) != len(other):
            raise ValueError, ("Instance of %s differs in size from %s"
                               % (self.__class__.__name__,
                                  other.__class__.__name__))
        return map(lambda x, y: x < y, self, other)

L = [2,3,4,5]
LC = listemulator([2,3,3,4])
print LC < L
```

The results from running jython richlist.py are:

```
[0, 0, 1, 1]
```

__hash__

Dictionary operations rely on the hash value of those objects used as keys. Jython objects can determine their own hash value for dictionary key operations and the built-in hash function by defining the special __hash__ instance method. The __hash__ method has only one parameter and it is self, and the return value should be an integer. A restriction in implementing __hash__ is that objects of the same value should return the same hash value. Because dictionary keys must be immutable, objects that define a comparison method but no __hash__ method cannot be used as dictionary keys.

Object "Truth"

The search for the truth in Jython objects follows these rules:

- If a class defines the special __nonzero__ method, its return value (1 or 0) determines the "truth" of the object.

- If an object does not define the __nonzero__ method, the interpreter calls the special method __len__. The __len__ method appears later in this chapter, but its meaning is sufficiently intuitive: It returns an integer representing the objects length. If this return value is non-zero, the object is true.

- If a class defines neither of the above special methods, instances of that class are always true.

Implementing trueness with the __nonzero__ method looks like this:

```
import random

class gamble:
    def __nonzero__(self):
        return random.choice([0,1])
```

The __nonzero__ parameter list includes only `self`, and the return value is `1` for true, and `0` for false.

Emulating Built-In Data Objects

Numerous occasions call for creating classes that emulate built-in data objects. Maybe a project requires a Jython dictionary, but needs that dictionary to maintain order, or maybe you need a list with a special lookup. Emulating built-in objects allows you to extend their behavior, add constraints and instrument object operations with minimal work, yet end up with a familiar interface. Implementing extended behavior with the familiarity of a built-in interface adds near zero complexity, which is the primary goal of objects. Jython's special methods allow user-defined classes to emulate Jython's built-in numeric, sequence and mapping objects. The emulation of objects that have associated methods requires implementations of those non-special methods as well to truly emulate that object.

The examples in this section often use a Jython class that internally uses a java object to illustrate this functionality. This is something that is not always required. Jython is very good about converting types to meet the situation. The `java.util.Vector` object already supports the `PyList` index syntax (`v[inex]`) and `java.util.Hashtable` and `java.util.HashMap` already support key assignment (`h[key]`), and numeric objects automatically convert to the appropriate types where needed. With this substantial intuitive support for Java objects there is often no need to wrap them in special methods; however, there may be little things like a `java.util.Vector` not supporting slice syntax in Jython:

```
>>> import java
>>> v = java.util.Vector()
>>> v.addElement(10)
>>> v.addElement(20)
>>> v[0]   # this works
10
>>> v[0:2]
Traceback (innermost last):
  File "<console>", line 1, in ?
TypeError: only integer keys accepted
```

Emulating built-in types allows you to specify every behavior to ensure an object acts indistinguishably similar to a built-in type. Because Jython and Java are so very integrated, passing objects between these languages is pervasive. It is often convenient to allow Java objects to better emulate Jython built-ins so users of your code need not care which is Java and which isn't. Java objects often already contain methods that do the same thing as a comparable method in a Jython built-in, but are named differently.

Listing 7.11 shows a convenient way to map such Java methods to Jython methods to further ease emulating built-in objects. The `HashWrap` class in Listing 7.11 is a subclass of `java.util.Hashtable` that assigns class identifiers to `Hashtable` methods that already perform the expected behavior. Notice that the `HashWrap` class doesn't define `values()`, `clear()`, or `get()`. These names already exist in the superclass, `java.util.Hashtable`, and perform close enough to what is expected. The only catch in Listing 7.11 is that some of the `Hashtable` functions return unexpected types, such as the `Enumeration` returned from `keys()` and `items()`. These methods are wrapped in a simple lambda expression to convert them into a list. Some of Jython's dictionary methods don't have direct parallels in Java `Hashtable`'s, so `setdefault()`, `popitem()`, and `copy()` are defined in the `HashWrap` class.

Listing 7.11 also contains special methods—those that begin and end with two underscores. The meaning of these special methods might be discernable from the Java methods they are mapped to, but the idea at this point is only to show how to map identifiers to Java methods.

Listing 7.11 **Assigning Java Methods to Jython Class Identifiers**

```
# file: hashwrap.py
import java
import copy


class HashWrap(java.util.Hashtable):
    #map jython names to Hashtable names
    has_key = java.util.Hashtable.containsKey
    update = java.util.Hashtable.putAll

    # Hashtable returns an Enumeration for
    keys = lambda self: map(None, java.util.Hashtable.keys(self))
    items = lambda self: map(None, java.util.Hashtable.elements(self))

    # these don't have direct parallels in Hashtable, so define here
    def setdefault(self, key, value):
        if self.containsKey(key):
            return self.get(key)
```

```
            else:
                self.put(key, value)
                return value

    def popitem(self):
        return self.remove(self.keys()[0])

    def copy(self):
        return copy.copy(self)

    # These are the special methods introduced in this section.
    # Read on to find out more.
    __getitem__ = java.util.Hashtable.get
    __setitem__ = java.util.Hashtable.put
    __delitem__ = java.util.Hashtable.remove
    __repr__ = java.util.Hashtable.toString
    __len__ = java.util.Hashtable.size


if __name__ == '__main__':
    hw = HashWrap()
    hw["A"] = "Alpha"
    hw["B"] = "Beta"
    print hw
    print hw.setdefault("G", "Gamma")
    print hw.setdefault("D", "Delta")
    print hw["A"]
    print "keys=", hw.keys()
    print "values=", hw.values()
    print "items=", hw.items()
```

Output from running jython hashwrap.py is:

```
{A=Alpha, B=Beta}
Gamma
Delta
Alpha
keys= ['A', 'G', 'D', 'B']
values= [Alpha, Gamma, Delta, Beta]
items= ['Alpha', 'Gamma', 'Delta', 'Beta']
```

Emulating Sequences

Built-in sequences come in two flavors: mutable and immutable. *Immutable sequences* (PyTuples) have no associated methods, while *mutable sequences* (PyLists) do; both flavors have similar sequence behaviors such as indexes and slices. Truly emulating a PyList would involve defining its associated methods (append, count, extend, index, insert, pop, remove, reverse, and sort) as well as the special methods associated with sequence length, indexes and slices. Emulating immutable sequences (PyTuples) requires only a subset of the special methods as some of those methods implement operations unique to mutable objects (they change object contents). A user-defined object need not implement all sequence behaviors, so you are free to define only those methods that suite your design. However, defining all sequence methods allows users to be blissfully unaware of inconsequential differences between your class and a built-in data object, which is really better for abstraction, reusability and the holy grail of objects: reduced complexity.

The following subsections delineate sequence behaviors, and their associated special methods. The descriptions used in subsections assume a sequence S, a PyList L and a PyTuple T. The use of sequence and S indicates special functions applicable to sequences in general. The use of PyTuple and T indicates implementation of an immutable sequence and the use of PyList and L indicates comments specific to mutable sequences.

__len__

A sequence should have a length equal to len(S).

The special method that returns an object's length is __len__(self). Calling len(S) is equivalent to S.__len__(). The __len__(self) method must return an integer >= 0. Note that there are no means of enforcing the accuracy of __len__. A list-like object with ten elements can define a __len__ method that returns 1.

Listing 7.12 keeps sequence elements in a java.util.Vector instance. The length method returns the results from the vector's size() method as the object's length:

Listing 7.12 **Implementing Sequence Length**

```
# file: seqlen.py

import java

class usrList:
    def __init__(self):
        # use name-mangled, private identifier for vector
        self.__data = java.util.Vector()

    def append(self, o):
        self.__data.add(o)

    def __len__(self):
```

```
            return self.__data.size()

    if __name__ == '__main__':
        L = usrList()
        L.append("A")
        L.append("B")
        L.append("C")
        print "The length of object L is:", len(L)
```

The output of jython seqlen.py is:

```
    The length of object L is: 3
```

__getitem__

S[i] gets the value at sequence index i. The index i can be a positive integer
(counted from the left side of a sequence), a negative integer (counted from
the right side), or a slice object.

The special method used to return an object designated by a specific index
or slice is __getitem__(self, index). Calling S[i] is equivalent to
S.__getitem__(i). The __getitem__ method should raise an IndexError exception when the specified index is out of range, and a ValueError for non-sup-
ported index types. To truly emulate built-in sequences, you must allow for an
index value of a positive integer, negative integer, or slice object.

The __getitem__ method is sometimes confused with the special class
attribute method __getattr__ so it's worth noting their differences. The
__getitem__ method retrieves what the object defines as list or mapping entries
(mapping implementations appear later) instead of attributes of the object
itself. Additionally, __getitem__ is called for each item retrieval, unlike
__getattr__, which is called only after a normal object attribute lookup fails.
Because __getitem__ is always called, it's a good candidate for implementing
persistence and other special behavior that require symmetry between setting
and getting objects.

Listing 7.13 is similar to Listing 7.12 in that it is a list-like class wrapped
around a java.util.Vector. Now we use this concept to illustrate the
__getitem__ method. The __getitem__ implementation in Listing 7.13 allows
for positive, negative, and slice indexes by converting the specified index value
into a list of positive integers.

The implementation should allow for positive, negative, and slice indexes
and should raise the IndexError and ValueError exceptions where appropriate.
Remember that negative indexes mean they are counted from the right, -1
being the last sequence item, -2 the penultimate, and so on. Jython slicing

conventions assume default values for missing slice elements, so a user-defined, list-like object should also allow for this. For the slice [::3], Jython assumes start of sequence and end of sequence for the first two missing values, then uses the 3 as the step value. Implementing all this in a user-defined object may sound daunting, but it need not be difficult or convoluted. An important tool in the battle against complexity is leveraging functionality already found in familiar objects. The premise of all this is that __getitem__ should emulate the behavior of a built-in PyList object—there couldn't be a bigger hint. Use a list object in the __getitem__ implementation. If the internal data is in a vector, make a list the size of the vector and apply the index or slice to the list—you've now handled positive, negative and slice indexes, as well as default index values and the IndexError and ValueError exceptions. That's the trick used in Listing 7.13. Here is an example of just the list trick to make it more clear:

```
>>> import java
>>> v = java.util.Vector()
>>> map(v.addElement, range(10))
[None, None, None, None, None, None, None, None, None, None]
>>> v  # take a peek at the vector
[0, 1, 2, 3, 4, 5, 6, 7, 8, 9]
>>> # create a slice object
>>> i = slice(2, -3, 4)
>>>
>>> ## Next line handles all slice logic, and appropriate exceptions
>>> indexes = range(v.size())[i]
>>> indexes
[2, 6] # remember- these are indexes of values, not values
```

Whereas the java.util.Vector object doesn't support slices, a PyList does. Make a PyList containing the vector's range of index numbers and apply the index or slice to that list. The result is a positive list of vector indexes or a single vector index number. Using the PyList also ensures that any ValueErrors or IndexErrors are raised as needed. Searching for ways to reuse existing functionality, especially that of built-ins, is vital in battling complexity.

Listing 7.13 acquires either a single, positive index or a list of positive indexes from using the list trick. Once the appropriate positive index values are determined, the __getitem__ method returns the appropriate value or values.

Listing 7.13 **Sequence Item Retrieval with __getitem__**

```
# file: seqget.py
import java
import types

class usrList:
```

```
    def __init__(self, initial_values):
        data = java.util.Vector()
        map(data.add, initial_values)
        self.__data = data

    def __getitem__(self, index):
        indexes = range(self.__data.size())[index]
        try:
            if not isinstance(indexes, types.ListType):
                return self.__data.elementAt(indexes)
            else:
                return map(self.__data.elementAt, indexes)
        except java.lang.ArrayIndexOutOfBoundsException:
            raise IndexError, "index out of range: %s" % index

if __name__ == '__main__':
    S = usrList(range(1,10))
    print "S=", S[:]
    print "S[3]=", S[3]
    print "S[-2]=", S[-2]
    print "S[1:7:2]=", S[1:7:2]
    print "S[-5:8]=", S[-5:8]
    print "S[-8:]=", S[-8:]
```

The output from running jython seqget.py is:

```
S= [1, 2, 3, 4, 5, 6, 7, 8, 9]
S[3]= 4
S[-2]= 8
S[1:7:2]= [2, 4, 6]
S[-5:8]= [5, 6, 7, 8]
S[-8:]= [2, 3, 4, 5, 6, 7, 8, 9]
```

Note that in Listing 7.13, using the vector's elementAt() method is inside a try/except. If an index is out of range, the more verbose Java exception and traceback is caught and replaced with a Jython IndexError exception. This is only an implementation choice—there is no obligation to wrap Java exceptions, but the IndexError helps the userList class act more like a built-in.

Although Listing 7.13 uses a PyList to do the dirty work, there may be instances requiring explicit handling of types. This introduces type testing. Normally in Jython a variable's type can be tested against a reference type such as one of these three following examples:

```
>>> import types
>>> a = 1024L
>>> if type(a) == types.LongType: "a is a LongType"
...
'a is a LongType'
```

```
>>> if type(a) == type(1L): "a is a LongType"
...
'a is a LongType'

>>> if type(a) in [types.IntType, types.LongType]: "a is an ok type"
...
'a is an ok type'
```

The test for appropriate types is interesting when you introduce Java types. Allowing for sufficient discrimination of Java types is a bit odd. For example, consider the following:

```
>>> import java
>>> v = java.util.Vector()
>>> i = java.lang.Integer(3)
>>> type(v) == type(i)
1
```

If type() can't tell the difference between an integer and vector, how can you allow for limited Java types? One way to do so is to test an object's class. All Jython objects have a __class__ attribute, including the Java ones, so you could do the following:

```
>>> import java
>>> i = java.lang.Integer(5)
>>> v = java.util.Vector()
>>> ok_types = [(1).__class__, (1L).__class__, java.lang.Integer,
java.lang.Long]
>>> i.__class__ in ok_types
1
>>> v.__class__ in ok_types
0
```

Another means of confirming the appropriateness of object types is the use of the built-in isinstance function. The isinstance function accepts an object and a class as arguments and returns 1 if the object is an instance of the specified class, 0 otherwise. Using isinstance to check types is preferred because of its appropriateness when working with inheritance hierarchies. Using isinstance to check types would look like this:

```
>>> import types
>>> a = 1024L
>>> if isinstance(a, types.LongType): "a is a LongType"
...
'a is a LongType'
```

__setitem__

The expression `L[i] = object` should bind `object` to index `i` in list-like object `L`. This is specific to classes designed to emulate lists, not immutable objects (`PyTuple`-like). Only mutable objects should implement this behavior.

The special method used to bind an object to a specific index is `__setitem__(self, index, value)`. This method should raise an `IndexError` exception when the specified index is out of range. The index value could be negative, positive or a slice object. Raise a `ValueError` exception for those index values the `__setitem__` implementation does not allow for.

Assigning to a slice has some special constraints, at least for the built-in `PyList`. You don't have to respect this behavior in user-defined objects, but it is recommended. The restrictions are that the `step` value must be 1, and the value need not be the same length as the slice. First, look at an assignment to a single index:

```
>>> S = ["a", "b", "c"]
>>> S[1] = [1, 2, 3]
>>> S
['a', [1, 2, 3], 'c']
```

The value assigned to index 1 is a list, which shows up as a single object in index 1. Assigning to a slice differs:

```
>>> S = ["a", "b", "c"]
>>> S[3:4] = [1, 2, 3]
>>> S
['a', 'b', 'c', 1, 2, 3]
```

There is still only 1 index involved which is index 3, but assigning to a slice means something different in that the right side must be a sequence, and the resulting list is the concatenation:

```
S[0:slice.start] + values + S[slice.stop:len(S)]
```

Listing 7.14 defines a class that implements the `__setitem__` method, but chooses to implement two constraints: All values must be strings and the list is a static size designated in a constructor parameter. Each list index internally represents a line in the file `usrList.dat`. Setting `L[2]=Some string` changes the second line of the file to `Some string`. This makes the internal list similar to class static variables considering all instances would be reading from a single file (this can be changed with another constructor argument however). The opening and closing of the file within each method is expensive, so this would only really occur if this file were a shared resource. The persistence could otherwise be implemented in the `__init__` method and possible a `close` method (note that `__del__` would work, but is often avoided because exceptions in __del__ are ignored and there's no guarantee of when that method gets called).

Listing 7.14 does support assignment to list indexes and slices, but because the lines of the file are stored in a real PyList as an intermediary, this functionality is automatic. Listing 7.14 raises ValueError and IndexError exceptions appropriately, but note that the IndexErrors would propagate from normal list operations rather than catching and re-raising the exception.

Listing 7.14 **Adding Persistence with __setitem__**

```
# file: seqset.py
import types
import os

class usrList:
    def __init__(self, size):
        self.__size = size
        self.__file = "usrList.dat"
        if not os.path.isfile(self.__file):
            f = open(self.__file, "w")
            print >> f, " \n" * size
            f.close()

    def __repr__(self):
        f = open(self.__file)
        L = f.readlines()[:self.__size]
        f.close()
        return str(map(lambda x: x[:-1], L))

    def __setitem__(self, index, value):
        f = open(self.__file, "r+")
        L = f.readlines()[:self.__size]
        if isinstance(index, types.SliceType):
            if len(L[index]) != len(value):
                raise ValueError, "Bad value: %s" % value
            for x in value:
                if not isinstance(x, types.StringType):
                    raise ValueError, "Only String values supported"
            L[index] = map(lambda x: x + "\n", value)

        if (isinstance(index, types.IntType) or
            isinstance(index, types.LongType)):
            if type(value) != types.StringType:
                raise ValueError, "Only String values supported"
            L[index] = value + "\n"
        f.seek(0)
        f.writelines(L)
        f.close()

if __name__ == '__main__':
```

```
S = usrList(10)
for x in range(10):
    S[x] = str(x)
print "First List=", S
S[4:-4] = "four", "five"
print "Second List =", S
for x in range(10, 20):
    S[x-10] = str(x)
print "Last list = ", S
```

Output from running `jython seqset.py`

```
First List= ['0', '1', '2', '3', '4', '5', '6', '7', '8', '9']
Second List = ['0', '1', '2', '3', 'four', 'five', '6', '7', '8', '9']
Last list =  ['10', '11', '12', '13', '14', '15', '16', '17', '18', '19']
```

The values in the usrList instance are stored in the usrList.dat file, so future instantiations of the usrList class will start with those values. You can confirm this in the interactive interpreter—just make sure to start the interpreter from within the same directory as the usrList.dat file (the usrList instance only looks in the current directory):

```
>>> import seqset
>>> L = seqset.usrList(10)
>>> print L    # <- print persistent values
['10', '11', '12', '13', '14', '15', '16', '17', '18', '19']
```

The convenience of an automatically persistent data type is great, but the performance of Listing 7.14 isn't. Using this same technique with a speedy database helps greatly.

Listing 7.14 is instructive, but there's little about handling the unique constraints of assignments to a slice within it because the internal data is a PyList. Listing 7.15 uses a java.util.Vector for the internal data so supporting slices in __setitem__ is clarified.

Listing 7.15 **Wrapping a Java Vector in a List Class**

```
#file: seqset1.py
import java
import types

class usrList:
    def __init__(self):
        self.__data = java.util.Vector()
        map(self.__data.addElement, range(10))
```

continues

Listing 7.15 **Continued**

```
    def __getitem__(self, index):
        indexes = range(self.__data.size())[index]
        if isinstance(index, types.SliceType):
            return map(self.__data.elementAt, indexes)
        else:
            return self.__data.elementAt(indexes)

    def __setitem__(self, index, value):
        if isinstance(index, types.SliceType):
            size = self.__data.size()
            if index.step != 1:
                raise ValueError, "Step size must be 1 for setting list slice"
            newdata = java.util.Vector()
            map(newdata.addElement, range(0, index.start))
            map(newdata.addElement, value)
            map(newdata.addElement, range(index.stop, size))
            self.__data = newdata
        else:
            self.__data.setElementAt(value, index)

    def __delitem__(self, index):
        indexes = range(self.__data.size())[index]
        indexes.reverse() # so we can delete High to Low
        for i in indexes:
            self.__data.removeElementAt(i)

    def __repr__(self):
        return str(map(None, self.__data))

if __name__ == "__main__":
    L = usrList()
    print "L=", L
    print "L[1:]=", L[1:7]
    print "L[-4:9]=", L[-4:9]
    L[3:6:1] = range(100, 110)
    print L
```

Output from running jython seqset1.py:

```
L= [0, 1, 2, 3, 4, 5, 6, 7, 8, 9]
L[1:]= [1, 2, 3, 4, 5, 6]
L[-4:9]= [6, 7, 8]
[0, 1, 2, 100, 101, 102, 103, 104, 105, 106, 107, 108, 109, 6, 7, 8, 9]
```

__delitem__

The expression `del L[i]` should delete an object from list-like object L. This is obviously specific to mutable objects (PyList-like object).

The special method used to delete a specific index is `__delitem__(self, index, value)`. This method should raise an `IndexError` exception when the specified index is out of range and a `ValueError` exception when the index type is unsupported.

Listing 7.16 defines a class that implements the `__delitem__` method. The class holds its list contents in an internal `java.util.Vector` object, so the `__delitem__` method must use the vector's `removeElementAt()` (or `remove()`) method for each index deleted. Adding support for slices is familiar from previous examples, but one additional trick is required to delete items from the vector. Deleting a slice becomes consecutive `removeElementAt()` operations on the vector. If indexes were deleted from low to high, the index of the next higher item to be removed is reduced by one every time an item is deleted. The list of indexes requiring deletion is reversed in Listing 7.16 to ensure that the indexes are in highest to lowest order. This allows deletion without decrementing indexes of future deletions.

Listing 7.16 **Implementing __delitem__**

```
# file: seqdel.py
import java
import types

class userList:
    def __init__(self):
        self.__data = java.util.Vector()

    def append(self, object):
        self.__data.addElement(object)

    def __repr__(self):
        return str(list(self.__data))

    def __delitem__(self, index):
        if isinstance(index, types.SliceType):
            if index.step != 1:
                raise ValueError, "Step size must be 1 for setting list slice"
            delList = range(self.__data.size())[index]
        else:
            delList = [range(self.__data.size())[index]]
        delList.reverse()
        map(self.__data.removeElementAt, delList)
```

continues

Listing 7.16   **Continued**

```
if __name__ == '__main__':
    S = userList()
    map(S.append, range(5, 20, 2))
    print "Before deletes:", S
    del S[3]
    del S[4:6]
    print "After deletes: ", S
```

Output from running `jython seqdel.py`:

```
Before deletes: [5, 7, 9, 11, 13, 15, 17, 19]
After deletes:  [5, 7, 9, 13, 19]
```

Sequence Concatenation and Multiplication

Table 7.2 contains the math operations a sequence-like object should support as well as the special methods associated with that operation.

Table 7.2   **Sequence Math Operations**

Operation	Description	Special Method
S1 + S2	The concatenation of two sequences.	__add__ and __radd__
L1 += L2	Changing L1 into the concatenation of L1 and L2 with augmented assignment.	__iadd__
S * i	Repeating a sequence for integer i times.	__mul__ and __rmul__
L *= i	Changing list L into i number of repetitions of L with augmented assignment.	__imul__

Implementing the concatenation and repetition operations requires implementing the special operator methods for addition and multiplication. Operator methods occur in threes: addition has __add__, __radd__, and __iadd__, whereas multiplication has __mul__, __rmul__, and __imul__. The first of these (__add__, or __mul__) is called when the object defining it is on the left side of an operation. For the sequence s it would mean s + x or s * x are really implemented as s.__add__(x) and s.__mul__(x). The second of these methods (__radd__, and __rmul__) are reflected versions of the first—for when the object is on the right side of the expression. The reflected methods are called only if objects on the left do not define __add__ or __mul__. If s defines

__radd__ and __rmul__, but X does not, then X + s and X * s become
s.__radd__(X) and s.__rmul__(X). The __iadd__ and __imul__ methods implement augmented assignment, meaning s += X and s *= X are implemented as
s.__iadd__(X) and s.__imul__(X).

Listing 7.17 implements all six methods listed in Table 7.2. The obligations
of these methods are that they raise exceptions for unsupported types, and that
only the augmented assignment operations modify self.

Listing 7.17 **Sequence Concatenation and Repetition**

```python
# file: seqmath.py
import types
import java

class usrList:
    def __init__(self):
        self.__data = java.util.Vector()
        map(self.__data.addElement, range(5,8)) # some default values

    def __add__(self, other):
        if isinstance(other, types.ListType):
            return map(None, self.__data) + other
        else:
            raise TypeError, "__add__ only defined for ListType"

    def __radd__(self, other):
        if isinstance(other, types.ListType):
            return other + map(None, self.__data)
        else:
            raise TypeError, "__radd__ only defined for ListType"

    def __iadd__(self, other):
        # Augmented assignments methods usually modify self, then return self
        if isinstance(other, types.ListType):
            map(self.__data.addElement, other)
            return self #map(None, self.__data) # act like a list type
        else:
            raise TypeError, "__iadd__ only defined for ListType"

    def __mul__(self, other):
        if (isinstance(other, types.IntType) or
            isinstance(other, types.LongType)):
            return map(None, self.__data) * other
        else:
            raise TypeError, "Only integers allowed for multiplier"

    def __rmul__(self, other):
        if (isinstance(other, types.IntType) or
            isinstance(other, types.LongType)):
```

continues

Listing 7.17   **Continued**

```
                    return map(None, self.__data) * other
            else:
                raise TypeError, "Only integers allowed for multiplier"

        def __imul__(self, other):
            if (isinstance(other, types.IntType) or
                isinstance(other, types.LongType)):
                map(self.__data.addElement,
                    [x for x in self.__data] * (other -1))
                return self
            else:
                raise TypeError, "Only integers allowed for multiplier"

        def __repr__(self):
            return str(map(None, self.__data))

    if __name__ == '__main__':
        L = usrList()
        print "start     :", L
        print "__add__   :", L + [1,0]
        print "__radd__  :", ["a", "b"] + L
        L += ["-", "-"]
        print "__iadd__  :", L
        print "__mull__  :", L * 2
        try:
            print "__rmull__ :", 2 * L
        except TypeError:
            print "__rmull__ raised a TypeError"

        L *= 2
        print "__imull__ :", L
```

Output from running jython seqmath.py is:

```
start     : [5, 6, 7]
__add__   : [5, 6, 7, 1, 0]
__radd__  : ['a', 'b', 5, 6, 7]
__iadd__  : [5, 6, 7, '-', '-']
__mull__  : [5, 6, 7, '-', '-', 5, 6, 7, '-', '-']
__rmull__ : [5, 6, 7, '-', '-', 5, 6, 7, '-', '-']
__imull__ : [5, 6, 7, '-', '-', 5, 6, 7, '-', '-']
```

Slices

Python deprecated the following methods in version 2.0. Support for these methods still exists in the Jython code base, so they are included here for completeness. Their inclusion is not meant to encourage their use, but instead is supplied just in case a reader encounters this in legacy code. For new code, use __setitem__, __getitem__, and __delitem__.

- **__getslice__(self, start, stop, step)**—Returns a sequence containing those elements of self designated by the slice parameters (start, stop and step). If L contains [1,2,3,4,5], then L[1:4:1] actually calls (if defined) L.__getslice__(1, 4, 1), and __getslice__(1, 4, 1) should return [2,3,4].

- **__setslice__(self, start, stop, step, value)**—Assigns indexes of self to value or values specified. If L contains [1,2,3,4,5], then L[2:4] = ["a", "b", "c"] actually calls (if defined) L.__setslice__(2, 4, 1, ["a", "b", "c"]). L.__setslice__ should set its internal list to L[0:start] + value + L[stop:].

- **__delslice__(self, start, stop, step)**—Removes the internal sequence values designated by the slice. If L contains [1,2,3,4,5], then del L[1:4] actually calls (if defined) L.__delslice__(1, 4, 1), which deletes internal values designated as elements 1, 2, and 3.

__contains__

Testing if an object o is a member of sequence s usually loops through s looking for o. If your design requires numerous membership tests like this, you are facing a harsh, quadratic performance penalty. You do, however, have the options to optimize this membership test with the special method __contains__. If the __contains__ method is defined, list membership tests instead call s.__contains__(o) rather than looping through s. The __contains__ method has the self parameter and a parameter slot for the item whose membership is in question. The __contains__ function should return 0 (false) if it does not contain the object and 1, or non-zero (true) if it does.

Listing 7.18 is a class that emulates a list, but also sets members as keys in an internal dictionary. The dictionary value is the number of times the object appears in the list. This allows speedy membership tests by checking if the dictionary has the key rather than looping through the sequence. The tradeoff is increased memory usage and a slower setting and deleting of items. Listing 7.18 adds the __setitem__ and __delitem__ methods as these operations must be intercepted to keep the internal dictionary and list in sync. Two helper methods, __incrementMember and __decrementMember, are defined to help in handling the syncing process by determining each key's count (value) and deleting or creating the key when necessary.

Listing 7.18 **Accelerating Membership Tests with __*contains*__**

```
# file: seqin.py
import types

class usrList:
    def __init__(self, initialValues):
        self.__data = initialValues
        self.__membership = {}
        map(self.__membership.update,
            [{key:1} for key in self.__data])

    def __contains__(self, item):
        return self.__membership.has_key(item)

    # for __contains__ to work, assignment and deletion must
    # change self.__data and self.__membership
    def __setitem__(self, index, value):
        if isinstance(index, types.SliceType):
            if index.step != 1:
                raise ValueError, "Assignment to slice requires step=1"
            indexes = self.__data[index]
        else:
            indexes = [self.__data[index]]

        # updated self.__data _and_ self.__membership
        self.__data[index] = value
        map(self.__decrementMember, indexes)
        map(self.__incrementMember, values)

    def __delitem__(self, index):
        indexes = self.__data[index]
        del self.__data[index]
        if isinstance(indexes, types.ListType):
            map(self.__decrementMember, indexes)
        else:
            self.__decrementMember(indexes) # it's really only one index

    def __incrementMember(self, member):
        if self.__membership.has_key(member):
            self.__membership[member] += 1
        else:
            self.__membership[member] = 1

    def __decrementMember(self, member):
        if self.__membership.has_key(member):
            if self.__membership[member] == 1:
                del self.__membership[member]
            else:
                self.__membership[member] -= 1
```

```
    def __repr__(self):
        return str(self.__data)

if __name__ == '__main__':
    from time import time

    t1 = time()
    pyList = range(0, 12000, 3)
    print "The PyList took %f seconds to fill." % (time()-t1,)

    t1 = time()
    newList = usrList(range(0, 12000, 3))
    print "The usrList took %f seconds to fill." % (time()-t1,)
    t1 = time()
    count = 0
    for x in range(10, 12000, 7):
        if x in pyList: count += 1
    print "Found %i items in pyList in %f seconds" % (count, time()-t1)

    t1 = time()
    count = 0
    for x in range(10, 12000, 7):
        if x in newList:
            count += 1
    print "Found %i items in newList in %f seconds" % (count, time()-t1)
```

Output from running `jython seqin.py` is:

```
The PyList took 0.000000 seconds to fill.
The usrList took 0.110000 seconds to fill.
Found 571 items in pyList in 6.430000 seconds
Found 571 items in newList in 0.220000 seconds
```

Listing 7.18 has a verbose testing section to illustrate the item setting penalty and the membership test benefit inherent in this approach.

UserList

The Jython (and Python) library contains a module aimed at easing the creating of list-like, user-defined objects. The previous examples used a class called usrList that was intended to foreshadow the introduction of this without creating naming confusion (note the spelling difference). The UserList module defines one class: UserList. This class optionally uses a PyList object internally to represent the list data, and supplies default methods for working with this data. If you choose not to use a PyList object for the internal data, you need to override all required methods.

Listing 7.19 uses the UserList class to keep statistics about the frequency items are requested from the list. The important points of Listing 7.19 are the internal data and the methods defined. The ListStats class in Listing 7.19 chooses to use the PyList object as internal data and passes that object to the UserList constructor. Not all methods require implementing to fully act like a built-in list because UserList handles everything not explicitly defined in the ListStats class of Listing 7.19. If it did not pass a PyList to the UserList super-class, much more work would need to be done to fully act like a list.

Listing 7.19   *UserList* **and List–Like Objects**

```
# file: liststats.py
import UserList

class ListStats(UserList.UserList):
    def __init__(self, data=[]):
        self.data = data
        assert type(data)==type([]), "Constructor arg must be a list"
        UserList.UserList(data)
        self.stats = {}
        self.requestCount = 0

    def __getitem__(self, index):
        items = self.data[index]
        if type(items) != type([]):
            # make plain integers into a list for convenience
            items = [items]
        for x in items:
            self.requestCount += 1
            self.stats[x] = self.stats.setdefault(x, 0) + 1
        return items

    def printStats(self):
        for x in self.data:
            use = self.stats.setdefault(x, 0)
            if not use: continue
            print ("%00.i, %1.3f%%  " %
                    (self.data[x],
                        float(use)/float(self.requestCount)*100)),
            print # to put prompt on a new line

if __name__ == '__main__':
    import random

    L = ListStats(range(10))
    for x in range(2000):
        L[random.randint(0, 9)] # access a random index
    L.printStats()
```

The output from running `jython liststats.py` is:

```
0, 9.100%   1, 9.600%   2, 11.000%   3, 10.900%   4, 11.350%   5, 8.750%   6,
10.850%   7, 9.500%   8, 9.550%   9, 9.400%
```

Emulating Mappings

Emulating a mapping type is extremely similar to emulating a list type, except you work with keys instead of indexes. A built-in mapping object implements the methods `clear`, `copy`, `get`, `has_key`, `items`, `keys`, `setdefault`, `update`, and `values`, so truly emulating a mapping type required implementing these methods. The special methods that a mapping object should implement are `__len__`, `__getitem__`, `__setitem__`, and `__delitem__`. These should look familiar from the section on lists.

- **`__len__(self)`**—Returns the number of `key:value` pairs within the mapping object.

- **`__getitem__(self, key)`**—Returns the values associated with the specified key.

- **`__setitem__(self, key, value)`**—Sets the specified key to the specified value in the internal mapping representation.

- **`__delitem__(self, key)`**—Deletes the specified key from the internal mapping.

Because the implementation of these special methods is so familiar from emulating lists, the following code listing should be sufficient to demonstrate these special mapping methods. Listing 7.20 borrows ideas from Listing 7.14 in that it also implements data elements as files, but adds a bit of a twist. The dictionary represents a directory, the keys represent files, and the values represent file contents.

Listing 7.20 also allows for numbers and data objects to be stored by using Jython's `pickle` module. Pickling is one of Jython's serialization mechanisms. The two `pickle` methods employed are `dumps()`, which converts from object to string, and `loads()`, which converts from string to object. To serialize the list in Listing 7.20, we use the following:

```
string = pickle.dumps(list)
```

To restore the list, we use this:

```
pickle.loads(string)
```

There is another trick used for safety sake in listing 7.20. A `JythonIDfile` is added to each directory created for this mapping. There are no checks to guarantee this class created a certain directory, or any file within it, so it must identify directories as special somehow (lest someone try this example with `/etc` or `C:\windows\system`).

Some of the library methods used have been introduced before, but for clarity, here is a list of methods and what they do:

- **os.mkdir(directory)**—Creates a directory. An OS that enforces file and directory permissions may raise an `OSError` if it unable to create the directory.

- **os.path.join(path, filename)**—Joins a path and filename, adding the platform-specific path separator where appropriate.

- **os.path.isdir(directory)**—Returns 1 if the specified directory exists, 0 otherwise.

- **os.path.isfile(filename)**—Returns 1 if the specified file exists, and is a file.

- **os.listdir(directory)**—Returns a list of all the names defined in the specified directory.

- **os.stat(file)**—Returns a nine-element `tuple` representing file statistics. Listing 7.20 uses only the file size, designated with `ST_SIZE` from the `stat` module.

- **pickle.dumps(object)**—Returns a string, which is the serialized object.

- **pickle.loads(string)**—Returns an object for which the string was the serialized data for.

Listing 7.20 **A Persistent Dictionary**

```
# file: specialmap.py
import types
import os
import pickle
from stat import ST_SIZE

class mappingDirectory:
    def __init__(self, directory):
        self.__ID = None
        self.__dir = directory
        if not os.path.exists(directory):
            os.mkdir(directory)
            idfile = os.path.join(directory, "JythonIDfile")
            f = open(idfile, "wb")
```

```
            print >> f, str(id(self))
            f.close()
        elif not os.path.isdir(directory):
            raise ValueError, "File %s already exists." % directory
        elif not os.path.isfile(os.path.join(directory,
                                "JythonIDfile")):
            msg = "Directory exists, but it isn't a mapping directory."
            raise ValueError, msg

    def __repr__(self):
        listing = os.listdir(self.__dir)
        results = {}
        for x in listing:
            if x == "JythonIDfile": continue
            size = os.stat(os.path.join(self.__dir, x))[ST_SIZE]
            results[x] = "<datafile: size=%i>" % size
        return str(results)

    def __setitem__(self, key, value):
        self.__testKey(key)
        pathandname = os.path.join(self.__dir, key)
        f = open(pathandname, "w+b")
        print >> f, pickle.dumps(value)
        f.close()

    def __getitem__(self, key):
        self.__testKey(key)
        pathandname = os.path.join(self.__dir, key)
        try:
            f = open(pathandname, "rb")
        except IOError:
            raise KeyError, key
        value = f.read()
        f.close()
        return pickle.loads(value)

    def __delitem__(self, key):
        self.__testKey(key)
        pathandname = os.path.join(self.__dir, key)
        if not os.path.isfile(pathandname):
            raise KeyError, key
        os.remove(pathandname)

    def __testKey(self, key):
        if not isinstance(key, types.StringType):
            raise KeyError, "This mapping restricts keys to strings"
        if key == "JythonIDfile":
            raise KeyError, "The name JythonIDfile is reserved."
```

continues

Listing 7.20   **Continued**

```
if __name__ == '__main__':
    md = mappingDirectory("c:\\windows\\desktop\\jythontestdir")
    md["odd"] = filter(lambda x: x%2, range(10000))
    md["even"] = filter(lambda x: not x%2, range(10000))
    md["prime"] = [2, 3, 5, 7, 11, 13, 17]
    print "Mapping =", md
    print "primes =", md["prime"]
    del md["prime"]
    print "primes deleted"
    print "Mapping =", md
```

Output from running jython `specialmap.py` is:

```
Mapping = {'prime': '<datafile: size=38>', 'odd': '<datafile: size=34452>',
'even': '<datafile: size=34452>'}
primes = [2, 3, 5, 7, 11, 13, 17]
primes deleted
Mapping = {'odd': '<datafile: size=34452>', 'even': '<datafile: size=34452>'}
```

Emulating Numeric Types

Emulating a numeric type requires defining the special methods for each numeric operation the object should support. The special methods associated with numeric operations are those that implement unary and binary operators, conversion to other types, and coercion. The majority of the special methods are for the binary operators, and these methods appear in triples. For example, implementing addition involves defining the __add__ method for when the object is on the left side of the addition operator, the __radd__ method for when the object is on the right side of the operator, or __iadd__ for when using augmented assignment (+=). These methods are sometimes called respectively normal, reflected, and augmented methods.

The augmented assignment methods (__i*__) are unique in that their implementation doesn't return a value, but instead modifies self. However, if a numeric object does not define the augmented method, it can still be used in an augmented assignment. If the object N defines __add__, but not __iadd__, the expression N += N executes the following:

```
N = N.__add__(N)
```

Table 7.3 lists numeric operations and their associated method. On the left side of Table 7.3 is the operation with N representing the user-defined, numeric object. The right side of Table 7.3 is the method signature of the associated special method. If a method should returns a specific type of object, the return type is noted by `-->` `type`. For example, the operation `N + 2` translates into `N.__add__(2)`, and the method signature is `__add__(self, other)`.

Something that plays an important role in the numeric operations is `__coerce__`. The `__coerce__` method is called whenever the two operands are of differing types. The operation `N1 + N2`, where `N1` and `N2` are different types, actually calls `N1.__coerce__(N2)`. The `__coerce__` method returns a `tuple` of `N1` and `N2` converted to a common type—let's call them `T1` and `T2`. Then `T1.__add__(T2)` is called. If the left operand does not have the `__coerce__` method, the right operand's `__coerce__` method is called.

Table 7.3 Numeric Binary Operators and Their Special Methods

Operators	Methods
`N + 2`	`__add__(self, other)`
`2 + N`	`__radd__(self, other)`
`N += 2`	`__iadd__(self, other) --> self`
`N - 2`	`__sub__(self, other)`
`2 - N`	`__rsub__(self, other)`
`N -= 2`	`__isub__(self, other) --> self`
`N * 2`	`__mul__(self, other)`
`2 * N`	`__rmul__(self, other)`
`N *= 2`	`__imul__(self, other) --> self`
`N / 2`	`__div__(self, other)`
`2 / N`	`__rdiv__(self, other)`
`N /= 2`	`__idiv__(self, other) --> self`
`N % 2`	`__mod__(self, other)`
`2 % N`	`__rmod__(self, other)`
`N %= 2`	`__imod__(self, other) --> self`
`divmod(N, 2)`	`__divmod__(self, other)`
`divmod(2, N)`	`__rdivmod__(self, other)`
`N ** 2`	`__pow__(self, other)`
`2 ** N`	`__rpow__(self, other)`
`N **= 2`	`__ipow__(self, other) --> self`
`pow(N, 2, 2)`	`__pow__(self, other, mod=1)`
`pow(2, N, 2)`	`__rpow__(self, other, mod=1)`
`N << 2`	`__lshift__(self, other)`

continues

Table 7.3 **Continued**

Operators	Methods
2 << N	__rlshift__(self, other)
N <<= 2	__ilshift__(self, other) --> self
N >> 2	__rshift__(self, other)
2 >> N	__rrshift__(self, other)
N >>= 2	__irshift__(self, other) --> self
N & 2	__and__(self, other)
2 & N	__rand__(self, other)
N &= 2	__iand__(self, other) --> self
N ¦ 2	__or__(self, other)
2 ¦ N	__ror__(self, other)
N ¦= 2	__ior__(self, other) --> self
N ^ 2	__xor__(self, other)
2 ^ N	__rxor__(self, other)
N ^= 2	__ixor__(self, other) --> self
- N	__neg__(self)
+ N	__pos__(self)
~ N	__invert__(self)
abs(N)	__abs__(self)
coerce(N, x)	__coerce__(self, other) --> some common type or None
complex(N)	__complex__(self) --> PyComplex
float(N)	__float__(self) --> PyFloat
hex(N)	__hex__(self) --> PyString
int(N)	__int__(self) --> PyInteger
long(N)	__long__(self) --> PyLong
oct(N)	__oct__(self) --> PyString

Jython Internals and Integrating Jython With Java

8

Compiling Jython with *jythonc*

JYTHON EXCELS BECAUSE OF ITS COMPREHENSIVE integration of Python and Java. Most multi-level language combinations have a semantic gap between the languages that discourages truly comprehensive integration. CPython, for example, cannot use C libraries without special steps, and writing C extensions must following specific guidelines unique to CPython. Jython, on the other hand, enables the seamless usage of arbitrary Java classes in a Python environment without requiring extra steps, modification, or special treatment in writing the Java class. That's only one side of the coin, however. To truly be comprehensive, Jython must also allow Java to seamlessly use Python. Jython meets this latter requirement, even if not fully transparently, thanks to `jythonc`.

`jythonc` allows you to compile Jython modules into Java `*.class` files. Jythonc can create runnable classes—those that Java can execute but still rely on Jython modules. `jythonc` can also create fully self-contained and runnable applications, meaning those that Java can execute and that have all dependant modules located and compiled. Additionally, `jythonc` can compile Jython classes that indistinguishably masquerade as Java classes—those that Java code can import and call.

To pique your interest, consider the advantages of being able to compile Jython applications into self-contained jar files runnable on most JVM's. Consider the development benefits of prototyping applications in Jython and later converting portions to Java—but only as needed. Consider the ease of writing servlets, applets and beans in Jython, and having them work within Java frameworks without regard for their original language. Consider the flexibility of composing, subclassing, and extending Java and Jython classes interchangeably. These rare abilities are the functionality supplied by jythonc.

What Is *jythonc?*

jythonc is a tool that generates Java code from Jython modules. jythonc can also create jar files, track dependencies, freeze associated modules, and more depending on the options supplied. Within the same directory as the Jython shell script (or batch file) should be another script called jythonc (or jythonc.bat). This script is really a wrapper around the file sys.prefix/Tools/jythonc/ jythonc.py that does the work of creating a java file and calling a java compiler to create *.class files. This means you must have an appropriate Java compiler such as Sun's javac, available at http://www.javasoft.com/j2se/, or IBM's jikes, currently available at http://www10.software.ibm.com/developerworks/ opensource/jikes/, to use in conjunction with jythonc. The Java Runtime Environmenta (JRE) is insufficient in itself because it does not include a compiler. You will need the Java Development Kit (JDK) or Jikes compiler. Note that Microsoft's jvc compiler is currently not a good choice for compiling Jython code.

Compiled Jython has no performance advantage over interpreted Python. It is often such an immediate concern for those new to Jython that it seems worth mentioning early. The current implementation produces compiled Jython code that performs similarly to using Jython itself to execute a module.

Compiling a Module with *jythonc*

If you run jython A.py it means that the module A runs as the top-level, or __main__, script. If you compile A.py with jythonc, you can instead use Java directly to execute the application. Listing 8.1 is a simple Jython module called guess.py. It will serve as a test subject for compiling a Jython module into runnable Java class files. The examples below assume that the Java compiler, *javac,* is in your path. If it is not, or if jythonc has difficulty locating the Java compiler, you can use jythonc's -C switch to specify the compiler. See the jythonc Options section later in this chapter for more on the -C switch.

Additionally, you may wish to exclude jython.jar from your classpath environment variable before running jythonc because some versions of jythonc fail when jython.jar is already in the classpath.

Listing 8.1 A Jython Guessing Module for Compiling into Runnable Classes

```
#file: guess.py
import random

print "I'm thinking of a number between 1 and 100. Guess what it is."
num = random.randint(1, 100)

while 1:
    guess = int(raw_input("Enter guess: "))
    if guess==num:
        print "Correct, the number was %i" % num
        break
    elif abs(guess - num) < 3:
        print "Close enough. The number was %i" % num
        break
    elif guess > num:
        print "Too high."
    else: print "Too low"
```

The shell command irequired to compile Listing 8.1 is this:

```
> jythonc guess.py
```

The preceding command assumes jythonc is in your path. If it is not, you must give the full path to jythonc—something like this:

```
c:\jython-2.1\jythonc guess.py
```

After running the jythonc command, you should see output similar to this:

```
processing guess

Required packages:

Creating adapters:

Creating .java files:
  guess module

Compiling .java to .class...
Compiling with args: ['javac', '-classpath',
'"C:\\jython\\jython.jar;.\\jpywork;;C:\\jython\\Tools\\jythonc;C:\\ch8
examples\\.;C:\\jython\\Lib;C:\\jython"', '.\\jpywork\\guess.java']
0
```

You may also receive the following warning depending on the version of the JDK you are iusing:

```
Note: Some input files use or override a deprecated API.
Note: Recompile with -deprecation for details.
```

Examining the output, we see that jythonc created a guess.java file from the guess.py module, and then called javac to compile the guess.java file into class files. The full command used to compile guess.java into classes is shown as a list (think .join(args) to get the actual command). We know jythonc called javac to do the compiling because javac is the first item in the args list. It is important to note that the generated Java file may have code specific to the JVM version you are using. This means that using the -target option may be insufficient as the generated code may contain references to unsupported classes. To compile Jython code for a specific JVM version, you should use that version of the JVM when running jythonc. This seems to be most often necessary for applets.

If javac is not the Java compiler you use, then you can specify a different compiler in the registry or on the command line. The Jython registry key python.jythonc.compiler and the -C command-line switch both specify which Java compiler to use. The appropriate registry line to use jikes instead of javac would be as follows:

```
python.jythonc.compiler = /path/to/jikes  # for *nix users
python.jythonc.compiler = c:\path\to\jikes # for win users
```

Specifying the jikes compiler with the -C option would appear as follows:

```
bash> jythonc -C /path/to/jikes guess.py
dos> jythonc -C c:\path\to\jikes guess.py
```

The results of jythonc guess.py is a directory called jpywork, which contains the files guess.java, guess.class, and guess$_PyInner.class. The guess.java file is what jythonc generates, and the two class files are the results of compiling guess.java. Compiling Jython code should result in at least two class files: one with the module's name and an associated $_PyInner class.

Running jythonc-compiled classes with a JVM executable requires that the jython.jar file and both compiled class files (guess.class and guess$_PyInner.class) are in the classpath. If you are within the same directory as the two class files generated from compiling listing 8.1, and you are using the Java executable from Sun's JDK, this would be the command to run the compiled guess files:

```
bash> java -cp /path/to/jython.jar:. guess
dos> java -cp \path\jython.jar;. guess
```

You should be prompted to guess a number. Sample output from running this program is as follows:

```
I'm thinking of a number between 1 and 100. Guess what it is.
Enter guess: 50
Too high.
Enter guess: 25
Close enough. The number was 23
```

It seems a somewhat common error to forget to include the appropriate directories in the classpath when first running jythonc-compiled files. Because jythonc-compiled files are often used within existing Java frameworks, the compiled class files are often moved into specific directories for that framework. This step seems prone to errors such as not copying all the required files. Remember that jythonc creates at least two files. Without the inner file (guess$_PyInner.class in our case) in the classpath, you should receive the following error message:

```
Error running main.  Can't find: guess$_PyInner
```

Additionally, jythonc-compiled classes required the classes found in the jython.jar file. These can be included in an archive by using special jythonc options, as we will see later. For now, we must ensure that the jython.jar file is in the classpath. If the jython.jar file is not included in the classpath, you should receive the following error message:

```
Exception in thread "main" java.lang.NoClassDefFoundError:
org/python/core/PyObject
```

The compiled version of Listing 8.1 still relies on the random module from the sys.prefix/Lib directory. If the sys.prefix or sys.path variables are wrong, you will receive the following error:

```
Java Traceback:
...
Traceback (innermost last):
  File "C:\WINDOWS\Desktop\ch8examples\guess.py", line 0, in main
ImportError: no module named random
```

Paths and Compiled Jython

Jython depends on a Java property called python.home to locate and read the Jython registry file as well as establish the sys.prefix, and thus certain sys.path entries. Jython also creates a cache directory in the python.home or sys.prefix directory, which is aptly named cachedir by default. Information discovered about Java packages is stored in this directory as an essential optimization, but this can be troublesome if `python.home` or `sys.prefix` have unexpected values. The `python.home` property is set as part of jython's startup script, but compiled Jython doesn't have this convenience.

This introduces issues concerning Jython's paths. A Jython module compiled into Java classes requires special steps to ensure it can find Jython modules and packages it depends on and make use of a specific `cachedir`. What follows is a list of options you can choose from to do so.

Set the *python.home* Property in the JVM

Sun's Java executables allow the setting of properties with the `-D` command-line option. Listing 8.2 is a Jython module designed to expose path problems.

Listing 8.2   **Jython Module for Clarifying Paths and Properties**

```
# file: paths.py

import sys
import java

print "sys.path=", sys.path
print "sys.prefix=", sys.prefix
print "python.home=", java.lang.System.getProperty("python.home")

# print a random number just so this depends on a
# module in the sys.prefix/Lib directory
import random
print "My lucky number is", random.randint(1,100)
```

Compile Listing 8.2 with `jythonc paths.py`. Compiling it this way creates class files dubbed runnable in Jython lingo. The word runnable infers that Jython code compiled so that the Java executable can execute it, but it still relies on Jython libraries and follows the standard Jython interpreter behavior. Executing a runnable class should act just like running a Jython script—meaning it would cache Java package information at startup and use the `sys.path` to locate modules. This means setting the `python.home` property or at least specifying library paths is required.

To continue testing Listing 8.2, change directories in a command shell to where the `paths.class` and `paths$_PyInner.class` files reside. Then execute `paths.class` using the `-D` option to set the `python.home` property. The command should look similar to that below only using the directories unique to your installation (the command "wraps" because of the long line, but is meant as a single command):

```
bash> java -Dpython.home="/usr/local/jython-2.1" -cp /usr/local/jython.jar:.
paths
```

```
dos> java -Dpython.home="c:\jython-2.1" -cp c:\jython-2.1\jython.jar;. paths
```

The results should appear similar to this:

```
sys.path= ['.', 'c:\\jython 2.1\\Lib']
sys.prefix= c:\\jython 2.1
python.home= c:\\jython 2.1
My lucky number is 96
```

This means Jython's registry file is found, the `sys.prefix` value is accurate, and modules, such as `random` in the `sys.prefix/Lib` directory, can be found and loaded.

What happens without the `-D` option? Without it, the command would look like this:

```
bash> java -cp /path/to/jython.jar:. paths
dos> java -cp c:\path\to\jython.jar;. paths
```

If the `jython.jar` file is still in the Jython installation directory, the results should be similar to that below (replace / with your platform–specific directory separator):

```
sys.path= ['.', '/usr/local/jython-2.1/Lib']
sys.prefix= /usr/local/jython 2.1a1/
python.home= None
My lucky number is 97
```

How does Jython know the correct `sys.prefix` value without having a proper `python.home` value? It's not part of Jython's documented behavior, but currently, if `jython.jar` is not in the current directory, the `sys.prefix` value becomes the directory in which the `jython.jar` file was found. If you copy the `jython.jar` file into the same directory as the `paths.class` file, the results would be different:

```
dos> java -cp jython.jar;. paths
sys.path= ['.', '\\Lib']
sys.prefix=.
python.home= None
Java Traceback:

        at org.python.core.Py.ImportError(Py.java:180)
...
        at paths.main(paths.java:72)
Traceback (innermost last):
  File "C:\WINDOWS\Desktop\ch8examples\paths.py", line 0, in main
ImportError: no module named random
```

The result in this last case is a `python.home` equal to `None`. This means that the Jython registry file is not located, and that modules in Jython's Lib directory (`random`) cannot be found. This can be resolved by moving the `random` module into the same directory as well, because `sys.path` will automatically include the current directory, or ..

Explicitly Add Directories to *sys.path* Within Modules

It can be easiest at times to explicitly append library paths to the `sys.path` variable within the module you intend to compile. This ensures modules within a certain directory are accessible. If you wanted to ensure that Listing 8.2 could find the random module in the `/usr/local/jython-2.1/Lib` directory, you can add the following line to `paths.py` (after importing `sys` of course):

```
sys.path.append("/usr/local/jython-2.1/Lib") # *nix
sys.path.append("c:\jython-2.1\Lib") # dos
```

With this being part of the compiled class, modules in that directory will always be found no matter where the `python.home` property and `sys.prefix` variable point. However, this lacks the flexibility of Java's `classpath`. If an application is moved to another machine, paths become troublesome and functionality across platforms suffers.

Add to the *python.path* or *python.prepath* Property

Just as you can set the `python.home` property with Java's `-D` switch, you can also set the registry's `python.path` or `python.prepath` property with the `-D` switch. Assume you have compiled Listing 8.2 with `jythonc paths.py`, and you have moved the `jython.jar` file into the same directory as the `paths.class` and `paths$_PyInner.class` files. You can run the application with a command similar to this:

```
dos>java -Dpython.path="c:\\jython-2.1\\Lib" -cp jython.jar;. paths
```

In this case, the `sys.path` list appends the `python.path` value as part its initialization, and therefore before loading modules. Our example application would locate and load the `random` module appropriately. Setting path properties in the command line allows batch files or scripts to dynamically determine this value—an improvement over placing static paths within code.

Freeze an Application

Freezing an application infers compiling a Jython module in a way that tracks all dependencies during compilation and results in class files for all required modules. A frozen application is self-contained: It does not depend on Jython's `sys.path` directories, it locates modules on Java's `classpath`, and it does not cache package information at startup. Freezing an application requires using `jythonc`'s `-d` or `--deep` option. To freeze Listing 8.2, use a command like the following:

```
dos> jythonc -d paths.py
dos> jythonc --deep paths.py
```

The compilation process will now include the `random` module. `jythonc` tracks dependencies, such as the `random` module, and compiles those modules to Java as well. The results of freezing the paths application (from Listing 8.2) should be four class files:

- `paths.class`
- `paths$_PyInner.class`
- `random.class`
- `random$_PyInner.class`

These class files, plus the classes found in `jython.jar`, are all that is required to run the paths application.

If you are at a command prompt, and you are in the same directory as the class files created from compiling Listing 8.2, you can execute the frozen paths program with the following command:

```
bash> java -cp /usr/local/jython-2.1/jython.jar:. paths
dos> java -cp c:\jython-2.1\jython.jar;. paths
```

Note that the classes within `jython.jar` are still required and must appear in the `classpath`.

It does not work to compile `paths.py` then `random.py` separately. `jythonc` must know if dependencies are to be Java classes or Jython modules at compile-time. This class/module dichotomy introduces another important point. The class files created from compiling a module with `jythonc` cannot be used within Jython as if they are modules. `jythonc` has made them Java classes and to revert them back into modules is tricky.

Write a Custom *__import__( )* Hook

Writing your own import tools allows greater control but also has some limitations. With a custom import, you can control the location from which modules load. This allows you to use zip files, jar files, `classpath` resources, remote URL resources, and more as the source for modules. The limitation, however, is the current difficulty in dealing with pre-compiled modules. The duality of

Python modules (*.py files) and Py classes (modules that are compiled into $py.class files) makes loading pre-compiled modules troublesome in Jython. The ability to load a compiled Jython module ($py.class) without having to freeze all module dependencies is a desired feature dubbed poor man freezing, but it is not yet implemented.

Listing 8.3 is a simple implementation of custom module loading that loads modules (*.py files) from the classpath. This allows access to *.py files that are packaged within jar files—something often desired for delivering applications. In Listing 8.3, loadmodule is the custom import function, and the myTest.py module is the simple companion module loaded with loadmodule.

The important aspects of the loadmodule function are as follows:

- The classloader
- Reading the module
- Creating a module instance with the new module
- The exec function

When examining the contents of the sys module, you will see three functions related to class loaders: classLoader, getClassLoader, and setClassLoader. Currently sys.classLoader is only set in a jythonc-compiled class. Listing 8.3 includes two extra lines for working with uncompiled code (they are commented out in the listing).

After acquiring a class loader, the loadmodule function begins loading the desired module. The steps to reading the module are as follows:

1. Create a byte[] buffer with the jarray module to use as an argument to the stream's read() method.
2. Read from the buffer.
3. Append data to the module string until the read() method reports the end of file (-1).

The new module enables the dynamic creation of classes, functions, methods, instances, and modules; the loadmodule function makes use of its dynamic module creation to create a module object. This module should be registered with the list of all modules loaded, which is held in the PyStringMap sys.modules, but also needs a reference in the current namespace, so both sys.modules[name] and mod are assigned the new module instance.

The remaining work in setting up the module is executing it, but it must be executed in the namespace of the new module instance created—mod (otherwise it executes in the top-level environment, or __main__). in mod.__dict__ is added after the exec statement to force bindings resulting from the execution to appear in the mod.__dict__ mapping object.

Listing 8.3 **Custom Module Import**

```
# file: customimp.py
import sys
import new
import jarray
import java

def loadmodule(name, bufferSize=1024):
    filename = name + ".py"
    cl = sys.getClassLoader()
    if cl == None:
        cl = java.lang.ClassLoader.getSystemClassLoader()
    r = cl.getResourceAsStream(filename)
    if not r:
        raise ImportError, "No module named %s" % name
    moduleString = ""
    buf = jarray.zeros(bufferSize, "b")
    while 1:
        readsize = r.read(buf)
        if readsize==-1: break
        moduleString += str(java.lang.String(buf[0:readsize]))
    sys.modules[name] = mod = new.module(name)
    exec(moduleString) in mod.__dict__
    return mod

myTest = loadmodule("myTest")
print myTest.test()
```

The simple `myTest` module used to test the custom loading is as follows:

```
# file: myTest.py
def test():
    return "It worked"
```

Listing 8.3 is a nice compromise because even if you freeze the application, you can still have flexibility with the `*.py` files that you load with `loadmodule`. Any required `*.py` files can be updated, added, or removed from a resource without having to recompile the anything.

To freeze Listing 8.3 and include required Jython classes all in a single `jar` file, use the following jythonc command:

```
jythonc -all --jar myapp.jar customimp.py
```

You can now add the `myTest.py` file to `myapp.jar` with the following:

```
jar -uf myapp.jar myTest.py
```

The `myapp.jar` file contains all you need to run the application, but you can easily update the `myTest.py` file without having to recompile anything. The following command runs the `customimp` module:

```
>java -cp myapp.jar customimp
It worked
```

jythonc Options

`jythonc` has a number of options that allow special treatment of the compiled files, dependencies, compiler options, and more. `jythonc`'s syntax requires that options are specified first, followed by the modules to be compiled:

```
jythonc options modules
```

The modules can be full paths to python modules, such as the following:

```
jythonc /usr/local/jython2.1/Lib/ftplib.py
```

Or, modules in the `sys.path` may be listed by just the module's name as it would be used in an `import` statement:

```
jythonc ftplib
```

Table 8.1 shows each of `jythonc`'s options and what it does. Notice that each option has a long and short form that may be used interchangeably. Some of the `jythonc` options are also available as registry keys. Equivalent registry keys are noted where applicable.

Table 8.1   *jythonc* Options

Option	Description
--deep -d	The --deep option locates and compiles all dependencies required for an application. It creates what is called a "frozen," or self-contained, application. A frozen application can run without access to the Jython Lib directory and does not cache Java package information at startup.
--jar jarfile -j jarfile	The --jar option automatically applies the --deep option and it places the results of the compilation in the specified jar file. A name jar file must appear

Table 8.1 *jythonc* **Options**

Option	Description
	with the `--jar` option. This does not update existing `jar` files, but instead over writes if a `jar` file of the specified name already exists.
`--core` `-c`	The `--core` option automatically applies the `--deep` option and adds the core Java classes to the `jar` file specified with the `--jar` option. The `--core` option is designed to be used in conjunction with the `--jar` option. If no `--jar` option appears, the `--core` option is ignored.
`--all` `-a`	The `--all` automatically applies the `--deep` option and it adds the classes from the `org.python.core`, `org.python.parser`, and `org.python.compiler` packages to the `jar` file specified with the `--jar` option. The resulting `jar` file contains all required files to run the Jython application. The `--all` option is designed to be used in conjunction with the `--jar` option. If no `--jar` option appears, the `--all` option is ignored.
`--addpackages packages` `-A`	The `--addpackages` option adds the specified Java packages to the `jar` file specified with the `--jar` option. The current implementation adds class files that are in package hierarchies (directories), but not the contents of `jar` files.
`--workingdir directory` `-w directory`	`jythonc` uses a directory called `jpywork` by default to create java files and compile to classes. The `--workingdir` option allows you to specify another directory for this to occur.

continues

Table 8.1   **Continued**

Option	Description
`--skip modules` `-s modules`	The `--skip` option requires a comma-separated list of module names. All module names in list are excluded from the compilation.
`--compiler compilerName` `-C compilerName`	The `--compiler` option allows you to specify which Java compiler to use. If the desired compiler is in the path, its name is sufficient; otherwise the path and name are required. You can use a `--compiler` option of `NONE` to have `jythonc` stop after the creation of the `.java` class. Jython's registry file also includes the key `python.jythonc.compiler`, which can be used to set the default compiler.
`--compileropts options` `-J`	The `--compileropts` options allows you to specify options that are passed to the Java compiler used. A `--compileropts -O` option would pass the optimize (`-O`) option to javac (if that is the compiler used).
`--package packageName` `-p packageName`	The `--package` option places the compiled code into the specified Java package. Accessing the compiled code then requires the package name to qualify the classes. Compiling module `A` with `-p test` means future references to `A` require `test.A`. The `--package` option is most useful in conjunction with the `--deep` option.
`--bean jarfile` `-b jarfile`	The `--bean` option creates a `jar file` that includes the appropriate bean manifest file. This is useful if the Jython class being compiled follows bean conventions and you wish to use the `jar` file created from within a bean box.

Table 8.1 *jythonc* **Options**

Option	Description
--falsenames names -f names	The --falsenames option sets a comma-separated list of names to false.
--help -h	The --help option prints usage information to the screen

Table 8.2 shows sample usages of jythonc coupled with explanations of how the options specified affect the compilation.

Table 8.2 **Usages of *jythonc***

Command	Result
jythonc test.p	This compiles test.py into runnable class files that will still potentially depend on Jython modules.
jythonc -d -A utest -j A.jar test.py	This compiles test.py into a frozen application. The -d (deep) option tracks all dependencies. The -A utest option adds java classes from the utest package to the resulting jar file. The -j A.jar option tells jythonc to put all resulting files into the file A.jar.
jythonc -p unit -j test.jar *.py	This compiles all modules in the current directory into Java class files. All class files will be part of the java package unit because of the -p option, and will be placed in the test.jar file because of the -j option.
jythonc -b myBean.jar namebean.py	This compiles the namebean.py module and places the resulting class files into the myBean.jar file. This also adds the appropriate bean manifest to the myBean.jar file.

continues

Table 8.2   **Continued**

Command	Result
`jythonc --core -j` `test.jar test.py`	This compiles the `test.py` into a frozen application. All dependencies are tracked down and compiled because the `--core` option implies the `--deep` option. Additionaly, Jython's core Java classes are also added to the `jar` file.

Java-Compatible Classes

A compiled Jython class can behave like a native Java class if it is Java-compatible. To make a Jython class Java-compatible, you must consider the following three guidelines:

- The Jython class must subclass a Java class or interface.
- The Jython class may include Java method signature hints called *sig-strings*.
- The Jython class must be within a module of the same name. The Java-compatible class A should be within the file A.py.

The first guideline is fairly simple: Subclass a Java class or interface. If you do not need the functionality from a specific Java class, subclass `java.lang.Object`. You may still inherit from one or more Jython classes—jythonc does not alter Jython's inheritance rules, it's just an additional requirement for those Jython classes used within Java. This doesn't apply to runnable or frozen applications, it is only when you require a compiled Jython class to masquerade as a Java class.

The second guideline is the use of `@sig` strings. A `@sig` string is really a `doc` string with a specific format. The format is the literal `@sig` followed by a valid Java method signature. Suppose you have the following Jython method:

```
def greet(self, name):
    return "Hello " + name
```

The same method with an added `@sig` string would appear as follows:

```
def greet(self, name):
    "@sig public String greet(String name)"
    return "Hello " + name
```

The @sig in this case specifies a public method with a String object as a return value and a String object as the parameter name. From Java, this method now acts as if it were Java code with the signature specified in the @sig string.

Not all methods require @sig strings. If you are overriding a method that appears in the Java superclass (see requirement #1), you need not specify the method signature. jythonc is smart enough to get this information from the Java superclass. In addition, if you never intend to call a certain method from Java, you need not specify a @sig string. In other words, if method A calls method B, and method A has a @sig string, then method A is callable from Java, while method B is not; however, method B is still callable from method A. Intra-class methods that are not accessible from Java are still accessible from Jython. This acts in a sense as enforced abstraction.

The third requirement is that the name of the class and the module that contains it must match. Listing 8.4 is a Jython module called message.py. Listing 8.4 also contains a class called message. Note the matching class and module name meet the third requirement for Java-compatible classes.

An Example Java-Compatible Jython Class

The message class in Listing 8.4 has two methods: __init__ and showMessage, of which, the showMessage method has a @sig string. The __init__ method does not, but it is still accessible from Java. Why? jythonc is able to determine this information from the Java superclass. The catch is that of the three constructors in the superclass, all three now point to the single __init__ method in the subclass. The subclass chooses to implement only the one signature, and fortunately, the number of parameters makes it clear which one. Remember that only methods that do not override base class methods require @sig strings. You may choose to supply a @sig string even where it is not required—there is no harm in that, but there is no advantage.

Listing 8.4 **Java-Compatible Jython Class**

```
# file: message.py
import java

class message(java.awt.Frame):
    def __init__(self, name):
        self.setTitle(name)
        self.label = java.awt.Label("", java.awt.Label.CENTER)
        action = lambda x: java.lang.System.exit(0)
        button = java.awt.Button('OK', actionPerformed=action)
        p = java.awt.Panel(java.awt.GridLayout(2,1,2,2))
        p.add(self.label)
```

continues

Listing 8.4   **Continued**

```
        p.add(button)
        self.add(p)

    def showMessage(self, text):
        "@sig public void showMessage(String text)"
        self.label.setText(text)
        self.pack()
        self.show()

if __name__ == '__main__':
    m = message("Test Message")
    m.showMessage("I look like Java, but I'm not")
```

To use the message class in Listing 8.4 from within Java, it must be compiled
with jythonc. No special options are required, so this is as simple as jythonc
message.py (assuming you are in the same directory as message.py and jythonc is
in your path). Again note that depending on your compiler version, you may
receive a warning message concerning the use of a deprecated API. The output
from running jythonc message.py should look similar to this:

```
processing message

Required packages:
  java.lang
  java.awt

Creating adapters:
  java.awt.event.ActionListener used in message

Creating .java files:
  message module
    message extends java.awt.Frame

Compiling .java to .class...
Compiling with args: ['C:\\JDK1.3.1\\bin\\javac', '-classpath', '"C:\\jython
2.1a1\\jython.jar;;.\\jpywork;;C:\\jython
2.1a1\\Tools\\jythonc;C:\\WINDOWS\\Desktop\\ch8examples\\.;C:\\jython
2.1a1\\Lib;C:\\jython 2.1a1;c:\\jython 2.1a1\\Lib\\site-python"',
'.\\jpywork\\message.java']
0
```

The messages you receive from jythonc are valuable. What is particularly valuable when compiling Java-compatible classes such as message.py is the information printed when jythonc is creating the *.java files:

```
Creating .java files:
  message module
    message extends java.awt.Frame
```

It is especially important to watch for the appropriate extends message, which ensures that you have met the first of the Java-compatible requirements.

Now that you have `message.class` and `message$_PyInner.class`, how do you use them from Java? The only requirement is placing both generated class files and the `jython.jar` file in the `classpath`. Otherwise, it acts no different than any other Java class. Listing 8.5 is a simple Java class that uses the message class as if it were native Java.

Listing 8.5 **Using a Compiled Jython Class in Java**

```
//file MessageTest.java
import message;

public class MessageTest {
    public static void main(String[] args) {
        message m = new message("Test");
        m.showMessage("I look like Java, but I\'m not");
    }
}
```

To compile Listing 8.5, include `jython.jar` and the `message` classes in the `classpath`. From within the directory containing `message.class` and `message$_PyInner.class`, and using javac from the Sun jdk, the command is as follows:

```
javac -classpath .;/path/to/jython.jar MessageTest.java
```

Running the `MessageTest` class also requires that the `jython.jar` and both message class files be in the classpath. If the classes `message.class`, `message$_PyInner.class`, and `MessageTest.class` are in the same directory, run `MessageTest` with the following command:

```
java -cp .;/path/to/jython.jar MessageTest
```

The small message box similar to that in Figure 8.1 should appear.

Figure 8.1 A Jython Message Box.

Providing a specific method signature in a `@sig` string does not automatically allow for overloaded methods. Yes, a `@sig` string specifies a unique signature, but as noted in Chapter 6, "Classes, Instances, and Inheritance," if Jython overrides a Java method, it must handle all overloaded methods of that name. You cannot add a `@sig` string in hopes of circumventing this generalization. Like-named methods in a Java superclass cannot automatically handle parameter types that differ from the `@sig` string. Nor can you define multiple, like-named methods in a Jython subclass to handle differing parameter types based solely on `@sig` strings.

Listing 8.6 demonstrates with three classes called `Base`, `sub`, and `App`.

Listing 8.6   **Overloaded Methods and *jythonc***

```
// file: Base.java

public class Base {
    public String getSomething(String s) {
        return "string parameter. Base class.";
    }

    public String getSomething(int i) {
        return "int parameter. Base class.";
    }

    public String getSomething(float f) {
        return "float parameter. Base class.";
    }
}

#- - - - - - -
#file: Sub.py

import Base

class Sub(Base):
    def getSomething(self, var):
        "@sig public String getSomething(String var)"
        return str(type(var)) + " Jython subclass."

//- - - - - - - -
//file: App.java

import Sub;

public class App {
    public static void main(String args[]) {
        Sub s = new Sub();
        System.out.println(s.getSomething("A string"));
        System.out.println(s.getSomething(1));
        System.out.println(s.getSomething((float)1.1));
```

```
    }
  }
```

The base Java class called `Base` has an overloaded method called `getSomething`. Three versions of this method collectively allow for `String`, `int`, and `float` parameter types. The Jython subclass, called `Sub`, overrides the `getSomething` method, but has a `@sig` string specifying only the `String` parameter type. This does not restrict it to overriding that specific method signature, however. Method signature information is also gleaned from the superclass, so all methods in the superclass with the same name, but different signatures, are automatically directed to the single method of that name in the Jython subclass.

To compile the files in Listing 8.6, place them all in the same directory, change the console's working directory to that where they reside, then compile with the following commands (in the specified order):

```
javac Base.java
jythonc -w . Sub.py
javac -classpath . App.java
```

Execute `App.java` with the following command from within the same directory:

```
dos>java -cp .;\path\to\jython.jar App
*nix>java -c; .:/path/to/jython.jar App
```

The results should appear similar to this:

```
org.python.core.PyString Jython subclass.
org.python.core.PyInteger Jython subclass.
org.python.core.PyFloat Jython subclass.
```

You can see that `jythonc` has automatically intercepted each of the `Base` class's overloaded methods with the name `getSomething`. The single Jython method by this name is expected to handle each of these conditions, and trying to circumvent this generalization with a `@sig` string gained nothing.

Module-Global Objects and Java-Compatible Classes

The rigidity of adding Java method signatures can feel contradictory to Jython's dynamic nature. Many common patterns that occur in Jython depend on dynamic special methods like `__getattr__` and `__setattr__`, or other mechanisms that don't easily translate into compile-time checks. Additionally, module-global objects might be unclear when using `jythonc` to create Java-compatible classes. The focus on the class shadows the value of *module-global identifiers*: those objects defined in a module, but not within the java-compatible class. Although a Jython class and those methods with `@sig` strings are callable from Java, module-global objects are not. However, the Jython class may use module-level code, and module-level code may even alter the details of a class used by Java (as in Listing 8.8). Listing 8.8 uses a bit of Jython's dynamicism in a compiled class as well as lends clarity to module-global objects.

To set the stage for Listing 8.8, imagine prototyping a Java application with compiled Jython classes. What do you do about static methods? `jythonc` doesn't allow you to specify static in a `@sig` string, so Listing 8.8 was invented to create the illusion of static methods in a compiled Jython class. It doesn't create a legitimate static method—the word "static" doesn't appear in it's signature, but it does emulate one. It does so with the use of other module-global code that is not callable from Java. It's useful to remember that Java may call only specific methods in the compiled Jython class, but Jython code has no restrictions. The generated method signatures are a hook into Jython and need not alter its flexibility.

Listing 8.8 defines a class called `JavaPrototype`, which contains one function definition: `test`. The `test` function is empty except for the `@sig` string. All this `test` function does is make `jythonc` generate a desired Java method signature; it does not have anything to do with the run-time functionality. Why? Because the last line of the module assigns a callable instance of another class to `test`. The `staticfunctor` class in Listing 8.8 defines `__call__`, and an instance of this class is what provides the desired method functionality. If you were wondering why the `arg` identifier appears in the test method's `@sig` string, it is because we are actually trying to generate a signature for the `__call__` method in the second class. Following is a summary of what happens in Listing 8.8:

1. Create a phony method and `@sig` string to trick `jythonc` into adding the desired Java method signature.

2. Define a class that implements `__call__`. The `__call__` definition is the actual functionality desired so the method signature (step 1) should fit its needs.

3. Assign the identifier from the phony method to an instance of a class containing the desired `__call__` method.

Listing 8.7   **Creating a Static-Like Method in Compiled Jython**

```
# file: JavaPrototype.py
import java.lang.Object

class JavaPrototype(java.lang.Object):
    def test(self):  # This will become static-like
        "@sig public void test(String arg)"

class staticfunctor(java.lang.Object):
    def __call__(self, arg):
        print "printing %s from static method" % arg

JavaPrototype.__dict__['test'] = staticfunctor()
```

How can it be static if the @sig string doesn't specify static? This is a stretch, but it acts static in the Jython sense. If you use the JavaPrototype module within Jython, you can test to see that multiple instances of the class share a single, common instance of the test function:

```
>>> import JavaPrototype
>>> p1 = JavaPrototype.JavaPrototype()
>>> p2 = JavaPrototype.JavaPrototype()
>>> p1.test == p2.test
1
>>> p1.test is p2.test
1
>>> print id(p1.test), id(p2.test)
5482965 5482965
```

The interactive example above uses the JavaPrototype module, not the compiled classes. This invites a warning about compiled Jython classes. A compiled Jython class is designed to work in Java, not in Jython. You should use modules in Jython and reserve jythonc-compiled classes for use within Java.

Listing 8.8 is a small Java test class that imports and uses the compiled JavaPrototype class to confirm that it behaves properly as a Java class as well. This assumes that you have used jythonc to compile the JavaPrototype module into class files with jythonc JavaPrototype.

Listing 8.8   **Using the *JavaPrototype* Class from Within Java**

```
// file: Test.java
import JavaPrototype;

public class Test {
    public static void main(String[] args) {
        JavaPrototype i1 = new JavaPrototype();
        JavaPrototype i2 = new JavaPrototype();
```

continues

Listing 8.8 **Continued**

```
        i1.test("THIS");
        i2.test("THAT");
    }
}
```


```
Place in the same direcotry as JavaPrototype.class and
JavaPrototype$_PyInner.class, then compile with:
javac -classpath . test.java
```

Output from running `"java -cp .;\path\to\jython.jar test" # dos`
`"java -cp .:/path/to/jython.jar test" # *nix:`

```
printing THIS from static method
printing THAT from static method
```

9

Embedding and Extending Jython in Java

JAVA APPLICATIONS THAT WOULD BENEFIT FROM Jython's high-level, dynamic nature can easily employ Jython through an embedding interpreter. Additionally, Jython applications in need of additional speed can contain modules written in Java, allowing them to take advantage of Java's efficient bytecode without affecting module-like functionality. These implementations are dubbed embedding and extending. Both are approaches to merging multiple languages in a single application.

Despite the fact that embedding and extending has long been commonplace in many languages, the Jython-Java combination may very well exceed all other languages in this regard. The C implementation of Python is highly praised for its utility in merging languages, or what Python programmers often call "gluing." Jython inherits this success, but also exceeds it by minimizing the seams and gaps between languages. Passing objects between Java and Jython is symmetrically seamless—Java objects can be passed into the interpreter, and Jython objects can be passed out to Java. Not specialized objects—any object. All of this happens without having to incur the cost of customizing these objects for the sake of the other language. Additionally, embedding and initializing the interpreter, setting and fetching objects, and other related tasks are very intuitive and easy with Jython. This ease, Jython's advantages, and the seamless integration of Java and Jython make Jython and Java the pinnacle combination for multi-language applications.

The conspicuous organization of this chapter is two sections, one on embedding and the other on extending Jython.

Embedding Jython

Embedding Jython within Java has many uses but is particularly helpful when needing an interactive command interpreter, when creating diverse forms of output (report generation), when employing dynamic configuration, and when specific elements of an application require frequent changes. Because many others are mining additional uses for embedded Jython, this list will no doubt grow. Even ignoring the design motivations, there is cause for embedding Jython just to leverage its advantages. You get increased readability, rapid development, a short learning curve and more with only the addition of an embedded interpreter. The only downsides are that you incur the memory overhead of the interpreter and require additional classes in your application.

Three classes from the `org.python.util` package provide the necessary means to embed Jython in Java. These classes are `PythonInterpreter`, `InteractiveInterpreter`, and `InteractiveConsole`. The order in which they appear also reflects their hierarchy. Each class is a subclass of the previous in the list. Figure 9.1 shows the hierarchy of these classes along with the methods associated with that class.

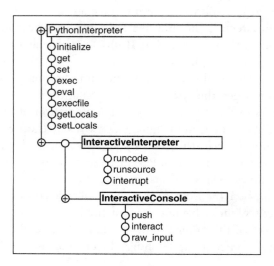

Figure 9.1   The interpreter hierarchy and associated methods.

PythonInterpreter

Embedding Jython most frequently equates to using an instance of the Java class `org.python.util.PythonInterpreter` within a Java application. The `jython.jar` file installed with Jython contains this class. Embedding this class within Java requires the addition of but two statements to Java code:

```
import org.python.util.PythonInterpreter;

PythonInterpreter interp = new PythonInterpreter;
```

The `interp` identifier in the preceding example, dubbed the interpreter instance, or just interpreter, is best thought of as a container, or bubble within Java. This analogy applies to most objects, but is especially valuable here because it enforces the distinction between using the Jython environment and using a Jython class. It is inside this bubble that the Jython interpreter runs. Java code surrounding the interpreter is unaware of what is within the bubble, and objects within the bubble are unaware of the outside world. Creating the bubble is extremely simple as noted in the two example lines above, so the concern is for steps preceding the instantiation of the interpreter and how to use it after its instantiation. The following sections detail how to initialize the Jython environment, how to instantiate the interpreter, how to use the interpreter instance, and how to pass Jython and Java object in and out of the embedded interpreter.

Initialization

The Jython environment depends on a number of properties. Properties such as the `python.home`, `python.path`, and `python.security.respectJavaAccessibility` are normally loaded from the registry file at startup or are set with command-line options. These properties and others ensure proper module loading and determine other aspects of Jython's behavior. Embedding Jython within Java allows opportunity for explicitly setting these properties before creating the interpreter object. Properties are set when you use the static initialize method in the `PythonInterpreter` class. This explicit control over properties, paths and settings is an advantage over using `jythonc`-compiled classes because you simply have more control when embedding.

Properties and Initialization

You should initialize the `PythonInterpreter` before creating an interpreter instance. The initialization is when Jython properties are set, when the registry file is processed, and when Jython's package manager searches as caches Java package information. The initialize step is meant literally because it uses the static initialize method in the `PythonInterpreter` class. Following is the signature for the initialize method:

```
public static void initialize(Properties preProperties,
                              Properties postProperties,
                              String[] argv)
```

The parameters can also be read as "old properties," "new properties," and "command-line arguments." The old, or `preProperties` are often set to `System.getProperties()`. When the `preProperties` are set to `System.getProperties()`, they contain those properties that were set with Java's `-D` command-line switch. The new, or `postProperties`, are most often set to a new `java.util.Properties` instance with some entries already added. The third and final argument of the initialize method is a `String` array. This string array becomes Jython's `sys.argv`.

If Jython is unable to find its home directory, it may not be able to read the registry file, or locate modules. You can ensure an embedded interpreter finds its home directory by setting the `python.home` property in the initialize method. To do so, you would use the following:

```
Properties props = new Properties();
props.put("python.home", "/usr/local/jython-2.1"); // *nix
//props.put("python.home", "c:\\jython2.1"); // windows
PythonInterpreter.initialize(System.getProperties(),
                             props, new String[0]);
```

Initializing the `PythonInterpreter` also processes Jython's registry file (if found). Settings within the registry file create a third set of properties. The three sets are old properties (from `System.getProperties()` in the above example), registry properties (those defined in the registry file), and the new properties that appear as the second argument to the initialize method ("props" in the preceding example). The order in which these properties appear in the previous sentence has significance. This order determines which property takes precedence when a given property is defined in multiple places. Old properties are loaded first, followed by registry properties, and finally new properties. This precedence means that registry properties override old properties, and that new properties override both registry and system properties.

Listing 9.1 is a Java class that embeds the `PythonInterpreter`. Not only does Listing 9.1 demonstrate the setting of properties and initializing the interpreter, but it also serves as a convenient base class for many of the examples in this chapter. A package called org.python.demo is used with Listing 9.1 and future Java listings to help organize examples. The `Embedding` class in the listing assumes that a property explicitly declared on the command-line with the `-D` option has the highest precedence, so it specifically sets command-line properties found in `System.getProperties()` that begin with the string `python` in the new properties, `postProps`. The `Embedding` class also sets the `python.home` property in the `sysProps` object, but only if it was not set on the command-line. This helps ensure that the interpreter finds and processes the registry file. In this scenario, the default `python.home` property has lowest priority, but that doesn't matter because it is usually not set in the registry. The registry properties load next. Then the new properties, altered to include those set with the `-D` switch, are set and override any previous values duplicate properties have.

Listing 9.1 **A Simple Embedded *PythonInterpreter***

```
// file: Embedding.java
package org.python.demo;

import java.util.Properties;
import org.python.util.PythonInterpreter;
import java.util.Enumeration;

public class Embedding {

    protected PythonInterpreter interp;

    public static void main(String[] args) {
        Embedding embed = new Embedding();
        embed.initInterpreter(args);
        embed.test();
    }

    protected void initInterpreter(String[] argv) {
        // Get preProperties postProperties, and System properties
        Properties postProps = new Properties();
        Properties sysProps = System.getProperties();

        // set default python.home property
        if (sysProps.getProperty("python.home")==null)
            sysProps.put("python.home", "c:\\jython 2.1a1");

        // put System properties (those set with -D) in postProps
        Enumeration e = sysProps.propertyNames();
        while ( e.hasMoreElements() ) {
            String name = (String)e.nextElement();
            if (name.startsWith("python."))
                postProps.put(name, System.getProperty(name));
        }

        // Here's the initialization step
        PythonInterpreter.initialize(sysProps, postProps, argv);
```

continues

Listing 9.1 **Continued**

```
        //instantiate- note that it is AFTER initialize
        interp = new PythonInterpreter();
    }

    public void test() {
        // Print system state values to confirm proper initialization
        interp.exec("import sys");
        interp.exec("print"); // Add empty line for clarity
        interp.exec("print 'sys.prefix=', sys.prefix");
        interp.exec("print 'sys.argv=', sys.argv");
        interp.exec("print 'sys.path=', sys.path");
        interp.exec("print 'sys.cachedir=', sys.cachedir");
        interp.exec("print"); // Another blank for clarity
    }
}
```

The test() method in Listing 9.1 is the method that many following example, will override. Within this method is where you will test the interpreter commands discussed in associated text. The test method in the preceding listing executes some Jython statements with the interpreter's exec method. The Jython statements import Jython's sys module, then use sys to print information confirming properties are set appropriately. The details of using the exec method appear later in the section, but for now it is sufficient to note the careful use of single and double quotations within each exec method.

Listing 9.1, and properties that use system paths in general, require special attention to make sure they comply with platform-specific rules for path and directory separators (such as ; and \\ for Windows and : and / for *nix). Also, note that Listing 9.1 assumes your python.home directory is C:\jython-2.1, and that you have sufficient permissions to use that directory. If that is not your python.home directory, change it to the proper value.

To compile the Embedding class in Listing 9.1, choose a working directory, and create the org/python/demo directories within it. Then place the Embedding.java file in the {working directory}/org/python/demo directory so the directory matches the package specified. Then from within your working directory, run the following command (replace / with \ for DOS):

```
javac -classpath /path/to/jython.jar org/python/demo/Embedding.java
```

The command to execute the Embedding class should look similar to the following. Remember to use paths specific to your platform:

```
java -classpath /path/to/jython.jar:. org.python.demo.Embedding
```

The following is a sample output from running the Embedding class:

```
sys.prefix= /usr/local/jython-2.1
sys.argv= []
sys.path= ['.', '/usr/local/jython-2.1/Lib']
sys.cachedir= /usr/local/jython-2.1/cachedir
```

The Embedding class supposedly uses properties set on the command line. Using a command line with -D switches added confirms correct property settings. The following demonstrates doing so on Windows. Note that the command is one line, but it wraps to occupy the first two lines below. Also, note that you must set the cachedir to a directory where you have sufficient privileges.

```
java -Dpython.cachedir="newcache" -Dpython.path="d:\devel\jython" -classpath
"c:\jython-2.1\jython.jar";. org.python.demo.Embedding
*sys-package-mgr*: processing new jar, 'C:\jython-2.1\jython.jar'
*sys-package-mgr*: processing new jar, 'C:\jdk1.3.1\jre\lib\rt.jar'
*sys-package-mgr*: processing new jar, 'C:\jdk1.3.1\jre\lib\i18n.jar'
*sys-package-mgr*: processing new jar, 'C:\jdk1.3.1\jre\lib\sunrsasign.jar'

sys.prefix= c:\jython-2.1
sys.argv= []
sys.path= ['.', 'c:\\jython-2.1\\Lib', 'd:\\devel\\jython']
sys.cachedir= c:\jython-2.1\newcache
```

You should see the caching messages if you do not already have a cache directory in the specified location. Searching for Java packages and caching the results obviously occurs when embedding Jython, just as it does when running the Jython program itself. In case timing matters in your applications, this caching occurs at initialization rather than when the PythonInterpreter is instantiated. Note that if you do not supply the system properties to the initialize method (the first parameter in Listing 9.1), the caching noted in the example above would not occur because the interpreter would not have the information required to find the jars.

Instantiating the Interpreter

Listing 9.1 already used the PythonInterpreter's empty constructor, but there are additional constructors that allow setting the namespace and system state of the interpreter. The PythonInterpreter class's three constructor signatures are as follows:

```
public PythonInterpreter()

public PythonInterpreter(PyObject dict)

public PythonInterpreter(PyObject dict, PySystemState systemState)
```

The first constructor is the intuitive, parameterless version. The second constructor accepts a `PyObject` as an argument. This `PyObject` becomes the interpreter's namespace; therefore, it is most frequently an `org.python.core.PyStringMap` object. A `PyDictionary` or another dictionary-like `PyObject` that implements some custom functionality would work as well, but unless there's reason to do otherwise, use a `PyStringMap`. Besides the potential for customizing the behavior of the namespace object, supplying the interpreter's namespace allows you to set objects in the interpreter's namespace before instantiating it, or store a namespace between script invocations. Setting objects in a `PyStringMap`, and then passing it to the `PythonInterpreter`'s constructor would look like this:

```
// the required imports
import org.python.core.*;
import org.python.util.PythonInterpreter;

// Assume the interpreter is already intitialized
PyStringMap dict = new PyStringMap();
dict.__setitem__("Name", new PyString("Strategy test"));
dict.__setitem__("Context", Py.java2py(new SomeContextClassOrBean()));
PythonInterpreter interp = new PythonInterpreter(dict);
```

Notice that using Jython objects within Java makes use of Jython's special methods described in Chapter 7, "Advanced Classes." In the preceding example, the `PyStringMap`'s `__setitem__` is used to set items in the namespace object. Java obviously does not automatically employ Jython's dynamic special methods (those with two leading and trailing underscores), so you must explicitly employ these special methods where appropriate when using Jython objects within Java.

The third constructor for the `PythonInterpreter` class allows you to set the namespace as well as the `PySystemState` object when you instantiate the interpreter. Later sections explain more about the `PySystemState` object, but for now it is enough to know that it is Jython's sys module in its Java persona. Using the `PySystemState` object to set the `sys.path` used by an interpreter would require the following lines:

```
PyStringMap dict = new PyStringMap();
dict.__setitem__("A", new PyInteger(1));
PySystemState sys = new PySystemState();
sys.path.append(new PyString("c:\\jython-2.1\\Lib"));
sys.path.append(new PyString("c:\\windows\\desktop"));
sys.path.append(new PyString("d:\\cvs"));

// instantiate with namespace and system state objects
interp = new PythonInterpreter(dict, sys);
```

If you embed multiple interpreters, they share the system state. This has implications for using a `PySystemState` with a constructor because even though the call looks isolated to the one interpreter instance being created, the system state of all embedded interpreters is changed when the `PySystemState` object is altered. The local namespace, however, is unique to each interpreter instance.

Setting Output and Error Streams

The `PythonInterpreter` instance has methods for setting the output stream and the error stream. These methods are `setOut` and `setErr`. Each of these methods accepts a single argument, but that argument may be a `java.io.OutputStream`, `java.io.Writer`, or even any `org.python.core.PyObject` that is a file-like object. Listing 9.2 makes use of the `setErr` method to redirect error messages to a file.

Listing 9.2 **Setting the Error Stream to a *FileWriter***

```
// file: ErrorRedir.java
package org.python.demo;

import org.python.demo.Embedding;
import java.io.*;

public class ErrorRedir extends Embedding {

    public static void main(String[] args) {
        ErrorRedir erd = new ErrorRedir();
        erd.initInterpreter(args);
        erd.test();
    }

    public void test() {
        // Redirect errors to a file
        try {
            interp.setErr(new FileWriter(new File("errors")));
        } catch (IOException e) {
            e.printStackTrace();
        }

        interp.exec("assert 0, 'This should end up in a file.'");
    }
}
```

After compiling Listing 9.2 with `javac -classpath c:\path\to\jython.jar;.`
`org\python\demo\ErrorRedir.java` and executing it with `java -cp`
`c:\path\to\jython.jar;. org.python.demo.ErrorRedir`, you should see only the
following message in the console:

```
Exception in thread "main"
```

The remaining traceback information appears in the file `errors` within your current working directory. Changing the error stream and the output stream to a network stream or other resource is also a likely scenario.

PySystemState

In Jython, the `sys` module contains information about the system state. Within Jython, you can view system state information by importing the `sys` module and printing variables within it. You can also change objects such as appending to `sys.path` or assigning new objects to the standard input, output and error objects. When you embed Jython, you can obviously use the `sys` object within the interpreter instance, but you can also use the `sys` module outside the interpreter. To use the `sys` module directory from Java, you must use its Java persona: `PySystemState`. Note that using methods from the `PythonInterpreter` class is the recommended API for embedding an interpreter. If an operation can be done with a `PythonInterpreter` method, that is how it should be done. However, the `PySystemState` object requires attention because it appears so frequently in Jython's code base, it contains methods that are very important to Jython's package manager (especially when embedding), and it is already familiar to users from using the `sys` module within Jython, making it an easy tool to use in Java as well.

What `import sys` is in Jython becomes the following in Java:

```
import org.python.core.*;
PySystemState sys = Py.getSystemState();
```

Because the `PySystemState` class and the `Py` class both appear in the `org.python.core` package, this package is first imported. After retrieving the `PySystemState` object with `Py.getSystemState()`, you can change the state inside the interpreter from Java code outside the interpreter. Listing 9.3 demonstrates how to append values to the `sys.path` variable by using the `PySystemState` object. Changes to the `sys.path` normally occur by setting the `python.path` property at initialization, or within Jython code such as the following:

```
import sys
sys.path.append("c:\\windows\\desktop")
```

This same operation can be done with the `PySystemState` object as demonstrated in Listing 9.3.

Listing 9.3 **Using the *sys* Module from Java**

```java
// file: SysState.java
package org.python.demo;

import org.python.demo.Embedding;
import org.python.core.*;

public class SysState extends Embedding {

    public static void main(String[] args) {
        SysState s = new SysState();
        s.initInterpreter(args);
        s.test();
    }

    public void test() {
        System.out.println("sys.path before changes to to sys:");
        interp.exec("import sys\n" +
                    "print sys.path\n" +
                    "print");

        // Get the system state and append to its path
        PySystemState sys = Py.getSystemState();
        sys.path.append(new PyString("c:\\windows\\desktop"));

        System.out.println("sys.path after changes to sys:");
        interp.exec("print sys.path");
    }
}
```

Compile the SysState class with the following command:

```
javac -classpath c:\path\to\jython.jar;. org.python.demo.SysState.java
```

The output from running the SysState class follows. Note that the command to execute the class is only one command (no returns) despite the fact that it wraps onto the second line in the example:

```
dos>\jdk1.3.1\bin\java -classpath "c:\jython-2.1\jy
thon.jar";. org.python.demo.SysState
The sys.path before changes to PySystemState:
['.', 'c:\\jython-2.1\\Lib', 'd:\\python20\\lib']

The sys.path after changes to PySystemState:
['.', 'c:\\jython-2.1\\Lib', 'd:\\python20\\lib', 'c:\\windows\\desktop']
```

The second time the example prints sys.path, the additional sys.path entry added through the PySystemState object appears. If you had embedded multiple interpreters, this change to the system state would have affected each of the interpreters.

Jython's `PySystemState` class (sys module) also contains three methods related to class loading: `add_package`, `add_classdir`, and `add_extdir`. These methods become important when embedding Jython because many Java applications will have their own classloaders. When an application's classloader differs from Jython's, Jython doesn't always properly recognize or find certain Java package. This creates situations where Jython needs help in identifying which Java classes it may import, and this is the reason for the three methods mentioned.

The `add_package` method places a specified Java package in Jython's package manager. If company A has an application with its own classloader, and embeds a Jython interpreter within it, the embedded interpreter might not properly identify Java packages such as `com.A.python` (assuming it exists). The interpreter would be unable to load classes within this package unless company A uses the `add_package` method to ensure proper package recognition, and thus loading. The following snippet demonstrates:

```
import org.python.core.*;
PySystemState sys = Py.getSystemState();
sys.add_package("com.A.python");
```

The `add_package` method does not import or load the package. The application's classloader does that work. The `add_package` method merely adds the package to the list of Java packages from which Jython may import classes.

The `add_classdir` and `add_extdir` methods are similar in that both add locations to the list where Jython searches for Java packages. The `add_classdir` method makes packages within a specified directory available. If you have a hierarchy of packages and classes beginning in the *nix directory `/usr/java/devel`, adding this tree to Jython's package manager is as follows:

```
import org.python.core.*;
PySystemState sys = Py.getSystemState();
sys.add_classdir("/usr/java/devel/");
```

The `add_extdir` method adds the contents of archives within a directory to the list of locations Jython searches for Java packages. If you store an application's required `jar` and `zip` files in the *nix directory `/usr/java/lib`, adding the contents of all these archives to Jython's package manager is as follows:

```
import org.python.core.*;
PySystemState sys = Py.getSystemState();
sys.add_extdir("/usr/java/lib/");
```

A good example of initializing the interpreter and employing the three `add_*` methods is the `org.python.util.PyServlet` class that comes with Jython. Listing 9.4 is an trimmed-down version of just the `init()` method in `PyServlet`, and within this method is where the interpreter is initialized and all the required Java packages are added to the package manager.

Listing 9.4 **Jython *PyServlet* Class**

```
public void init() {
    Properties props = new Properties();
    if (props.getProperty("python.home") == null &&
        System.getProperty("python.home") == null)
    {
        props.put("python.home", rootPath + "WEB-INF" +
                    File.separator + "lib");
    }

    PythonInterpreter.initialize(System.getProperties(),
                                    props, new String[0]);

    PySystemState sys = Py.getSystemState();
    sys.add_package("javax.servlet");
    sys.add_package("javax.servlet.http");
    sys.add_package("javax.servlet.jsp");
    sys.add_package("javax.servlet.jsp.tagext");

    sys.add_classdir(rootPath + "WEB-INF" +
                        File.separator + "classes");

    sys.add_extdir(rootPath + "WEB-INF" +
                    File.separator + "lib");
}
```

Remember that `add_package`, `add_classdir`, and `add_extdir` do not load anything. The application's classloader does the actual work and the `add_*` methods merely make additional Java packages available to import. These methods are available in Jython's sys module. This description of the `add_*` methods appears here because they are most frequently used when embedding, but there is no intent to imply they are restricted only to embedding Jython. You may call these methods from within an embedded Jython interpreter with `sys.add_*` (after importing sys), and you may have need to use such methods in Jython even when not embedding. Below is a small interactive interpreter session where the `sys.add_extdir` method is used to make all the packages within the jar files in a Tomcat web server's `lib` directory importable from Jython (Tomcat is a web server available from Apache's Jakarta project at `http://jakarta.apache.org`. More on Tomcat appears in Chapter 12, "Server-Side Web Programming"):

```
>>> import sys
>>> sys.add_extdir("c:\\web\\tomcat\\lib")
*sys-package-mgr*: processing new jar, 'C:\web\tomcat\lib\ant.jar'
*sys-package-mgr*: processing new jar, 'C:\web\tomcat\lib\jaxp.jar'
*sys-package-mgr*: processing new jar, 'C:\web\tomcat\lib\servlet.jar'
```

```
*sys-package-mgr*: processing new jar, 'C:\web\tomcat\lib\parser.jar'
*sys-package-mgr*: processing new jar, 'C:\web\tomcat\lib\webserver.jar'
*sys-package-mgr*: processing new jar, 'C:\web\tomcat\lib\jasper.jar'
*sys-package-mgr*: processing new jar, 'C:\web\tomcat\lib\zxJDBC.jar'
*sys-package-mgr*: processing new jar, 'C:\web\tomcat\lib\tools.jar'
*sys-package-mgr*: processing new jar, 'C:\web\tomcat\lib\ecs.jar'
*sys-package-mgr*: processing new jar, 'C:\web\tomcat\lib\jython.jar'
>>> from javax.servlet import http
>>> dir()
['__doc__', '__name__', 'http', 'sys']
```

We see that the http package was made available, but add_extdir makes only packages available, not classes. If the interactive session is continued with an attempt to import a class from ext_dirs, we see the following:

```
>>> from javax.servlet.http import HttpServlet
Traceback (innermost last):
  File "<console>", line 1, in ?
ImportError: cannot import name HttpServlet
```

Using the Interpreter

Running code within the interpreter requires the use of one of the interpreter's exec, execfile, or eval methods.

exec

The interpreter's exec method allows you to execute a string of Python code or a pre-compiled code object. When executing a string of Python code, you must use complete, syntactically correct statements in each call to exec. In other words, you cannot exec the first line of a function and complete the function definition in subsequent calls to exec. There are no static restrictions on the length of the string executed. The exec string can contain statements, assignments, functions, and anything normally found in a Jython script file. The exec method does not return any objects: The entire product of executing strings of Jython code remains inside the interpreter bubble.

Previous listings in this chapter demonstrate the exec method, but they only used simple statements. Compound statements are more difficult because of their need for special formatting. Formatting strings used in the exec method is part of the embedding craft, but the extent of the formatting is escaping double-quotes or replacing them with single-quotes, adding newlines where required, and using proper indention. In other words, if you print the string you intend to send to the exec method, it should look like a syntactically correct Jython script. Listing 9.5 shows a simple function definition in Jython, and then shows the same thing re-written to work in an embedded interpreter.

Listing 9.5 **Formatting Jython for the Interpreter's *exec* Method**

```
# in Jython
def movingAverage(datalist, sampleLen):
    """movingAverage(list, sampleLen) -> PyList"""
    add = lambda x, y: x + y
    return [reduce(add, datalist[x:x+10])/sampleLen
            for x in range(len(datalist) - sampleLen)]

import random
L = [random.randint(1,100) for x in range(100)]
print movingAverage(L, 10)

// in Java
interp.exec("def movingAverage(datalist, sampleLen):\n" +
            "    '''movingAverage(list, sampleLength) -> PyList'''\n" +
            "    add = lambda x, y: x + y\n" +
            "    return [reduce(add, datalist[x:x+10])/sampleLen " +
            "            for x in range(len(datalist)-sampleLen)]\n" +
            "import random\n" +
            "L = [random.randint(1,100) for x in range(100)]\n" +
            "print movingAverage(L, 10)");
```

The Java version in the preceding example concatenates strings to create a string equivalent to the Jython version. The stacked quotes, or placement of each line's starting quote directly below that on the previous line, eases reproduction of proper Jython indention. The quoting required by the Jython code uses single quotes to avoid confusion with the Java quotes. If double quotes are required within the string, make sure to escape them. The newline (\n) character must also be added where required in the exec string to comply with Jython's syntax.

An embedded interpreter often gets code from an external resource such as a network stream, portions of a file or archive resource. Some applications may dynamically generate code used by the interpreter. However, if the code is the entire contents of a file, the interpreter's execfile method fits the situation better than exec.

execfile

The PythonInterpreter's execfile method allows you to execute a file or an InputStream. There are three versions of the execfile method. The first accepts a single string argument that is the name of the file to execute. The second version accepts a single InputStream object. Because there is no name associated with an InputStream, error messages will show <iostream> in the file name location of error messages. The third version of the execfile method accepts an `InputStream` object and a `String` object to use in the file name field of error messages. The Java method signatures of these three methods are as follows:

```
public void execfile(String s)
public void execfile(java.io.InputStream s)
public void execfile(java.io.InputStream s, String name)
```

Listing 9.6 contains a class that implements all three `execfile` methods. Listing 9.6 requires a command-line argument to specify the file to execute. This argument is not an absolute path to that file, but is instead just the name of a file that actually resides in the user's home directory. The user's home directory is pre-pended to the file name to create the fully qualified path. If my home directory, `/home/rbill`, contains the file `exectest.py`, the command-line argument should be just `exectest.py`. If you are unsure of your home directory, run the following with Jython:

```
>>> import java
>>> print java.lang.System.getProperty("user.home")
```

Listing 9.6   **Demonstration of the *execfile* methods**

```java
// file: ExecFileTest.java
package org.python.demo;

import org.python.demo.Embedding;
import java.io.*;
import org.python.core.*;

public class ExecFileTest extends Embedding {

    public static void main(String[] args) {
        ExecFileTest eft = new ExecFileTest();
        eft.initInterpreter(args);
        eft.test();
    }

    public void test() {
        PySystemState sys = Py.getSystemState();
        if (sys.argv.__len__() == 0) {
            System.out.println("Missing filename.\n " +
                            "Usage: ExecFileTest filename");
            return;
        }

        String home = System.getProperty("user.home");
        String filename = home + File.separator +
                        sys.argv.__getitem__(0);

        // Using a file name with execfile
```

```
        interp.execfile(filename);

        // Using an InputStream with execfile
        try {
            FileInputStream s = new FileInputStream(filename);
            interp.execfile(s);
        } catch (FileNotFoundException e) {
            e.printStackTrace();
        }

        // Using an InputStream and a name with execfile
        try {
            FileInputStream s = new FileInputStream(filename);
            interp.execfile(s, sys.argv.__getitem__(0).toString());
        } catch (FileNotFoundException e) {
            e.printStackTrace();
        }
    }
}
```

You can compile the `ExecFileTest.java` file with the following command:

```
javac -classpath c:\path\to\jython.jar;.
org\python\demo\ExecFileTest.java
```

Create a Python file called `test.py` within your home directory which contains the line `print 'It worked.'`. You can execute this file three times in a row—one for each of the `execfile` methods, with the following command:

```
java -cp c:\path\to\jython.jar;. org.python.demo.ExecFileTest test.py
It worked.
It worked.
It worked.
```

eval

The `eval` method differs from the `exec` methods in three ways. The `eval` method always returns the results of the expression it evaluates as an `org.python.core.PyObject`—Jython's equivalent to Java's `java.lang.Object` class. In contrast, the return type of `exec` and `execfile` is always void. The interpreter's `eval` method currently only accepts strings of code. In contrast, the `exec` method accepts either a `String` or compiled code object. Finally, the interpreter's `eval` method only evaluates expressions while the `exec` methods execute any arbitrary Jython code.

Introducing the interpreter's `eval` method is also a good opportunity to introduce the use of Jython's built-in functions from within Java. The interpreter's `eval` method is a wrapper around Jython's built-in `eval` method. The interpreter's `eval` accepts a string of code, and in turn calls the built-in `eval` method with two small modifications. The first modification is that it adds the interpreter's local namespace as the second argument to the built-in `eval` method. The second modification is that it changes the code string from a `java.lang.String` to an `org.python.core.PyString` object. The following code shows an `eval` operation using both the interpreter's `eval` method and the built-in `eval` method:

```
// The interpreter's eval shortcut
interp.eval("1 or 0")  // The interpreter's eval()
// The built-in version
__builtin__.eval(new PyString("1 or 0"), interp.getLocals())
```

You can see the Jython's built-in functions are available through the class `org.python.core.__builtin__`. It is not just the `eval` method available this way; most of Jython's built-in functions are available through `__builtin__`. These built-in functions are usable directly from Java. Using Jython's built-in functions in Java often comes in handy when working with `PyObjects`. Because the `eval` method always returns a `PyObject`, you can experiment using built-in methods on the objects that `eval` returns.

The built-in `eval` function, and thus the interpreter's `eval` method, evaluates an expression. An `eval` expression has the same restrictions as `lambda` expressions: It cannot contain assignments or statements. Instead, the code string must only use functions, methods, data objects, literals, and those operators that do not perform a name-binding operation.

Listing 9.7 creates an interactive loop for evaluating expressions with an embedded interpreter. The listing subclasses the `Embedding` class discussed earlier in this chapter, so it inherits the interpreter initialization and instantiation from the `Embedding` class. The highlights of Listing 9.7 are that it confirms how the `eval` method returns a `PyObject`, and it shows how to use the built-in function `type()` on that object. The command loop in the `EvalTest` class also gives an opportunity to examine expressions.

Listing 9.7   **An *eval* Loop**

```
// file: EvalTest.java
package org.python.demo;

import org.python.demo.Embedding;
import java.io.*;
import org.python.core.*;

public class EvalTest extends Embedding {
    private static BufferedReader terminal;

    public static void main(String[] args) {
```

```
        EvalTest et = new EvalTest();
        et.initInterpreter(args);
        et.test();
    }

    public void test() {
        System.out.println("Enter strings to evaluate at the prompt");
        interact("eval> ");
     }

    public void interact(String prompt) {
        terminal = new BufferedReader(new InputStreamReader(System.in));
        System.out.println("Enter \"exit\" to quit.");

        String codeString = "";
        while (true) {
            System.out.print(prompt);
            try {
                codeString = terminal.readLine();
                if (codeString.compareTo("exit")==0) System.exit(0);
                processInput(codeString);
            } catch (IOException e) {
                e.printStackTrace();
            }
        }
    }

    public void processInput(String input) {
        PyObject o = interp.eval(input);
        System.out.println("Results is of type " +
                            __builtin__.type(o));
        System.out.println(o);
    }
}
```

Compile with the EvalTest class with the following:

```
javac -classpath c:\path\to\jython.jar;. org\python\demo\EvalTest.java
```

Execute the EvalTest class with the following:

```
java -cp c:\path\to\jython.jar;. org.python.demo.EvalTest
```

Following is sample output from running the EvalTest class:

```
Enter strings to evaluate at the prompt
Enter "exit" to quit.
eval> 0 or 10
Results is of type <jclass org.python.core.PyInteger at 6851381>
10
eval> 1 and "A string"
Results is of type <jclass org.python.core.PyString at 7739053>
```

```
A string
eval> [x for x in range(2,37) if 37%x == 0] == []
Results is of type <jclass org.python.core.PyInteger at 6851381>
1
eval> a = 10  # Assignments are not allowed
Exception in thread "main" Traceback (innermost last):
  (no code object) at line 0
  File "<string>", line 1
        a = 10  # Assignments are not allowed
            ^
SyntaxError: invalid syntax
```

Compiling Code Object for Later Use

Calling the `exec` and `eval` methods in the Jython interpreter with strings of code causes the interpreter to first compile, and then to execute that code. The compiling step takes time; therefore, if an application has large strings of Jython code, or code that is used multiple times, it may benefit from compiling this code outside of time-critical sections of the application. Maybe you have a statistics application that cycles through many different data sets but applies the same Jython code to each. Rather than calling `exec` or `eval` with a string of Jython code each iterations, it is better to compile that code before the loop, maybe even compile it at startup and squirrel away the compiled code objects for later use. Doing this requires Jython's built-in `compile` function.

Using Jython's built-in `compile` function from within Java to create a compiled code object involves three steps: import required classes, create a `java.lang.String`, and compile the `String` into a code (`PyCode`) object. The import must include the `__builtin__` and `PyCode` classes found in the `org.python.core` package. Accessing Jython's built-in functions occurs through the Java class `org.python.core.__builtin__`. The `compile` function requires a `java.lang.String` object as an argument, and the `compile` function returns an `org.python.core.PyCode` object. You will most often see `import org.python.core.*` used to cover the import requirements. The `compile` function returns a `PyCode` object, and this is the compiled object desired. You may execute or evaluate (depending on the third argument given to the `compile` function) this object at future times without incurring the compile cost. Here are the lines that create a `PyCode` object for use with the `exec` method:

```
// Import required classes (PyCode and __builtin__)
import org.python.core.*;

// Create a java.lang.String
String s = "print 'Hello World'";
```

```
// compile with "<>" for the file-name, and "exec" for type of object
PyCode code = __builtin__.compile(s, "<>", "exec");

// exec with interpreter. Note: no return object
interp.exec(code);
```

The built-in `compile` function requires three arguments: the `PyString` of code, the file name (used in error messages), and the mode. The mode may be `exec`, `eval`, or `single` if it is just a single statement. Because the `compile` statement in the example above creates a code object with the `exec` mode, you can pass that object to the embedded interpreter's `exec` method. The embedded interpreter's `exec` method works with code objects as well as strings. The interpreter's `eval` method, however, works only with strings. This is because it is easy enough to use the built-in `eval` to execute a compiled code object. To use the built-in `eval` with a compiled code object, call the `__builtin__.eval` method, and include the interpreter's namespace as the second argument. The following demonstrates this:

```
import org.python.core.*;
String s = "1 and 0 or 10";
PyCode code = __builtin__.compile(s, "<>", "eval");

// Fetch the interpreter's local namespace
PyCode locals = interp.getLocals();

// use __builtin__.eval with interp's locals
PyObject o = __builtin__.eval(code, locals);
```

The preceding lines are often shortened to the following:

```
import org.python.core.*;
PyCode code = __builtin__.compile("1 and 0 or 10", "<>", "eval");
PyObject o = __builtin__.eval(code, interp.getLocals());
```

Handling Exceptions in the Interpreter

What happens if something goes wrong in the interpreter? The answer is that the interpreter raises the exception `org.python.core.PyException`. If Jython's open function failed to open a file, the Java code would not get an `IOError` exception as Jython does, but would instead get a `PyException`. The following shows a try/except statement in Jython and what it looks like if you try to move the exception handling into Java code surrounding the embedded interpreter:

```
# in Jython
try:
    f = open("SomeNonExistingFile")
except IOError:
```

```
        e, i, tb = sys.exc_info()
        print e, "\n", tb.dumpStack()

    // in Java
    try {
        interp.exec("f = open('SomeNonExistingFile')");
    } catch (PyException e) {
        e.printStackTrace();
    }
```

The `PyException` stack trace would include the information about the actual
Jython exception, but it would not aid in discriminating the type of Jython
exception in the `catch` clause. Even if you use a Java object within the interpreter that raises a Java exception, the Jython wrapping around it turns the
exception into a `PyException`. Trapping a specific Jython exception in a Java
catch clause is not possible; therefore, you must a use a `try`/`except` statements
within the Jython interpreter object, avoid Jython exceptions by negotiating
errors in surrounding Java code, or you must discern the actual exception type
within Java's catch block by using `Py.matchException`.

    Suppose you have a command loop and need to catch only an `IOException`
within it. Just catching the `PyException` within Java doesn't allow that speci-
ficity, so you could instead use a `try`/`except` within the interpreter like so:

```
    interp.exec("try:\n" +
        "    _file = open(" + filename + ")\n" +
        "except:\n" +
        "    print 'File not found. Try again.');
```

Alternately, you could negotiate error trapping within the Java code and later
use objects, or pass objects into the interpreter, that have been verified. The
following example assumes again that there is a command loop in which
someone enters a file name, additionally, the `FileNotFoundException` or Jython's
`IOError` needs to be avoided so that the command loop continues. This example first tests the file before opening it in the interpreter. This example assumes
that a readable file is safe to open from within the interpreter:

```
        File file = new File(filename);
        if (file.canRead()!=true) {
            System.out.println("File not found. Try again.");
            break;
        }
        // File was found and is readable- safe to open.
        interp.exec("file = open(" + filename + ")");
```

The `org.python.core.Py` class contains the function `matchException` and Jython's
exception objects; and using the `Py.matchException` function to compare a
`PyException` to specific Jython exceptions allows you to discern specific Jython

exceptions within a catch clause's associated block of code. The
Py.matchException function takes a PyException as the first argument, a PyObject
that is a Jython exception (such as Py.IOError) as the second argument, and
returns a Boolean value indicating if the PyException is of the specific Jython
exception type. Suppose you wrap an interpreter's exec statement in a
try/catch statement like so:

```
try {
    interp.exec("f = open('SomeNonExistingFile')");
} catch (PyException e) {
    //fill in later
}
```

Then, you can add tests for specific Jython exception like this:

```
try {
    interp.exec("f = open('SomeNonExistingFile')");
} catch (PyException e) {
    if (Py.matchException(e, Py.AttributeError)) {
        //handle Jython's AttributeError here
    } else if (Py.matchException(e, Py.IOError)) {
        //handle Jython's IOError here
    }
}
```

The *set* and *get* Methods

The PythonInterpreter's get and set methods respectively return or set objects
in the interpreter's local namespace. It's worth mentioning, for the sake of
foreshadowing the getLocals and setLocals methods, that this namespace is a
PyStringMap object identified as locals within the interpreter. The bi-direc-
tional mobility that objects have between Jython and Java with the get and set
methods reintroduces type conversions of data objects. If you set a
java.lang.Integer object in the interpreter, does it remain a java.lang.Integer?
The short answer is no, but the reason for the answer lies in the following sections. The purpose of the following sections is to show how to set objects in
the interpreter, how to get objects from the interpreter, and to clarify what
happens to the type of such objects when they traverse the interpreter's
boundary.

set

The `PythonInterpreter` class has two `set` methods that allow interpreter instances to bind an identifier (`name`) within the interpreter to an object originating outside the interpreter. The signatures for these two methods are as follows:

```
public void set(String name, Object value)

public void set(String name, PyObject value)
```

Both methods accept a `java.lang.String` object for the name (first parameter), but their second parameter differs. The second parameter is the actual object bound to the specified name. If this object is a Java Object (the first of the methods listed previously), the interpreter converts that object to an appropriate Jython type. If this object is a `PyObject`, then the interpreter places it directly in the namespace dictionary without modification. The following shows how to set some simple objects in the embedded interpreter with the set method:

```
interp.set("S", "String literals becomes a PyStrings in the interp");
interp.set("V", java.util.Vector()); //V becomes a PyInstance type
```

Strings and Java instances are easy, but what about the primitive types? A Java int is not a `java.lang.Object`. The following two lines are both errors:

```
interp.set("I", 1);

interp.set("C", 'c');
```

These types require the use of their `java.lang` counterparts. Revising the preceding two lines to use the `java.lang` classes looks like this:

```
interp.set("I", new Integer(1));

interp.set("C", new Character('c'));
```

Part of the logic of the set method is that it converts Java objects to appropriate `PyObjects`. The section on "Java types" in Chapter 2, "Operators, Types, and Built-In Functions," describes how Jython converts certain types of objects. The example of setting a variable to a string earlier in this section makes note of this type conversion. A string object becomes a `PyString` when set in the interpreter. A `java.lang.Integer` becomes a `PyInteger`, a `java.lang.Long` becomes a `PyLong`, and so on, according to Jython's rules for type conversion.

get

The `PythonInterpreter`'s get method retrieves an object from the interpreter. There are two method signatures for the get method, and they are as follows:

```
public PyObject get(String name)

public Object get(String name, Class javaclass)
```

The name parameter designates a key in the interpreter's namespace mapping object (`locals`), and the return value of the get methods is the value associated with that specified key. The first get method requires only the name parameter, and returns a `PyObject`. The second get method, however, has an additional parameter to specify the class of the object returned.

The automatic type conversion of Java objects in the interpreter's set method is not reciprocal in the get method. To retrieve a Java object instead of a `PyObject` with the get method, you must specify the Java class you wish returned and cast it to the desired object. To retrieve a `java.lang.String` object with the get method, you would use this:

```
interp.set("myStringObject", "A string");

String s = (String)interp.get("myStringObject", String.class);
```

The return value is an object, so it must be cast if you are assigning the results to a less generic type. Also, remember that the second parameter must be a class; a string describing the class is insufficient. You can use `Classname.class` as was done previously, or `Objectname.getClass()`:

```
interp.set("myStringObject", "A string");
String s = (String)interp.get("myStringObject", String.class);
```

Listing 9.8 demonstrates both the set and get methods. What the listing does is create some Java objects, uses set to place them in the interpreter, and then uses get to retrieve the objects back in Java. The object's class is printed at each step—in Java, in Jython, and back in Java, so that it produces a table detailing what automatic type conversions the interpreter applied. Without any command-line arguments, the `TypeTest` class uses the generic, single-argument get method. When the user specifies the command-line option `symmetrical`, the `TypeTest` class applies the two-parameter get method to convert each object back to its original class.

Listing 9.8 **Type Converter**

```
// file: TypeTest.java
package org.python.demo;

import org.python.demo.Embedding;
import org.python.core.*;
import java.util.Vector;

public class TypeTest extends Embedding {
    private boolean simple = true;

    public TypeTest( ) { ; }

    public static void main(String[] args) {
        TypeTest tt = new TypeTest();
        tt.initInterpreter(args);
        tt.test();
    }

    public void test() {
        String codeString;
        Object[] jTypes = {"A string", new Short("1"), new Integer(3),
            new Long(10), new Float(3.14), new Double(299792.458),
            new Boolean(true), new int[] {1,2,3,4,5}, new Vector(),
            new PyInteger(1), new Character('c')};

        interp.exec("print 'In Java'.ljust(20), " +
                    "'In Jython'.ljust(20), " +
                    "'Back in Java'");
        interp.exec("print '-------'.ljust(20), " +
                    "'---------'.ljust(20), " +
                    "'------------'");

        // get first command-line argument- argv[0]
        PyObject argv = Py.getSystemState().argv;
        if (argv.__len__() > 0) {
            String option = argv.__getitem__(0).toString();
            if (option.compareTo("symmetrical")==0) simple = false;
        }

        for ( int i=0; i < jTypes.length; i++ ) {
            showConversion(jTypes[i]);
        }
    }

    public void showConversion(Object o) {
        interp.set("testObject", o);
        interp.set("o", o.getClass().toString());
        String newClass = null;

        if (simple) {
            newClass = interp.get("testObject").getClass().toString();
        } else {
```

```
            newClass = interp.get("testObject",
                            o.getClass()).getClass().toString();
        }
        interp.set("n", newClass); // n for newJavaClass
        interp.exec("pyClass = str(testObject.__class__) \n" +
                "print o[o.rfind('.') + 1:].ljust(20), " +
                "pyClass[pyClass.rfind('.') + 1:].ljust(20), " +
                "n[n.rfind('.') + 1:]");
    }
}
```

Compile the TypeTest class in Listing 9.8 with the following command:

```
javac -classpath c:\path\to\jython.jar;. org\python\demo\TypeTest.java
```

Running the TypeTest class without a command-line argument produces the following:

```
dos>java -classpath "c:\jython-2.1\jython.jar";. or
g.python.demo.TypeTest
```

In Java	In Jython	Back in Java
String	PyString	PyString
Short	PyInteger	PyInteger
Integer	PyInteger	PyInteger
Long	PyLong	PyLong
Float	PyFloat	PyFloat
Double	PyFloat	PyFloat
Boolean	PyInteger	PyInteger
class [I	PyArray	PyArray
Vector	Vector	PyJavaInstance
PyInteger	PyInteger	PyInteger
Character	PyString	PyString

You can see from the results that the interpreter's automatic conversion is one way. Adding the symmetrical option to the command will show what happens when you try to convert each type back to its original Java class.

```
C:\WINDOWS\Desktop\ch9examples>java -classpath "c:\jython-2.1\jython.jar";.
org.python.demo.TypeTest symmetrical
```

In Java	In Jython	Back in Java
String	PyString	String
Short	PyInteger	Short
Integer	PyInteger	Integer
Long	PyLong	Long
Float	PyFloat	Float
Double	PyFloat	Double
Boolean	PyInteger	Boolean
class [I	PyArray	class [I
Vector	Vector	Vector
PyInteger	PyInteger	PyInteger
Character	PyString	Character

There is also another means of converting Py* objects into Java objects, which are used more frequently. This is the __tojava__ method, which appears in the following section.

__tojava__

Instances of Jython classes (PyObjects) have a special method called __tojava__. The __tojava__ method requires a Java class as a parameter, and returns the instance coerced into the requested Java class. If the coercion is not possible, the method returns a Py.NoConversion object. The following lines show converting PyString to a java.lang.String object:

```
interp.set("A = 'A test string'");
PyObject po = interp.get("A");
String MyString = (String)po.__tojava__(String.class);
```

The preceding example assumes that __tojava__ is successful. The __tojava__ method would instead return the Py.NoConversion object if it failed to convert the object into an instance of the String class. The Py.NoConversion value would raise a ClassCastException because of the (String) cast. Handling the exception means either wrapping the cast in a try/except, or testing for the Py.NoConversion object before casting. Listing 9.9 chooses to test for the Py.NoConversion object. The Convert class in this listing is another subclass of the Embedding class. The test() method in this case walks through the getting, converting, and casting of a PyInteger object into a java.lang.Character. The conversion fails in this case; testing for Py.NoConversion before casting as a Character prevents ClassCastException.

Listing 9.9 **Testing for *Py.NoConversion* with __tojava__**

```
// file: Convert.java
package org.python.demo;

import org.python.demo.Embedding;
import org.python.core.*;

public class Convert extends Embedding {
    public Convert() { ; }

    public static void main(String[] args) {
        Convert c = new Convert();
        c.initInterpreter(args);
        c.test();
    }

    public void test() {
        // Set an identifier in the interpreter
```

```
    interp.exec("test = 'A'");

    // Get object out of interpreter as PyObject
    PyObject retrievedObject = interp.get("test");

    // Convert PyObject to instance of desired Class
    Object myObject = retrievedObject.__tojava__(Character.class);

    // See if conversion failed- meaning Py.NoConversion returned
    if (myObject == Py.NoConversion) {
        System.out.println("Unable to convert.");
    } else {
        Character myChar = (Character)myObject;
        System.out.println("The Character is: " + myChar);
    }
  }
}
```

Converting user-defined, Jython classes into Java objects with the __tojava__ method allows classes written in Jython to be used where certain Java classes are required. Consider an application that uses the Java class A, and that you require a great number of unique versions of this class. You could write these classes in Jython as subclasses of A, and convert them to objects of class A when required by certain method signatures. This may allow rapid development of these required classes. Listings 9.10, 9.11, and 9.12 form a trio of files that employ such a process. The Report class in Listing 9.10 is meant to simulate a report generation tool. Admittedly the pairing down of the report generation portion to avoid distracting from the __tojava__ focus leaves a lot to the imagination, but the pattern is an effective venue for Jython scripts. The Report class loads a Jython script specified on the command line. Listing 9.12 contains a Jython script that handles the details of a specific report. This allows a multitude of reports formats to exist without having to recompile the Report class. The trick to using scripts this way is to have them inherit from a Java class. Listing 9.11 is a simple abstract ReportSpec class that serves as an appropriate superclass for the Jython script in Listing 9.12.

Listing 9.10   Using __*tojava*__ for Report Generator

```
// file: Report.java
package org.python.demo.reports;

import org.python.demo.Embedding;
import org.python.demo.reports.ReportSpec;
import java.io.*;
import org.python.core.*;
```

continues

Listing 9.10 **Continued**

```java
public class Report extends Embedding {

    public static void main(String[] args) {
        Report rpt = new Report();
        rpt.initInterpreter(args);
        try {
            rpt.generateReport();
        } catch (Exception e) {
            e.printStackTrace();
        }
    }

    public void generateReport() throws FileNotFoundException, PyException {
        String fileName;
        ReportSpec rs = null;

        // Check #1- user supplied command-line arg
        PySystemState sys = Py.getSystemState();
        if (sys.argv.__len__() == 0) {
            System.out.println("Missing filename.\n " +
                               "Usage: 'Report' filename");
            return;
        } else {
            fileName = sys.argv.__getitem__(0).toString();
        }

        // Check #2- Command-line arg is in fact a *.py file
        if (new File(fileName).isFile() != true)
            throw new FileNotFoundException(fileName);
        if (fileName.endsWith(".py") != true)
            throw new PyException(
                new PyString(fileName + " is not a *.py file"));
        try {
            rs = getReportSpecInstance(fileName);
        } catch (InstantiationException e) {
            e.printStackTrace();
        }
        rs.fillTitle();
        rs.fillHeadings();
        while (rs.fillRow()) {}
    }

    protected ReportSpec getReportSpecInstance(String fileName)
    throws InstantiationException
    {
        String className;

        // Exec the file
        interp.execfile(fileName);
```

```
        // Get the name of the file without path and extension.
        // This should be the name of the class within the file
        int start = fileName.lastIndexOf(File.separator);
        if (start < 0)
            start = 0;
        else
            start++;
        className = fileName.substring(start, fileName.length() - 3);
        PyObject reportSpecClass = interp.get(className);
        if (reportSpecClass == null)
            throw new InstantiationException(
                "No ReportSpec Class named " + className +
                "exists in " + fileName);
        PyObject m_args = (PyObject) new PyInteger(70);
        PyObject reportSpecInstance = reportSpecClass.__call__(m_args);
        ReportSpec rs =
            (ReportSpec)reportSpecInstance.__tojava__(ReportSpec.class);
        if (rs == Py.NoConversion)
            throw new InstantiationException(
                "Unable to create a ReportSpec instance from " +
                className);
        return rs;
    }
}
```

Listing 9.11 **A Java Class Jython Report Scripts Subclass**

```
// file: ReportSpec.java
package org.python.demo.reports;

public abstract class ReportSpec extends Object {
    public abstract String fillTitle();
    public abstract void fillHeadings();
    public abstract boolean fillRow();
}
```

Listing 9.12 **The Jython Report Generation Script**

```
# file: ReportTest.py
from org.python.demo.reports import ReportSpec

class ReportTest(ReportSpec):
    def __init__(self, reportWidth):
        # "@sig public ReportTest(int reportWidth)"
        # plug in data (a database in a real implementation)
        self.width = reportWidth
```

continues

Listing 9.12   **Continued**

```
        self.data = [ [1,2,3],
                      [4,5,6],
                      [7,8,9] ]
        self.pad = reportWidth/(len(self.data[0]) - 1)

    def fillTitle(self):
        print "Test of Report Generator".center(self.width)

    def fillHeadings(self):
        """Prints column headings."""
        # This would be database metadata in a real implementation
        for x in ["A", "B", "C"]:
            print x.ljust(self.pad - 1),
        print

    def fillRow(self):
        if not self.data:
            return 0
        row = self.data.pop()
        for x in row:
            print str(x).ljust(self.pad - 1),
        print
        return 1
```

The abstract Java class that the report scripts must inherit from is the abstract ReportSpec class from Listing 9.11. The Jython script merely needs to meet the protocol specifications of the required superclass, as the ReportTest.py class in Listing 9.12 does. Notice that the class is retrieved from the interpreter, not the instance. It is just as plausible to create the instance in the interpreter and get it; however, in a long-lived process, it may be a bit easier to minimize the interpreter's namespace pollution. Note that the creation of the instance uses the __call__() method on the class object. Revisit Chapter 7, "Advanced Classes," for the importance of the __call__ method for callable Jython objects.

Compile the Report class in Listing 9.10 and the ReportSpec class from Listing 9.11 with the following commands:

```
javac -classpath \path\to\jython.jar;.
org\python\demo\reports\Report.java

javac -classpath \path\to\jython.jar;.
org\python\demo\reports\ReportSpec.java
```

Running the `Report` class with Listing 9.12 as the command-line argument produces the following:

```
>java -classpath "c:\jython-2.1\jython.jar";.
org.python.demo.reports.Report ReportTest.py
                      Test of Report Generator
  A                         B                         C

  7                         8                         9

  4                         5                         6

  1                         2                         3
```

The *getLocals* and *setLocals* Methods

`Locals` means the interpreter's local namespace. The `set` and `get` methods described above actually bind a key in the locals mapping object, or retrieve a key's associated object. The `setLocals` and `getLocals` methods instead allow you to set or retrieve the entire namespace mapping object. There are various reasons for doing so, but the obvious one is maintaining isolated namespaces for multiple scripts. If module A and module B execute sequentially in the interpreter, and both define the same module-global variable, then module B redefined that variable. This will likely have an unfortunate consequence if module A executes again. Fetching and restoring the `locals` object eliminates this risk of incidental side effect.

The `getLocals` and `setLocals` methods respectively return or require a dictionary-like `PyObject`. This is usually an `org.python.core.PyStringMap` object. The method signatures for the `getLocals` and `setLocals` methods are as follows.

```
public PyObject getLocals()

public void setLocals(PyObject d)
```

Listing 9.13 is yet another subclass of the earlier `Embedding` example. The class in this listing sets a test value into a `PyStringMap` object which it sets in the interpreter. Within the interpreter, that test value is printed to confirm it's there, and then another test value is set in the interpreter. The `getLocals` method retrieves the locals and prints it to confirm the both identifiers exist in it.

Listing 9.13 **Using *setLocals* and *getLocals***

```
// file: LocalsTest.java
package org.python.demo;
```

continues

Listing 9.13 **Continued**

```
import org.python.demo.Embedding;
import org.python.core.*;

public class LocalsTest extends Embedding {
    public LocalsTest() { ; }

    public static void main(String[] args) {
        LocalsTest L = new LocalsTest();
        L.initInterpreter(args);
        L.test();
    }

    public void test() {
        PyStringMap locals = new PyStringMap();
        locals.__setitem__("Test1", new PyString("A test string"));
        interp.setLocals(locals);
        interp.exec("print Test1");
        interp.exec("Test2 = 'Another teststring'");
        PyObject dict = interp.getLocals();
        System.out.println(dict);
    }
}

Compile with javac -classpath c:\path\to\jython.jar;.
org\python\demo\LocalsTest.java
```

The output from running Listing 9.13 is as follows:

```
dos>java -cp "c:\jython\jython.jar";. org.python.demo.LocalsTest
A test string
{'Test2': 'Another teststring', 'Test1': 'A test string'}
```

imp and the Top-Level Script

Many Jython modules make use of the top-level script environment to conditionally run a main section of code. While this description may not ring a bell, the related statement should be extremely familiar:

```
if __name__ == '__main__':
```

A script employs this to run specific code when the script is the main script. The __name__ identifier is automatic in Jython, but when embedding Jython, you must explicitly add this to the interpreter if you require a script to execute the code associated with the __name__ == '__main__' condition. Listing 9.14 is another subclass of the Embedding class, which executes a file specified on the command line. This example, however, adds the __main__ so that __name__ == '__main__' is true.

Listing 9.14   **Setting __*name*__ == '__*main*__'**

```
// file: TopLevelScript.java
package org.python.demo;

import org.python.demo.Embedding;
import java.io.*;
import org.python.core.*;

public class TopLevelScript extends Embedding {

    public static void main(String[] args) {
        TopLevelScript tls = new TopLevelScript();
        tls.initInterpreter(args);
        tls.test();
    }

    public void test() {
        PySystemState sys = Py.getSystemState();
        if (sys.argv.__len__() == 0) {
            System.out.println("Missing filename.\n " +
                               "Usage: TopLevelScript filename");
            return;
        }
        String filename = sys.argv.__getitem__(0).toString();

        // Set __name__
        PyModule mod = imp.addModule("__main__");
        interp.setLocals(mod.__dict__);

        // Using a file name with execfile
        interp.execfile(filename);
    }
}

Compile with javac -classpath \path\to\jython.jar
org\python\demo\TopLevelScript.java
```

You can use a minimal Jython module like the following to test the __name__
setting:

```
# file: mainname.py
if __name__ == '__main__':
    print "It worked."
```

The command and output from running this is as follows:

```
dos> java -classpath \path\to\jython.jar;. ort.python.demo.TopLevelScript
mainname.py
It worked.
```

The same effect could be achieved by creating a `PyStringMap` with the `__name__` key set to `__main__`:

```
// Set __name__
PyStringMap dict = new PyStringMap();
dict.__setitem__("__name__", new PyString("__main__"));
interp.setLocals(dict);
```

Listing 9.14 instead uses the `imp.addModule` method because Jython does it this way, and because it introduces the `imp` class.

The `imp` class implements Jython's import facility. The `addModule` method used in Listing 9.14 loads a module, and then returns that `PyModule` object. It also places the module name in the list of imported modules: `sys.modules`. More details about the `imp` class appear in the later section "Extending Jython."

Embedding the *InteractiveInterpreter*

The `InteractiveInterpreter` is a subclass of `PythonInterpreter`. The `InteractiveInterpreter` provides the `runcode`, `runsource`, and `interrupt` methods for a higher level of interaction. The two behaviors that are important in this class are exception trapping and management of statement completeness. If an exception occurs in the `runcode` or `runsource` methods, it is trapped within the methods so that it is not fatal, thus allowing interaction to continue. The interpreter does print such exceptions, however, so that the user is aware of what happened. Additionally, the `runsource` method returns a Boolean value that indicates the completeness of the source string. This helps determine which prompt to print and when to reset the statement buffer.

Table 9.1 shows the method signatures and use of each of the `InteractiveInterpreter`'s methods.

Table 9.1   *InteractiveInterpreter* **Methods**

Method Signature	Summary
`public InteractiveInterpreter()` `public InteractiveInterpreter (PyObject locals)`	These are the constructors for the `InteractiveInterpreter` class. The second constructor accepts a `PyStringMap` object just like the `PythonInterpreter`'s one-argument constructor.

Table 9.1 *InteractiveInterpreter* **Methods**

Method Signature	Summary
| ```
public Boolean
    runsource(String source)
public Booleanstring.
runsource(String source,
        String filename)
``` | The runsource method tries to compile and execute a code It also displays exception information, but does not propagate exceptions. The return values are as follows: |
| ```
public Boolean
    runsource(String source,
            String filename,
            String symbol)
``` | Success -> false<br><br>Exception occurred -> false<br><br>Incomplete statement -> true<br><br>The true when incomplete is what allows easy control of the loop gathering user input. The second and third parameters are the same as for the built-in compile method. |
| ```
public void
    runcode(PyObject code)
``` | The runcode method executes a code object and displays any exception that occurred during the execution. Note that the exception is only displayed; it does not propagate. |
| ```
public void
    showexception(PyException exc)
``` | Writes exception information to sys.stderr. This is mostly for internal uses. |
| ```
public void write(String data)
``` | This writes a string to sys.stderr. This is mostly for internal uses. |
| ```
public void
    interrupt(ThreadState ts)
    throws InterruptedException
``` | The interrupt method pauses the code to insert an exception in a thread-friendly way. |

The following loop leverages the runsource return value to loop until the user has entered a syntactically complete statement:

```
while (interp.runsource(codeString)) {
    System.out.print(ps2);
    codeString += "\n" + terminal.readLine();
}
```

Listing 9.15 demonstrates both the special handling of exceptions and the return value from the runsource method. Note that the initialize step is still required. The initialize method is the same method used when embedding a PythonInterpreter because that is the InteractiveInterpreter's superclass.

Listing 9.15   **Embedding the *InteractiveInterpreter***

```java
// file: InteractiveEmbedding.java
package org.python.demo;

import org.python.demo.Embedding;
import org.python.util.InteractiveInterpreter;
import java.util.Properties;
import java.io.*;

public class InteractiveEmbedding extends Embedding {

    protected InteractiveInterpreter interp;

    public static void main(String[] args) {
        InteractiveEmbedding ie = new InteractiveEmbedding();
        ie.initInterpreter(args);
        ie.test();
        ie.interact();
    }

    public void initInterpreter(String[] argv) {
        // set Properties
        if (System.getProperty("python.home") == null)
            System.setProperty("python.home", "c:\\jython-2.1");

        // no postProps, all properties but python.home put in registry file
        InteractiveInterpreter.initialize(System.getProperties(), null, argv);

        //instantiate- note that it is AFTER initialize
        interp = new InteractiveInterpreter();
    }

    public void test() {
        interp.runsource("print 'this is a syntax error");
        interp.runsource("print 'This is not'");
    }

    public void interact() {
        String ps1 = ">>>";
        String ps2 = "...";
        BufferedReader terminal = new BufferedReader(
            new InputStreamReader(System.in));
        interp.write("Enter \"exit\" to quit.");

        String codeString = "";
        interp.write("\n");
        while (true) {
            interp.write(ps1);
            try {
```

```
            codeString = terminal.readLine();
        } catch (IOException e) {
            e.printStackTrace();
        }
        if (codeString.compareTo("exit")==0) System.exit(0);

        while (interp.runsource(codeString)) {
            interp.write(ps2);
            try {
                codeString += "\n" + terminal.readLine();
            } catch (IOException e) {
                e.printStackTrace();
            }
        }
    }
}
}
```

Listing 9.15 initializes the interpreter, runs a quick `test` method, then begins an interaction loop. The `test` method intentionally includes a misquoted string to produce a `SyntaxError`. This demonstrates how the `runsource` method reports the error without terminating the interpreter. After the `test` method, the example continues with a command loop. The command loop prints a prompt, reads input, and then feeds that input to the interpreter's `runsource` method. The `runsource` method returns true if the statement is incomplete, and this return value is what allows a succinct inner loop that collects input for compound statements until the statement is complete. This inner loop for compound statements also uses the secondary prompt (...) to indicate the continuation of the statement.

Compile Listing 9.15 with a command similar to the following:

```
javac -classpath \path\to\jython.jar;.
org\python\demo\InteractiveEmbedding.java
```

Ouput from a sample usage of the `InteractiveEmbedding` class follows. Remember that the `SyntaxError` and the `This is not` statement at the start of the execution are part of the `test` method:

```
dos>java -cp \path\to\jython;. org.python.demo.InteractiveEmbedding
Traceback (innermost last):
  (no code object) at line 0
  File "<input>", line 2
SyntaxError: Lexical error at line 2, column 0.  Encountered: <EOF> after :
```

```
" "
This is not
Enter "exit" to quit.
>>>print "Hello World!"
Hello World!
>>>try:
...    assert 0, "Assertion error for testing compound statements"
...except AssertionError:
...    import sys
...    e = sys.exc_info()
...    print "%s\n%s\n%s" % e
...
exceptions.AssertionError
Assertion error for testing compound statements
<traceback object at 2147462>
>>>exit
```

Embedding an *InteractiveConsole*

The InteractiveConsole adds one more layer of abstraction to embedding, but this one is specific to the console interaction so common in Jython, such as used in Listing 9.13. Creating console interaction involves using the InteractiveConsole's three methods: interact, raw_input, and push. Table 9.2 summarizes these methods.

Table 9.2   *InteractiveConsole* **Methods**

Method	Summary

public InteractiveConsole()
 	
public InteractiveConsole
    (PyObject locals)
 	
public InteractiveConsole
    (PyObject locals,
     String filename)
	The InteractiveConsole's three constructors allow for optionally setting the interpreter's local namespace and setting a file name for use in error messages.

public void interact() public void interact(String banner)	The interact method mimics the Jython interpreter. The optional banner argument is a message printed before the first interaction only.

Table 9.2   *InteractiveConsole* **Methods**

Method	Summary
`public boolean push(String line)`	The push method pushes a single line that does not end with \n into the interpreter. This method returns `true` or `false` just as the `InteractiveInterpreter`'s runsource method does—true again means that additional input is required.
`public String` `raw_input(PyObject prompt)`	The `InteractiveConsole`'s `raw_input` method is the same as the built-in `raw_input` method.

Listing 9.16 shows how easy it is to create an embedded console. The initialize step is required as always, but beyond that, the `interact` method does all the work.

Listing 9.16   **Embedding the *InteractiveConsole***

```
// file: Console.java
package org.python.demo;

import org.python.util.InteractiveConsole;
import java.util.Properties;
import java.io.*;

public class Console {
    protected InteractiveConsole interp;

    public Console() {
        // set Properties
        if (System.getProperty("python.home") == null)
            System.setProperty("python.home", "c:\\jython-2.1");

        // no postProps, registry values used
        InteractiveConsole.initialize(System.getProperties(),
                            null, new String[0] );
        interp = new InteractiveConsole();
    }

    public static void main(String[] args) {
        Console con = new Console();
```

continues

Listing 9.16 **Continued**

```
        con.startConsole();
    }

    public void startConsole() {
        interp.interact("Welcome to your first embedded console");
    }
}
```

Listing 9.16 initializes the `InteractiveConsole`, and calls its `interact` method. The initialization is the same procedure as before, but the interaction loop is greatly simplified with the `interact` method. Executing Listing 9.16 produces Jython's interactive console, so an example is unnecessary. Note that the `InteractiveConsole`'s `push` and `raw_input` methods are usable, but they were not necessary for this listing. These methods are designed for interaction, just like the `InteractiveInterpreter`'s `runsource` method, and therefore are not ideal to performance critical situations. If your application need not interact with the interpreter, use the `PythonInterpreter` object and its `exec` and `eval` methods.

Extending Jython

Extending Jython means writing Jython modules in Java. *Jython modules* is used here to mean Java classes that specifically behave like Jython modules. There is a distinction between this and just writing Java classes. Jython can use most any Java class, so there is no requirement to take additional steps to make that Java class look and act like a Jython module. However, there are situations where design begs for a true Jython module. The distinction occurs when a class should allow Jythonisms such as ordered and keyword parameters.

Listing 9.17 shows a sample Jython module written in Java. You can see that it is nothing more than a Java class. The parts of interest, however, are the `ClassDictInit` interface, the related `classDictInit` method, static modifiers on each method, the `__doc__` strings, and the `PyException`. Although the `mymod` class is very simple, it demonstrates many aspects of creating Jython modules in Java.

Listing 9.17 **A Jython Module Written in Java**

```
// file mymod.java
package org.python.demo.modules;
import org.python.core.*;

public class mymod implements ClassDictInit {
```

```
    public static void classDictInit(PyObject dict) {
        dict.__setitem__("__doc__",
                         new PyString("Test class to confirm " +
                                      "builtin module"));
        dict.__delitem__("classDictInit");
    }

    public static PyString __doc__fibTest =
        new PyString("fibTest(iteration) "+
                     "-> integer");

    public static int fibTest(PyObject[] args, String[] kw) {
        ArgParser ap = new ArgParser("fibTest", args, kw, "iteration");
        int iteration = ap.getInt(0);
        if (iteration < 1)
            throw new PyException(Py.ValueError,
                                  new PyString("Only integers >=1 allowed"));
        if (iteration == 1 || iteration == 2)
            return iteration;

        return fibTest(new PyObject[] { new PyInteger(iteration-1) },
                       new String[0]) +
               fibTest(new PyObject[] { new PyInteger(iteration-2) },
                       new String[0]);
    }
}
```

Following is example output from running the `mymod` class as a module within Jython's interactive shell:

```
>>> from org.python.demo.modules import mymod
>>> import time
>>>
>>> def test(method, iteration):
...     t1 = time.time()
        results = apply(method, (iteration,))
...     print "The 25th fibonacci iteration is: ", results
...     print "Time elapsed: ", time.time() - t1
...
>>> test(mymod.fibTest, 25)
The 25th fibonacci iteration is:  121393
Time elapsed:  0.8799999952316284
```

If we continue this example with a comparable `fibonacci` function in Jython, it clarifies one advantage to writing Java modules: performance. You could additionally minimize some of the instantiations in the `fibTest` method if you passed on implementing Jython's flexible parameter scheme and use just `public static int fibTest(int iteration)`.

```
>>> def fib(iteration):
...     if iteration < 1: raise ValueError, "Iteration must be >=1"
...     if iteration < 3: return iteration
```

```
...         return fib(iteration - 1) + fib(iteration -2)
...
>>> test(fib, 25)
The 25th fibonacci iteration is:    121393
Time elapsed:   1.590000033378601
```

ClassDictInit

A Jython module written as a Java class may control the module's __dict__ attribute if it implements the ClassDictInit interface. A class that implements the ClassDictInit interface must have a method like the following:

```
public static void classDictInit(PyObject dict)
```

Jython calls the classDictInit method when the class is initialized, allowing control over attribute names visible within Jython and their implementations. The mymod class in Listing 9.17 uses the classDictInit to set a __doc__ string and to remove itself, classDictInit, from names visible from Jython. In reality, this is unnecessary because the __doc__ string could be defined as follows:

```
public static String __doc__="Test class to confirm builtin module";
```

Without the __doc__ string assignment in classDictInit, the classDictInit need not be included in the class and therefore would not appear in Jython anyway. The real usefulness comes when you have a complicated module implemented in multiple classes or the class includes multiple attributes you need to hide from Jython.

There is an additional means for controlling a Java method's visibility in Jython that is promising because of its simplicity, but is somewhat experimental at the time this was written. This involves the exception org.python.core.PyIgnoreMethodTag. The exception is never actually thrown, but any Java method that declares that it throws this exception is automatically removed from Jython's view.

__doc__ Strings

You can define a module's doc string by including a static PyString member named __doc__:

```
public static __doc__ = new PyString("Some documentation");
```

The static methods within a class become module functions in Jython. In Listing 9.17, the static fibTest method behaves like the fibTest function within a Jython module. To add a doc string to this function means adding a static PyString called __doc__fibTest. Listing 9.15 uses this to assign documentation to the fibTest method than can be retrieved from Jython as mymod.fibTest.__doc__.

Exceptions

To raise a Jython exception requires throwing the `PyException` class with two arguments: the actual Jython exception, and the exception message (what is referred to as the exception argument in Jython). Jython's built-in exceptions are located in the `org.python.core.Py` class. So, a `ValueError` is really a `Py.ValueError`.

```
raise ValueError, "Invalid Value"
```

The preceding Jython statement is shown in Java form as follows.

```
throw PyException(Py.ValueError, "Invalid Value")
```

Listing 9.17 uses the `PyException` to raise a Jython `ValueError` exception in the interpreter.

Parameters

Jython functions benefit from a rich parameter scheme that includes ordered parameter, keyword parameters, default values, and wild cards. It is possible to emulate this behavior in Java. The following method allows a Java method to handle positional and keyword arguments:

```
public PyObject MyFunction(PyObject[] args, String[] kw);
```

The `args` array holds all argument values, whereas the `kw` array holds only the specified keys. Following is and example call of the previously mentioned `MyFunction`:

```
MyFunction(1, 2, D=4, C=9)
```

The args and kw arrays would then look like the following:

```
args = [1, 2, 4, 9]
kw = ["D", "C"]
```

The class `org.python.core.ArgParser` eases parsing these parameters into more useful forms. The `ArgParser` class has four constructors:

```
public ArgParser(String funcname, PyObject[] args,
                 String[] kws, String p0)

public ArgParser(String funcname, PyObject[] args,
                 String[] kws, String p0, String p1)

public ArgParser(String funcname, PyObject[] args,
                 String[] kws, String p0, String p1, String p2)

public ArgParser(String funcname, PyObject[] args,
                 String[] kws, String[] paramnames)
```

Each constructor requires the function's name as the first parameter. The function using `ArgsParser` should use the parameters `PyObject[]` args and `String[]` kw. These two objects become the second and third arguments to the `ArgParser` constructor. The remaining parameters are the list of arguments expected by a method. These can be separate args if there are three or fewer; otherwise, they are a `String[]`. Listing 9.17 shows a Java method that implements Jython's argument style with the help of `ArgParser`. Some example Jython methods and their Java method plus `ArgParser` counterparts presented as follows to clarify.

```
Jython Method:
def test(A, B, C=2)

Java implementation:
public static PyObject test(PyObject[] args, String[] kws) {
    ArgParser ap = new ArgParser("test", args, kws, "A", "B", "C");
}

Jython Method:
def addContact(name, addr, ph=None)

Java implementation:
public static PyObject addContact(PyObject[] args, String[] kws) {
    ArgParser ap = new ArgParser("addContact", args, kws,
                              new String[] {"name", "addr", "ph"});
}
```

The parameter values are retrieved from the `ArgParser` instance with one of its `get*` methods. The `get*` methods listed here have either one or two parameters. Those with two parameters retrieve parameters with default values. Note that the position of the argument (`pos`) starts with position 0, not 1.

```
public String getString(int pos)

public String getString(int pos, String def)

public int getInt(int pos)

public int getInt(int pos, int def)

public PyObject getPyObject(int pos)

public PyObject getPyObject(int pos, PyObject def)

public PyObject getList(int pos)
```

For the Jython method:

```
def test(A, B, C=2)
```

The Java implementation, which allows for the default value, is this:

```
public static PyObject test(PyObject[] args, String[] kws) {
    ArgParser ap = new ArgParser("test", args, kws, "A", "B", "C");
    int A = ap.getInt(0);
    // or...
    // String A = ap.getString(0);
    // PyObject A = ap.getPyObject(0);
    // PyTuple A = (PyTuple)ap.getList(0);

    String B = ap.getString(1);
    // or...
    // int B = ap.getInt(1);
    // PyObject B = ap.getPyObject(1);
    // PyObject B = ap.getList(1);

    // here's the two argument version to allow for defaults
    int C = ap.getInt(2, 2);// first 2=position, second 2=default value
}
```

Importing Jython Modules in Java

Importing a Jython module in Java usually uses the `__builtin__.__import__` function. The `__import__` function has four signatures:

```
public static PyObject __import__(String name)

public static PyObject __import__(String name, PyObject globals)

public static PyObject __import__(String name, PyObject globals,
                                  PyObject locals)

public static PyObject __import__(String name, PyObject globals,
                                  PyObject locals,PyObject fromlist)
```

Importing the random module from within Java would be as follows:

```
PyObject module = __builtin__.__import__(random);
```

Working with *PyObjects*

Calling Jython classes in Java, and writing Jython modules in Java requires extensive use of Jython's special methods. Special methods are those methods that begin and end with two underscores and are described in Chapter 7. Jython's flexible operation creates special means of calling `PyObjects` from within Java.

Jython's dynamic operation means that the finding, getting, setting, and calling of attributes all happens through methods that provide opportunity to customize or extend each step. Chapter 7 covered the special methods for getting, setting, and calling, but there are additional methods for finding. These methods are __findattr__ and __finditem__. The __findattr__ method returns object attributes, and the __finditem__ method returns sequence or dictionary values designated by a key. Usage of these methods create the following signatures:

```
public PyObject __finditem__(PyObject key)
public PyObject __finditem__(int index)
public PyObject __finditem__(String key)

public PyObject __findattr__(String name)
public PyObject __findattr__(PyObject name)
```

The __finditem__ and __findattr__ methods that accept a String object as a parameter both require that the string object be interned. String literals are automatically interned, but otherwise, this string must be explicitly interned.

If you import the random module and intend to use the randint method, you cannot just call its directory:

```
// This doesn't work
PyObject random = __builtin__.__import__("random");
random.randint(new PyInteger(10), new PyInteger(100));
```

Instead, you should use the __findattr__ method combined with the call method:

```
PyObject random = __builtin__.__import__("random");
random.__findattr__("randint").__call__(new PyInteger(10),
                                        new PyInteger(20));
```

The shortcut method invoke exists to help in calling a method on a PyObject from Java. Specifically, the correct and generic way to call methods on all kinds of Jython mapping objects (such as PyDictionary and PyStringMap) is with the invoke method. Calling the invoke method on a PyObject's method is the equivalent of calling the following:

```
myPyObject.__getattr__(name).__call__(args, keywords)
```

Following are the different method signatures of the invoke method:

```
public PyObject invoke(String name)
public PyObject invoke(String name, PyObject arg1)
public PyObject invoke(String name, PyObject arg1, PyObject arg2)
public PyObject invoke(String name, PyObject[] args)
public PyObject invoke(String name, PyObject[] args, String[] keywords)
```

The different signatures respectively allow for differing sets of arguments passed to the invoked method, but what does not differ is that the first argument is a string representing the name of the PyObject's method to call. This name parameter must be an interned string. Remember that string literals are automatically interned.

The following example shows the creation of a PyDictionary and the retrieval of its keys from within Java using the invoke method. This example uses PyDictionary's empty constructor and subsequently adds values with the __setitem__ special method:

```
PyDictionary dct = new PyDictionary();
dct.__setitem__(new PyString("G"), new PyInteger(1));
dct.__setitem__(new PyString("D"), new PyInteger(2));
dct.__setitem__(new PyString("A"), new PyInteger(3));
dct.__setitem__(new PyString("E"), new PyInteger(4));
dct.__setitem__(new PyString("B"), new PyInteger(5));
PyObject keys = dct.invoke("keys");

PyObject keys = dict.invoke("keys");
```

The invoke method above uses the keys method of the PyDictionary object to retrieve its keys. Because the method name (keys) is a string literal in the previous example, it is automatically interned.

Looping through the keys returned in the previous example also requires special care. Because a PyObject's __len__ method may return wrong values, the only way to safely loop through Jython sequences in Java is to test for each index value until reaching a non-existing index. If we continue the dictionary keys example from above with a loop through those keys, the proper and generic way to loop through them is implemented as follows:

```
PyObject key;
for (int i = 0; (key = keys.__finditem__(i)) != null; i++) {
    System.out.println("K: " + key + ", V: " + dict.__getitem__(key));
}
```

Writing Jython Classes in Java

When a Java class emulates a Jython module, functions within that module are often implemented as static class members. Emulating a Jython class in Java can therefore be implemented as a static inner class; however, the ClassDictInit interface allows more flexibility in this regard. To emulate a Jython class with Java, it is best to subclass the most appropriate Py* class found in the org.python.core package and then implement all the special methods required for the desired type of class. All classes written in Java may subclass PyObject and implement the __findattr__, __setattr__, and __delattr__ methods. A Mapping object would subclass PyDictionary or PyStringMap and implement __finditem__, __setitem__, __delitem__, and the associated mapping methods. The same is true for Jython's other data types.

Adding a Java Class as a Built-In Jython Module

When you write a Jython module in Java, you also have the option to designate this module as a built-in module. The registry key `python.modules.builtin` allows you to add modules to the list of built-in modules written in Java. The `python.modules.builtin` property is a comma-separated list of entries. The entries may appear in three forms. Table 9.3 shows each form of a module entry and an explanation of its use.

Table 9.3   **Built-In Modules Entry Syntax and Description**

Entry Syntax	Description
`name`	Just the name of the Java class. This assumes that the class is in the `org.python.modules` package. Adding this entry to the `python.modules.builtin` list allows you to use "import name" in Jython. If you wish to add the class `org.python.modules.jnios`, the entry would appear as follows: `python.modules.builtin = jnios`

`name:class`	This form requires a name and fully qualified class, separated by a colon. The name need not be the class name; it is simply the name Jython uses to refer to this class. If the name duplicates a pre-existing name, the pre-existing module is overridden. To add the class `com.mycompany.python.agent` as the name `mycompanyagent` use the following:
	
	`python.modules.builtin =`
	`mycompanyagent:org.mycompany.python.agent`

`name:null`	This removes the module name from the list of built-in modules. To remove the `os` module, use the following: `python.modules.builtin = os:null`

The `python.modules.builtin` property is unique in how it is set. Currently setting this property with the `-D` command-line switch does not add a module to this built-in list. It must be set in the registry file, or in the post-properties (second arg) in the initialize method.

To add `mymod` as a module, compile it, and ensure that it is in the correct directory tree for its package and in the `classpath`. Then edit the registry file, adding the following:

```
python.modules.builtin = "mymod:org.python.demo.modules.mymod"
```

The name, or portion left of the colon, could be any legal identifier, but the class, or right side of the colon, must be a full `package.class` string uniquely identifying the appropriate class. Once a Java class is added as a built-in, it is available in Jython with just an import of its simple name. The `mymod` from the preceding example is available with the following:

```
>>> import mymod
```

This same mechanism for defining a built-in allows you to substitute a module for an existing built-in, or remove a built-in. All of this contributes to the ease of which Jython is extended and customized with Java.

Applications with Jython

10

GUI Development

THE PRIMARY TOOLKITS FOR DEVELOPING graphical user interfaces (GUIs) in Jython are Java's Abstract Windowing Toolkit (AWT) and Swing classes. These toolkits are the logical choice considering that Jython is written in Java, and excels at using Java classes within Python's syntax. This doesn't mean that the AWT and Swing are the only choices for implementing GUIs. An increasing number of bindings to other toolkits also allow Java, and thus Jython, to use those toolkits as well. This chapter, however, is limited to AWT and Swing GUIs written with Jython.

This chapter does not cover AWT and Swing basics. Previous Java knowledge is assumed of the reader, so basics are unnecessary, but a bigger reason is that the scope of such and undertaking grossly exceeds the bounds of this book. Fortunately, shelves at local bookstores appear fully saturated with quality AWT and Swing material.

What you can expect from this book are details concerning what Jython brings to developing GUI applications with the AWT and Swing toolkits. Jython brings automatic bean properties, event properties, convenient keyword arguments and some convenience tools located in Jython's pawt package.

Translating Java GUI examples into Jython code is the fastest way to understand Jython GUI development; therefore, Java-to-Jython translations begins this chapter. Additionally, Jython has two valuable contributions to ease and accelerate development with the AWT and Swing classes: automatic bean attributes and the pawt package. Both of these are detailed in this chapter. The remaining sections develop larger examples to help reinforce techniques used in writing Jython GUIs.

Comparing a Java and Jython GUI

Writing a GUI in Jython is very similar to doing so in Java. Most any Java GUI is easily translated to Jython with minimal effort and will work as expected. Once accustomed to using the AWT and Swing from Jython, the prototyping of GUIs in Jython, and later translating into Java (as needed) becomes more appealing. Listing 10.1 shows a simple Java GUI followed by Listing 10.2, which shows a similar GUI written in Jython.

Listing 10.1 **A Simple Java GUI**

```
// file SimpleJavaGUI.java
import java.awt.*;
import java.awt.event.*;

class SimpleJavaGUI implements ActionListener {
    private Button mybutton = new Button("OK");
    private Label mylabel = new Label("A Java GUI", Label.CENTER);

    public SimpleJavaGUI() {
        Frame top_frame = new Frame();
        Panel panel = new Panel();
        top_frame.setTitle("A Basic Jython GUI");
        top_frame.setBackground(Color.yellow);

        //WindowListener needed for window close event
        top_frame.addWindowListener(
            new WindowAdapter() {
                public void windowClosing(windowEvent e) {
                    System.exit(0);
                }
            });

        mybutton.addActionListener(this);
        panel.add(mylabel);
        panel.add(mybutton);
        top_frame.add(panel);

        // pack and show
```

```
        top_frame.pack();
        Dimension winSz = Toolkit.getDefaultToolkit().getScreenSize();
        top_frame.setLocation(winSz.width/2 - top_frame.getWidth()/2,
                              winSz.height/2 - top_frame.height()/2);
        top_frame.setVisible(true);
    }

    public static void main(String[] args) {
        SimpleJavaGUI s = new SimpleJavaGUI();
    }

    public void actionPerformed(ActionEvent event) {
        System.exit(0);
    }

}
```

The GUI produced from running the class in Listing 10.1 is shown in
Figure 10.1.

Figure 10.1   A simple Java GUI.

Note the use of AWT classes, bean properties, and bean events in Listing 10.1.
The example uses the Frame, Panel, Button, and Label classes from the AWT.
These classes employ bean attribute assignments such as the .setVisible()
method. Additionally, the example sets event listeners with methods such as the
.addWindowListener method. These elements are important points of comparison with Jython.

Implementing the same GUI in Jython requires the obvious changes to
syntax. Java's type declarations, access modifiers, semicolons, and braces are
absent from Jython. Take the instantiation of the Button component in Java:

```
import java.awt.*;
private Button mybutton = new Button("OK");
```

In Jython, this becomes the following:

```
from java import awt
mybutton = awt.Button("OK")
```

Instantiating the button in Jython uses the `awt` package prefix. The reason why is because `from java.awt import *` is discouraged in Jython (we know this from Chapter 5, "Modules and Packages"), so you would instead import the package or explicit class names. Using `from java import awt` is the more common approach, but this requires that the package name be used in subsequent references to `AWT` classes, such as `awt.Button`.

Jython does automatic type conversion to and from Java types, and translating Listing 10.1 in Jython requires attention to the type of object used in Jython. The `setVisible` method, for example, requires a Java Boolean argument. Jython converts a `PyInteger` of 1 to Boolean true, and 0 to a Boolean false. This means that the `visible` property should be set to 1 in Jython. An interesting point that foreshadows the discussion of Jython's automatic bean properties is that Jython is not required to use the `setVisible` method, but can instead assign 1 to the `visible` property.

A class is not required in Jython. A Jython class would certainly work, and might be a more accurate translation of Listing 10.1, but a class is certainly optional in Jython. Listing 10.2 chooses to not use a class, yet implements a GUI nearly identical to that in Listing 10.1. If a class had been used, it would be important to point out how Jython methods require an explicit `self` parameter in the first parameter slot. Previous chapters make this clear, but it is common enough of a slip when converting Java code to Jython that it warrants another reminder. Listing 10.2 does not define a class just to show how it is possible to implement a GUI without a class; however, the nature of the `AWT` and `Swing` classes make complex classless GUIs difficult to implement.

The `window` event and `button` event in Listing 10.1 are simple tasks within a very basic `AWT` application; however, these tasks already begin to tie the proverbial Gordian knot. An anonymous inner class implements `WindowAdapter` so that it may handle the `windowClosing` event. The `SimpleJavaGUI` class itself implements the `ActionListener` interface so that it may handle the button action in the `actionPerformed` method. The `addWindowListener` and `addActionListener` methods set the appropriate instances for the handling of these events. Now look at Listing 10.2 and notice that `WindowAdapter`, `addWindowListener`, and `addActionListener` do not even exist in the `SimpleJythonGUI`! Instead, the Jython version uses assignments to handle these properties and events. These assignments are another first-rate device for simplicity that Jython offers by automatically adding bean properties and events as class attributes.

Listing 10.2   **A Simple Jython GUI**

```
# File: simpleJythonGUI.py
import java
from java import awt

# Make an exit function
def exit(e):
    java.lang.System.exit(0)

#Make root frame and the panel it will contain
top_frame = awt.Frame(title="A Basic Jython GUI",
                      background = awt.Color.yellow,
                      windowClosing=exit)
panel = awt.Panel()

#Add stuff to look at inside frame
mylabel = awt.Label("A Jython GUI", awt.Label.CENTER)
mybutton = awt.Button("OK", actionPerformed=exit)

panel.add(mylabel)
panel.add(mybutton)
top_frame.add(panel)

# pack and show
top_frame.pack()

# set location
toolkit = awt.Toolkit.getDefaultToolkit()
winSz = toolkit.screenSize
top_frame.setLocation(winSz.width/2 - top_frame.size.width/2,
                      winSz.height/2 - top_frame.height/2)

top_frame.visible = 1
```

The GUI produced from running the Jython implementation is visually similar to that in Figure 10.1 only with the appropriate name change. Figure 10.2 shows the Jython implementation of this simple GUI.

Figure 10.2   A simple Jython GUI.

Bean Properties and Events

A quick review of beans is in order before describing Jython automatic bean attributes. A *bean* is any class that follows appropriate conventions for methods, properties, and events. A bean's methods are all of the methods within the bean designated as public. A bean's properties are data objects manipulated through get and set methods. A bean defines events by designating listener objects with add and remove methods. The class below can be read as "bean A with the read-only property name."

```
public class A {
    private String name;
    public String getName() {
        return name;
    }
}
```

Whereas Java would directly use the getName() method in the preceding bean, Jython adds a valuable shortcut—not just for properties like the name property above, but for properties and events. Jython uses inspection to determine bean properties and events, and then it allows you to use these bean properties and events as instance attributes. Java would use the following to retrieve the above bean's name property:

```
import A;
bean = new A();
String name = bean.getName();
```

Within Jython, you can simply treat the name property as an attribute, and you can therefore access the name property with just the following:

```
>>> import A
>>> b = A()
>>> name = b.name
```

You need not call any methods to retrieve the name property because Jython automatically treats bean properties as class attributes. You still may use the getName() method from within Jython, but you do not have to because its functionality is done behind the scenes with Jython's automatic bean properties. The same simplicity applies to setter methods. A setName method in bean A would translate into the following Java usage:

```
import A;
A bean = new A();
bean.setName("new name");
```

In Jython, however, it is only an attribute assignment:

```
import A
bean = A()
bean.name = "new name"
```

Although these examples are with simple properties, the principle is the same for events. This principle, combined with Jython's keyword parameters simplifies many aspects of GUI's. The following lines from Listing 10.2 use Jython's keyword arguments in a constructor to set a couple properties in a component's state:

```
top_frame = awt.Frame(title="A Basic Jython GUI",
                      background = awt.Color.yellow,
                      windowClosing=exit)
mybutton = awt.Button("OK", actionPerformed=exit)
```

Jython's automatic bean property and bean event attributes are a shortcut, as noted earlier, but this should not imply they are less valid than using the methods themselves as Java does. The use of automatic bean properties is very apropos in Jython's syntax, and they are especially valuable when working with GUIs because beans permeate the AWT and Swing classes. The feature that makes them so apropos within Jython is keyword parameters. Using keyword parameters to set bean properties works exceptionally well, although this only works in Java constructors. Following is Java pseudo-code and Jython code that sets up a frame. Notice the difference that keyword parameters make.

```
// In Java   (pseudo-code)
import java.awt.*;
Frame myframe = new Frame("A test Frame");
myframe.setBackground(Color.gray);
myframe.addWindowListener(new SomeWindowListenerClass());
myframe.setBounds(20, 20, 200, 300);


# In Jython
from java import awt
myframe = awt.Frame("A test Frame", background=awt.Color.gray,
                    bounds=(20, 20, 200, 300),
                    actionPerformed=someCallableObject)
```

Although this doesn't always save space, lines, or typing, it is more legible due to the close visual association properties and events have with their component when set with keyword arguments.

Looking back at Listing 10.1, we see how Java classes interact with bean properties by explicitly using get and set methods. Listing 10.1 demonstrated this with the following methods:

```
Dimension winSz = Toolkit.getDefaultToolkit().getScreenSize();
top_frame.setLocation(winSz.width ... winSz.height);
top_frame.setTitle("A Basic Jython GUI");
top_frame.setBackground(Color.yellow);
top_frame.setVisible(true);
```

Additionally, Java specifies `bean` events with `add` and `remove` methods, of which, the `add` method appears twice in Listing 10.1.

```
top_frame.addWindowListener(new exitClass());
mybutton.addActionListener(this);
```

Jython could use the same methods as the Java application does. `top_frame.setBounds(...)` would work the same in Jython along with all the others mentioned above. Jython, however, adds the ability to work with bean properties and events as if they were normal Jython class attributes. Looking back at Listing 10.2 we see the attribute assignments that have supplanted bean property methods:

```
winSz = toolkit.screenSize
title="A Basic Jython GUI"
background = awt.Color.yellow
actionPerformed=exit
```

Additionally, Listing 10.2 registers event handlers with simple attribute assignments that specify a Jython function:

```
windowClosing=exit
actionPerformed=exit
```

The justification for this long diversion into bean properties lies in the prominence bean properties have in `AWT` and `Swing` classes. Just looking at the `java.awt.Frame` class shows how basic bean properties are in the `AWT`. The Frame class itself has thirteen bean property methods listed in the jkd1.3 API documentation:

```
getAccessibleContext, getCursorType, getFrames, getIconImage,
getMenuBar, getState, getTitle, setCursor, setIconImage,
setMenuBar, setResizable, setState, setTitle.
```

The `Frame` class also inherits 10 additional `accessor` methods from the `java.awt.Window` class:

```
getFocusOwner, getGraphicsConfiguration, getInputContext, getListeners,
getLocale, getOwnedWindows, getOwner, getToolkit, getWarningString, setCursor
```

`Frame` also inherits fourteen accessor methods from the `java.awt.Container` class:

```
getAlignmentX, getAlignmentY, getComponent, getComponentAt, getComponentAt,
getComponentCount, getComponents, getInsets, getLayout, getMaximumSize,
getMinimumSize, getPreferredSize, setFont, setLayout
```

This class also inherits thirty-nine methods from the `java.awt.Component` class:

```
getBackground, getBounds, getBounds, getColorModel, getComponentOrientation,
getCursor, getDropTarget, getFont, getFontMetrics, getForeground,
getGraphics, getHeight, getInputMethodRequests, getLocation, getLocation,
getLocationOnScreen, getName, getParent, getPeer, getSize, getSize,
getTreeLock, getWidth, getX, getY, setBackground, setBounds, setBounds,
setComponentOrientation, setDropTarget, setEnabled, setForeground, setLocale,
setLocation, setLocation, setName, setSize, setSize, setVisible
```

And let's not forget the most basic of bean properties defined in `java.lang.Objects`:

```
getClass
```

Interacting with just a simple `Frame` container involves a repletion of bean properties that work just like class attributes in Jython. The following interactive example demonstrates what Jython does with the `Frame` object's bean properties. Of special interest is the keyword arguments used in instantiating the `frame` class.

```
>>> import java, sys
>>> myframe = java.awt.Frame(title="Test", background=(220,220,4))
>>> myframe.bounds=(40, 30, 200, 200)
>>> myframe.visible=1
>>> myframe.background = 150, 240,25  # Change color interactively
>>> # Try clicking on the window close icon here- it does nothing.
>>> myframe.windowClosing = lambda x: sys.exit(0)
>>> # now try closing the frame- it works.
```

Jython's keyword arguments make it possible to establish numerous bean properties and events in a component's constructor. Even ignoring the keyword parameters, the `Frame` container doesn't have a stock constructor that allows such arguments. Instead, Jython's magic bean attributes make it possible to establish so much of the bean state in the constructor. Better yet is what Jython does with `tuple` arguments like those assigned to `bounds` and `background` in the preceding interactive example.

Bean Properties

Beans are mostly about convention. A `bean` property called `extent` has the associated accessor and mutator methods `getExtent` and `setExtent`. Notice the capitalization convention. The property and its pair of associated methods are lowercase-first with each successive word capitalized. This convention determines the name of the `bean` attributes defined in Jython. If a Java class has a method named `setAMultiWordName`, then Jython adds an automatic bean property name `aMultiWordName`.

A bean property is read-only if it only defines the `get` method, whereas a property with only an associated `set` method becomes write-only. Defining both creates a read-write property. The `get` and `set` method signatures need to complement each other for the full read and write access. This means that if a set method's signature has a string parameter, then the complimentary `get` method must return a string object. The following Java bean wrongly sets the `setName` parameter to the generic `Object`.

```
public class A {
    private String name = "";

    public String getName() {
        System.out.println("Getting name");
        return name;
    }

    public void setName(Object s) {
        name = (String)s;
        System.out.println("Setting name");
    }
}
```

Using the preceding bean with Jython's automatic `bean` attributes creates the following output:

```
>>> import A
>>> b = A()
>>> b.name
Getting name
''
>>> b.name = "this"
Traceback (innermost last):
  File "<console>", line 1, in ?
AttributeError: read-only attr: name
```

If the class were rewritten to have the appropriate complementary signatures, it would then interact properly with Jython's bean attribute assignments:

```
public class A {
    private String name = "";

    public String getName() {
        System.out.println("Getting name");
        return name;
    }

    public void setName(String s) {
        name = s;
```

```
        System.out.println("Setting name");
    }
}
```

A quick interactive test of the new bean confirms proper read–write access to the name property.

```
>>> import A
>>> b = A()
>>> b.name = "New name"
Setting name
>>> b.name
Getting name
'New name'
```

Bean properties may also be a sequence. This creates four accessor methods if you desire full read–write access to a sequence, or *indexed bean*. The four methods would be as follows:

```
setProperty([])            // Sets the entire sequence
setProperty(int, Object)   // Sets a specific index
getProperty()              // Gets the entire sequence
getProperty(int)           // Gets a specific index
```

However, Jython's automatic bean properties only use the getProperty() and setProperty([]) methods of the four.

Listing 10.3 is a Java bean with an indexed property called items.

Listing 10.3 **A Bean with an Indexed Property**

```
// file: ItemBean.java
public class ItemBean {
    private String[] data = {"A", "B", "C"};

    public ItemBean() { ; }

    public String[] getItems() {
        return data;
    }

    public String getItems(int i) {
        return data[i];
    }

    public void setItems(String[] items) {
        data = items;
    }

    public void setItems(int index, String item) {
        data[index] = item;
    }
}
```

The following interactive console session demonstrates the interaction with the items property from Listing 10.3.

```
>>> import ItemBean
>>> ib = ItemBean()
>>>
>>> # This calls ib.getItems()
>>> ib.items
array(['A', 'B', 'C'], java.lang.String)
>>>
>>> # The following does not call ib.getItems(int i), but instead
>>> # calls ib.getItems() and applies the index to the returned array
>>>
>>> # The following calls ib.setItems([])
>>> ib.items = ["1", "2", "3"]
```

Bean Properties and Tuples

Jython automatically interprets `tuples` assigned to bean properties as constructors for the type of property being set. The three-member `tuple` assigned to the background property automatically becomes constructor values to the `Java.awt.Color` class because the bean property type is `java.awt.Color`. The `tuple` assignment to the bounds property automatically becomes a `Rectangle` type.

This automatic property type construction further simplifies Jython GUI code. Again, note that Jython's automatic `bean` attributes are most effective in conjunction with Jython's keyword parameters. The difference between `f.setVisible(1)` and `f.visible = 1` is negligible, but the keyword parameters often makes a valuable difference.

```
// In Java  (pseudo-code)
import java.awt.*;
Frame f = new Frame();
Label L = new Label("This is a Label");
L.setBackground( new Color(50, 160, 40));
L.setForeground( new Color(50, 255, 50));
L.setFont(new Font("Helvetica Bold", 18, 24));
f.add(L);
f.setVisible(true);

# In Jython
from java import awt
f = awt.Frame()
L = awt.Label("This is a Label", background=(50, 160, 40),
              foreground=(50, 255, 50), font=("Helvetica Bold", 18, 24))
f.add(L)
f.visible = 1
```

Bean Events

Bean events are those events registered with add*Event*Listener and remove*Event*Listener. (*Event* is a placeholder for the actual type of event). For example, the java.awt.Window class, or Window bean, registers window events with the addWindowListener method. The addWindowListener method requires a class that implements the WindowListener interface as an argument.

If you wish to handle an event in a Java GUI, you need to add a class that implements an event listener for that type of event. The windowClosing event, for example, is defined in the interface WindowListener. Therefore, a Java application must use the bean event addWindowListener to add a class that implements the WindowListener interface or extend a class that does. This class would then be required to implement the method windowClosing. Java also allows an anonymous inner class to satisfy the interface, and therefore handle the event.

Jython, however, uses automatic event properties as attributes. This allows Jython to leverage its first-class functions. Although using first-class functions is the common implementation of this, it actually works with any callable Jython object. Jython's automatic bean event attributes let you assign a callable object to an event's bean name. To implement the windowClosing event, just assign a callable object to the container's windowClosing attribute. The callable object should accept one parameter, the event. The event action does not need to be a class, nor must it have a specific name. In other words, an event's name acts like a class attribute in Jython. Events such as windowClosing, windowOpened, and windowActivated are simple, assignable attributes in Jython as demonstrated in the following interactive interpreter example:

```
>>> def wclose(e):
...     print "Processing the windowClosing Event"
...     e.getSource().dispose()
...
>>> def wopen(e):
...     print "Processing the windowOpened Event"
...
>>> def wact(e):
...     print "Processing the windowActivated event"
...
>>> import java
>>> f = java.awt.Frame("Jython AWT Example")
>>> f.windowClosing = wclose
>>> f.windowOpened = wopen
>>> f.windowActivated = wact
>>> f.visible = 1
>>> Processing the windowActivated event
Processing the windowOpened Event          # click out of window here
Processing the windowActivated event       # click on window here
Processing the windowClosing Event         # click on window close box
```

All the event attribute assignments may be included in the constructor as keyword arguments as well:

```
f = java.awt.Frame("Jython AWT Example", windowOpened=wopen,
                   windowClosing=wclose, windowActivated=wact)
```

Name Priorities

Jython supports instance methods, class-static fields, bean properties, and bean event properties. This allows for potential naming conflicts, where a method may have the same name as a bean property or event property. What happens in cases where multiple properties share the same name? Jython resolves name conflicts by assigning priorities. Preference is given to instance methods. A method name will always precede other conflicting property names. Class-static attributes appear next in the hierarchy. The following Jython class defines a class-static property called windowClosing. This is a class field, not an event, and it will precede the event of the same name because of its priority:

```
>>> class f(java.awt.Frame):
...       windowClosing="This"
...
>>> myf = f()
>>> myf.windowClosing = lambda x: java.lang.System.exit(0)
>>> myf.visible=1   # try to close the window now
```

Event properties and bean properties follow in the hierarchy, in that order. The summary of this order is as follows:

```
(1) Methods
(2) Class-static attributes
(3) Event Properties
(4) Bean properties
```

The *pawt* Package

Jython's pawt package adds a few convenience modules for using AWT and Swing in Jython. GridBag, colors, test, and swing are the import functionality within the pawt package.

GridBag

The pawt.GridBag class is a wrapper class designed to help with java.awt.GridBagLayout and java.awt.GridBagConstraints. There are two methods in the GridBag class: add and addRow. Working with most layout managers, such as BorderLayout, CardLayout, FlowLayout, and GridLayout, within

Jython varies little from working with the same layout managers in Java.
Jython does allow the shortcut assignment of a layout manager in a container's
constructor. The following snippet shows how to establish a container's layout
manager with keywords in a constructor:

```
from java import awt
from java.lang import System

f = awt.Frame("Test", bounds=(100,100,200,200),
            layout=awt.FlowLayout(),
            windowClosing=lambda e: System.exit(0)
)
```

The GridBagLayout does differ from other layouts in Jython because Jython
has a class that adds convenience to this complicated layout manager.
Components display according to their attached layout constraints with
the GridBagLayout, but working with both the GridBagLayout and
GridBagConstraints is awkward. Bean properties are again useful in
reducing this awkwardness, but Jython's pawt.GridBag class helps reduce
this awkwardness.

To use the pawt.GridBag class with a Java container, supply an instance of
the container to the pawt.GridBag constructor. The following lines create a
java.awt.Frame instance and add that frame to the pawt.GridBag class. Once
added, the frame uses the GridBagLayout:

```
from java import awt
import pawt
top_frame = awt.Frame("GridBag frame")
bag = pawt.GridBag(top_frame)
```

The instantiation of the pawt.GridBag class optionally accepts keyword arguments for default constraints. The following instantiation of the pawt.GridBag
class sets fill to GridBagConstraints.VERTICAL as a default. Note the use of
"VERTICAL" in quotes as opposed to the more verbose
GridBagConstraints.VERTICAL.

```
bag = pawt.GridBag(top_frame, fill="VERTICAL")
```

The pawt.GridBag class uses two methods to add components to a container
that uses the GridBagLayout: add and addRow. To add a label and a TextField in
Java with GridBagConstraints looks like the following (pseudo-code):

```
import java.awt.*;

Panel pane = new Panel();
GridBagLayout bag = new GridBagLayout();
GridBagConstraints bagconstraints = new GridBagConstraints();

pane.setLayout(bag);
```

```
Label nameLabel = new Label("name: ");
bagconstraints.anchor = GridBagConstraints.WEST;
bagconstraints.fill = GridBagConstraints.NONE;
bagconstraints.gridwidth = 1;
pane.add(nameLabel, bagconstraints);

TextField nameField = new textField(25);
bagconstraints.anchor = GridBagConstraints.WEST;
bagconstraints.fill = GridBagConstraints.HORIZONTAL;
bagconstraints.gridwidth = 3;
pane.add(nameLabel, bagconstraints);
```

With Jython's `pawt.GridBag` class, you can shorten this to the following
(pseudocode):

```
from java import awt
from pawt import GridBag

pane = awt.Panel()
bag = GridBag(pane, fill='HORIZONTAL')
nameLabel = awt.Label("Name: ")
nameField = awt.TextField(25)
bag.add(nameLabel, anchor="WEST", fill="NONE", gridwidth=1)
bag.addRow(nameField, anchor="WEST", fill="HORIZONTAL", gridwidth=3)
```

The `add` method adds the specified component with the constraints specified
as keyword arguments. The `addRow` method does the same except that it also
completes the row, with the subsequent component beginning on the following row.

Listing 10.4 uses the `pawt.GridBag` module to simplify the setup of a address
book entry. The listing requires only minimal use of keyword constraints. The
container that uses the `GridBaglayout` is the first argument to the `pawt.GridBag`
class. Following this are default constraints, and the fill constraint is set to `"HOR-
IZONTAL"` by default in this example. The addition of the category choice com-
ponent is the only component that uses keyword constraints. To set the `fill`
constraint to `NONE`, the keyword parameter `fill` is set to the string `"NONE"`
instead of to `GridBagConstraints.NONE`. This abbreviation applies to all of the
`GridBagConstraint` fields. This allows the simple keyword argument
`anchor="WEST"` to set a component's anchor constraint.

Listing 10.4 ***GridBagConstraints* the Easy Way:** *pawt.GridBag*

```
from java import awt
from java.awt.event import ActionListener
from pawt import GridBag
from java.lang import System
```

```
frame = awt.Frame("GridBag Test", visible=1,size=(200,200),
                    windowClosing=lambda e: System.exit(0))

pane=awt.Panel(background=(200,200,255))
frame.add(pane)

bag = GridBag(pane, fill='HORIZONTAL')

labelFactory = lambda x: awt.Label(x, background=awt.Color.yellow)

title = awt.Label("Jython GridBag Address Book", awt.Label.CENTER)
bag.addRow(title)

category = awt.Choice()
map(category.add, ["Family", "Friends", "Business"])
bag.add(labelFactory("Category: "))
bag.addRow(category, anchor="WEST", fill="NONE")

name = awt.TextField(25)
bag.add(labelFactory("Name: "))
bag.addRow(name)

address = awt.TextField(35)
bag.add(labelFactory("Address: "))
bag.addRow(address)

city = awt.TextField(25)
bag.add(labelFactory("City: "))
bag.add(city)

state = awt.TextField(2)
bag.add(labelFactory("State: "))
bag.add(state)

zip = awt.TextField(5)
bag.add(labelFactory("zip: "))
bag.addRow(zip)

homephone_areacode = awt.TextField(3)
homephone_prefix = awt.TextField(3)
homephone_suffix = awt.TextField(4)

cellphone_areacode = awt.TextField(3)
cellphone_prefix = awt.TextField(3)
cellphone_suffix = awt.TextField(4)


frame.pack()
```

Executing the module in Listing 10.4 produces the output shown in Figure 10.3.

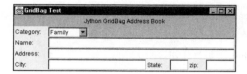

Figure 10.3   Address book entry with *pawt. GridBag.*

colors

The `colors` module within the `pawt` package is a set of many named colors. Because people often remember names better than numbers, these predefined colors add names just for their convenience. For example, the color `papayawhip` is very easy to remember, but its RGB component (255, 239, 213) is less memorable.

To get a full listing of the colors defined within `pawt.colors`, examine the contents of the `sys.prefix/Lib/pawt/colors.py` file, or execute the following in Jython's interactive interpreter:

```
>>> import pawt
>>> dir(pawt.colors)
['__doc__', '__file__', '__name__', 'aliceblue', 'antiquewhite', 'aqua',
'aquamarine', 'azure', 'beige', 'bisque', 'black', 'blanchedalmond', 'blue',
'blueviolet', 'brown', 'burlywood',
...
'snow', 'springgreen', 'steelblue', 'tan', 'teal', 'thistle', 'tomato',
'turquoise', 'violet', 'wheat', 'white', 'whitesmoke', 'yellow',
'yellowgreen']
```

test

The `test` function within the `pawt` package allows a simple test of graphic components. To test a button color without having to use a `Frame` or `Panel` to see it, use `pawt.test`.

```
>>> import java
>>> import pawt
>>> b = java.awt.Button("help", background=(212,144,100))
>>> pawt.test(b)
```

The `test` function optionally accepts a size argument. The size argument should be a `tuple` or list with integers for width and height:

```
>>> from java.awt import Label
>>> import pawt
>>> L = Label("Test", background=(255,10,10), foreground=(10, 10, 100))
>>> pawt.test(L, (200,140))
```

The `test` function returns the root frame used so that you may continue to interact with the test:

```
>>> from java.awt import Label
>>> import pawt
>>> L = Label("Test", background=(110,10,10), foreground=(10,110,100))
>>> f = pawt.test(L, (200,250))
>>> f.resize(100,140)
>>> L.font="Helvetica Bold", 20,24
>>> f.dispose()
>>> # note the prompt is still available for further tests this way
```

pawt.swing

The `pawt.swing` module does two things: It selects the appropriate `Swing` library for your JDK, and it has a `test` function specific to `Swing` components.

Retrieving the correct `Swing` library is useful for those who work in both 1.1 and 1.2 JDKs. Its need diminishes with time, but it allows developers to write Jython `Swing` code that works in both java1.1 and java1.2 without changes.

This module also adds in a test function equivalent to `pawt.test`, but using `Swing` widgets:

```
>>> import pawt
>>> cb = pawt.swing.JCheckBox("Test Check Box")
>>> myframe = pawt.swing.test(cb)
>>> myframe.dispose()
>>> myframe = pawt.swing.test(cb, (100,200))
```

There are drawbacks to using the `pawt.swing` module however. It is a very dynamic module, which creates problems in compiled Jython. Because of this, it is best not to use the `pawt.swing` module when you subclass a swing component, or when you are compiling the Jython application into class files. Instead, use `javax.swing` directly.

Examples

This section contains a number of examples that clarify using the AWT and Swing toolkits in Jython.

Simple *AWT* Graphics

Listing 10.5 is a simple banner drawn in the java.awt.Canvas's paint method. The paint method receives a Graphics2D object, and the listing uses that object to print the Jython banner. Listing 10.5 uses Jython's automatic bean properties for the canvas's height and width properties, and the Graphics' font and color properties. It also uses Jython's automatic event properties to establish the windowClosing event in the Frame's constructor.

Listing 10.5 **A Jython Banner**

```
# file: jythonBanner.py
from java import awt
import java

class Banner(awt.Canvas):
    def paint(self, g):
        g.color = 204, 204, 204
        g.fillRect(15, 15, self.width-30, self.height-30)
        g.color = 102, 102, 153
        g.font = "Helvetica Bold", awt.Font.BOLD, 28
        message = ">>> Jython"
        g.drawString(message,
                        self.width/2 - len(message)*10,   #approx. center
                        self.height/2 + 14)               #same here

top_frame = awt.Frame("Jython Banner", size=(350, 150),
                    windowClosing=lambda e: java.lang.System.exit(0))
top_frame.add( Banner() )
top_frame.visible = 1
```

Running the jythonBanner.py script should produce a banner similar to Figure 10.4. The paint method is called on each resize event. You can resize the banner to notice how it adjusts.

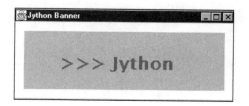

Figure 10.4 A Jython banner.

Adding Events

Events in Jython, as noted earlier, are simple attribute assignments. Previous examples demonstrate this with the `windowClosing` event and a button's `actionPerformed` event. Listing 10.6, however, demonstrates the use of mouse events defined in `java.awt.event.MouseListener` and `java.awt.event.MouseMotionListener` interfaces. Implementing event handlers for these events still acts just like an attribute assignment thanks to Jython's automatic event properties.

Listing 10.6 is a polar graph that displays the radius (r) and angle (theta) of the mouse location as the mouse traverses a graph canvas. The `PolarCanvas` class is the component that implements the graph, and it is a subclass of `java.awt.Canvas`. Subclassing the `java.awt.Canvas` class allows `PolarCanvas` to implement the `paint` method, which draws the graph. The intent of the application is to display coordinates in labels when the mouse is over the `PolarCanvas` component. This means that the `PolarCanvas` class is the one that should register the mouse motion listener. The following line is what defines the `mouseMoved` event handler:

```
self.graph.mouseMoved = self.updateCoords
```

The assignment in the preceding line means that whenever the mouse moves over the `PolarCanvas` component, the `Main` class's `updateCoords` method is called. The `updateCoords` method is what displays the desired coordinates at the top of the window.

In addition to displaying mouse coordinates, Listing 10.6 displays points registered by the release of the mouse button. The `mouseReleased` event, which registers a display point, is set in the `PolarCanvas` constructor. The `mouseReleased` event is handled by the `onClick` method, which adds a display point and repaints the canvas.

Listing 10.6   **Graphing Polar Coordinates**

```
# file: PolarGraph.py
import java
from java.lang import System
from java import awt
from java.lang import Math

class Main(awt.Frame):
    def __init__(self):
        self.background=awt.Color.gray
        self.bounds=(50,50,400,400)
        self.windowClosing=lambda e: System.exit(0)
```

continues

Listing 10.6 **Continued**

```python
        self.r = awt.Label("r:          ")
        self.theta = awt.Label("theta:           ")
        infoPanel = awt.Panel()
        infoPanel.add(self.r)
        infoPanel.add(self.theta)
        self.graph = PolarCanvas()
        self.add("North", infoPanel)
        self.add("Center", self.graph)
        self.visible = 1
        self.graph.mouseMoved = self.updateCoords

    def updateCoords(self, e):
        limit = self.graph.limit
        width = self.graph.width
        height = self.graph.height
        x = (2 * e.x * limit)/width - limit
        y = limit - (2 * e.y * limit)/height
        r = Math.sqrt(x**2 + y**2)
        if x == 0:
            theta = 0
        else:
            theta = Math.atan(Math.abs(y)/Math.abs(x))
        if x < 0 and y > 0:
            theta = Math.PI - theta
        elif x < 0 and y <= 0:
            theta = theta + Math.PI
        elif x > 0 and y < 0:
            theta = 2 * Math.PI - theta
        self.r.text = "r: %0.2f" % r
        self.theta.text = "theta: %0.2f" % theta

class PolarCanvas(awt.Canvas):
    def __init__(self, interval=100, limit=400):
        self.background=awt.Color.white
        self.mouseReleased=self.onClick
        self.interval = interval
        self.limit = limit
        self.points = []

    def onClick(self, e):
        x = (2 * e.x * self.limit)/self.width - self.limit
        y = self.limit - (2 * e.y * self.limit)/self.height
        self.points.append(awt.Point(x, y))
        self.repaint()

    def paint(self, g):
        rings = self.limit/self.interval
        step = (self.width/(rings*2), self.height/(rings*2))
        # Draw rings
```

```
            for x in range(1, rings + 1):
                r = awt.Rectangle(x*step[0], x*step[1],
                                  step[0] *(rings-x)*2,
                                  step[1]*(rings-x)*2)
                lambda x, y: max(y - x * 20, 10)
                g.color = (max(140-x*20,10), max(200-x*20,10),
                           max(240-x*20,10))
                g.fillOval(r.x, r.y, r.width, r.height)
                g.color = awt.Color.black
                g.drawOval(r.x, r.y, r.width, r.height)
                g.drawString(str((rings*self.interval)-(x*self.interval)),
                             r.x - 8, self.height/2 + 12)

            # draw center dot
            g.fillOval(self.width/2-2, self.height/2-2, 4, 4)

            # draw points
            g.color = awt.Color.red
            for p in self.points:
                x = (p.x * self.width)/(2 * self.limit) + self.width/2
                y = self.height/2 - (p.y * self.height)/(2 * self.limit)
                g.fillOval(x, y, 4, 4)

    if __name__ == '__main__':
        app = Main()
```

Figure 10.5 shows the results from running the PolarGraph.py module.

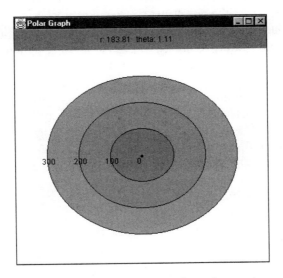

Figure 10.5 Mouse events and a polar graph.

Images

Although there is little innovation in displaying images with Jython, it makes for yet another good comparison with Java. Listing 10.7 displays a simple image in an AWT frame. The implementation in Listing 10.7 is similar to how it would be done in Java, especially considering how the application's top frame is a class that subclasses the java.awt.Frame. This is done to make use of the component's paint method, which is difficult to use without creating a subclass because of the way update and repaint work. Aspects that differ from Java are again the bean properties, event properties, and keyword assignments that appear in the jyimage class constructor.

Listing 10.7 displays an image designated by a name in the jyimage constructor. The image displayed in this example is the logo from Jython's website (http://www.jython.org). You can download this image to reproduce the same results as Listing 10.7. Listing 10.7 assumes that this image is within the current working directory so that it can just use the file name without qualifying the path.

Interesting points in Listing 10.7 are the getDefaultToolkit() method and the MediaTracker object. It is common to assume that getDefaultToolkit() translates into a bean property accessible with awt.Toolkit.defaultToolkit; however, it doesn't qualify as a static class method, so you must use the full call awt.Toolkit.getDefaultToolkit(). Listing 10.7 uses the default toolkit to load the displayed image. To make sure that the entire image is loaded before painting it, Listing 10.7 uses the awt.MediaTracker. This makes it unnecessary to define an imageUpdate and other issues related to incremental loading of images. A Java application would require a try/catch statement surrounding the mt.waitForID() method, and while this is likely good practice in Jython, it is not required.

It is potentially common knowledge in the Java community, but it's worth repeating the use of addNotify and insets. The (0,0) coordinate of a frame is under the title bar. This necessitates using the frames inset information to determine the total dimensions of the frame, and getInsets is only usable after creating a peer with the addNotify() method.

Listing 10.7 **Displaying Images**

```
# file jyimage.py
from java.lang import System
from java import awt

class jyimage(awt.Frame):
    def __init__(self, im):
```

```
        self.im = awt.Toolkit.getDefaultToolkit().getImage(im)
        self.bounds=100,100,200,200
        self.title="Jython Image Display"
        self.windowClosing=lambda e: System.exit(0)

        mt = awt.MediaTracker(self)
        mt.addImage(self.im, 0)
        mt.waitForID(0)
        self.addNotify()   # add peer to get insets
        i = self.insets
        self.resize(self.im.width + i.left + i.right,
                    self.im.height + i.top + i.bottom)

    def paint(self, g):
        g.drawImage(self.im, self.insets.left, self.insets.top, self)


if __name__ == '__main__':
    f = jyimage("jython-new-small.gif")
    f.visible = 1
```

Figure 10.6 shows the results of executing the `imagedisplay.py`.

Figure 10.6   Displaying an image with Jython.

Menus and Menu Events

Frames have a menu bar property that designates which instance of the
`java.awt.MenuBar` class acts as its menu bar. The instance of `java.awt.MenuBar`
contains instances of the `java.awt.MenuItem` class for each menu item you wish
to implement. The steps to create a menu bar in Jython are fill a `MenuBar`
instance with `MenuItem` instance(s), then assign the `MenuBar` to the frame's
`menuBar` property.

Implementing menu item actions requires only an assignment to each
`MenuItem`'s `actionPerformed` property. Listing 10.8 shows the ease in which
menus and their associated actions are added to a frame in Jython. The use of
Jython's `getattr` function in this listing makes tying menu actions to methods
a snap.

Listing 10.8 *AWT* **Menus**

```python
# file: jythonmenus.py
from java import awt
from java.awt import event
from java.lang import System

menus = [
    ('File', ['New', 'Open', 'Save', 'Saveas', 'Close']),
    ('Edit', ['Copy', 'Cut', 'Paste']),
]

class MenuTest(awt.Frame):
    def __init__(self):
        bar = awt.MenuBar()
        for menu, menuitems in menus:
            menu = awt.Menu(menu)
            for menuitem in menuitems:
                method = getattr(self, 'on%s' % menuitem)
                item = awt.MenuItem(menuitem, actionPerformed=method)
                menu.add(item)
            bar.add(menu)
        self.menuBar = bar
        self.windowClosing = lambda e: System.exit(0)
        self.eventLabel = awt.Label("Event: ")
        self.bounds = 100, 100, 200, 100
        self.add(self.eventLabel)

    def onNew(self, e):
        self.eventLabel.text = "Event: onNew"

    def onOpen(self, e):
        self.eventLabel.text = "Event: onOpen"

    def onSave(self, e):
        self.eventLabel.text = "Event: onSave"

    def onSaveas(self, e):
        self.eventLabel.text = "Event: onSaveas"

    def onClose(self, e):
        self.eventLabel.text = "Event: onClose"
        System.exit(0)

    def onCopy(self, e):
        self.eventLabel.text = "Event: onCopy"

    def onCut(self, e):
        self.eventLabel.text = "Event: onCut"

    def onPaste(self, e):
```

```
        self.eventLabel.text = "Event: onPaste"

f = MenuTest()
f.visible = 1
```

Figures 10.7 and 10.8 show how the `jythonmenus` module from Listing 10.8 works. Figure 10.7 shows the File menu pulled down, and Figure 10.8 show the updated label as a result of the menu selection.

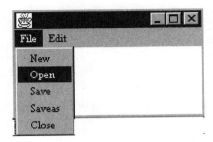

Figure 10.7   *AWT* Menu and Events File menu.

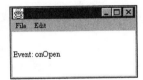

Figure 10.8   *AWT* Menu and Events After the label update.

Drag and Drop

Jython has no abbreviation mechanism for implementing drag and drop (DnD) functionality. Just as in Java, the implementation involves implementing the required DnD interfaces: `DragGestureListener`, `DragSourceListener`, and `DropTargetListener`. The class(es) that implement these interfaces then establish a drag source and a drop target.

Establishing a drag source requires two steps: instantiating the `java.awt.dnd.DragSource` class, and using that class to create the drag source recognizer. The Jython code for these two steps is as follows:

```
from java.awt import dnd
myDragSource = dnd.DragSource()
myDragRecognizer = myDragSource.createDefaultDragGestureRecognizer(
```

```
                          some_component,
                          dnd.DnDConstants.ACTION_COPY_OR_MOVE,
                          implementation_of_dnd.DragGestureListener)
```

The three arguments to create the recognizer are the drag source component, the action and the drag listener. The drag source is any component that you wish to drag things from. The action is a value designating which actions are appropriate for the drag gestures. The action values are in the `java.awt.dnd.DnDConstants` class. The third argument is an instance of a class that implements the `java.awt.dnd.DragGestureListener` interface. The `JythonDnD` class in Listing 10.9 instantiates the gesture recognizer with a `java.awt.List` for the drag source, copy or move for the action, and itself (self) as the `DragGestureListener`.

Once a drag source and drag gesture recognizer are established, the application needs a place to drop items. Listing 10.9 uses a class that extends `java.awt.List` appropriately called `DropList`. The drop portion of DnD requires a class that implements the `java.awt.dnd.DropTargetListener`, which the `DropList` class in Listing 10.9 does.

Listing 10.9   **Drag and Drop Lists**

```python
# file: ListDnD.py
from java import awt
from java.awt import dnd
from java.lang import System
from java.awt import datatransfer

class JythonDnD(awt.Frame, dnd.DragSourceListener, dnd.DragGestureListener):
    def __init__(self):
        self.title="Jython Drag -n- Drop Implementation"
        self.bounds = 100, 100, 300, 200
        self.windowClosing = lambda e: System.exit(0)

        self.draglist = awt.List()
        map(self.draglist.add, ["1","2","3","4","5"])
        self.droplist = droplist([])
        self.dropTarget = dnd.DropTarget(self,
            dnd.DnDConstants.ACTION_COPY_OR_MOVE, self.droplist)

        self.layout = awt.GridLayout(1, 2, 2, 2)
        self.add(self.draglist)
        self.add(self.droplist)
        self.dragSource = dnd.DragSource()
        self.recognize = self.dragSource.createDefaultDragGestureRecognizer(
                        self.draglist,
                        dnd.DnDConstants.ACTION_COPY_OR_MOVE,
                        self)

    def dragGestureRecognized(self, e):
        item = self.draglist.getSelectedItem()
```

```
        e.startDrag(self.dragSource.DefaultCopyDrop,
                    datatransfer.StringSelection(item), self)

    def dragEnter(self, e): pass
    def dragOver(self, e): pass
    def dragExit(self, e): pass
    def dragDropEnd(self, e): pass
    def dropActionChanged(self, e): pass

class droplist(awt.List, dnd.DropTargetListener):
    def __init__(self, datalist):
        map(self.add, datalist)
        self.dropTarget = dnd.DropTarget(self, 3, self)

    def drop(self, e):
        transfer = e.getTransferable()
        data = transfer.getTransferData(datatransfer.DataFlavor.stringFlavor)
        self.add(data)
        e.dropComplete(1)

    def dragEnter(self, e):
        e.acceptDrag(dnd.DnDConstants.ACTION_COPY_OR_MOVE)

    def dragExit(self, e): pass
    def dragOver(self, e): pass
    def dropActionChanged(self, e): pass

win = JythonDnD()
win.visible=1
```

The product of Listing 10.9 is two lists. The leftmost list contains items that you can drag and drop into the empty, rightmost list. Figure 10.9 shows the GUI produced by this DnD example after a few items have already been dropped on the rightmost list.

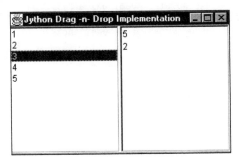

Figure 10.9   Drag and drop lists.

Swing

Using the Swing classes are not very different from using the AWT. Swing is a substantial change to the internal implementation of GUIs and provides an overwhelming wealth of components to choose from, but it does not fundamentally change how graphical applications are built. This combined with the continued prevalence of beans makes Jython equally effective for developing Swing applications.

Writing a Swing application in Jython still benefits from automatic bean properties and event properties. These combined with the keyword parameters drastically improve working with Swing components just as they do for AWT components.

Listing 10.10 shows a simple tree display in a Swing application. The only subtle difference between the JFrame in Listing 10.10 and earlier AWT Frame examples is the use of the JFrame's contentPane. Besides this subtle difference, studying this example mostly reinforces the similarities between working with the AWT and the Swing. Jython's role is expediting component properties and events that a component fires with automatic bean properties and event properties.

Listing 10.10 **A *Swing* Tree**

```
# file: SwingTree.py
from javax import swing
from javax.swing import tree
import sys

top_frame = swing.JFrame("A Simple Tree in Jython and Swing",
                         windowClosing=lambda e: sys.exit(0),
                         background=(180,180,200),
                         )
data = tree.DefaultMutableTreeNode("Root")
data.add(tree.DefaultMutableTreeNode("a leaf"))
childNode = tree.DefaultMutableTreeNode("a node")
childNode.add(tree.DefaultMutableTreeNode("another leaf"))
data.add(childNode)
t = swing.JTree(data)

t.putClientProperty("JTree.lineStyle", "Angled")
top_frame.contentPane.add(t)
top_frame.bounds = 100, 100, 200, 200
top_frame.visible = 1
```

The graphics produced from Listing 10.10 appear in Figure 10.10.

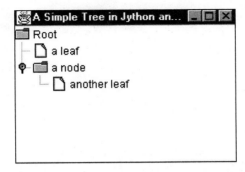

Figure 10.10   Jython tree display.

11

Database Programming

T HIS CHAPTER DETAILS THE USE OF DATABASES with Jython. Jython can use any database tool Java can, but this chapter focuses on the DBM database files, the MySQL database server and the PostgreSQL object–relational database management system (ORDBMS). This chapter also includes Jython object serialization and persistence. Topics include DBM, serialization, persistence, MySQL, PostgreSQL, the JDBC API, the zxJDBC API, and transactions.

DBM Files

DBM files are hashed database files that act similarly to a dictionary object. This similarity is somewhat limited because current implementations do not use all dictionary methods and because all DBM keys and values must be strings. Various DBM tools will work with Jython, but only one is currently bundled with Jython: dumbdbm. The name isn't necessarily enticing, and the implementation is simple and slow; however, it is a moderately effective DBM clone. In the future, it is likely that other DBM modules will be available for Jython as well.

The following simple interactive example using the `dumbdbm` module shows how using `dumbdbm` requires calling its module's `open()` method, then you can use the opened object much like a dictionary—with restrictions.

```
>>> import dumbdbm
>>> dbm = dumbdbm.open("dbmtest")
>>> dbm['Value 1'] = 'A'
>>> dbm['Value 2'] = 'B'
>>> dbm['Value 3'] = 'B'
>>> for key in dbm.keys():
...     print key, ":", dbm[key]
...
Value 3 : B
Value 2 : B
Value 1 : A
>>>
>>>dir(dbm.__class__)
['__delitem__', '__doc__', '__getitem__', '__init__', '__len__',
'__module__', '__setitem__', '_addkey', '_addval', '_commit', '_setval',
'_update', 'close', 'has_key', 'keys']
>>>
>>> dbm.close()
```

The `dir(dbm.__class__)` method shows how the `dbm` object differs from a dictionary. Of the dictionary methods, only `keys` and `has_key` are implemented. The minimum special methods expected of dictionary objects (`__setitem__`, `__delitem__`, `__getitem__`, and `__len__`) do appear. Because a DBM object behaves like a dictionary, there is no need to explain its usage, and although it lacks some of the dictionary methods, it does have one distinct advantage: It is persistent. Re-opening the `dbmtest` catalog shows the values previously entered:

```
>>> import dumbdbm
>>> dbm = dumbdbm.open("dbmtest")
>>> for key in dbm.keys():
...     print key, ":", dbm[key]
...
Value 3 : B
Value 2 : B
Value 1 : A
>>> dbm.close()
```

Opening a new `dumbdbm` catalog actually creates two files: one with a `.dir` extension, and another with a `.dat` extension. No extension is required in the open function, only the catalog name. Other DBM implementations allow for flags and mode arguments in the open function, but `dumbdbm` ignores such arguments.

Serialization

Serializing makes an object into a stream suitable for transmission or storage. The storage part is what warrants including this topic with databases, as that is where such serialized objects often reside. To serialize a Jython object, use the marshal, pickle, or cPickle module. The *marshal module* works only on built-in types, whereas the *pickle* module works with built-in objects, module-global classes and functions, and most instance objects. The *cPickle module* is a high-performance, Java version of the pickle module. Its name is borrowed from CPython's cPickle module and does not mean it is written in C. The shelve module combines databases with pickle to create persistent object storage. Jython's PythonObjectInputStream is an ObjectInputStream that helps with resolving classes when deserializing Jython objects that inherit from Java classes.

The *marshal* Module

The marshal module serializes code objects and built-in data objects. It is most frequently foregone in favor of the cPickle module described next, but it nonetheless sometimes appears in projects. Note that one draw the marshal module has for CPython is its ability to compile code objects; however, this is currently not true for Jython objects, leaving the marshal module less used.

The marshal module has four methods: dump, dumps, load, and loads. The dump and load methods serialize and restore an object to and from a file. Therefore, the arguments to dump are the object to serialize and the file object, while the arguments for load are just the file object. The file object given to the dump and load functions must have been opened in binary mode. The dumps and loads methods serialize and restore an object to and from a string.

The following interactive example demonstrates using marshal with a list object. Remember that the marshal module does not serialize arbitrary objects, only the common built-in objects. In the current implementation, if marshal cannot serialize the object, a KeyError is raised.

```
>>> import marshal
>>> file = open("myMarshalledData.dat", "w+b") # Must be Binary mode
>>> L = range(30, 50, 7)
>>> marshal.dump(L, file)  # serialize object L to 'file'
>>>
>>> file.flush() # flush or close after the dump to ensure integrity
>>> file.seek(0) # put file back at beginning for load()
>>>
>>> restoredL = marshal.load(file)
```

```
>>> print L
[30, 37, 44]
>>> print restoredL
[30, 37, 44]
```

The *pickle* and *cPickle* Modules

The `pickle` and `cPickle` modules are the preferred means of serializing Jython objects. The difference between `pickle` and `cPickle` is only implementation and performance, but there is no usage difference between the two. Most objects, except Java objects, code objects and those Jython objects that have tricky `__getattr__` and `__setattr__` methods, may be serialized with `pickle` or `cPickle`. Note that future references to the `pickle` module refer to either `pickle` or `cPickle`, but all examples will use the `cPickle` module because of its marked performance advantage.

The `pickle` module defines four functions that appear in Table 11.1. The `dump` and `dumps` functions serialize objects and the `load` and `loads` functions deserialize them.

Table 11.1 **Pickle Methods**

Method	Description
Dump(object, file[, bin])	Serializes a built-in data object to a previously opened file object. If the object cannot be serialized, a `PicklingError` exception is raised. `pickle` can use a text or binary format. A zero or missing third argument means text format, and a nonzero third argument indicates binary.
Load(file)	Reads and deserializes data from a previously opened file object. If the pickled data was written with the file in binary mode, the file object supplied to load should also be in binary mode.
dumps(object[, bin])	Serializes an object to a string object rather than to a file. A `PicklingError` is raised if the object cannot be serialized. A zero or missing second argument means text format, and a nonzero second argument indicates binary.
loads(string)	Deserializes a string into a data object.

The `pickle` module also defines a `PicklingError` exception that is raised when it encounters an object that cannot be pickled.

Following is a simple interactive example using `pickle` to store an instance of a class called `product`. This example specifies binary mode for the file object and specifies the binary `pickle` mode by adding a non-zero, third argument to `cPickle.dump`:

```
>>> import cPickle
>>> class product:
...     def __init__(self, productCode, data):
...         self.__dict__.update(data)
...         self.productCode = productCode
...
>>> data = {'name':'widget', 'price':'112.95', 'inventory':1000}
>>> widget = product('1123', data)
>>> f = open(widget.productCode, "wb")
>>> cPickle.dump(widget, f, 1)
>>> f.close()
```

Now the `widget` product is stored in a file named `1123`—the product's `productCode`. Restoring this instance uses the `cPickle.load` function, but in order to re-create the instance properly, its class must exist in the namespace where it is unpickled. Assume the following interactive example is a new session that reconstructs the `widget` product. The `product` class must be defined again to ensure it is available for the instance's reconstruction. Because the original file was opened in binary mode, subsequent access to the file must specify binary mode:

```
>>> import cPickle
>>> class product:
...     def __init__(self, productCode, data):
...         self.__dict__.update(data)
...         self.productCode = productCode
...
>>> f = open("1123", "rb")
>>> widget = cPickle.load(f)
>>> f.close()
>>> vars(widget)
{'name': 'widget', 'productCode': '1123', 'price': '112.95', 'inventory':
1000}
```

An object can control its pickling and unpickling by defining the special methods __getstate__ and __setstate__. If __getstate__ is defined, its return value is what is serialized when an object is pickled. If __setstate__ is defined, it is called with the de-serialized data (what __getstate__ returned) when reconstructing an object. The __getstate__ and __setstate__ methods are complementary, but both are not required. If you do not define __setstate__, then __getstate__ must return a dictionary. If you do not define __getstate__, then __setstate__ receives a dictionary (the instance __dict__) when loading.

You can alternatively use `pickler` and `unpickler` objects. To create these objects, supply the appropriate file object to the `pickle.Pickler` or `pickle.Unpickler` class.

```
>>> import cPickle
>>> f = open("picklertest", "w+b")
>>> p = cPickle.Pickler(f)
>>> u = cPickle.Unpickler(f)
>>>
>>> L = range(10)
>>> p.dump(L)   # use pickler object to serialize
>>> f.seek(0)
>>> print u.load()
[0, 1, 2, 3, 4, 5, 6, 7, 8, 9]
```

`pickle` handles recursive data structures, objects that contain a reference to themselves, and nested data structures, such as a dictionary that contains a list that contains a `tuple` and so on. A `Pickler` object stores a reference to all the previously pickled objects, ensuring that no serialization happens for later references to the same object, whether additional references are from recursion or nesting. Reusing a `Pickler` object allows shared objects to be pickled only once, and `Pickler.dump()` only writes a short reference for those objects it encounters that where previously pickled.

Shelves

Jython's *shelve module* combines the convenience of DBM catalogs with `pickle`'s serialization to create a persistent object storage. A `shelve` acts like a dictionary, similar to the `dumbdbm` module, but the difference is that a `shelve` allows any picklable object as values, even though keys still must be strings. Following is an interactive example of using the `shelve` module:

```
>>> import shelve, dumbdbm
>>> dbm = dumbdbm.open("dbmdata")
>>> shelf = shelve.Shelf(dbm)
>>> shelf['a list'] = range(10)
>>> shelf['a dictionary'] = {1:1, 2:2, 3:3}
>>> print shelf.keys()
['a list', 'a dictionary']
>>> shelf.close()
```

You may alternately use the `shelve` open method itself, as shown here, skipping the `dumbdbm.open(...)` step:

```
>>> import shelve
>>> shelf = shelve.open("dbmdata")
```

PythonObjectInputStream

The process of serializing Jython objects from within Java is the same as for serializing Java objects with but one exception: `org.python.util.`
`PythonObjectInputStream`. Normally, Jython objects serialize and deserialize as expected from Java, but the `PythonObjectInputStream` helps resolve classes when deserializing Jython objects that inherit from a Java class. This doesn't mean that it only works for those that subclass a Java object. It works with any Jython object, but is most valuable when deserializing those Jython objects with Java superclasses.

Serializing a Jython object from Java requires the steps shown in the following pseudo-code:

```
// Import required classes
import java.io.*;
import org.python.core.*;

// Identify the resource
String file = "someFileName";

// To serialize, make an OutputStream (FileOutputStream in this case)
// and then an ObjectOutputStream.
FileOutputStream oStream = new FileOutputStream(file);
ObjectOutputStream objWriter = new ObjectOutputStream(oStream);

// Write a simple Jython object
objWriter.writeObject(new PyString("some string"));

// clean up
objWriter.flush();
oStream.close();
```

Deserializing the object from the example above can use either the `ObjectInputStream` or the `PythonObjectInputStream`. The steps required appear in the following pseudo-code:

```
// Import required classes
import java.io.*;
import org.python.core.*;
import org.python.util.PythonObjectInputStream;

// Identify the resource
String file = "someFileName;

// Open an InputStrea (FileInputStream in this case)
FileInputStream iStream = new FileInputStream(file);

// Use the input stream to open an ObjectInputStream or a
// PythonObjectInputStream.
```

```
PythonObjectInputStream objReader =
    new PythonObjectInputStream(iStream);

// It could be this for objects without java superclasses
// ObjectInputStream objReader = new ObjectInputStream(iStream);

// Read the object
PyObject po = (PyObject)objReader.readObject();

// clean up
iStream.close();
```

Database Management Systems

This section details using Jython to interact with the MySQL and PostgreSQL database management systems (DBMS). Jython can work with any database that has a Java driver, but these two were chosen because they are extremely popular, freely available, very stable, commonly deployed, and have a lot of documentation. Additionally, New Riders has the books *MySQL*, by Paul DuBois, and *PostgreSQL Essential Reference*, by Barry Stinson. Both these books are useful resources in exploring these databases, and you can investigate these books further at http://www.newriders.com. Examples within this chapter are each written using a specific database, but most will actually work with either database, or even other databases not mentioned here, with slight modifications. The exception is that examples using features that exist in PostgreSQL, but not MySQL, obviously will not work without those underlying features (such as transactions).

The differences between MySQL and PostgreSQL are speed and features. This might be an oversimplification when comparing complex data systems, but the general guideline is that MySQL is fast—very fast—and PostgreSQL is very advanced in respect to features. An update or select operation is faster with MySQL, but PostgreSQL provides transaction integrity, constraints, rules, triggers, and inheritance. *MySQL* is a SQL database server that follows the relational database model (it stores data in separate tables) while PostgreSQL is an object-relational database management system (ORDMS). MySQL uses only tabular data, but when using object-oriented languages, it is sometimes difficult to get objects to fit the tabular structure. This gives cause for *ORDBMS*, allowing representation of non-traditional data structures within an underlying relational model.

Using PostgreSQL or MySQL has security implications because each is available to network connections. The administration of these database systems is well beyond the scope of this book, but it is important to encourage those users new to these databases to explore the relevant security and administrative documentation available for each system.

MySQL

MySQL is an SQL database server that runs on most UNIX-like platforms and on Windows. To run the MySQL-specific examples in this chapter, you must download and install MySQL and its associated JDBC driver, or alter the examples to work with whichever database system you decide to use. MySQL is available from `http://www.mysql.com/` in the "downloads" section. The MySQL JDBC driver is located in the same downloads section of the website, but the most current driver and release information is at `http://mmmysql.sourceforge.net/`. The version of the JDBC driver used in this chapter is `mm.mysql-2.0.4-bin.jar`. This is actually just one of the drivers available for MySQL, but it is currently the most commonly used and best JDBC driver available for MySQL.

Installation instructions are unnecessary because MySQL comes as a Windows installer or in `*nix` package format. Just run the installer or package manager as required. The MySQL JDBC driver requires no installation, it just needs to be added to the `classpath`. After installing MySQL, however, you must add a user and a database. Examples in this chapter will use the user `jyuser`, the password `beans`, and the database `test` unless specified otherwise. To start the server, use the command appropriate to your platform from the commands below:

```
# *nix. "user" designates the name of the user to own the process
/pathToMysql/bin/safe_mysqld &

# windows
\pathToMysql\bin\winmysqladmin.exe
```

The `test` database used in this chapter should be automatically created when MySQL is installed, but if for some reason the `test` database does not exist, create it. To create the `test` database, connect to the server from a command shell with the MySQL client program `mysql`, then enter the `CREATE DATABASE` command. The client program `mysql` is located in the bin directory within MySQL's installation directory. You need to run this program as the user who has appropriate privileges. Note that the SQL commands are terminated with `;`, `\g`, or `\G`.

```
C:\mysql\bin>mysql
Welcome to the MySQL monitor.  Commands end with ; or \g.
Your MySQL connection id is 3 to server version: 3.23.39

Type 'help;' or '\h' for help. Type '\c' to clear the buffer.

mysql> CREATE DATABASE test;
Query OK, 1 row affected (0.33 sec)
```

You can confirm the database exists with the SHOW DATABASES statement:

```
mysql> SHOW DATABASES\g
+----------+
| Database |
+----------+
| mysql    |
| test     |
+----------+
2 rows in set (0.00 sec)mysql>
```

Next, add the user jyuser. This user will require all permissions to the test database. To do this, use the GRANT statement. There are four parts to the GRANT statement that equate to what, where, who and how. Following is a summary of the GRANT statement's syntax:

```
GRANT what ON where TO who IDENTIFIED BY how
```

what designates which permissions are being granted. We shall grant ALL permissions to the user *jyuser*. *where* means in which databases and tables these permissions apply—the test database in our case. *who* specifies not only the username, but also the source machine from which requests may originate. The user for examples within this chapter is jyuser, and the source location should be from the machine you will use to connect to the database. The example GRANT statement below assumes all jyuser connections originate from the localhost. To add additional source addresses, use the percent sign as a wild card, such as 192.168.1.%, or even just % to allow from anywhere. Note that allowing users to connect from any host is troublesome. *how* is the means of authentication, or in other words, the password. This chapter uses the password beans. An example of the GRANT statement that fulfills the requirements of examples in this chapter is this:

```
mysql> USE test;
mysql> GRANT ALL ON test TO jyuser@localhost IDENTIFIED BY "beans";
Query OK, 0 rows affected (0.05 sec)
```

The setup for examples in this chapter is complete. The following section follows the same setup procedures for the PostgreSQL database, so skip ahead to the section "JDBC" if you are only using the MySQL database.

PostgreSQL

PostgreSQL is a very advanced and full-featured ORDBMS. PostgreSQL runs on most UNIX-like platforms and Windows 2000/NT. The PostgreSQL examples that appear in this chapter require the use of a PostgreSQL server and the PostgreSQL JDBC driver, which are available from `http://www.post-gresql.org/`. This chapter assumes an installation on a `*nix` system. Because Windows lacks much of the UNIX-like functionality, installing PostgreSQL on Windows requires additional packages and is generally more troublesome. To install on a UNIX-like system, download the package format appropriate for your system and run your package manager. To Install PostgreSQL on a Windows 2000/NT system, first download the `Cygwin` and `cygipc` packages required to emulate a UNIX environment on a Windows OS. The `Cygwin` package is available at `http://sources.redhat.com/cygwin/` and the `cygipc` package is available at `http://www.neuro.gatech.edu/users/cwilson/cygutils/V1.1/cygipc/`. Then follow the instructions found in the file `doc/FAQ_MSWIN` within the PostgreSQL distribution or the instructions found in Chapter 2 of the PostgreSQL Administrator's guide that is freely available at `http://www.ca.postgresql.org/users-lounge/docs/7.1/admin/install-win32.html`.

After the server has been installed, you will need to initialize a database cluster. This should be done as the user who administers the PostgreSQL database—usually *postgres*. You should not perform administrative operations on the database as `root` or `administrator`. The command to initialize a database cluster is the following:

```
initdb -D /path/to/datadirectory
```

The `initdb` file comes with PostgreSQL. The data directory is usually `/usr/local/pgsql/data`, making the command as follows:

```
initdb -D /usr/local/pgsql/data
```

Within the data directory created with the preceding command is the file `pg_hba.conf`. This file controls which hosts connect to the database. Before you can connect to the database with the JDBC driver, there must be a host entry in the `pg_hba.conf` file for the machine you will use to connect from. A host entry requires the word "host," the database name that host is allows to connect to, the IP address of the connection machine, a bit mask indicating significant bits in the IP address, and the authentication type. If you will connect from the local machine, the host entry would look like this:

```
host test 127.0.0.1 255.255.255.255 crypt
```

The authentication type can be any of the following:

- **Trust**—No authentication required.
- **Password**—Match username with a password.
- **Crypt**—Same as "password," but the password in encrypted when sent over the network.
- **Ident**—Authenticate with the ident server.
- **Krb4**—Use Kerberos V4 authentication.
- **Krb5**—Use Kerberos V5 authentication.
- **Reject**—Connections from the specified IP are rejected.

Next, you will need to create the user jyuser. PostgreSQL comes with a utility program appropriately called createuser that you should use to create the new user. The command to do so is as follows:

```
[shell prompt]$ createuser -U postgres -d -P jyuser
Enter password for user "jyuser":
Enter it again:
Shall the new user be allowed to create more new users? (y/n) n
CREATE USER
```

The password beans was entered at the password prompts, but it is not echoed back to the terminal. The output CREATE USER confirms that the action was successful. With the creation of a new user, you can now minimize tasks done as the postgres user. Performing subsequent tasks as jyuser is safer, such as the creation of the test database.

To create the test database, use the PostgreSQL utility program createdb. The command to create the test database with the createdb program is as follows:

```
[shell prompt]$ createdb -U jyuser test
CREATE DATABASE
```

The output CREATE DATABASE confirms that the creation was successful.

Now you can start the server. You should start the server under the username of the person who administers the server—most often *postgres*. To start the server, use the following command (replace the data directory path with the one you chose for your installation):

```
postmaster -i -D /usr/local/pgsql/data &
```

You must use the -i option because that is the only way PostgreSQL will accept network socket connections (required to connect with JDBC).

Now PostgreSQL is ready for the examples in this chapter.

JDBC

Java uses the JDBC and `java.sql` package to interact with SQL databases. This means Jython can also use JDBC and the `java.sql` package. Using the JDBC API and `java.sql` package to interact with SQL databases requires only the appropriate JDBC driver for the database used (and the database of course). Examples in this chapter rely on the MySQL and PostgreSQL drivers described in the earlier section "Database Management Systems." The actual interaction matches those steps taken in Java, only using Jython's syntax. Interacting requires a connection, a statement, a result set, and the ever present need to handle errors and warnings. Those are the basics, and using those basics from Jython is what appears in this section. Additionally, advanced features such as transactions, stored procedures appear here as well.

Connecting to the Database

A database connection requires a JDBC URL and most likely a username and password. Before continuing with the connection process, you should understand JDBC URLs.

JDBC URLs

A URL is a string that uniquely identifies a database connection. The syntax is as follows:

```
jdbc:<subprotocol>:<subname>
```

The URL begins with `jdbc:`, followed by the subprotocol, which most often coincides with the database vendor product name (such as Oracle, MySQL, PostgreSQL). Beyond that, URLs are driver-specific, meaning that the `subname` depends on the `subprotocol`. Below is the JDBC URL syntax for the MySQL database and the URL syntax for the PostgreSQL database:

```
jdbc:mysql://[hostname][:port]/databaseName[parameter=value]
jdbc:postgresql://[hostname][:port]/databaseName[parameter=value]
```

There is only one word difference between these two URLs and that is the subprotocol (product) name. To connect to the `test` database on the local machine, use command below with the protocol matching the database system you wish to connect to:

```
jdbc:mysql://localhost:3306/test
jdbc:postgresql://localhost:5432/test
```

The default host is localhost, so it is actually not required in the URL. The default ports for MySQL and PostgreSQL are 3306 and 5432 respectively, so those numbers are also unnecessary as the default value is correct. This shortens localhost connections to the test database to the following:

```
jdbc:mysql:///test
jdbc:postgresql:///test
```

Note that the number of slashes remains the same, but the colon that separates the host and port number is omitted when no port specified.

Below are some example JDBC URLs for other database drivers. These URLs assume that the database name is test:

```
Driver: COM.ibm.db2.jdbc.net.DB2Driver
URL: jdbc:db2//localhost/test

Driver: oracle.jdbc.driver.OracleDriver
URL: jdbc:oracle:thin:@localhost:ORCL

Driver: sun.jdbc.odbc.JdbcOdbcDriver
URL: JDBC:ODBC:test

Driver: informix.api.jdbc.JDBCDriver
URL: jdbc:informix-sqli://localhost/test
```

At the end of a JDBC URL, you may specify connection parameters. *Parameters* can be any number of the database driver's allowed parameters separated by the & character. Table 11.2 shows each parameter, its meaning, its default value, and which of the two databases (MySQL or PostgreSQL) allows this parameter. The `java.sql` package also contains the class `DriverPropertyInfo`, which is another way of exploring and setting connection properties.

Table 11.2 **Driver Parameters**

Parameter	Meaning	Default Value	Database
User	Your database user name	none	Both
password	Your password	none	Both
autoReconnect	Attempt to reconnect if the connection dies? (true | false)	false	MySQL
maxReconnects	How many times should the driver try to reconnect? (Assuming autoReconnect is true.)	3	MySQL

Parameter	Meaning	Default Value	Database
`initialTimeout`	How many seconds to wait before reconnecting? (Assuming `autoReconnct` is true.)	2	MySQL
`maxRows`	The maximum number of rows to return (0 = all rows)	0	MySQL
`useUnicode`	Use Unicode—true or false?	false	MySQL
`characterEncoding`	Use which Unicode character encoding (if `useUnicode` is true)	none	MySQL

The following is an example URL that specifies the `test` database on the local machine, and it specifies to use Unicode character encoding for strings. The port is missing, but that is only required if it is other than the default:

```
jdbc:mysql://localhost/test?useUnicode=true
jdbc:postgresql://localhost/test?useUnicode=true
```

If the hostname is again excluded because `localhost` is already the default value, then these URLs become the following:

```
jdbc:mysql:///test?useUnicode=true
jdbc:postgresql:///test?useUnicode=true
```

Specifying the `products` database on a machine with the IP address 192.168.1.10, on port 8060, username `bob` and password `letmein` would look like this:

```
jdbc:mysql://192.168.1.10:8060/products?user=bob&password=letmein
jdbc:postgresql://192.168.1.10:8060/products?user=bob&password=letmein
```

In practice, the username and password are rarely specified as parameters because the actual connection methods already accept such parameters. Parameters can be burdensome in the URL string.

JDBC Connection

The steps to establishing a database connection using Java's database connectivity are as follows:

1. Include the appropriate driver in the `classpath`.
2. Register the driver with the JDBC `DriverManager`.
3. Supply a JDBC URL, username, and password to the `java.sql.DriverManager.getConnection` method.

You must ensure that an appropriate database driver exists in the classpath, either as an environment variable, or with Java's -classpath option in a Jython startup script. The filenames of the jar files for the MySQL and PostgreSQL JDBC drivers used in this chapter are mm.mysql-2_0_4-bin.jar and jdbc7.1-1.2.jar. Adding these jar files to the classpath requires the following shell commands:

```
# For MySQL
set CLASSPATH=\path\to\mm_mysql-2_0_4-bin.jar;%CLASSPATH%

# For PostgreSQL
set CLASSPATH=\path\to\jdbc7.1-1.2.jar;%CLASSPATH%
```

Once the drivers exist in the classpath, using JDBC requires that the drivers are also loaded, or registered with the DriverManager. There are two basic ways of loading the driver. You can set the jdbc.drivers property to the appropriate driver on the command line with the -D switch, or you can use the java.lang.Class.forName(classname) method.

Registering a driver with the -D options would require creating a new batch or script file to launch Jython. Two commands appear below, one which registers the MySQL driver, and another that registers the PostgreSQL driver.

```
dos>java -Djdbc.drivers=org.gjt.mm.mysql.Driver \
-Dpython.home=c:\jython-2.1 \
-classpath c:\jython-2.1\jython.jar;\path\to\mm.mysql-2_0_4-bin.jar \
org.python.util.jython

dos>java -Djdbc.drivers=org.postgresql.Driver \
-Dpython.home=c:\jython-2.1 \
-classpath c:\jython-2.1\jython.jar;\path\to\jdbc7.1-1.2.jar \
org.python.util.jython
```

You can also use Java's dynamic Class.forName(classname) syntax to load a driver. Remember that classes in the java.lang package are not automatically available in Jython as they are in Java, so you must import java.lang.Class or one of its parent packages before calling this method. The following example loads the MySQL and PostgreSQL drivers with Class.forName:

```
import java
try:
    java.lang.Class.forName("org.gjt.mm.mysql.Driver")
    java.lang.Class.forName("org.postgresql.Driver")
except java.lang.ClassNotFoundException:
    print "No appropriate database driver found"
    raise SystemExit
```

Just as it would in Java, the preceding example catches the Java ClassNotFoundException.

With the driver in the `classpath` and registered with the `DriverManager`, we are ready to connect to the database. For this, use the `java.sql.DriverManager`'s getConnection method. The getConnection method has three signatures:

```
public static Connection getConnection(String url) throws SQLException

public static Connection getConnection(String url, Properties info)
    throws SQLException

public static Connection getConnection(
    String url, String user, String password) throws SQLException
```

Assume the local database `test` exists, and that you are connecting to this database as `jyuser` with the password beans. The possible syntaxes for connecting are as follows:

```
from java.sql import DriverManager
from java.util import Properties

# Using the getConnection(URL) method
mysqlConn = DriverManager.getConnection(
    "jdbc:mysql://localhost/test?user=jyuser&password=beans")

postgresqlConn = java.sql.DriverManager.getConnection(
    "jdbc:postgresql://localhost/test?user=jyuser&password=beans")

# Using the getConnection(URL, Properties) method
params = Properties()
params.setProperty("user", "jyuser")
params.setProperty("password", "beans")

mysqlConn = DriverManager.getConnection("jdbc:mysql://localhost/test",
                                        params)

postgresqlConn =
    DriverManager.getConnection("jdbc:postgresql://localhost/test",
                                params)


# Using the getConnection(URL, String, String) method
mysqlConn =
    DriverManager.getConnection("jdbc:mysql://localhost/test",
                                "jyuser", "beans")

postgresqlConn =
    DriverManager.getConnection("jdbc:postgresql://localhost/test",
                                "jyuser", "beans")
```

Each of these methods returns a database connection that allows you to then interact with the database system.

Connection Scripts

Jython's interactive interpreter makes an ideal database client tool. Both MySQL and PostgreSQL have interactive, console client applications that are included with them, so using Jython's interactive interpreter would parallel those tools. However, you would also inherit Jython functions, classes, and so on, and have a consistent interface for any database with a JDBC driver.

The only thing Jython needs to become an interactive client is a connection. Typing in the database connection statements interactively in Jython each time you need to work with a database isn't a very good approach. Alternatively, you could use Jython's -i command-line option. When run with the -i option, Jython continues in interactive mode, even after the execution of a script. This allows you to setup database connection in a script, and continue to interact with the objects created by the script after its execution. The problem with the -i switch is that there is no mechanism to explicitly close database resources automatically. When working with databases, it is considered best to always explicitly close any database resource, so this would mean typing in the close method before quitting the interpreter each time you are finished working with the database—still not the best approach.

Wrapping an interactive console in the required connection and close statements, or using Java's `Runtime.addShutdownHook` could ensure connections are closed. Because the `addShutdownHook` is not available in all versions of Java, the best approach seems to be wrapping an `InteractiveConsole` instance in the required connection and close statements. Listing 11.1 does just that. The database connection and a statement object are created, then the inner `InteractiveConsole` is started with those objects in its namespace. When this inner `InteractiveConsole` exits, the connection and statement objects are closed.

Listing 11.1 **Database Client Startup Script**

```
# File: mystart.py

from java.lang import Class
from java.sql import DriverManager
from org.python.util import InteractiveConsole
import sys

url = "jdbc:mysql://localhost/%s"
user, password = "jyuser", "beans"
```

```
# Register driver
Class.forName("org.gjt.mm.mysql.Driver")

# Allow database to be optionally set as a command-line parameter
if len(sys.argv) == 2:
    url = url % sys.argv[1]
else:
    url = url % "test"

# Get connection
dbconn = DriverManager.getConnection(url, user, password)

# Create statement
try:
    stmt = dbconn.createStatement()
except:
    dbconn.close()
    raise SystemExit

# Create inner console
interp = InteractiveConsole({"dbconn":dbconn, "stmt":stmt}, "DB Shell")

try:
    interp.interact("Jython DB client")
finally:
    # Close resources
    stmt.close()
    dbconn.close()
    print
```

To connect to the test database, all you need to do is make sure the appropriate driver is in the `classpath`, then run `jython mystart.py`. Following is a sample interactive session that uses `mystart.py`.

```
shell-prompt> jython mystart.py
Jython DB Client
>>> dbconn.catalog
'test'
>>> # Exit the interpreter on the next line
>>>
```

A PostgreSQL startup script would be similar to the one in Listing 11.1 except for the `postgresql` name in the JDBC URL. Note that `dbconn.catalog` with PostgreSQL is empty.

Connection Dialog

Another common connection task is acquiring connection information with a dialog box. Client applications requiring a database login often acquire connection information with a dialog window. The frequency of this task warrants an example, and Listing 11.2 is just that. Listing 11.2 is a dialog window that establishes a database connection and returns that connection to a registered client object. The *client* object is any callable object that accepts one parameter: the connection. When the connection is successfully retrieved, the dialog box then forwards this connection to the registered client object. It is then the client's duty to close the connection.

Acquiring the connection occurs in the `login` method of the `DBLoginDialog` class in Listing 11.2. Two important `try`/`except` clauses exist in the `login` method. The first `try`/`except` catches the `ClassNotFoundException` in case the appropriate driver doesn't exist in the `classpath`, and the second `try`/`except` catches any `SQLException` that occurs while trying to actually get a connection to the database.

The `dummyClient` function defined in Listing 11.2 serves as the dialog's client for when the module is ran as the main script. A successful connection is passed to the `dummyClient`, and it is then the `dummyClient`'s duty to close that object.

Listing 11.2   **Database Connection Dialog Box**

```
# File: DBLoginDialog.py

import sys
import java
from java import awt
from java import sql
import pawt

class DBLoginDialog(awt.Dialog):
    '''DBLoginDialog prompts a user of database information and
    establishes a database login. A connection receiver is registered
    as client- for example:
        def connectionClient(dbconnection):
            # do something with database connection
        dbl = DBLoginDialog(parentframe, message)
        dbl.client = connectionClient'''

    def __init__(self, parentFrame, message):
        awt.Dialog.__init__(self, parentFrame)
        self.client = None
        self.background = pawt.colors.lightgrey
        bag = pawt.GridBag(self, anchor='WEST', fill='NONE')
```

```
    # Make required components
    self.Hostname = HighlightTextField("localhost", 24)
    self.DBMS = awt.Choice(itemStateChanged=self.updatePort)
    self.Port = HighlightTextField("3306", 5)
    self.Database = HighlightTextField("test",12)
    self.User = HighlightTextField("jyuser", 10)
    self.Password = HighlightTextField("", 10, echoChar='*')

    # Fill the choice component with opions
    self.DBMS.add("MySQL")
    self.DBMS.add("PostgreSQL")

    # add message
    bag.addRow(awt.Label(message), anchor='CENTER')

    # Put components in the bag
    for x in ["Hostname", "DBMS", "Port", "Database",
              "User", "Password"]:
        bag.add(awt.Label(x + ":"))
        bag.addRow(self.__dict__[x])

    # Add action buttons
    bag.add(awt.Button("Login", actionPerformed=self.login),
            fill='HORIZONTAL')
    bag.addRow(awt.Button("Cancel", actionPerformed= self.close),
               anchor='CENTER')

    self.pack()
    bounds = parentFrame.bounds
    self.bounds = (bounds.x + bounds.width/2 - self.width/2,
                   bounds.y + bounds.height/2 - self.height/2,
                   self.width, self.height)

def login(self, e):
    db = self.DBMS.selectedItem
    if db == "MySQL":
        driver =  "org.gjt.mm.mysql.Driver"
    else:
        driver = "org.postgresql.Driver"

    try:
        java.lang.Class.forName(driver)
    except java.lang.ClassNotFoundException:
        self.showError("Unable to load driver %s" % driver)
        return
    url = "jdbc:%s://%s:%s/%s" % (db.lower(), self.Hostname.text,
                                  self.Port.text,
                                  self.Database.text)
    try:
        dbcon = sql.DriverManager.getConnection(url,
                                                self.User.text,
                                                self.Password.text)
```

continues

Listing 11.2 **Continued**

```python
            self.dispose()
            self.client(dbcon)
        except sql.SQLException:
            self.showError("Unable to connect to database")

    def updatePort(self, e):
        if self.DBMS.selectedItem == 'MySQL':
            port = '3306'
        elif self.DBMS.selectedItem == 'PostgreSQL':
            port = '5432'
        self.Port.text= port

    def setClient(client):
        self.client = client

    def showError(self, message):
        d = awt.Dialog(self.parent, "Error")
        panel = awt.Panel()
        panel.add(awt.Label(message))
        button = awt.Button("OK")
        panel.add(button)
        d.add(panel)
        d.pack()
        bounds = self.parent.bounds
        d.bounds = (bounds.x + bounds.width/2 -d.width/2,
                    bounds.y + bounds.height/2 - d.height/2,
                    d.width, d.height)
        d.windowClosing = lambda e, d=d: d.dispose()
        button.actionPerformed = d.windowClosing
        d.visible = 1

    def close(self, e):
        self.dispose()

class HighlightTextField(awt.TextField, awt.event.FocusListener):
    def __init__(self, text, chars, **kw):
        awt.TextField.__init__(self, text, chars)
        self.addFocusListener(self)
        for k in kw.keys():
            exec("self." + k + "=kw[k]")

    def focusGained(self, e):
        e.source.selectAll()

    def focusLost(self, e):
        e.source.select(0, 0)

def dummyClient(connection):
```

```
     if connection != None:
         print "\nDatabase connection successfully received by client."
         print "Connection=", connection
         connection.close()
         print "Database connection properly closed by client."

 if __name__ == '__main__':
     # make a dummy frame to parent the dialog window
     f = awt.Frame("DB Login", windowClosing=lambda e: sys.exit())
     screensize = f.toolkit.screenSize
     f.bounds = (screensize.width/2 - f.width/2,
                 screensize.height/2 - f.height/2,
                 f.width, f.height)

     # create and show the dialog window
     dbi = DBLoginDialog(f, "Connection Information")
     dbi.client = dummyClient
     dbi.windowClosing = dbi.windowClosed = lambda e: sys.exit()
     dbi.visible = 1
```

To execute the DBLoginDialog, you must make sure the appropriate database drivers are in the classpath, then execute jython DBLoginDialog.py. You should see the login window shown in Figure 11.1

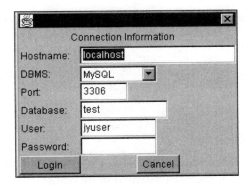

Figure 11.1 DB Login dialog box.

DatabaseMetaData

Once connected, you may explore information about the database and connection, or metadata. A Java connection object (java.sql.Connection) has the method getMetaData, which returns a java.sql.DatabaseMetaData object. The

DatabaseMetaData object provides thorough information about its related data-base connection. The DatabaseMetaData object has numerous methods, and you should consult its javadoc page for full details.

Metadata becomes very important when learning a new database tool and when trying to support multiple databases. You can interactively explore meta-data with Jython to discover a database's features and properties. Suppose you need to know a MySQL's system functions, numeric functions, and support for transactions. Interactively discovering this looks like the following:

```
>>> import java
>>> from java.sql import DriverManager
>>>
>>> # Register driver
>>> java.lang.Class.forName("org.gjt.mm.mysql.Driver")
<jclass org.gjt.mm.mysql.Driver at 650329>
>>>
>>> # Get Connection
>>> url, user, password = "jdbc:mysql:///test", "jyuser", "beans"
>>> dbconn = DriverManager.getConnection(url, user, password)
>>>
>>> # Get the DatabaseMetaData object
>>> md = dbconn.getMetaData()
>>>
>>> # Use the metadata object to find info about MySQL
>>> print md.systemFunctions
DATABASE,USER,SYSTEM_USER,SESSION_USER,PASSWORD,ENCRYPT,LAST_INSERT_ID,
VERSION
>>> md.numericFunctions
'ABS,ACOS,ASIN,ATAN,ATAN2,BIT_COUNT,CEILING,COS,COT,DEGREES,EXP,FLOOR,LOG,
LOG10,MAX,MIN,MOD,PI,POW,POWER,RADIANS,RAND,ROUND,SIN,SQRT,TAN,TRUNCATE'
>>> md.supportsTransactions()
0
>>>
>>> # Don't forget to close connections
>>> dbconn.close()
```

Of the overwhelming number of methods in the DatabaseMetaData Object, only some illuminate differences between the MySQL and PostgreSQL data-bases. Listing 11.3 uses the methods that highlight differences to create a visual report comparing MySQL and PostgreSQL. Many differences are somewhat trivial, but other, such as transactions, schema, and unions, are not. Listing 11.3 uses the DBLoginDialog defined in Listing 11.1 to create the connections. The DBLoginDialog.py file must therefore be in the sys.path, preferably the current working directory. When running Listing 11.3, you are given two dialog boxes for database connections. The first must select a MySQL database, and the sec-ond, a PostgreSQL database. The script then produces the report by looping through a list of the desired methods. Within this loop, Jython's `exec` statement executes a constructed statement string. What is normally:

```
value = metaData.supportsTransactions()
```

becomes something like this:

```
cmd = "supportsTransactions"
exec("value = metaData.%s()" % cmd)
```

The results for each database then appear in a `TextArea` after all the information is collected.

Listing 11.3 **Retrieving MetaData with JDBC**

```
# File: jdbcMetaData.py
from DBLoginDialog import DBLoginDialog
from java import awt
import sys

class MetaData(awt.Frame):
    def __init__(self):
        self.windowClosing=lambda e: sys.exit()
        self.databases = ["MySQL", "PostgreSQL"]
        self.panel = awt.Panel()
        self.infoArea = awt.TextArea("", 40, 60,
                            awt.TextArea.SCROLLBARS_VERTICAL_ONLY,
                            font=("Monospaced", awt.Font.PLAIN, 12))
        self.panel.add(self.infoArea)
        self.add(self.panel)
        self.pack()
        screensize = self.toolkit.screenSize
        self.bounds = (screensize.width/2 - self.width/2,
                        screensize.height/2 - self.height/2,
                        self.width, self.height)
        self.data = {}
        self.visible = 1
        self.dialog = DBLoginDialog(self, "Select a Connection")
        self.dialog.client = self.gatherMetaInfo
        self.dialog.visible = 1

    def showResults(self):
        infoWidth = self.infoArea.columns
        info = 'Method' + 'MySQL    PostgreSQL\n'.rjust(infoWidth - 7)
        info += '-' * (infoWidth - 1) + '\n'
        keys = self.data.keys()
        keys.sort()
        for x in keys:
            info += x
            mysql = str(self.data[x]['MySQL'])
            postgresql = str(self.data[x]['PostgreSQL'])
```

continues

Listing 11.3   **Continued**

```
                results = mysql.ljust(18 - len(postgresql)) + postgresql
                info += results.rjust(self.infoArea.columns - len(x) - 2)
                info += "\n"
        self.infoArea.text = info

    def nextDatabase(self):
        if len(self.databases):
            self.dialog.visible = 1
        else:
            self.showResults()

    def gatherMetaInfo(self, dbconn):
        if dbconn==None:
            return
        metaData = dbconn.getMetaData()
        dbname = metaData.databaseProductName
        for cmd in self.getCommands():
            value = ""
            try:
                exec("value = metaData.%s()" % cmd)
            except:
                value = "Test failed"
            if self.data.has_key(cmd):
                self.data[cmd][dbname] = value
            else:
                self.data.update({cmd:{dbname:value}})
        dbconn.close()  # close the database!
        self.databases.remove(dbname)
        self.nextDatabase()

    def getCommands(self):
        return ['getCatalogTerm', 'getMaxBinaryLiteralLength',
                'getMaxCatalogNameLength', 'getMaxCharLiteralLength',
                'getMaxColumnsInGroupBy', 'getMaxColumnsInIndex',
                'getMaxColumnsInOrderBy', 'getMaxColumnsInSelect',
                'getMaxColumnsInTable', 'getMaxConnections',
                'getMaxCursorNameLength', 'getMaxIndexLength',
                'getMaxProcedureNameLength', 'getMaxRowSize',
                'getMaxStatementLength', 'getMaxStatements',
                'getMaxTablesInSelect', 'getMaxUserNameLength',
                'supportsANSI92EntryLevelSQL', 'supportsBatchUpdates',
                'supportsCatalogsInDataManipulation',
                'supportsCoreSQLGrammar',
                'supportsDataManipulationTransactionsOnly',
                'supportsDifferentTableCorrelationNames',
                'supportsFullOuterJoins', 'supportsGroupByUnrelated',
                'supportsMixedCaseQuotedIdentifiers',
                'supportsOpenStatementsAcrossCommit',
                'supportsOpenStatementsAcrossRollback',
```

```
                'supportsPositionedDelete', 'supportsUnion',
                'supportsSubqueriesInComparisons',
                'supportsTableCorrelationNames', 'supportsTransactions']

if __name__ == '__main__':
    md = MetaData()
```

To execute Listing 11.3, ensure that both the database drivers are in the class-path. Then run the following command:

```
jython jdbcMetaData.py
```

You should first see the same dialog window as in Listing 11.2. Enter a MySQL connection there. The dialog will return; enter a PostgreSQL connection then. Following that, you should see a metadata comparison between the two databases that is similar to that shown in Figure 11.2.

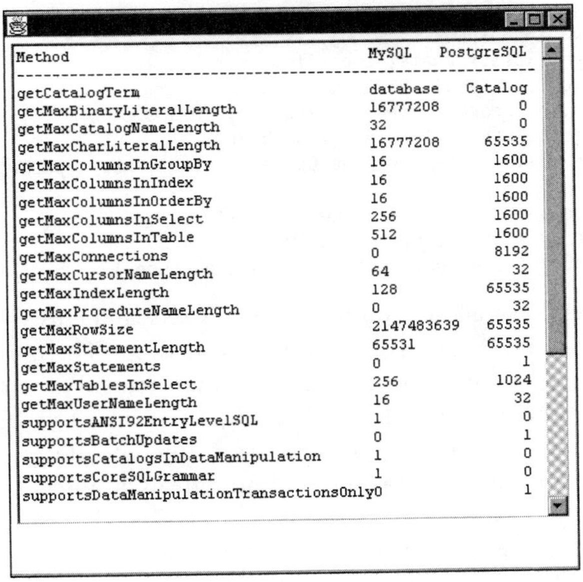

Method	MySQL	PostgreSQL
getCatalogTerm	database	Catalog
getMaxBinaryLiteralLength	16777208	0
getMaxCatalogNameLength	32	0
getMaxCharLiteralLength	16777208	65535
getMaxColumnsInGroupBy	16	1600
getMaxColumnsInIndex	16	1600
getMaxColumnsInOrderBy	16	1600
getMaxColumnsInSelect	256	1600
getMaxColumnsInTable	512	1600
getMaxConnections	0	8192
getMaxCursorNameLength	64	32
getMaxIndexLength	128	65535
getMaxProcedureNameLength	0	32
getMaxRowSize	2147483639	65535
getMaxStatementLength	65531	65535
getMaxStatements	0	1
getMaxTablesInSelect	256	1024
getMaxUserNameLength	16	32
supportsANSI92EntryLevelSQL	1	0
supportsBatchUpdates	0	1
supportsCatalogsInDataManipulation	1	0
supportsCoreSQLGrammar	1	0
supportsDataManipulationTransactionsOnly	0	1

Figure 11.2   MySQL-PostgreSQL comparison results.

Statements

The bulk of interacting with MySQL and PostgreSQL involves SQL statements. Issuing SQL statements requires a `statement` object. To create a `statement` object, use the connection's `createStatement()` method.

```
>>> import java
>>> java.lang.Class.forName("org.gjt.mm.mysql.Driver")
<jclass org.gjt.mm.mysql.Driver at 1876475>
>>> db, user, password = "test", "jyuser", "beans"
>>> url = "jdbc:mysql://localhost/%s" % db
>>> dbconn = java.sql.DriverManager.getConnection(url, user, password)
>>> stmt = dbconn.createStatement()
```

The `createStatement` method may also set type and concurrency parameters for the result set. Before a result set can use its `update*` methods, the statement must be created with concurrency set to `updatable`. The following example creates an updateable result set by setting the type and concurrency:

```
>>> import java
>>> from java import sql
>>> java.lang.Class.forName("org.gjt.mm.mysql.Driver")
<jclass org.gjt.mm.mysql.Driver at 1876475>
>>> db, user, password = "test", "jyuser", "beans"
>>> url = "jdbc:mysql://localhost/%s" % db
>>> dbconn = sql.DriverManager.getConnection(url, user, password)
>>>
>>> type = sql.ResultSet.TYPE_SCROLL_SENSITIVE
>>> concurrency = sql.ResultSet.CONCUR_UPDATABLE
>>> stmt = dbconn.createStatement(type, concurrency)
```

The `statement` object allows you to execute SQL statements with its `execute()`, `executeQuery()`, and `executeUpdate()` methods. These three methods differ in what they return. The `execute()` method returns 0 or 1 indicating whether or not there is a `ResultSet`. Actually, it returns a Java Boolean that Jython interprets as 1 or 0. The `executeQuery()` method always returns a `ResultSet`, and the `executeUpdate()` method returns an integer indicating the number of affected rows.

```
>>> query = "CREATE TABLE random ( number tinyint, letter char(1) )"
>>> stmt.execute(query)
0
```

In the preceding example, the query updates the database, meaning there is no `ResultSet`. You can confirm this with the statement's `getResultSet()` method or `resultSet` automatic bean property.

```
>>> print stmt.resultSet
None
```

Now that a table exists, you can fill the table with data. This would use the
`executeUpdate()` method. The following interactive example continues previous examples (the `statement` object already exists) by adding some data to the
random table:

```
>>> import string, random
>>> for i in range(20):
...     number = random.randint(0, 51)
...     query = "INSERT INTO random (number, letter) VALUES (%i, '%s')"
...     query = query % (number, string.letters[number - 1])
...     stmt.executeUpdate(query)
1
...
```

You should see an output of many 1s, indicating that one row was altered for
each update. Note the use of single quotes around the `'%s'` in the query
string. The letter, as all strings, must be in quotes. Using internal single quotes
makes this easy, but what if the string is a single quote. A single quote for the
letter would create an `SQLException`. Single quotes must be doubled in query
strings, meaning the string `"It's a bird"` should be `"It''s a bird"` in query
strings. Even then, you must negotiate this within Jython's syntax, and include
escaped double quotes to maintain proper SQL format. Using escaped double
quotes to allow for a single quote string is shown here:

```
>>> query = "INSERT INTO random (number, letter) VALUES (%i, \"%s\")"
>>> query = query % (4, "'")
```

Now that the `random` table has data, you can use the `executeQuery()` method
to select that data. Still continuing the same interactive session from above, the
following example selects all the data from the random table:

```
>>> rs = stmt.executeQuery("SELECT * FROM random")
```

Now we need to use the `ResultSet` object (`rs`) to inspect the results of the
`SELECT` statement.

The *ResultSet*

When you use `executeQuery`, the object returned is a `ResultSet`. The
`java.sql.ResultSet` object contains numerous methods to navigate through
the results and retrieve them as Java native types. Remember that Jython automatically converts Java native types to appropriate Jython types. Using the
`ResultSet`'s `getByte()` returns a value that becomes a `PyInteger`, `getDouble()`
returns a `PyFloat`, and so on, all according to the Java type conversion rules
listed in Chapter 2, "Operators, Types, and Built-In Functions."

To query the `random` table created earlier, and loop through all its entries uses the `ResultSet`'s `next()` and `get*` methods. In the following example, the number field is retrieved with `getInt()` and the letter field is retrieved with `getString()`. This creates the Jython types `PyInteger` and `PyString`:

```
>>> import java
>>> java.lang.Class.forName("org.gjt.mm.mysql.Driver")
<jclass org.gjt.mm.mysql.Driver at 1876475>
>>> db, user, password = "test", "jyuser", "beans"
>>> url = "jdbc:mysql://localhost/%s" % db
>>> dbconn = java.sql.DriverManager.getConnection(url, user, password)
>>> stmt = dbconn.createStatement()
>>>
>>> rs = stmt.executeQuery("SELECT * FROM random")
>>> while rs.next():
...     print rs.getString('letter'), ": ", rs.getInt('number')
...
...
U : 46
K : 36
h : 7
Q : 42
l : 11
u : 20
n : 13
z : 25
U : 46
Y : 50
j : 9
o : 14
i : 8
s : 18
d : 3
A : 26
K : 36
j : 9
n : 13
g : 6
>>> stmt.close()
>>> dbconn.close()
```

Note that your output will look different due to the use of the `random` module.

Navigation through the set involves moving through records with the `ResultSet`'s navigation methods. These differ depending on which version of the JDBC you are using, and the type of statement you created. Before JDBC 2.0, navigation is restricted to just the `next()` method. Current JDBC versions work with `next()`, `first()`, `last()`, `previous()`, `absolute()`, `relative()`, `afterLast()`, `beforeFirst()`, `moveToCurrentRow()`, and `moveToInsertRow()`. Of

S

x

these, `moveToInsertRow()` and `moveToCurrentRow()` are not implemented in the PostgreSQL driver, and require special conditions with the MySQL driver.

Most of these navigation methods are obvious from their names, but four of these methods are less obvious. The `relative(int)` navigation method moves the cursor `int` number of rows from the current position. The `absolute(int)` moves the cursor to the `int`'s row of the result set regardless of the current position. The `moveToInsertRow()`, currently available with MySQL, moves the cursor to a special row that is a construction zone unrelated to data retrieved from the database. In this area, you build a row that you intend to insert. After you have called `moveToInsertRow()`, and wish to return to the row you were at before jumping to the construction zone, use `moveToCurrentRow()`. Note that the `moveToInsertRow()` and `moveToCurrentRow()` methods require an updateable `ResultSet` object.

Besides navigating through rows, the result set can update rows if the driver supports this. Currently, PostgreSQL does not, but the MySQL driver does. There are conditions, however, that restrict which result sets are updateable. In MySQL a result set is updateable only if the query includes only one table, the query does not use a join and the query selects the table's primary key. An additional requirement that applies to all JDBC drivers is that the statement must set the concurrency type to `ResultSet.CONCUR_UPDATABLE`. To perform inserts, you must also ensure that the query generating the updateable result set includes all rows without default values and all `NON NULL` rows.

Because the `random` table created earlier lacks a primary key, it must be altered to include one before its result set can be updateable. The following interactive example shows the update to the `random` table followed by scrolling and update demonstrations:

```
>>> import java
>>> from java import sql
>>> java.lang.Class.forName("org.gjt.mm.mysql.Driver")
<jclass org.gjt.mm.mysql.Driver at 1876475>
>>> user, password = "jyuser", "beans"
>>> url = "jdbc:mysql://localhost/test"
>>> dbconn = sql.DriverManager.getConnection(url, user, password)
>>>
>>> type = sql.ResultSet.TYPE_SCROLL_SENSITIVE
>>> concurrency = sql.ResultSet.CONCUR_UPDATABLE
>>> stmt = dbconn.createStatement(type, concurrency)
>>>
>>> # Update table to include primary key (excuse the wrap)
>>> query = "ALTER TABLE random ADD pkey INT UNSIGNED NOT NULL AUTO_INCREMENT
PRIMARY KEY"
>>> stmt.execute(query)
0
```

```
>>>
>>> # Now get an updatable result set.
>>> rs = stmt.executeQuery("select * from random")
>>> rs.concurrency  # 1008 is "updatable"
1008
>>>
>>> # Insert a row
>>> rs.moveToInsertRow()
>>> rs.updateInt('number', 7)
>>> rs.updateString('letter', 'g')
>>> rs.updateInt('pkey', 22)
>>> rs.insertRow()  # This puts it in the database
>>> rs.moveToCurrentRow()
>>>
>>> rs.relative(5)  # scroll 5 rows
1
>>> # Print current row data
>>> # Remember, data is random- odds are yours will differ
>>> print rs.getString('letter'), rs.getInt('number')
h 8
>>> rs.updateInt('number', 3)
>>> rs.updateString('letter', 'c')
>>> rs.updateRow()  # this puts it in the database
>>> stmt.close()
>>> dbconn.close()
```

Prepared Statements

Pre-compiling SQL statements that are frequently used often helps with efficiency. A java.sql.PreparedStatement allows you to create such a prepared statement. To create a prepared statement, use the connection object's prepareStatement method, instead of createStatement. A simple prepared statement that updates a row in the random database would look like this:

```
>>> import java
>>> from java import sql
>>> java.lang.Class.forName("org.postgresql.Driver")
<jclass org.gjt.mm.mysql.Driver at 1876475>
>>> dbconn = sql.DriverManager.getConnection(url, user, password)
>>> query = "INSERT INTO random (letter, number) VALUES (?, ?)"
>>> preppedStmt = dbconn.prepareStatement(query)
```

Notice the question marks (?) in the query. A prepared statement allows you to leave placeholders for values that you can fill at execution time. Filling these placeholders requires that you set the value for each placeholder based on their positional identity with the set* methods. A set method exists for each supported Java type. Additionally, you should first clear parameters before setting new parameters and executing the update:

```
>>> # continued from previous interactive example
>>> preppedStmt.clearParameters()
>>> preppedStmt.setString(1, "f")
>>> preppedStmt.setInt(2, 6)
>>> preppedStmt.executeUpdate()
1
>>> preppedStmt.close()
>>> dbconn.close()
```

Transactions

Transactions are database operations where a set of statements must all complete successfully, or the entire operation is undone (rolled back). PostgreSQL is the database we will use for transaction examples, so that means the random table must now be created in the PostgreSQL `test` database. Following is an interactive example of creating the random table:

```
>>> import java
>>> from java import sql
>>> java.lang.Class.forName("org.postgresql.Driver")
<jclass org.postgresql.Driver at 5303656>
>>> db, user, password = "test", "jyuser", "beans"
>>> url = "jdbc:postgresql://localhost/%s" % db
>>> dbconn = sql.DriverManager.getConnection(url, user, password)
>>> stmt = dbconn.createStatement()
>>> query = "CREATE TABLE random ( number int, letter char(1),
            pkey INT UNSIGNED NOT NULL AUTO_INCREMENT PRIMARY KEY)"
>>> stmt.execute(query)
0
>>> import string, random
>>> for i in range(20):
...     number = random.randint(0, 51)
...     query = "INSERT INTO random (number, letter) VALUES (%i, '%s')"
...     query = query % (number, string.letters[number - 1])
...     stmt.executeUpdate(query)
1
1
...
>>> stmt.close()
>>> dbconn.close()
```

To use JDBC transactions from Jython, you must set the connections `autoCommit` bean property to 0, begin the set of statements, and call the connection's `rollback()` method if any of the statements fail. Following is a simple example of a transaction with PostgreSQL and the random table:

```
>>> import java
>>> from java import sql
>>> java.lang.Class.forName("org.postgresql.Driver")
```

```
<jclass org.postgresql.Driver at 5711596>
>>> url = "jdbc:postgresql://localhost/test"
>>> con = sql.DriverManager.getConnection(url, "jyuser", "beans")
>>> stmt = con.createStatement()
>>> con.autoCommit = 0
>>> try:
...     # Insert an easy-to-find character for letter
...     query = "INSERT INTO random (letter, number) VALUES ('.', 0)"
...     stmt.executeUpdate(query)
...     print "First update successful."
...     stmt.execute("Create an exception here")
...     con.commit()
... except:
...     print "Error encountered, rolling back."
...     con.rollback()
...
1
First update successful.
Error encountered, rolling back.
>>>
>>> # now confirm that the first update statement was in fact undone
>>> rs = stmt.executeQuery("SELECT * FROM random WHERE letter='.'")
>>> rs.next()
0
```

The final zero at the end of the preceding example indicates that there is no result set for the query. This confirms that the first SQL insert statement was rolled back.

zxJDBC

Working with JDBC from Jython is no doubt valuable. It allows prototyping in Jython and leverages JDBC skill sets; however, the numerous methods specific to Java types makes it clear that it is a Java API. Java, databases, and therefore JDBC are type-rich. The down side is that methods specific to Java native type are seemingly contrary to Jython's high-level, polymorphic dynamic types.

In contrast, Python has a database API referred to as just the Python DB API, currently at version 2.0. Python's DB API 2.0 has been a standard API for interacting with databases from CPython; however, database drivers used by CPython are often useless to Jython because of underlying C implementations. Although Jython easily makes use of Java's database connectivity, it was still left wanting for a Java implementation of Python's DB API. Brian Zimmer, an avid Jython, Java, and Python developer, wrote zxJDBC to fill this void. In reality, zxJDBC does more that just implement the DB API, it also adds extensions to this API. Brian's zxJDBC tools are freely available, include source code, are well documentation, and are available at `http://sourceforge.net/projects/zxjdbc/` or `http://www.ziclix.com/zxjdbc/`. The zxJDBC tools may be incorporated into Jython proper by the time you read this, eliminating the need for a separate download. Check `http://www.jython.org`, or the Jython information at `http://www.newriders.com/` for more information on this. If it isn't included in your version of Jython, you will need to download zxJDBC, and include the `zxJDBC.jar` file in your `classpath`.

The zxJDBC package contains more tools than are shown here, including a package implementing the pipe pattern and the easy creation of datahandlers and `DataHandlerFilters`.

Connecting to the Database

When you use the zxJDBC package, all that is required before calling the connection function is that `zxJDBC.jar` and the required JDBC driver exist in the `classpath`. The actual loading of the driver occurs behind the scenes when creating a connection to the database. The two steps to establishing a database connection with zxJDBC are as follows:

1. Include the appropriate driver and the `zxJDBC.jar` file in the `classpath`.
2. Supply a JDBC URL, username, password, and the name of the database `Driver` class to the `zxJDBC.connect()` method.

An appropriate `classpath` setting for using zxJDBC looks like this:

```
# For MySQL
set CLASSPATH=mm_mysql-2_0_4-bin.jar;\path\to\zxJDBC.jar;%CLASSPATH%

# For PostgreSQL
set CLASSPATH=\path\to\jdbc7.1-1.2.jar;\path\to\zxJDBC.jar;%CLASSPATH%
```

The `zxJDBC.connect` method returns the database connection and has the following syntax:

```
zxJDBC.connect(URL, user, password, driver) -> connection
```

Retrieving the connection with the `zxJDBC.connect` method looks like this:

```
from com.ziclix.python.sql import zxJDBC
mysqlConn = zxJDBC.connect("jdbc:mysql://localhost/test",
                           "jyuser", "beans",
                           "org.gjt.mm.mysql.Driver")

postgresqlConn = zxJDBC.connect("jdbc:postgresql://localhost/test",
                                "jyuser", "beans",
                                "org.postgresql.Driver")
```

Special parameters required by drivers may appear as keyword arguments to the connect function. To set `autoReconnect` to true when connecting to a MySQL database include that parameter as a keyword argument as follows:

```
url = "jdbc:mysql://localhost/test"
user = "jyuser"
password = "beans"
driver = "org.gjt.mm.mysql.Driver"
mysqlConn = zxJDBC.connect(url, user, password, driver,
                          autoReconnect="true")
```

Connection errors raise the exception `DatabaseError`, so handling errors with a connection attempt requires an `except` statement like the following:

```
url = "jdbc:mysql://localhost/test"
user = "jyuser"
password = "beans"
driver = "org.gjt.mm.mysql.Driver"
try:
    mysqlConn = zxJDBC.connect(url, user, password, driver,
                              autoReconnect="true")
except zxJDBC.DatabaseError:
    pass
    #handle error here
```

If you use a connection factory from the `javax.sql` package, or a class that implements `javax.sql.DataSource` or `javax.sql.ConnectionPoolDataSource`, you can connect with the `zxJDBC.connectx` method. Note that the `javax.sql` package is not included in the normal JDK installation, except for the enterprise edition. The MySQL JDBC drive does, however, include the `MysqlDataSource` class used in the example below. The `zxJDBC.connectx` method requires the `DataSource` class and all the database connection parameters as keyword arguments, or as a dictionary object:

```
from com.ziclix.python.sql import zxJDBC
userInfo = {'user':'jyuser', 'password':'beans'}
con = zxJDBC.connectx("org.gjt.mm.mysql.MysqlDataSource",
                      serverName="localhost", databaseName='test',
                      port=3306, **userInfo)
```

The bean property names are set with keyword parameters in the preceding example, but could also be included in the dictionary containing the username and password information:

```
from com.ziclix.python.sql import zxJDBC
userInfo = {'user':'jyuser', 'password':'beans',
            'databaseName':'test', 'serverName':'localhost',
            'port':3306}
con = zxJDBC.connectx("org.gjt.mm.mysql.MysqlDataSource", **userInfo)
```

You can also obtain a connection through a `jndi` lookup with the `zxJDBC.lookup` method. The `lookup` method only requires a string representing the JNDI name bound to the specific connection or `DataSource` you desire. Keyword parameters may be included and are converted to the static field values of `javax.jndi.Context` when the keywords match a Context's static field name.

Cursor

A *zxJDBC cursor* is the object used to actually interact with the data in the database. A `zxJDBC` cursor is actually a wrapper around the JDBC `Statement` and `ResultSet` objects. The handling of the result sets is what differentiates the static and dynamic cursor types. A dynamic cursor is lazy. It iterates through the result set only as needed. This saves memory and evenly distributes processing time. A static cursor is not lazy. It iterates through the entire result set immediately, and incurs the memory overhead of doing so. The advantage of a static cursor is that you know the row count soon after executing a statement, something you cannot know when using a dynamic cursor.

To get a cursor, call the `zxJDBC` connection object's `cursor()` method. An example of connecting to the database and retrieving a cursor object appears here:

```
from com.ziclix.python.sql import zxJDBC
url = "jdbc:mysql://localhost/test"
user = "jyuser"
password = "beans"
driver = "org.gjt.mm.mysql.Driver"
con = zxJDBC.connect(url, user, password, driver,
                     autoReconnect="true")
cursor = con.cursor()  # Static cursor

# Alternatively, you can create a dynamic cursor
cursor = con.cursor(1)  # Optional boolean arg for dynamic
```

A cursor object's execute method executes SQL statements. The following example shows how to execute an SQL statement that selects all the data in the random table.

```
>>> from com.ziclix.python.sql import zxJDBC
>>> url = "jdbc:mysql://localhost/test"
>>> user, password, driver = "jyuser", "beans", "org.gjt.mm.mysql.Driver"
>>> con = zxJDBC.connection(url, user, password, driver)
>>> cursor = con.cursor()
>>> cursor.execute("SELECT * FROM random")
```

To iterate through the results of a statement, you must use the cursor's fetchone, fetchmany, and fetchall methods. The fetchone and fetchall methods do exactly as their names imply, fetch one result set row, or fetch all rows. The fetchmany method accepts an optional argument which specifies the number of rows to return. Each time multiple rows are returned, they are returned as a sequence of sequences (list of tuples). You can see the usage of these three methods as the preceding example is continued:

```
>>> cursor.fetchone()
(41, '0', 1)
>>> cursor.fetchmany()
[(6, 'f', 2)]
>>> cursor.fetchmany(4)
[(49, 'W', 4), (35, 'I', 5), (43, 'Q', 6), (37, 'K', 3)]
>>> cursor.fetchall()  # All remaining in this case
[(3, 'c', 7), (17, 'q', 8), (29, 'C', 9), (36, 'J', 10), (43, 'Q', 11), (23,
'w', 12), (49, 'W', 13), (25, 'y', 14), (40, 'N', 15), (50, 'X', 16), (46,
'T', 17), (51, 'Y', 18), (8, 'h', 19), (25, 'y', 20), (7, 'g', 21), (11, 'k',
22), (1, 'a', 23)]
```

After a query has been executed, you can view the row information for those rows in the result set with the cursor's description attribute. The description attribute is read-only, and contains a sequence for each row in the result set. Each sequence includes the name, type, display size, internal size, precision, scale, and nullable information for a column of the row set. A description of the previous query looks like this:

```
>>> cursor.description
[('number', -6, 4, None, None, None, 1), ('letter', 1, 1, None, None, None,
1), ('pkey', 4, 10, None, 10, 0, 0)]
```

Table 11.3 shows the complete set of the cursor object's methods and attributes.

Table 11.3 **The *Cursor* Object's Methods and Attributes**

Method/Attribute	Description
description	Information describing each column that appears in the results of a query. The information is a seven-item tuple containing name, type code, display size, internal size, precision, scale, and nullability.
rowcount	The number of rows in the results. This only works when the cursor is a static cursor, or after completely traversing the result set with a dynamic cursor.

Method/Attribute	Description
callproc(procedureName, [parameters])	Calls stored procedures and applies only to those databases that implement stored procedures.
close()	Closes the cursor.
execute(statement)	Executes a statement.
executemany(statement, parameterList)	Executes a statement with a parameter list. With this, you can use question marks in the statement for values and include a `tuple` of values to the `parameterList` which are replaced in the statement.
fetchone()	Retrieves one row of the query results.
fetchmany([size])	Retrieves `arraysize` number of rows if no argument is given. If the argument `arg` is supplied, it returns `arg` numbers of result rows.
fetchall()	Retrieves all remaining result rows.
nextset()	Continues with the next result set. This applies only to those databases that support multiple result sets.
arraysize	The number of rows `fetchmany()` should return without arguments.

zxJDBC and MetaData

The Python DB API does not contain metadata specifications, but `zxJDBC` does provide some connection metadata with a number of connection and cursor attributes. These attributes match bean properties found in the JDBC `java.sql.DatabaseMetaData` object discussed earlier in this chapter. Table 11.4 shows the `zxJDBC` cursor fields and the underlying `DatabaseMetaData` bean methods.

Table 11.4   *zxJDBC* MetaData

zxJDBC Attribute	*DatabaseMetaData* Accessor
connection.dbname	getDatabaseProductName
connection.dbversion	getDatabaseProductVersion
cursor.tables(catalog, schemapattern, tablepattern, types)	getTables

continues

Table 11.4 **Continued**

zxJDBC Attribute	*DatabaseMetaData* Accessor
cursor.columns(catalog, schemapattern, tablenamepattern, columnnamepattern)	getColumns
cursor.foreignkeys(primarycatalog, primaryschema, pimarytable, foreigncatalog, foreignschema, foreigntable)	getCrossReference
cursor.primarykeys(catalog, schema, table)	getPrimaryKeys
cursor.procedures(catalog, schemapattern, procedurepattern)	getProcedures
cursor.procedurecolumns(catalog, schemapattern, procedurepattern, columnpattern)	getProcedureColumns
cursor.statistics(catalog, schema, table, unique, approximation)	getIndexInfo

Here is an example of extracting some metadata from the MySQL random database created earlier:

```
>>> from com.ziclix.python.sql import zxJDBC
>>> url = "jdbc:mysql://localhost/test"
>>> driver = "org.gjt.mm.mysql.Driver"
>>> dbconn = zxJDBC.connect(url, "jyuser", "beans", driver)
>>> dbconn.dbname
'MySQL'
>>> dbconn.dbversion
'3.23.32'
```

The remaining metadata is accessible through a cursor object. When the cursor retrieves information, it stores it internally waiting for the user to fetch it. To view metadata provided by the cursor, each metadata method must be called, then the cursor must be used to retrieve the data:

```
>>> cursor.primarykeys(None, "%", "random")
>>> cursor.fetchall()
[('', '', 'random', 'pkey', 1, 'pkey')]
>>> cursor.tables(None, None, "%", None)
>>> cursor.fetchall()
[('', '', 'random', 'TABLE', '')]
>>> cursor.primarykeys('test', '%', 'random')
>>> cursor.fetchall()
[('test', '', 'random', 'pkey', 1, 'pkey')]
>>> cursor.statistics('test', '', 'random', 0, 1)
```

```
>>> cursor.fetchall()
[('test', '', 'random', 'false', '', 'PRIMARY', '3', 1, 'pkey', 'A', '23',
None, '')]
```

Prepared Statements

The executemany() cursor method is the Python DB API Java's prepared statement. In reality, other statement executed are prepared, but the executemany() method allows you to use question marks for values in the SQL statement. The second argument to executemany() is a tuple of values that replaces the question marks in the SQL statement:

```
>>> sql = "INSERT INTO random (letter, number) VALUES (?, ?)"
>>> cur.executemany(sql, ('Z', 51))
>>>
>>> # view the row
>>> cur.execute("SELECT * from random where letter='Z'")
>>> cur.fetchall()
[('Z', 51, 24)]
```

Errors and Warnings

Exceptions that may be raised in zxJDBC are the following:

- **Error**—This is the generic exception.

- **DatabaseError**—Raised for database-specific errors. The connection object and all the connection methods (connect, lookup, conntectx) may raise this.

- **ProgrammingError**—Raised for programming errors such as missing parameters, bad SQL statements. The cursor object and the lookup connection may raise this.

- **NotSupportedError**—This exception is raised when a method is not implemented.

Each of these exceptions are within the zxJDBC package, so except clauses should look like the following:

```
>>> try:
...     pass #Assume a method that raises and error is here
... except zxJDBC.DatabaseError:
...     pass # Handle DatabaseError
... except zxJDBC.ProgrammingError:
...     pass # handle ProgrammingError
... except notSupportedError:
...     pass # handle not supported error
... except zxJDBC.Error:
...     pass # Handle the generic Error exception
```

You can also get warnings with the cursor's `warnings` attribute. If no warnings exist, then use the `cursor.warnings` attribute in None.

dbexts

Another extension available with the `zxJDBC` package is `dbexts`. `dbexts` is a Python module that adds another layer of abstraction around the Python DB API 2.0. With `DBexts`, you can specify connection information in a configuration file, and then use the higher-lever `dbexts` methods on the connections defined. In order to use `dbexts`, the `dbexts.py` module that comes with `zxJDBC` must be added to the `sys.path`.

The configuration file can be any file, but the default is a file named `dbexts.ini` that resides in the same directory as the `dbexts.py` file. To use another file, include the filename in the `dbexts` constructor. Listing 11.4 is a configuration file that defines connections to the two databases used in this chapter.

Listing 11.4   **Sample *dbexts* Configuration**

```
[default]
name=mysqltest

[jdbc]
name=mysqltest
url=jdbc:mysql://localhost/test
user=jyuser
pwd=beans
driver=org.gjt.mm.mysql.Driver

[jdbc]
name=pstest
url=jdbc:postgresql://localhost/test
user=jyuser
pwd=beans
driver=org.postgresql.Driver
```

Once the configuration file is defined, you can connect to the database by instantiating the `dbexts` class. In the following example, the `dbexts.ini` file is placed in the current working directory. You can alternatively place it in the directory on the `sys.path` where you placed the `dbexts.py` module:

```
>>> from dbexts import dbexts
>>> mysqlcon = dbexts("mysqltest", "dbexts.ini")
>>> psgrscon = dbexts("pstest", "dbexts.ini")
>>>
>>> # execute raw sql and get a list of headers and results
```

```
>>> psgrscon.raw("SELECT * from random")
([('letter', 1, 1, None, None, None, 1), ('number', 4, 11, None, 10, 0, 1)],
[('A', 4), ('f', 6), ('a', 1)])
>>>
>>> # execute interactive sql
>>> psgrscon.isql("select * from random")

LETTER | NUMBER
----------------
A      | 4
f      | 6
a      | 1

3 rows affected
>>>
>>> # Display schema- this works with postgresql, not MySQL
>>> psgrscon.schema("random")
Table
  random

Primary Keys

Imported (Foreign) Keys

Columns
  letter               bpchar(1), nullable
  number               int4(4), nullable

Indices
>>>
>>> # show tables in MySQL 'test' database
>>> mysqlcon.table()

TABLE_CAT | TABLE_SCHEM | TABLE_NAME ¦ TABLE_TYPE | REMARKS
----------------------------------------------------------
          |             | random     ¦ TABLE      |

1 row affected
```

Table 11.5 lists the primary dbexts methods. Some of the methods have additional optional arguments and there are some additional methods, but they are bit beyond the scope of this chapter. For more details, consult the excellent documentation that comes with zxJDBC.

Table 11.5 *dbexts* **Methods**

Method	Description
`__init__(dbname, cfg, resultformatter, autocommit)`	The `dbexts` constructor. All parameters have default values, so they are all optional. The `dbname` is the name you specified for the connection in the `dbexts.ini` file. The `cfg` is the location of the `dbexts.ini` file if it does not reside in the same directory as the `dbexts.py` file. The `resultformatter` is a callable object that accepts a list of rows as one argument and optionally accepts a list of headers. The `resultformatter` object is called to display data. The `autocommit` argument is set to 1, or true, by default, but can be set to 0 if included in the call to the constructor.
`isql(sql, params, bindings, maxrows)`	The `isql` method interactively executes SQL statements. *Interactive* means that results are displayed with the `resultformatter` immediately after executing the statement, much like the MySQL and pSQL client programs. All parameters have default values except for the `sql` statement. The `sql` parameter is the SQL statement itself. The `params` parameter is a `tuple` of value parameters used to replace `?` in SQL statements. The `bindings` parameter allows you to bind a `datahandler`. See the documentation on `zxJDBC` for more about `datahandlers`. The `maxrows` specifies the maximum number of rows to return, where zero or None means no limit.
`raw(sql, params, bindings)`	Executes the `sql` statement and returns a `tuple` containing headers and results. The `params` and `bindings` arguments are the same as for the `isql` method.
`schema(table, full, sort)`	Displays a table's indices, foreign keys, primary keys, and columns. If the `full` parameter is nonzero, the results include the table's referenced keys. A nonzero `sort` value means the table's column names will be sorted.

Method	Description
`table(table)`	The table parameter is optional. Without a table argument, this method displays a list of all tables. Otherwise, the specified table's columns are displayed.
`proc(proc)`	The `proc` parameter is optional. Without it, all procedures are listed. With it, the parameters for the specified procedure are displayed.
`bcp(src, table, where='(1=1)')`	This method copies data from specified database and table (`src` and `table`) to the current instance's database.
`begin(self)`	Creates a new cursor.
`rollback(self)`	Rolls back statements executed since the creation of a new cursor.
`commit(self, cursor=None, maxrows=None)`	Commits statements executed since the creation of a new cursor.
`display(self)`	Displays the results using the current formatter.

12

Server-Side Web Programming

WHERE DOES JYTHON FIT INTO WEB DEVELOPMENT? The answer is wherever Java fits. Jython especially fits those Java venues where people desire faster development and increased flexibility. Server-side Java web programming is primarily implemented as Servlets and Java Server Pages (JSP); therefore, Jython's primary implementation is Servlets and JSP. This isn't the entire story. Java's enterprise packages (j2ee) figures prominently in developing web applications. EJB's, JNDI, JDBC and more are integral to most Java web applications, and Jython is equally effective with all those technologies; however, the primary focus of this chapter is Servlets and JSP.

There are also places where Jython does not fit. CPython is a very popular language for implementing CGI scripts, but Jython is not. In CGI, a web server receives a request, starts a process to respond, and shuts down that sub-process when the response is completed. It is possible to use Jython in this manner, but it is not a good way. The startup time of the JVM itself makes this a poor choice. Servlets and JSP on the other hand, are persistent—they remain in memory between web requests.

There are many advantages to using Jython for web programming. High-quality Servlet containers are readily available and near ubiquitously deployed. Java Servlet applications can benefit from Jython's flexibility and high-level language characteristics, and you get to leverage all that Java's and Jython's libraries have to offer. Some of the many quality Servlet containers include WebLogic, WebSphere, Tomcat, Jigsaw, Resin, and Jetty. The number of organizations that have deployed such containers is astounding, which makes Jython immediately usable in a huge percentage of situations.

What you can expect in this chapter is Servlets and JSP written with Jython. The basic topics include setting up a Servlet container, the basic Servlet classes, implementing cookies, sessions and database connections, and using Jython with JSP pages. The slightly more advanced topic of creating your own Jython Servlet mappings appears after the basics. Implementation-specific topics appear toward the end of this chapter, and they include topics such as templates, XML, Cocoon, IBM's Bean Scripting Framework, and Enterprise Java Beans.

Jython Servlet Containers

Jython works with any compliant Java Servlet container, and there are a great many of these from which to choose. This chapter uses Tomcat, which is the reference implementation of the Servlet and Java Server Page specifications. Some of the popular and freely available Servlet containers are Tomcat from Apache's Jakarta project, Apache's JServ, the Jigsaw web server from the W3C and Jetty from Mort Bay Consulting. Following is a brief description of each of these tools.

Jakarta's *Tomcat* is the reference implementation of the Servlet and Java Server Pages specifications, and the server used in this chapter. Tomcat is available at `http://jakarta.apache.org/` and the stable release version as of the writing of this chapter is 3.2.3. This version of Tomcat supports the 2.2 Servlet and 1.1 JSP specifications. By the time you read this, Tomcat 4.0 will have been released, which implements the 2.3 Servlet and 1.2 JSP specifications. All Jython Servlets in this chapter were tested with Tomcat 3.2.3. All examples should work with any Servlet 2.2/JSP 1.1-compliant container available according to Sun's "Write Once, Run Anywhere" motto. The Tomcat distribution includes the Servlet and JSP classes that are required for this chapter, so there are no additional downloads required.

Apache JServ is a Servlet (version 2.0) engine created for Apache and is commonly deployed. This is an easy means of using Servlets with Jython and may be a good choice if your current development already employs JServ as many do. Information about Apache and JServ can be found at `http://java.apache.org/`. JServ requires the accompanying Java Servlet Development Kit 2.0 available separately at `http://java.sun.com/products/servlet/index.html`. Java Server Pages require an external module that is currently located at `http://java.apache.org/jserv/`.

Jigsaw is the W3C's experimental web server. The term "experimental" may be misleading because it is more mature than that label indicates. Jigsaw is a fully HTTP/1.1-compliant web server and caching proxy server written entirely in Java. Jigsaw also supports the Servlet 2.2 specification and Java Server Pages 1.1. Jigsaw is available at `http://www.w3.org/Jigsaw/` and includes the required Servlet and JSP files.

Jetty is a compact and efficient Java web server that supports the Servlet 2.2 and JSP 1.1 specifications, supports HTTP 1.1, includes SSL support, and easily integrates with EJB servers such as JBoss. Jetty is available at `http://jetty.mortbay.com/`.

The documentation for these tools is extensive, so installation guidelines for these should be gleaned from their respective web sites.

Defining Simple Servlet Classes

This section compares a simple Java Servlet with a simple Jython Servlet. The section on testing these Servlets describes how to install the `jython.jar` file in a Tomcat web application.

A Simple Java Servlet

Listing 12.1 is the most basic of Java Servlets.

Listing 12.1 **A Basic Java Servlet**

```
"""// Filename:  JavaServlet.java
import javax.servlet.*;
import java.io.*;

public class JavaServlet extends GenericServlet {

    public void service(ServletRequest req, ServletResponse res)
    throws ServletException, IOException {
```

continues

Listing 12.1   **Continued**

```
        res.setContentType("text/html");
        PrintWriter toClient = res.getWriter();

        toClient.println("<html><body>" +
                        "This is a Java Servlet." +
                        "</body></html>");
    }
}
```

A base class from the Servlet API is required, and Listing 12.1 uses `GenericServlet`, imported from the `javax.servlet` package in the first line. The `service` method in `GenericServlet` is abstract, so it must be implemented in any subclasses. This is the method invoked in response to a web request for `JavaServlet` (the name of the file in Listing 12.1). Output destined for the client is sent through a `PrintWriter` object retrieved from the `ServletResponse` object. This could also be an `OutputStream` for binary data.

A Simple Jython Servlet

Implementing a Jython Servlet comparable to Listing 12.1 should be similar in what it imports, inherits, and implements, but done in Jython's syntax. Listing 12.2 demonstrates.

Listing 12.2   **A Basic Jython Servlet**

```
# Filename:  JythonServlet.py
from javax import servlet
import random  # Not used, just here to test module imports

class JythonServlet(servlet.GenericServlet):
    def service(self, req, res):
        res.setContentType("text/html")
        toClient = res.getWriter()
        toClient.println("""<html><body>
                        This is a Servlet of the Jython variety.
                        </body></html>""")
```

Listing 12.2 is a subclass of `GenericServlet` just like its Java counterpart in Listing 12.1. It also implements the `service()` method of `GenericServlet` as required. Syntactic differences in Listing 12.2 include parentheses after the class definition to designate the superclass, the omission of the `throws` statement, an explicit `self` parameter in the `service` method, and, of course, the absence of semicolons and explicit type declarations. Additionally, the import statements differ in Jython. As stated earlier, the `from module import *` syntax is strongly discouraged; instead, Listing 12.2 imports the `parent` package. One additional import in Listing 12.2 is the `random` module. This module is not actually used, and only exists to test module imports.

Testing the Java and Jython Servlets

Testing the Servlets in Listings 12.1 and 12.2 requires the installation of Tomcat. The Jython Servlet in Listing 12.2 additionally requires including the `jython.jar` file in Tomcat. This section first describes the steps to installing Tomcat, then addresses the installation and testing of the two Servlets discussed.

Installing Tomcat

The first step is to download Tomcat from `http://jakarta.apache.org`. This section addresses the installation of a binary release of Tomcat in stand-alone mode. The suggested version to download is `jakarta-tomcat-3.2.3`. Download the `zip` or `tar.gz` file appropriate for your platform.

Next, unzip or untar the archive to the directory in which you have sufficient permissions. If you unzip the archive into the `C:\jakarta-tomcat-3.2.3` directory, this becomes the Tomcat home directory. If you use `/usr/local/jakarta-tomcat-3.2.3`, this becomes the Tomcat home directory. You should set an environment variable to the Tomcat home directory. For the directory `C:\jakarta-tomcat-3.2.3` on Windows, add the following to your environment settings:

```
set TOMCAT_HOME=c:\jakarta-tomcat-3.2.3
```

For the directory `/usr/local/jakarta-tomcat-3.2.3` on *nix, add the following to your bash environment:

```
export TOMCAT_HOME=/usr/local/jakarta-tomcat-3.2.3
```

If you do not set the `TOMCAT_HOME` environment variable, you must start Tomcat from within its home or bin directory.

Next, set the environment variable `JAVA_HOME` to the root directory of your JDK installation. Here's an example using JDK1.3.1:

```
# on Windows
set JAVA_HOME=c:\jdk1.3.1
# bash (*nix) setup
export JAVA_HOME=/usr/java/jdk1.3.1
```

The installation is complete. You can start Tomcat with the startup script appropriate for your platform:

```
# Windows
%TOMCAT_HOME%\bin\startup.bat
# bash (*unix)
$TOMCAT_HOME/bin/startup.sh
```

You should see startup information printed to the screen as the Tomcat server loads. An important line to look for is this:

```
date time - PoolTcpConnector: Starting HttpConnectionHandler on 8080
```

This designates the port that you will be using to connect to the Servlet container: 8080 is the default. When you see this, Tomcat is running and ready to accept connections on port 8080.

When you wish to stop Tomcat, use the following shutdown scripts:

```
# Windows
%TOMCAT_HOME%\bin\shutdown.bat
# bash (*nix)
$TOMCAT_HOME/bin/shutdown.sh
```

The Servlet 2.2 specification designates a directory hierarchy for web applications that begins in the directory `%TOMCAT_HOME%\webapps`. Folders within this directory are web applications, or contexts, and each follows a specific directory hierarchy. The examples in this chapter use the context named `jython`. The directory structure required for the `jython` context is shown here:

```
%TOMCAT_HOME%\webapps\
%TOMCAT_HOME%\webapps\jython                    The context's root
%TOMCAT_HOME%\webapps\jython\WEB-INF
%TOMCAT_HOME%\webapps\jython\WEB-INF\classes     Servlet classes
%TOMCAT_HOME%\webapps\jython\WEB-INF\lib         Library archives
```

You should create these directories before continuing with the examples. If you restart Tomcat, you should see an additional line of information when it restarts. The following line confirms that Tomcat has loaded the new context:

```
date time - ContextManager: Adding context Ctx( /jython )
```

Installing the Java Servlet

To install the Java Servlet from Listing 12.1, first place the `JavaServlet.java` file in the directory `%TOMCAT_HOME%\webapps\jython\WEB-INF\classes`. This directory is the root directory for class files. Because `JavaServlet` is not within a package, it belongs in the root of the `classes` directory. Note that Listing 12.1 is not within a package; if you had chosen to designate a package, such as the package `demo` for example, you would have then placed the compiled class file in the `classes\demo` directory in order to comply with Java class directory structures. This is only a note for those Servlets placed within a package, which is not the case for our example, however.

From within that directory, compile the `JavaServlet.java` file with the following command:

```
javac -classpath %TOMCAT_HOME%\lib\servlet.jar JavaServlet.java
```

After compiling JavaServlet, you are ready to view it. First, start the Tomcat server, and then point your browser to `http://localhost:8080/jython/servlet/JavaServlet`. You should see the simple string message `This is a Java Servlet`.

Installing the Jython Servlet

There are two ways to use Jython Servlets. One is to compile the Servlet with `jythonc` and place the resulting class files in the `%TOMCAT_HOM%\jython\WEB-INF\classes` directory. The other is to use Jython's `PyServlet` mapping class. This section uses `jythonc`. The `PyServlet` mapping is often a better way to deploy Jython Servlets, but `jythonc`-compiled Servlets are equally sensible at times.

The three steps required to install a `jythonc`-compiled Servlet in Tomcat are as follows:

1. Compile the Jython Servlet module with `jythonc`.
2. Add the `jython.jar` file to the web application.
3. Make the modules from Jython's `lib` directory available to Jython Servlets.

Compiling a Jython Servlet with jythonc

Compiling with `jythonc` requires that the `servlet.jar` file exists within the classpath. The `servlet.jar` file contains the `javax.Servlet.*` classes and packages, and it is found in Tomcat's `lib` directory (`%TOMCAT_HOME%\lib`). If you use `jythonc` to compile a Servlet without `servlet.jar` in the `classpath`, there are no errors or warnings during the compilation; however, when you try to run a Servlet compiled that way, you will get a `java.lang.ClassCastException` (at least that is the case for `jythonc` at the time of this writing).

Place the `JythonServlet.py` file from Listing 12.2 to the directory `%TOM-CAT_HOME%\jython\WEB-INF\classes`. Ensure that your environment `CLASSPATH` variable does in fact include `Servlet.jar`, and then use `jythonc` to compile the Jython code into Java classes by using the following command from within the `%TOMCAT_HOME%\jython\WEB-INF\classes directory`:

```
jythonc -w . JythonServlet.py
```

Specifying the current working directory with the -w switch eliminates the need to copy the generated class files from the jpywork directory. There should be two class files in the classes directory. Remember that a compiled Jython file will have at least two associated class files. The files produced from compiling JythonServlet.py with *jythonc* should be JythonServlet.java, JythonServlet.class, and JythonServlet$_PyInner.class. Both the class files are required to use the Servlet and must both be in the WEB-INF\classes directory.

During the compilation with jythonc, it is important to look for the lines that read as follows:

```
Creating .java files:
  JythonServlet module
     JythonServlet extends javax.servlet.GenericServlet
```

If you do not see these lines, something is wrong and the Servlet will not work. Double-check the CLASSPATH and setup options and compile the file again until you see the lines noted previously.

Adding **jython.jar** *to the* **classpath**

All Jython Servlets must have access to the classes within the jython.jar file. There are three ways to add the jython.jar file to Tomcat's classpath:

- Add jython.jar to the context's lib directory. This is the preferred way.
- Add jython.jar to Tomcat's lib directory. This method is discouraged.
- Leave jython.jar in Jython's installation directory, but add it to the classpath before running Tomcat. This is reasonable, but not as good as placing it in the context's lib directory.

The preferred approach is to place the jython.jar file in the context's lib directory. The context should include the directory {context}\WEB-INF\lib. For the jython context used in this chapter, it is %TOMCAT_HOME%\webapps\jython\WEB-INF\lib. Class archive files, such as jython.jar, belong in this directory. This is preferred because it makes a self-contained web application. As soon as a web application requires access to archives outside of its context, archiving, packaging, and installing the application on other servers becomes troublesome. You are strongly urged to keep all web applications self-contained unless you are sure it is not necessary in your situation.

You can also place the `jython.jar` file in Tomcat's `lib` directory
(`%TOMCAT_HOME%\lib`). Jar files in this directory are automatically added to the
`classpath`. However, this is the least preferred of the three approaches. You
may reduce duplicate `jython.jar` files, but your web application is no longer
self-contained. Additionally, you do not get automatic access to Jython's `lib`
directory as you do with the third approach.

The third option is to leave the `jython.jar` file in Jython's installation
directory, and add it to the `classpath` before starting Tomcat. This also eliminates duplicate `jython.jar` files; however, it has the added advantage of providing access to the registry file and Jython's `lib` directory. Remember that the
registry is sought in the `python.home` directory, or in the location in which the
`jython.jar` file was found if there is no `python.home` property. Leaving the
`jython.jar` file in Jython's installation directory is therefore an advantage over
placing it in Tomcat's `lib` directory. It's worth mentioning again, however, that
a self-contained context is preferred.

Making Jython's **lib** *Directory Available to Servlets*

There are three ways to make the modules in Jython's `lib` directory available
to Servlets:

- Set the `python.home` property.
- Freeze required modules.
- Have each Servlet explicitly append module locations to the `sys.path`.

If you chose to leave the `jython.jar` file in Jython's installation directory, no
additional steps are required to gain access to Jython's `lib` directory. If you
chose to place the `jython.jar` file in the context's `lib` directory, you must set
the `python.home` property, explicitly append a directory to `sys.path`, or freeze
the modules before your Jython Servlets can use the Jython module library.

To set the `python.home` property you can set the `TOMCAT_OPTS` environment
variable. Before you do this, you must decide where the modules will be
located. Again, the best way is to create a self-contained web application. A
good recommendation is to create an additional directory within the context's
`WEB-INF` directory. The name of this directory will be `jylib` for the purposes of
this section. Create the directory `%TOMCAT_HOME%\webapps\jython\WEB-
INF\jylib`. Because Jython looks for the `lib` directory within `python.home`,
continue by also making the directory `%TOMCAT_HOME%\webapps\jython\
WEB-INF\jylib\Lib`. Place any required modules within this directory, and

specify the `jylib` directory as the `python.home`. Here are some examples that set `TOMCAT_OPTS` to the proper `python.home` property setting:

```
# Windows
set TOMCAT_OPTS=-Dpython.home=%TOMCAT_HOME%\webapps\jython\WEB-INF\jylib
```

```
# bash (*nix)
export TOMCAT_OPTS=-Dpython.home=$TOMCAT_HOME/webapps/jython/WEB-INF/jylib
```

Note that some versions of Windows do not allow an equals sign in an environment string. In this case, you must edit the `tomcat.bat` file to include the `python.home` parameter setting.

It is possible to just begin Servlets by explicitly adding the module directory to `sys.path`. The problem is that this often requires explicit, machine-dependent paths, and thus limits cross-platform portability. Here is an example of what would appear at the top of a Servlet where you wish to explicitly append to the `sys.path`:

```
import sys
libpath = "c:/jakarta-tomcat_3.2.3/webapps/jython/WEB-INF/jylibs/Lib"
sys.path.append(libpath)
```

Another useful approach to making Jython's modules available is to freeze them. The `jythonc --deep` option compiles all required modules, making the `python.home` and Jython's `lib` directory unimportant. To freeze the `JythonServlet.py` file from Listing 12.2, use the following command from within the Jython context's `classes` directory:

```
jythonc -w . --deep JythonServlet.py
```

Class files for the `JythonServlet` and for all the modules it requires are now located within the context's `classes` directory. In other words, the Servlet and modules are now installed in a self-contained web application. Note that compiling other Jython Servlets this way will overwrite any previously compiled modules. This means you must be careful when updating modules, as a newer version may adversely affect an older Servlet. Compiling with the `--deep` options creates a number of files, but the generated `*.java` files may be deleted after compilation.

Freezing is beneficial because changes to modules are infrequent, and because it is an easy way to make a fully self-contained web application. You don't need to set the `python.home` property. A web application set up this way can simply be archived as a .war file and plugged into any other compliant server without a single extra installation step required.

Testing the Jython Servlet

With the Servlet from Listing 12.2 compiled with `jythonc`, the `jython.jar` in the `classpath`, and Jython's modules accessible, you can now view it. Point you browser to `http://localhost:8080/jython/servlet/jythonServlet`. You should see the simple message "This is a Servlet of the Jython variety." If this is not what you see, the likely alternatives are one of three error messages. If the `Servlet.jar` file was not in the `classpath` while compiling the `JythonServlet`, you will likely see a `ClassCastException`. You will also see a `ClassCastException` if the filename and classname differ, even if only in capitalization. If one of the class files generated from compiling the Servlet with `jythonc` is in the context's `classes` directory, you will see an `AttributeError`. If Jython's modules are not available, you will see an `ImportError`.

More About *GenericServlet*

Listing 12.2 inherits from `javax.Servlet.GenericServlet`. This class is just what its name implies: a Servlet class that is not specific to any protocol. The `HttpServlet` class is more common for web programming because it is specific to the HTTP protocol; however, `GenericServlet` is `HttpServlet`'s superclass, and its methods are important to know. Table 12.1 has a summary of Java method signatures for `GenericServlet` and examples of how a Jython subclass of `GenericServlet` would use those methods. These are not all the methods—just those easily used from Jython. Table 12.1 lists methods in two categories:

- Methods overridden in the Jython subclass, noted by the `def` statements.

- Superclass methods invoked from the Jython subclass, noted by qualifying the method with `self`.

Table 12.1   *GenericServlet* **Methods**

Java Signature	Usage in Jython Subclass
METHODS YOU SUBCLASS:	
`public void init(ServletConfig config)` `throws ServletException;`	`def init(self, config):`
`public void destroy();`	`def destroy(self):`
`public abstract void service(` `ServletRequest request,` `ServletResponse response) throws` `Servletexception, IOException;`	`def service(self, request,` `response):`

continues

Table 12.1 **Continued**

`public String getServletInfo();`	`def getServletInfo(self):`
	`    return "Info string"`

METHODS YOU USE WITH THE *SELF.METHOD* SYNTAX:

`public void log(String message);`	`self.log("message")`
`public ServletConfig`	
`    getServletConfig();`	`config = self.getServletConfig()`
`public java.util.enumeration`	
`    getInitParameterNames();`	`nameList =`
	`    self.getInitParameterNames()`
`public String`	
`    getInitParameter(String name)`	`param = self.getInitParameter(`
	`    "paramName")`
`public ServletContext`	
`    getServletContext()`	`context = self.getServletContext`

You have already seen an example of overloading the `public abstract void service()` method in Listing 12.2. The other methods available for overloading get attention in the following hit counter Servlet.

A *hit counter* Servlet is almost as obligatory as a `Hello World` application in the pedagogy of programming. Here it is in the name of tradition. The `hitCounter` Servlet (see Listing 12.3) shows the use of the `init`, `service`, and `destroy` methods. A discussion of each of these methods appears following the listing.

Listing 12.3 *HitCounter* **Servlet**

```
# filename: HitCounter.py
from javax import servlet
from time import time, ctime
import os

class HitCounter(servlet.GenericServlet):
    def init(self, cfg=None):
        if cfg:
            servlet.GenericServlet.init(self, cfg)
        else:
            servlet.GenericServlet.init(self)

        # Construct a path + filename to file storing hit data
        contextRoot = self.servletContext.getRealPath(".")
```

```
        self.file = os.path.join(contextRoot, "counterdata.txt")

        if os.path.exists(self.file):
            lastCount = open(self.file, "r").read()
            try:
                # within 'try' just in case the file is empty
                self.totalHits = int(lastCount)
            except:
                self.totalHits = 0
        else:
            self.totalHits = 0

    def service(self, req, res):
        res.setContentType("text/html")
        toClient = res.getWriter()
        toClient.println("<html><body>")
        toClient.println("Total Hits: %i<br>" % (self.totalHits,))
        self.totalHits += 1
        toClient.println("</body></html>")

    def destroy(self):
        f = open(self.file, "w")
        f.write(str(self.totalHits))
        f.close()
```

Place the `HitCounter.py` in the context's `classes` directory
(`%TOMCAT_HOME%\webapps\jython\WEB-INF\classes`), and compile it with
`jythonc` from within the same directory.

```
jythonc -w . --deep HitCounter.py
```

Test the `HitCounter` Servlet by pointing you browser to `http://local-host:8080/jython/servlet/HitCounter`. You should see the message "Total
Hits: 0" The first time you visit this URL. Each subsequent hit increments the
count. If you shut down Tomcat with `%TOMCAT_HOME%\bin\shutdown.bat` ($TOM-CAT_HOME/bin/shutdown.sh` for bash) and restart Tomcat, the hit count should
continue at its last number.

The three methods `init`, `service`, and `destroy` are essential to Servlets, and
each one matches a stage of a Servlet's life cycle. A Servlet is first loaded and
initialized: the `init()` method. A Servlet then handles client requests: the `ser-vice()` method. A Servlet handles requests until it is unloaded or removed
from the Servlet `container()`: the `destroy` method.

init(ServletConfig) **Method**

The init() method is called at Servlet startup, and only called that one time. This makes it useful for time-intensive tasks such as setting up database connections, compiling regular expressions or loading ancillary files. The purpose of including an init() method in Listing 12.3 is to establish the file that stores the hit information, and to set the counter to the last stored integer in that file. This implementation ensures that the hit counter is not reset to 0 unless the Servlet is restarted and the counter.txt file is missing.

The 2.2 version of the Servlet API has two init() methods: a parameterless version and one that accepts an instance of the ServletConfig class. Listing 17.3 uses the variable cfg for this object. It's important to remember that when Jython overrides a Java method, it overrides all methods with that name. This means that defining an init() method in a Jython Servlet overrides both the parameterless init() and the init(ServletConfig cfg) methods. Listing 17.3 handles the functionality of both methods by specifying a default argument of None for the cfg variable, then testing for None to determine if that cfg variable should be used when calling the superclass's init() method.

service(ServletRequest, ServletResponse) **Method**

This is the method called in response to each client request. A Servlet must define this method because it is abstract in GenericServlet. The arguments passed to this method are the ServletRequest and the ServletResponse objects. ServletRequest contains client information sent in the request to the server such as the request headers, request method, and request parameters. ServletResponse is used for sending the response stream in the appropriate mime-encoded format back to the client.

destroy() **Method**

This is called when shutting down or unloading a Servlet. Cleanup code goes here, including closing database connections, flushing and closing files, and so on.

The destroy method in Listing 12.3 writes the hit counter value to a file so that the information is not lost when the Servlet is unloaded. This isn't the best means of persistence, however. The hit count value only gets stored if the server is shutdown politely. If the Servlet container is not shutdown properly, the destroy method may not be called. When you are using Tomcat, you usually start and stop the server with the startup and shutdown shell scripts. These are the polite and proper ways to start and stop Tomcat; however, if you choose to stop Tomcat with an impolite "Ctrl+C", the proper shutdown sequence is skipped. Additionally, an error that unexpectedly terminated Tomcat causes the same results, and the hit count would be lost. Higher quality persistence would require that the data be stored in a way that the assignment and commit are in a transaction framework.

HttpServlet

GenericServlet is truly generic because it is applicable to any chat-type protocol; however, web development is mostly about the HTTP protocol. To chat in HTTP, javax.Servlet.http.HttpServlet is best to extend. HttpServlet is a subclass of GenericServlet. Therefore, the init, service, and destroy methods from GenericServlet are available when extending HttpServlet.

HttpServlet defines a method for each of the HTTP methods. These methods are doGet, doPost, doPut, doOptions, doDelete, and doTrace. When Tomcat receives a client request of the GET type, the requested Servlet's doGet() method is invoked to reply to that client. Additionally, HttpServlet has an HTTP-specific version of the service method. The only change in the HttpServlet service method over the GenericServlet's version is that HTTP-specific request and response objects are the parameters (javax.servlet.http.HttpServletRequest and javax.servlet.http.HttpServletResponse).

To write a Servlet by subclassing HttpServlet, implement each HTTP method desired (such as doGet or doPost), or define the service method. The HttpServlet class also has a getlastModified method that you may override if you wish to return a value (milliseconds since the 1970 epoch) representing the last time the Servlet or related data was updated. This information is used by caches.

HttpServlet **Methods**

Table 12.2 includes all of the methods for the javax.servlet.http. HttpServlet class, and example usage in Jython. Those methods that are overridden have a def statement in Jython, and those methods invoked on the superclass begin with self. Java signatures in Table 12.2 do not include return values or permission modifiers. For permissions, all methods are protected except for service(ServletRequest req, ServletResponse res), it has no permissions modifier (package private). All return values are void except for getLastModified, which returns a long type representing milliseconds since the epoch.

Table 12.2 *HttpServlet* **Methods**

Java Signature	Usage in Jython Subclass
doDelete(HttpServletRequest req, HttpServletResponse resp)	def doDelete(self, req, res):
doGet(HttpServletRequest req, HttpServletResponse resp)	def doGet(self, req, res):
doHead(HttpServletRequest req, HttpServletResponse resp)	def doHead(self, req, res): *in J2EE version 1.3*

doOptions(HttpServletRequest req,
          HttpServletResponse resp)
	def doOptions(self, req,
	                         res):

doPost(HttpServletRequest req, HttpServletResponse resp)	def doPost(self, req, res):
doPut(HttpServletRequest req, HttpServletResponse resp)	def doPut(self, req, res):
doTrace(HttpServletRequest req, HttpServletResponse resp)	def doTrace(self, req, res):
getLastModified(HttpServletRequest req)	def getLastModified(self, req):
service(HttpServletRequest req, HttpServletResponse resp)	def service(self, req, res):
service(ServletRequest req, ServletResponse res)	def service(self, req, res):

The service method that accepts HTTP-specific request and response object redispatches those request to the appropriate do* method (if it isn't overridden). The service method that accepts a generic Servlet request and response object redispatches the request to the HTTP-specific service method. The redispatching makes the service methods valuable when implementing Servlet mappings.

HttpServlet **Example**

Listing 12.4 demonstrates a Servlet that subclasses `javax.servlet.http.HttpServlet`. The example implements both the `doGet` and `doPost` methods to demonstrate how those methods are called depending on the type of request received from the client. A web client should not allow a `POST` operation to be repeated without confirmation. Because of this, database updates, order commits, and so on should be in a `doPost` method, whereas the forms to do so can reside safely in a `doGet`.

The `get_post.py` file in Listing 12.4 shows how to get parameter names and values by using the `HttpServletRequest`'s (`req`) `getParameterNames` and `getParameterValues`. The list returned from `getParameterNames` is a `java.util.Enumeration`, which the `doPost` method uses to display the request's parameters. Jython lets you use the `for x in list:` syntax with the enumeration returned from `getParameternames`. Note that the `getParameterValues()` method is plural. Parameters can have multiple values as demonstrated in the hidden form fields. To prevent redundancy in the `doGet` and `doPost` methods of the Servlet, Listing 12.4 adds a `_params` method. This method is not defined anywhere in `HttpServlet` or its bases, and because no Java class calls it, no `@sig` string is required. The purpose of the method is merely to keep similar operations in only one place.

Listing 12.4   **Implementing a Servlet with *HttpServlet***

```
#file get_post.py
from time import time, ctime
from javax import servlet
from javax.servlet import http

class get_post(http.HttpServlet):
    head = "<head><title>Jython Servlets</title></head>"
    title = "<center><H2>%s</H2></center>"

    def doGet(self,req, res):
        res.setContentType("text/html")
        out = res.getWriter()

        out.println('<html>')
        out.println(self.head)
        out.println('<body>')
        out.println(self.title % req.method)

        out.println("This is a response to a %s request" %
                    (req.getMethod(),))
        out.println("<P>In this GET request, we see the following " +
                    "header variables.</P>")
```

continues

Listing 12.4   **Continued**

```
        out.println("<UL>")
        for name in req.headerNames:
            out.println(name + " : " + req.getHeader(name) + "<br>")
        out.println("</UL>")

        out.println(self._params(req))
        out.println("""
            <P>The submit button below is part of a form that uses the
                "POST" method. Click on this button to do a POST request.
            </P>""")

        out.println('<br><form action="get_post" method="POST">' +
                    '<INPUT type="hidden" name="variable1" value="one">' +
                    '<INPUT type="hidden" name="variable1" value="two">' +
                    '<INPUT type="hidden" name="variable2" value="three">' +
                    '<INPUT type="submit" name="button" value="submit">')

        out.println('<br><font size="-2">time accessed:  %s</font>'
                    % ctime(time()))
        out.println('</body></html>')

    def doPost(self, req, res):
        res.setContentType("text/html");
        out = res.getWriter()

        out.println('<html>')
        out.println(self.head)
        out.println('<body>')
        out.println(self.title % req.method)

        out.println("This was a %s<br><br>" % (req.getMethod(),))
        out.println(self._params(req))
        out.println('<br> back to <a href="get_post">GET</a>')
        out.println('<br><font size="-2">time accessed:  %s</font>'
                    % ctime(time()))
        out.println('</body></html>')

    def _params(self, req):
        params = "Here are the parameters sent with this request:<UL>"
        names = req.getParameterNames()

        if not names.hasMoreElements():
            params += "None<br>"
        for name in names:
            value = req.getParameterValues(name)
            params += "%s : %r<br>" % (name, tuple(value))
        params += "</UL>"
        return params
```

After placing the `get_post.py` file in the `$TOMCAT_HOME/webapps/jython/WEB-INF/classes` directory, compile it with the following:

```
jythonc -w . --deep get_post.py
```

To test it, point your browser at `http://localhost:8080/jython/servlet/get_post`. You should see a browser window similar to that in Figure 12.1.

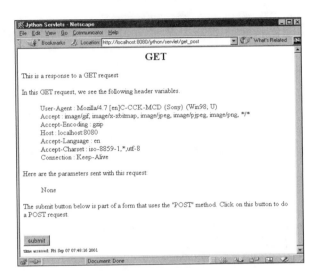

Figure 12.1 The *GET* view from *get_post.py*.

The parameters for the GET operation are None in this example, but test other parameters in the doGet method by adding some to the end of the URL(such as `http://localhost:8080/servlet/get_post?variable1=1&variable2=2`).

Because the Submit button on the bottom of the first view is part of a form implemented as a POST, clicking on the Submit button executes the doPost method of the same Servlet. The results of the doPost method should match what is shown in Figure 12.2.

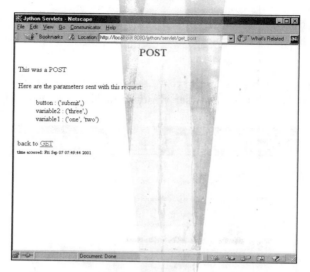

Figure 12.2 The *POST* view from *get_post.py*.

HttpServletRequest and *HttpServletResponse*

Communication with client connections happens through the
HttpServletRequest and HttpServletResponse object. These are abstractions of
the literal request stream received from and sent to the client. Each of these
objects adds higher-level, HTTP-specific methods to ease working with
requests and responses.

Table 12.3 is a list of the methods within the HttpServletRequest object. A
great majority of the methods are bean property accessors, which means that
you can reference them with Jython's automatic bean properties. This may not
be as great of an advantage here as it is for GUI programming because there is
no opportunity to leverage this facility in method keyword arguments. Table
12.3 shows the methods and bean property names from the
HttpServletRequest object.

Table 12.3   *HttpServletRequest* **Methods and Properties**

Method and Property	Description
Method: `getAuthType()` Property name: `AuthType`	Returns a string (`PyString`) describing the name of the authentication type. The value is `None` if the user is notauthenticated.
Method: `getContextPath()` Property name: `contextPath`	Returns a string (`PyString`) describing the path information that identifies the context requested.
Method: `getCookies()` Property name: `cookies()`	Returns all cookies sent with the client's request as an array of j `avax.servlet.http.Cookie` objects.
Method: `getDateHeader(name)`	Retrieves the value of the specified header as a long type.
Method: `getHeader(name)`	Returns the value of the specified header as string (`PyString`).
Method: `getHeaderNames()` Property name: `headerNames`	Returns all the header names contained within the request as an Enumeration.
Method: `getHeaders(name)`	Returns all the values of the specified header name as an Enumeration.
Method: `getIntHeader(name)`	Retrieves the specified header value as a Java `int`, which Jython converts to a `PyInteger`.
Method: `getMethod()` Property name: `method`	Returns the type of request made a string.

continues

Table 12.3 **Continued**

Method and Property	Description
Method: getPathInfo() Property name: pathInfo	All extra path information sent by the client.
Method: getPathTranslated() Property name: pathTranslated	Returns the real path derived from extra path information in the client's request.
Method: getQueryString() Property name: queryString	Returns the query string from the client's request (the string after the path).
Method: getRemoteUser() Property name: remoteUser	Returns the login name of the client. None if the client is not authenticated.
Method: getRequestedSessionId() Property name: requestedSessionId	Returns the clients session ID.
Method: getRequestURI() Property name: requestURI	Returns that segment of the between the protocol name and the query string.
Method: getServletPath() Property name: servletPath	Returns the portion of the URL that designates the current Servlet.
Method: getSession() Property name: session	Returns the current session, or creates on if needed. A session is an instance of javax.servlet.http.HttpSession.
Method: getSession(create)	Returns the current session if one exists. If not, a new session is created if the create value is true.

Method and Property	Description
Method: getUserPrincipal() Property name: userPrincipal	Returns a java.security.Principal object with the current authentication information userPrincipal
Method: isRequestedSessionIdFromCookie()	Returns 1 or 0 depending on whether the current session ID was from a cookie.
Method: isRequestedSessionIdFromURL()	Returns 1 or 0 depending on whether the current session ID was from the requested URL string.
Method: isRequestedSessionIdValid()	Returns 1 or 0 depending on whether the requested session ID is still valid.
Method: isUserInRole(role)	Returns 1 or 0 indicating whether the user is listed in the specified role.

The HttpServletResponse object is used to send the mime-encoded stream back to the client. HttpServletResponse defines additional HTTP-specific methods that do not exist in a generic ServletResponse object. The methods within the HttpServletResponse object appear in Table 12.4. Whereas Jython adds numerous automatic bean properties to the HttpServletRequest object, the HttpServletResponse object only has one: status.

Table 12.4   *HttpServletResponse* **Methods and Properties**

Method and Property	Description
addCookie(cookie)	Add a cookie to the response.
addDateHeader(headerName, date)	Adds a header name with a date (long) value.
addHeader(headerName, value)	Adds a header name and value.
addIntHeader(headerName, value)	Adds a header name with an integer value.
containsHeader(headerName)	Returns a 1 or 0 depending whether the specified header.
encodeRedirectUrl(url)	Encodes a URL for the sendRedirect method. For version 2.1 and greater, use encodeRedirectURL instead.

continues

Table 12.4 **Continued**

Method and Property	Description
encodeRedirectURL(url)	Encodes a URL for the sendRedirect method.
encodeURL(url)	Encodes a URL by including the session ID in it.
sendError(sc)	Sends an error using the status code.
sendError(sc, msg)	Sends an error using the specified status code and message.
sendRedirect(location)	Sends a temporary redirect to the specified location.
setDateHeader(headerName, date)	Sets a header name to the specified date (long) value.
setHeader(headerName, value)	Sets a header name to the specified value.
setIntHeader(headerName, value)	Sets a header name to the specified integer value.
setStatus(statusCode) status	Sets the response status code.

The HttpServletResponse class also contains fields that correspond to the standard HTTP response codes. You can use these with sendError(int) and setStatus(int). Table 12.5 lists the number and error code for these status codes.

Table 12.5 *HttpServletResponse* **Status CodesError**

Code	Status
100	SC_CONTINUE
101	SC_SWITCHING_PROTOCOLS
200	SC_OK
201	SC_CONTINUE
202	SC_ACCEPTED
203	SC_NON_AUTHORITATIVE_INFORMATION
204	SC_NO_CONTENT
205	SC_RESET_CONTENT

206	SC_PARTIAL_CONTENT
300	SC_MULTIPLE_CHOICES
301	SC_MOVED_PERMANENTLY
302	SC_MOVED_TEMPORARILY
303	SC_SEE_OTHER
304	SC_NOT_MODIFIED
305	SC_USE_PROXY
400	SC_BAD_REQUEST
401	SC_UNAUTHORIZED
402	SC_PAYMENT_REQUIRED
403	SC_FORBIDDEN
404	SC_NOT_FOUND
405	SC_METHOD_NOT_ALLOWED
406	SC_NOT_ACCEPTABLE
407	SC_PROXY_AUTHENTICATION_REQUIRED
408	SC_REQUEST_TIMEOUT
409	SC_CONFLICT
410	SC_GONE
411	SC_LENGTH_REQUIRED
412	SC_PRECONDITION_FAILED
413	SC_REQUEST_ENTITY_TOO_LARGE
414	SC_REQUEST_URI_TOO_LONG
415	SC_UNSUPPORTED_MEDIA_TYPE
500	SC_INTERNAL_SERVER_ERROR
501	SC_NOT_IMPLEMENTED
502	SC_BAD_GATEWAY
503	SC_SERVICE_UNAVAILABLE
504	SC_GATEWAY_TIMEOUT
505	SC_HTTP_VERSION_NOT_SUPPORTED

PyServlet

A great advantage of `HttpServlet` programming for Jython programmers is that the Jython distribution comes with the Servlet `org.python.util.PyServlet`. This Servlet loads, executes and caches Jython files so that you can write and view a Jython Servlet without any compiling step in the middle. This works with a Servlet mapping. A *Servlet mapping* is an association between a specific Servlet, `PyServlet` in this case, and a certain URL pattern, such as `*.py`. With a proper `web.xml` file, Jython's `PyServlet` class is mapped to all `*.py` files, so as requests for `*.py` files arrive, the `PyServlet` class loads, caches, and invokes methods in the `*.py` files as needed to respond.

   `PyServlet`'s design creates some restrictions on the Jython files it serves. A Jython file must contain a class that subclasses `javax.servlet.http.HttpServlet`. The name of that class must match the name of the file without the `.py` extension. In other words, the file `Test.py` must contain the class `Test`, which must be a subclass of `javax.servlet.http.HttpServlet`. Additionally, it is unsafe to use module–global identifiers other than the one class which subclasses `HttpServlet`.

   A note on naming: With Servlets, `PyServlet`, and Jython modules that implement servlets, names get a bit confusing. To clarify any confusion, the term servlet appears in a generic sense regardless of which language implements it. `PyServlet` refers to the specific Servlet `org.python.util.PyServlet`. The confusion arises with those Jython modules that `PyServlet` actually serves. Files matching the `*.py` pattern within the context that are loaded, executed, and cached by PyServlet, need a name of their own to distinguish them. There is no precedence for any such term, but dubbed *jylets* they are for the sake of this chapter.

Installing *PyServlet*

All that is required to install the `PyServlet` is to define a Servlet mapping and make sure the `jython.jar` file is in the context's `lib` directory. A Servlet mapping is defined in the context's deployment descriptor file: `web.xml`. The `web.xml` file for the Jython context belongs in the location `$TOMCAT_HOME/webapps/jython/WEB-INF/web.xml`. In Tomcat, the default `web.xml` file from `$TOMCAT_HOME/conf/web.xml` is used for all the settings that are not explicitly included in the context's `web.xml`. Therefore, there may not be a `web.xml` file in your context yet, and you need not define all properties in that context because default values already exist.

Listing 12.5 is an example deployment descriptor for the *Jython* context, which establishes `PyServlet` as the handler for context requests matching the `*.py` pattern. The essential additions to the `web.xml` file are a Servlet definition for `PyServlet` and a Servlet mapping that associates URLs with the `PyServlet`. Because Tomcat has default values for items not defined, Listing 12.5 is a sufficiently complete `web.xml` file for the Tomcat server.

Listing 12.5 A Sample Deployment Descriptor for *PyServlet*

```
<web-app>
    <servlet>
        <servlet-name>PyServlet</servlet-name>
        <servlet-class>
            org.python.util.PyServlet
        </servlet-class>
        <load-on-startup>1</load-on-startup>
    </servlet>
    <servlet-mapping>
        <servlet-name>PyServlet</servlet-name>
        <url-pattern>*.py</url-pattern>
    </servlet-mapping>
</web-app>
```

The Servlet definition defines the Servlet name and the Servlet's class. Listing 12.5 defines the name as `PyServlet` and the class as `org.python.util.PyServlet`. The class is the full package-class hierarchy that uniquely identifies the Servlet class: `PyServlet`. The actual class resides in the `jython.jar` file, which should be in the context's `lib` directory.

The Servlet definition for `PyServlet` may optionally include initialization parameters (init-params). `PyServlet` uses such parameters in the initialization of Jython; therefore, this is where you would place any of the Jython property settings such as `python.home`, `python.path`, `python.respectJavaAccessibility` or any of the other properties normally set in Jython's registry file. Listing 12.6 is a `web.xml` file supplies a `python.home` and `python.path` value as init-params.

Listing 12.6 *PyServlet* init-params in *web.xml*

```
<web-app>
    <servlet>
        <servlet-name>PyServlet</servlet-name>
        <servlet-class>
            org.python.util.PyServlet
        </servlet-class>
        <load-on-startup>1</load-on-startup>
        <init-param>
            <param-name>python.home</param-name>
```

continues

Listing 12.6   **Continued**

```
                <param-value>c:\jython-2.1</param-value>
            </init-param>
            <init-param>
                <param-name>python.path</param-name>
                <param-value>
                    c:\jython-2.1\lib\site-packages
                </param-value>
            </init-param>
    </servlet>
    <servlet-mapping>
        <servlet-name>PyServlet</servlet-name>
        <url-pattern>*.py</url-pattern>
    </servlet-mapping>
</web-app>
```

Properties that define locations of Jython resources, such as `python.home` and `python.path` are of special concern. These affect whether a context is self contained and affect cross-platform portability. If the `python.home` property points outside the context, or if the `python.path` property includes a directory outside the context, the context is no longer self contained. Additionally, the property values must be platform-specific paths. Notice the `python.home` and `python.path` properties in Listing 12.6. They would not work on other platforms, and there is no mechanism to create platform-neutral paths for these property values. Fortunately, `PyServlet` has a default value for the `python.home` property that creates both a self-contained and a platform-neutral context.

The default `python.home` value for `PyServlet` is the context's `lib` directory. This makes the default `python.home` value for the *Jython* context one of the following (depending on platform).

```
%TOMCAT_HOME\webapps\jython\WEB-INF\lib
$TOMCAT_HOME/webapps/jython/WEB-INF/lib
```

Additionally, Jython's `lib` directory automatically becomes one of the following:

```
%TOMCAT_HOME%\webapps\jython\WEB-INF\lib\Lib
$TOMCAT_HOME/webapps/jython/WEB-INF/lib/Lib
```

This keeps all of Jython's resources within the context, keeping it self contained. The additional advantage is that `PyServlet` adds the default `python.home` path in a platform-independent manner, making those contexts that use the default value platform independent.

Testing *PyServlet*

You con confirm that the Servlet mapping is working by starting Tomcat and viewing a simple jylet (Jython-Servlet) in a browser. Below is a simple test jylet:

```
# File ServletMappingTest.py
from javax.servlet.http import HttpServlet

class ServletMappingTest(HttpServlet):
    def doGet(self, req, res):
        out = res.writer
        res.contentType = "text/html"
        print >> out, "Greetings from a jylet."
```

Save this test file as `%TOMCAT_HOME%\webapps\jython\ServletMappingTest.py`, then point your browser to `http://localhost:8080/jython/ServletMappingTest.py`. If you see the greeting message, the `PyServlet` mapping is correct. To complete the installation, create Jython's `lib` directory `%TOMCAT_HOME%\webapps\jython\WEB-INF\lib\Lib`. This is the directory where you will place any Jython modules used in your jylets. After that, installation is complete.

Cookies

Cookies allows storage on the client's machine information that is to be included in subsequent requests. To create and manipulate cookies from Jython, use the `javax.Servlet.http.Cookie` class. Creating a new cookie requires instantiating `javax.servlet.http.Cookie` with a name and value as parameters. If you were using cookies to track book purchases, you could set the author and title with a cookie like this:

```
from javax.servlet import http
name = "book1"
value = "Lewis Carroll, Alice In Wonderland"
MyNewCookie = http.Cookie(name, value)
```

Now you have a new cookie with a name of *book1*, the value is the Rev. Dodgson's pen name, and the title *Alice in Wonderland*. To send this cookie to the client you need to use `HttpServletResponse`'s `addCookie(cookie)` method:

```
res.addCookie(MyNewCookie)
```

Adding cookies should take place before sending other content through the response stream.

Cookies often require more attention than that, thus the cookie instance has methods to set the specifics of the cookie. Each cookie instance can use get and set methods or Jython's automatic bean properties for each of the following properties:

- comment
- domain
- maxAge
- name
- path
- secure
- value
- version

Listing 12.7 makes use of the cookie object's automatic bean properties to create and read cookies defined in a web form.

Listing 12.7   **Cookies with Jython**

```
# File: cookies.py
from javax import servlet
from javax.servlet import http

class cookies(http.HttpServlet):
    def doGet(self, req, res):
        res.setContentType("text/html")
        out = res.getOutputStream()

        print >>out, "<html><head><title>Cookies with Jython</title></head>"
        print >>out, """
            <body>\n<H2>Cookie list:</H2>
            Remember, cookies must be enabled in your browser.<br><br>"""

        # Here's the list of Cookies
        for c in req.cookies:
            print >>out, """
                <b>Cookie Name</b>= %s  
                <b>Value</b>= %s<br><br>""" % (c.name,c.value)

        print >>out, """<br><br><br>
            <HR><P>Use this form to add a new cookie</P>
            <form action="cookies.py" method="POST">
            <P>Name:<br><INPUT type="text" name="name" size="30"></P>
            <P>Value:<br><INPUT type="text" name="value" size="30"></P>
            <P>Use the MaxAge field to set the cookie's time-to-expire.
                A value of "0" deletes the cookie immediately, a value of
```

```
                    "-1" saves the cookie until the browser exits, and
                    any other integer represents seconds until it expires
                    (i.e.- using "10" would expire 10 seconds after being set).</P>
               <P>MaxAge:<br><INPUT type="text" name="maxAge" size="30"></P>
               <INPUT type="submit" name="button" value="submit">
               \n</body>
               \n</html>
               """

     def doPost(self, req, res):
         res.setContentType("text/html");
         out = res.getWriter()
         name = req.getParameterValues("name")[0]
         value = req.getParameterValues("value")[0]
         maxAge = req.getParameterValues("maxAge")[0]

         if name:
             newCookie = http.Cookie(name, value)
             newCookie.maxAge = int(maxAge or -1)
             newCookie.comment = "Jython test cookie"
             res.addCookie(newCookie)

             print >>out, """
                 <html><body>Cookie set successfully\n\n
                 <P>click <a href="cookies.py">here</a>
                 to view the new cookie.</P>
                 <P>If cookies are enabled in your
                 browser that is.</P>
                 \n</body>
                 \n</html>"""
         else:
             print >>out, """
                 <html>\n<body>
                 Cookie not set
                 <P>No cookie "Name" provided</P>
                 <P>click <a href="cookies">here</a>
                 to try again</P>
                 \n</body>
                 /n</html>"""
```

To test the jylet in Listing 12.7, first make sure your browser is set to allow cookies. Then place the cookies.py file in the directory %TOMCAT_HOME%\webapps\jython and point your browser to http://localhsot:8080/jython/cookies.py. You should only see a heading and a form on your first visit to this servlet. Proceed to add a form entry—possibly "Jython Cookie" for the name and "My first Jython cookie" for the value, and click the Submit button (maxAge is optional). You should see confirmation that adding the cookie was successful. To confirm that the cookie was truly added, return to `doGet` method and see if it shows up in the cookie list. Figure 12.3 shows what a browser might display after returning to the `doGet` method. Note that Figure 12.3 assumes certain cookie names and values were entered, and your result page will depend on the names and values you use.

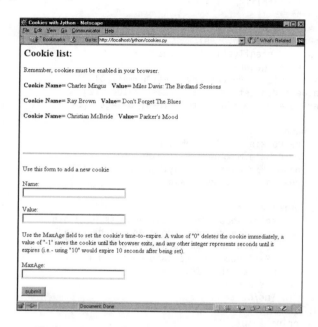

Figure 12.3　Defined Cookies with *cookies.py*.

Sessions

Cookies are the most common means of creating sessions with clients. *Sessions* are a means of tracking client information through a series of requests. The cookie example (see Listing 12.7) could have been used to store a sessions ID, but the Java `HttpSession` class makes session tracking much easier.

To create a session, use `HttpRequest`'s `getSession()` method. This returns a `HttpSession` instance. `HttpSession` is a simple interface to the more complicated behavior of a session management subsystem. Using the `HttpSession` object from Jython differs only from Java in the syntax and the automatic bean properties for the object's `get*` methods.

Listing 12.8 creates a session object with the simple `req.session` bean property. Listing 12.8 allows the cookie or the URL to contain the session value. Because cookies may store the session value, you should use the `req.session` bean property or the `req.getSession()` method before sending other data to the output stream. If the client has cookies disabled, however, the session object still works because all URLs are rewritten with the `encodeUrl` method. Actually, it is just one URL that needs rewritten, and that is the form action. If there were any other URLs, they would also necessarily go through the `res.encodeUrl()` method to support cookie-less sessions.

Once you have a `HttpSession` instance, passing data through the session is just a matter of using `key`, `value` pairs with `putValue(key, value)` and `value = getValue(key)`.

Listing 12.8   **Session Management**

```
# File: session.py
from javax import servlet
from javax.servlet import http

class session(http.HttpServlet, servlet.RequestDispatcher):
    def doGet(self, req, res):
        sess = req.session
        res.contentType = "text/html"
        out = res.getWriter()

        name = req.getParameterValues("name")
        value = req.getParameterValues("value")
        if name and value:
            sess.putValue(name[0], value[0])

        print >>out, ("""
            <html>
            <body>
            <H3>Session Test</H3>
            Created at %s<br>
            Last Accessed = %s<br>
            <u>Values:</u>""" %
            (sess.creationTime, sess.maxInactiveInterval)
        )

        print >>out, "<ul>"
        for key in sess.getValueNames():
            print >>out, "<li>%s:  %s</li>" % (key, sess.getValue(key))
        print >>out, "</ul>"

        print >>out, """
            <HR><P>Use this form to add a new values to the session</P>
```

continues

Listing 12.8 **Continued**

```
<form action="session.py" method="GET">
<P>Name:<br><INPUT type="text" name="name" size="30"></P>
<P>Value:<br><INPUT type="text" name="value" size="30"></P>
<INPUT type="submit" name="button" value="submit">
</body>
</html>
"""
```

After saving the session.py file from Listing 12.8 in the %TOMCAT_HOME%\
webapps\jython directory, point your browser to http://localhost:8080/
jython/session.py. Use the web form to add some variables to the session to
confirm it is working, and even try disabling cookies to see how the URL
rewriting works. Figure 12.4 is the session.py results after adding a series of
arbitrary values (results depend on the values added).

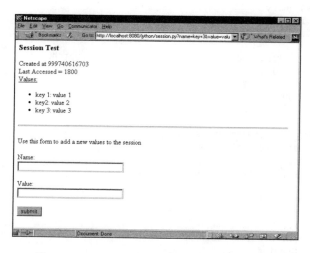

Figure 12.4 Session variables with *session.py*.

Databases and Servlets

Connecting to a database, executing statements and traversing result sets is no
different in a jylet than it is in other Jython database applications. Managing
connections and other database resources, however, is a primary concern
because many web applications contain numerous jylets that use database content. Creating a database connection in each jylet quickly consumes the database resources, which has bad consequences. Alternatively, creating and closing
a database connection for each request is unacceptable overhead.

There are many options for managing database resources, but two primary approaches are a connection per jylet, or connection pooling. Using a connection for each jylet is a popular but resource intensive approach. This approach involves establishing a database connection in the jytlet's `init` method, and closes that connection only when they jylet is unloaded. This eliminates any connection overhead while responding to client requests. However, this is only reasonable if the number of connections you require is well within resource limits. Most situations call for more prudent resource management.

Listing 12.9 implements a jylet that obtains a database connection and cursor object in its `init` method, which are closed in its destroy method. Therefore, the jylet incurs the connection overhead only at initialization, not during each client request. The database implementation in Listing 12.9 uses the `zxJDBC` package and MySQL database described in Chapter 11, "Database Programming." You must therefore include the classes required for MySQL and `zxJDBC` in the context's `lib` directory. For Listing 12.9, the `mm_mysql-2_0_4-bin.jar` file and the `zxJDBC.jar` file should be placed in the directory `%TOMCAT_HOME%\webapps\jython\WEB-INF\lib`. You should restart Tomcat after adding `jar` files to the `lib` directory to ensure it detects the new `jar` files.

Listing 12.9 Jython Servlet with Database Connection

```
# file: DBDisplay.py
from javax.servlet import http
from com.ziclix.python.sql import zxJDBC

class DBDisplay(http.HttpServlet):
    def init(self, cnfg):
        #define the JDBC url
        url = "jdbc:mysql://192.168.1.77/products"
        usr = "productsUser"      # replace with real user name
        passwd = "secret"         # replace with real password
        driver = "org.gjt.mm.mysql.Driver"

        #connect to the database and get cursor object
        self.db = zxJDBC.connect(url, usr, passwd, driver)
        self.c = self.db.cursor()

    def doGet(self, req, res):
        res.setContentType("text/html")
        out = res.getWriter()

        print >>out, """
            <html>
            <head>
              <title>Jylet Database Connection</title>
            </head>
```

continues

Listing 12.9 **Continued**

```
                <body>
                <table align="center">
                  <tr>
                    <td><b>ID</b></td>
                    <td><b>Title</b></td>
                    <td><b>Description</b></td>
                    <td><b>Price</b></td>
                  </tr>"""

        self.c.execute("select code, name, description, price from products")
        for row in self.c.fetchall():
            print >>out, """
                <tr>
                  <td>%s</td>
                  <td>%s</td>
                  <td>%s</td>
                  <td>%s</td>"""  % row

        print >>out, """
            </table>
            </body>
            </html>"""

    def destroy(self):
        self.c.close()
        self.db.close()
```

Listing 12.9 assumes there is a database named products that includes the products table, and that the products table has at least the fields code, name, description, and price. To create such a database, use the following SQL statement:

```
create database products
```

To create the products table, use the following SQL statements:

```
CREATE TABLE products (
  primarykey int(11) NOT NULL auto_increment,
  code varchar(55) default NULL,
  name varchar(255) default NULL,
  description text,
  price float(5,2) default NULL,
  PRIMARY KEY (primarykey)
) TYPE=MyISAM;
```

After creating the database and table, creating some arbitrary values for each of the fields and placing the DBDisplay.py file in the context's root directory, you should be able to point your browser to http://localhost:8080/jython/ DBDisplay.py to see the database data.

If your web application begins using excessive connections, consider instead using connection pooling. *Connection pooling* allows for both prudent resource management and elimination of connection overhead. A connection pool maintains a certain number of active database connections that jylets borrow when replying to client requests and return to the pool when done. This creates a predictable, static number of connections. It is also possible to use a statement pool, giving statements the same advantage. A popular, free, tested, and well-documented connection-pooling tool is PoolMan from `http://www.codestudio.com/`. Other Java connection-pooling packages exist as well, and all should work seamlessly with Jython.

JSP

Java Server Pages (JSP) is the templating system espoused by Sun as a compliment to Servlets. A JSP file contains a web page's markup code and text unaltered, but also contains special tags that designate dynamic content. Currently, Tomcat only implement the Java language in JSP, so the big question is how do you use Jython with JSP. Currently, the answer is that you do not use Jython directly. You cannot include a code tag (`<% code %>`) where the code is in the Jython language. What you can do is use `jythonc`-compiled classes, use an embedded `PythonInterpreter`, or create a Jython-specific, custom tag library.

jythonc-Compiled Classes and JSP

Using `jythonc`-compiled classes with JSP requires creating a Java-compatible Jython class. One that has the same name as the module within it, inherits from a Java class, and includes `@sig` strings for each method not derived from the superclass. Placing class files generated with `jythonc` in the context's classes directory allows JSP pages to use those classes just like any native Java class. Of course, this also requires that the `jython.jar` file is placed in the context's `lib` directory.

A JSP file can use a `jythonc`-compiled class one of two ways, in scriptlets, or as a bean. If it is to be used as a bean, the Jython class must comply with bean conventions and include a `getProperty` and `setProperty` method for each read-write property. A scriptlet, however, can use any class. Whether as a bean or in a scriptlet, you must first load the `jythonc`-compiled class into the appropriate scope. To import a non-bean class, use the page import directive:

```
<%@ page import="fully.qualified.path.to.class" %>
```

For a bean, use the `jsp:useBean` tag to load the bean:

```
<jsp:useBean name="beanName"
              class="fully.qualified path.to.class"
              scope="scope(page or session)">
```

To use a non–bean class, include Java code using that class in scriplet tags (<% %>) or in expression tags (<%= %>). If you imported the hypothetical class `ProductListing`, you could use that class in something similar to the following contrived JSP page:

```
<%@ page import="ProductListing" %>

<html>
<body>

<!--The next line begins the scriptlet -->
<% ProductListing pl = new ProductListing(); %>

<table>
  <tr>
    <td><%= pl.productOne %></td>
    <td><%= pl.productTwo %></td>
  </tr>
</table>
```

Scriplets are often discouraged because they complicate the JSP page. The preferred implementation uses `jythonc`-compiled beans along with the JSP `useBean`, `setProperty`, and `getProperty` tags. Listing 12.10 is a very simple bean written in Jython that stores a username. It will serve as an example on how to use a bean written in Jython.

Listing 12.10   **A Simple Bean Written in Jython**

```
# file: NameHandler.py
import java

class NameHandler(java.lang.Object):
    def __init__(self):
        self.name = "Fred"
    def getUsername(self):
        "@sig public String getname()"
        return self.name
    def setUsername(self, name):
        "@sig public void setname(java.lang.String name)"
        self.name = name
```

Place the `nameHandler.py` file from Listing 12.10 in the
`%TOMCAT_HOME%\webapps\jython\WEB-INF\classes` directory and compile it from
within that directory with the following command:

```
jythonc -w . Namehandler.py
```

Listing 12.11 is a simple JSP page that uses the `NameHandler` bean.

Listing 12.11 **Using a Jython Bean in a JSP page**

```
<!--file: name.jsp -->
<%@ page contentType="text/html" %>

<jsp:useBean id="name" class="NameHandler" scope="session"/>

<html>
<head>
  <title>hello</title>
</head>
<body bgcolor="white">
Hello, my name is

<jsp:getProperty name="name" property="username"/>
<br>

No, wait...

<jsp:setProperty name="name" property="username" value="Robert"/>

,  It's really <%= name.getUsername() %>.

</body>
</html>
```

Notice that the `jsp:setProperty` does the same as the `<%= beanName.property
= value %>` expression and the `jsp:getProperty` is the same as the `<%=
beanName.property %>` expression.

To use the JSP page in Listing 12.11, place the `name.jsp` file in the context's
root directory (`%TOMCAT_HOME%\webapps\jython`), and then point your browser
to `http://localhost:8080/jython/name.jsp`. You should see the default name
Fred and the revised name Robert.

Embedding a *PythonInterpreter* in JSP

If you did wish to use Jython code within a JSP scriptlet, you could indirectly do so with a `PythonInterpreter` instance. This would require that you use an import directive to import `org.python.util.Pythoninterpreter`. Listing 12.12 shows a simple JSP page that uses the `PythonInterpreter` object to include Jython code in JSP pages.

Listing 12.12 **Embedding a *PythonInterpreter* in a JSP Page**

```
<!--name: interp.jsp-->
<%@ page contentType="text/html" %>
<%@ page import="org.python.util.PythonInterpreter" %>

<% PythonInterpreter interp = new PythonInterpreter();
    interp.set("out, out); %>


<html>
<body bgcolor="white">
<% interp.exec("out.printIn('Hello from JSP and the Jython interpreter.')"); %>
</body>
</html>
```

To use the `interp.jsp` file, make sure that the `jython.jar` file is in the context's `lib` directory, and place the `interp.jsp` file in the context's root directory (`%TOMCAT_HOME%\webapps\jython`). If you then point your browser at `http://localhost:8080/jython/interp.jsp` you should see the simple message from the Jython interpreter.

Note that many consider scriptlets poor practice anyway, so adding another level of complexity by using Jython from Java in scriptlets is obviously suspect. There are better ways to create dynamic content, such as bean classes and taglibs.

A Jython Taglib

Taglibs are custom tag libraries that you can use within JSP pages. You can create taglibs in Jython by using `jythonc` to compile Jython taglib modules into Java classes. A Jython taglib module must then comply with certain restrictions before it transparently acts as a Java class. The module must contain a class with the same name as the module (without the `.py` extension). The class must subclass the `javax.servlet.jsp.tagext.Tag` interface or a Java class that implements this interface. The `org.python.*` packages and classes, and Jython library modules (if the taglib imports any) must be accessible to the compiled class file.

To make all the required classes and libraries available to a taglib, you can compile it with jythonc's `--all` option much like was done with jythonc-compiled Servlets earlier in this chapter. Doing so would create a jar file that you would then place in the context's `lib` directory. The problem is that it is very likely that numerous resources will use the Jython core files, so repeatedly compiling with `--core`, `--deep`, or `--all` creates wasteful redundancy. The better plan is to include the `jython.jar` file in the context's `lib` directory, establish a Jython `lib` directory for Jython's modules somewhere in the context (`{context}\WEB-INF\lib\Lib` is recommended—see the earlier section "PyServlet" for an explanation), and then compile the Jython taglib modules without dependencies.

Listing 12.13 is a simple Jython taglib module that serves as the specimen used to dissect taglibs. All Listing 12.13 does is add a message, but it implements all the essential parts of a taglib. The basic requirements implemented in Listing 12.13 are as follows:

- The name of the file in Listing 12.13 is the same as the class it contains.
- The class implements (subclasses) the `javax.servlet.jsp.tagext.Tag` interface. Other options for the superclass (interfaces) include the `BodyTag` and `IterationTag` interfaces, and the `TagSupport` or `BodyTagSupport` classes from the `javax.servlet.jsp.tagext` package.
- The `JythonTag` class implements all the methods required to complete the `Tag` interface.

Listing 12.13 **A Jython Taglib**

```
# file: JythonTag.py
from javax.servlet.jsp import tagext

class JythonTag(tagext.Tag):
    def __init__(self):
        self.context = None
        self.paren = None

    def doStartTag(self):
        return tagext.Tag.SKIP_BODY

    def doEndTag(self):
        out = self.context.out
        print >>out, "Message from a taglib"
        return tagext.Tag.EVAL_PAGE

    def release(self):
        pass
```

continues

Listing 12.13 **Continued**

```
def setPageContext(self, context):
    self.context = context

def setParent(self, parent):
    self.paren = parent

def getParent(self):
    return self.paren
```

The instance variables holding the `pageContext` and parent tag information
(`self.context` and `self.paren`) deserve a special warning. These variables
either must not be identified as `self.pageContext` and `self.parent`, or all
access to these variables must go through the instance's `__dict__`. The Tag
interface requires that implementations of the `setPageContext()`, `setParent()`,
and `getParent()` methods, but because these methods exist, Jython creates an
automatic bean property for their associated property names. This makes circular references and `StackOverflowExceptions` easy to make. Imagine the following code:

```
def setPageContext(self, context):
    self.context = context
```

The `setPageContext` method assigns the context to the instance attribute
`self.context`. However, `self.context` is an automatic bean property, meaning
that `self.context` really calls `self.setPageContext(context)`. This type of circular reference is always a concern when using `jythonc`-compiled classes in
Java frameworks, but it is the explicit requirement of `get*` and `set*` methods
due to the interface that increases the likelihood here.

To install the classes required for the taglib in Listing 12.13, first ensure the
`jython.jar` file is in the context's `lib` directory, then compile the `JythonTag.py`
file with the following command:

```
jythonc -w %TOMCAT_HOME%\webapps\jython\WEB-INF\classes JythonTag.py
```

This will create the `JythonTag.class` and `JythonTag$_PyInner.class` files in
the context's classes directory. The classes themselves are insufficient to use the
taglib, however. You must also create a taglib library description file before
using the tag in a JSP page. Listing 12.14 is a taglib library description file
appropriate for describing the tag defined in Listing 12.13.

Listing 12.14 **Tag Library Descriptor**

```
<?xml version="1.0" encoding="ISO-8859-1" ?>
<!DOCTYPE taglib
  PUBLIC "-//Sun Microsystems, Inc.//DTD JSP Tag Library 1.2//EN"
  "http://java.sun.com/dtd/web-jsptaglibrary_1_2.dtd">

<taglib>
    <tlibversion>1.0</tlibversion>
    <jspversion>1.1</jspversion>
    <shortname>JythonTag</shortname>
    <info>A simple Jython tag library</info>
    <tag>
        <name>message</name>
        <tagclass>JythonTag</tagclass>
    </tag>
</taglib>
```

Place the tag library descriptor information from Listing 12.14 in the file
`%TOMCAT_HOME%\webapps\jython\WEB-XML\jython-taglibs.tld`. JSP pages will
use this file to identify tags used within the page.

The tag library descriptor identifies characteristics of the tag library such as
its version number, and the version of JSP it is designed for. It also specifies a
name `<shortname>` for referencing this tag library. The remaining elements
define the one specific tag library created in listing 12.13. The tag element
identifies the fully qualified class name and assigns a name to that class. The
`JythonTag` is not in a package, so it is a fully qualified name on its own, and
this class is associated with the name *taglet*.

With `JythonTag` compiled and the tag library descriptor saved, that remaining step is to use the tag library from a JSP page. A JSP page must include a
directive that designates the path to the tag library descriptor and assigns a
simple name that library. All subsequent references to tags within this library
will begin with the name assigned in this directive. A JSP directive for the tag
library created in Listings 12.13 and 12.14 would look like the following:

```
<%@ taglib uri="/WEB-INF/jython-taglibs.tld" prefix="jython" %>
```

Remember that the `.tld` file specified the name *message* for our example tag,
so after declaring this tag library, you may subsequently use the message tag
with the following:

```
<jython:message/>
```

The `jython` portion of the tag comes from the name assigned in the JSP declaration, while the `message` portion comes from a tag class's assigned name as
specified in the tag library description. Listing 12.15 is a JSP file that uses the
tag defined in Listing 12.13 and the taglib descriptor in Listing 12.14. Save the

test.jsp file in Listing 12.14 as %TOMCAT_HOME%\webapps\jython\test.jsp, then point your browser to http://localhost:8080/jython/test.jsp, and you should see the custom tag message.

Listing 12.15   **A JSP File that Employs the *JythonTag***

```
<%@ taglib uri="/WEB-INF/jython-taglibs.tld" prefix="jython" %>
<html>
<body>

<jython:message />

</body>
</html>
```

Implementing taglibs with compiled jython modules again raises issues with Jython's home directory and Jython's lib directory. A jythonc-compiled taglib will not know where python.home is or where to find library modules unless that information is established in the PySystemState. You can set the python.home property in the TOMCAT_OPTS environment variable, but you could also leverage the PyServlet class to establish this system state information. If the context you are in loads the PyServlet class, then the python.home and sys.path information may already be correct for the taglibs that need it. With the default PyServlet settings, python.home is %TOMCAT_HOME%\webapps\jython\WEB-INF\lib, and therefore Jython's lib directory is %TOMCAT_HOME%\webapps\jython\WEB-INF\lib\Lib. With PyServlet loaded, taglibs may load Jython modules from the same lib directory.

BSF

IBM's *Bean Scripting Framework (BSF)* is a Java tool that implements various scripting languages. Jython is one of the languages that BSF currently supports. The Apache Jakarta project includes a subproject called taglibs, which is an extensive collection of Java tag libraries ready for use; however, the interesting taglib is the BSF tag library. The BSF tag library combined with the BSF jar file itself allows you to quickly insert Jython scriptlets and expression directly into JSP pages.

The BSF distribution currently requires a few tweaks to work with Jython. Because the BSF distribution will eventually include these small changes, there is no advantage to detailing them here; however, this does mean you need to confirm your version of BSF includes these changes. To make this easy, the website associated with this book (http://www.newriders.com/) will include a link to where you can download the correct `bsf.jar` file. After downloading the `bsf.jar` file, place it in the context's `lib` directory (`%TOMCAT_HOME%\webapps\jython\WEB-INF\lib`). The website associated with this book will also contain download links for the BSF taglibs and `bsf.tld` files. Place the `jar` file containing the BSF taglibs in the context's `lib` directory, and place the `bsf.tld` file in the context's `WEB-INF` directory (`%TOMCAT_HOME%\webapps\jython\WEB-INF\bsf.tld`).

With these files installed, you can use Jython scriptlets within JSP files. You first must include a directive to identify the BSF taglib:

```
<%@ taglib uri="/WEB-INF/bsf.tld" prefix="bsf" %>
```

Then you can use the `bsf.scriptlet` tag, including Jython code in the tag body like so:

```
<bsf.scriptlet language="jython">
import random
print >>, out random.randint(1, 100)
</bsf.scriptlet>
```

The scriptlet has a number of JSP objects automatically set in the interpreter, and these objects are listed below with their Java class names:

- `request`   `javax.servlet.http.HttpServletRequest`
- `response`   `javax.servlet.http.HttpServletResponse`
- `pageContext`   `javax.servlet.jsp.PageContext`
- `application`   `javax.servlet.ServletContext`
- `out`   `javax.servlet.jsp.JspWriter`
- `config`   `javax.servlet.ServletConfig`
- `page`   `java.lang.Object`
- `exception`   `java.lang.Exception`
- `session`   `javax.servlet.http.HttpSession`

Most of the objects are familiar from Servlets, but the BSF scriptlet tag lets you use them within JSP pages. Listing 12.16 shows a JSP page that uses the `bsf:scriptlet` tag to create a timestamp in a JSP file.

Listing 12.16   **BSF Scriptlet**

```
<%@ taglib uri="/WEB-INF/bsf.tld" prefix="bsf" %>
<html>
<body>

<center><H2>BSF scriptlets</H2></center>
```

continues

Listing 12.16 **Continued**

```
<b>client info:</b><br>

<bsf:scriptlet language="jython">
for x in request.headerNames:
    print >>out, "%s:  %s<br>\n" % (x, request.getHeader(x))
</bsf:scriptlet>

<br><br>
<b>Time of request:</b><br>

<bsf:scriptlet language="jython">
import time
print >>out, time.ctime(time.time())
</bsf:scriptlet>

</body>
</html>
```

After saving Listing 12.16 as the file %TOMCAT_HOME%\webapps\jython\ scriptlets.jsp, point your browser to http://localhost:8080/jython/ scriptlets.jsp. You should see all the client information as well as the access time.

IV

Appendix

A

Jython Statements and Built-In Functions Quick Reference

Tᴴɪꜱ ᴀᴘᴘᴇɴᴅɪx ɪɴᴄʟᴜᴅᴇꜱ ᴛᴡᴏ ᴀʟᴘʜᴀʙᴇᴛɪᴄᴀʟʟʏ sorted, quick-reference tables. Table A.1 shows built-in functions, and Table A.2 shows Jython statements.

Table A.1   **Built-In Functions Quick Reference**

Function	Description
abs	Returns the absolute value of the number x. **Syntax:** `abs(number)` **Example:** `>>> abs(-5.43)` `5.43`
apply	Calls an object, the object supplied as the first argument to the apply function. This can be a function, class, or any callable object. If the optional second argument is supplied, it must be a `tuple` and is used as ordered arguments when the object is called. The optional third argument can be a `Pydictionary` or `PyStringMap` and is used as keyword arguments when the object is called.

continues

Table A.1 **Continued**

Function	Description

Syntax:

```
apply(object[, args[, kwargs]])
```

Example:

```
>>> def printKWArgs(**kw):
...     print kw
...
>>> apply(printKWArgs, (), globals())
{'__name__': '__main__', 'printKWArgs': <function
printKWArgs at 2744202>, '__doc__': None}
>>>
>>> def product(x, y):
...     return x * y
...
>>> print apply(product, (3, 4))
12
```

callable — Returns 1 or 0 (true or false) as to whether the object in question is a callable type.

Syntax:

```
callable(object)
```

Example:

```
>>> def myFunction():
...     return
...
>>> callable(myFunction)
1
>>> callable("a string")
0
```

chr — For integers <= 65535, chr returns the character (PyString of length 1) that has the specified integer value.

Syntax:

```
chr(integer)
```

Example:

```
>>> chr(119)
'w'
>>> chr(88)
'X'
>>> chr(50000)
u'\uC350'
```

Function	Description
cmp	Requires two parameter and returns a value of -1, 0, or 1 is returned based on whether x<y, x==y, or x>y, respectively.

cmp

Syntax:

```
cmp(x, y)
```

Example:

```
>>> cmp(1, 3)
-1
>>> cmp(3, 1)
1
>>> cmp(3, 3)
0
```

coerce

Accepts two objects as parameters, tests if there is a common type that can represent the values of each object. The two values are returned in a **tuple** of same-type objects if there is a common type. If not, coerce raises a **TypeError**.

Syntax:

```
coerce(x, y)
```

Example:

```
>>> coerce(3.1415, 6) # float and int
(3.1415, 6.0)
>>>results = coerce("a", 2.3)
Traceback (most recent call last):
  File "<stdin>", line 1, in ?
TypeError: number coercion failed
```

compile

Compiles a string to a code object. The first parameter is the source string. The second must be a string usually representing the filename. This second argument is used only to make a more descriptive error message so can be any arbitrary string without affecting functionality. The third argument is the mode of compilation, which must be one of three modes:

exec for modules or larger code strings
single for a single statement
eval for an expression

The returned code object can be executed with the **exec** or **eval** statement.

Table A.1 **Continued**

Function	Description
	Syntax:
	```compile(source, filename, mode)```
	Example:

	```>>> co = compile("0 and 'This' or 1 and 'that'", "-", "eval")```
	```>>> exec(co)```
	```>>> eval(co)```
	```'that'```
	```>>> co = compile("for x in range(10):\n\tprint x,", "<console>", "single")```
	```>>> exec(co)```
	```0 1 2 3 4 5 6 7 8 9```

complex	Returns a complex number where the real and imaginary parts are created from the two arguments supplied to the function. The complex portion (second argument) is optional, and 0 is used when this argument is not supplied.
	Syntax:
	```complex(real[, imag])```
	Example:

	```>>> complex(2) # int to complex```
	```(2+0j)```
	```>>> complex(3.1, 0.123) # floats to complex```
	```(3.1+0.123j)```
	```>>> complex("2.1", "0.1234")```
	```(2.1000000000000001+0j)```

delattr	Deletes a specified attribute from an object.
	Syntax:
	```delattr(object, name)```
	Example:

	```>>> class cache:```
	```... pass # empty class to store arbitrary objects```
	```...```
	```>>> c = cache()```
	```>>> c.a = 1```
	```>>> c.b = 2```
	```>>> vars(c)```
	```{'a': 1, 'b': 2}```
	```>>> delattr(c, "a")```
	```>>> vars(c)```
	```{'b': 2}```

Function	Description
dir	If an object is specified, `dir` returns a list of names defined in that object. If no object is specified, it returns names defined in the current scope.

Syntax:

```
dir([object])
```

Example:

```
>>> a = 1
>>> b = "a string"
>>> def aFunction():
...     return
...
>>> dir()
['__doc__', '__name__', 'a', 'aFunction', 'b', 'file']
>>> dir(aFunction)
['__dict__', '__doc__', '__name__', 'func_closure',
'func_code', 'func_defaults', 'func_doc',
'func_globals', 'func_name']
```

divmod	Returns both the integer division and modulus of x divided by y as a `tuple`.

Syntax:

```
divmod(x, y)
```

Example:

```
>>> divmod(9,4)
(2, 1)
>>> divmod(7, 2)
(3, 1)
```

eval	Evaluates a string of code, or a code object created with `compile`. If namespaces are not specified, the current namespaces are used. If only the `globals` namespace is supplied, it serves `locals` as well. Namespaces can be PyDictionaries or PyStringMap.

Syntax:

```
eval(source[, globals[, locals]])
```

continues

Table A.1   **Continued**

Function	Description
	Example:

```
>>> eval("x>3 and x or 0", {'x':4})
4
>>> eval("x>3 and x or 0", {'x':2})
0
>>> co = compile("map(lambda x: divmod(x,3), L)",
"console", "eval")
>>> eval(co, {'L':range(15)})
[(0, 0), (0, 1), (0, 2), (1, 0), (1, 1), (1, 2), (2,
0), (2, 1), (2, 2), (3, 0), (3, 1), (3, 2), (4, 0),
(4, 1), (4, 2)]
```

Function	Description
execfile	Executes a file containing Jython code in the specified namespaces. If namespaces are not specified, the current namespaces are used. If only the `globals` namespace is supplied, it serves `locals` as well. Namespaces can be PyDictionaries or PyStringMap.

Syntax:

```
execfile(filename[, globals[, locals]])
```

Example:

```
>>> # first use an anonymous dictionary for globals
>>> execfile("c:\\windows\\desktop\\testfile.py", {})
a b 7
>>> globals()
{'__name__': '__main__', '__doc__': None}
>>>
>>> # Now use current namespaces
>>> execfile("c:\\windows\\desktop\\testfile.py")
a b 7
>>> globals()
{'var2': 'b', 'var1': 'a', '__doc__': None, 'var3': 7,
'__name__': '__main__'}
```

Function	Description
filter	The `filter` function requires a function and a sequence as arguments and returns a list of those members of the argument sequence for which the function evaluates to true. The function can be None. In that case, `filter` returns a list of those members of the argument sequence that evaluate to true.

Syntax:

```
filter(function, sequence)
```

Function	Description

Example:

```
>>> filter(lambda x: x%2, [1,2,3,4,5,6,7,8,9])
[1, 3, 5, 7, 9]
>>> filter(None, [1, 0, [], 3-3, {}, 7])
[1, 7]
```

float   Returns the first argument, converted to a float (PyFloat type) when possible.

Syntax:

```
float(x)
```

Example:

```
>>> float(2)  # int to float
2.0
>>> float(7L)  # long to float
7.0
>>> float(abs(1.1+2.1j))
2.37065391822259396
>>> float("2.1")  # string to float
2.1
```

getattr   Returns a reference to the specified object attribute. The two arguments required are the object and the attribute name as a string. An optional third argument is the default value to return if the object does not contain the specified attribute. In the case where the object lacks the desired attribute, and the optional third parameter is absent, an AttributeError is raised.

Syntax:

```
getattr(object, name[, default])
```

Example:

```
>>> from time import time
>>> class util:
...     def __init__(self):
...         self.inittime = time()
...
>>> u = util()
>>> getattr(u, "inittime")
9.8829678293E8
>>> getattr(u, "currenttime", time())
9.8829681275E8
```

continues

Table A.1   **Continued**

Function	Description
globals	Returns a dictionary-like object representing the variables defined in the globals namespace.

Syntax:

```
globals()
```

Example:

```
>>> num = 1
>>> string = "a String"
>>> globals()
{'num': 1, '__name__': '__main__', '__doc__': None,
'string': 'a String'}
```

| hasattr | Tests whether an object has a specified attribute and returns 1 or 0 accordingly. |

Syntax:

```
hasattr(object, name)
```

Example:

```
>>> class add:
...     def __init__(self):
...         pass
...     def methodA(self):
...         pass
...
>>> hasattr(add, "methodA")
1
>>> hasattr(add, "methodB")
0
```

| hash | Returns an integer that is the specified object's hash value. |

Syntax:

```
hash(object)
```

Example:

```
>>> a = 1
>>> hash(1)
1
>>> hash(a)
1
>>> c = "dog"
>>> hash(c)
1528775661
```

Function	Description

hex	Returns the hexadecimal representation of an integer as a string.
	
	Syntax:
	
	`hex(number)`
	
	Example:
	
	```\n>>> hex(16)\n'0x10'\n>>> hex(15)\n'0xf'\n```

id	Returns an integer representing the unique identification of the specified object.
	
	Syntax:
	
	`id(object)`
	
	Example:
	
	```\n>>> string = "A"\n>>> id("A")\n6262933\n```

input	The function `input` is the same as `raw_input` except that what is entered at the prompt is evaluated.
	
	Syntax:
	
	`input([prompt])`
	
	Example:
	
	```\n>>> input("Enter a Jython expression: ")\nEnter a Jython expression: 2+3\n5 <— the evaluated result of 2+3\n```

int	Returns the first argument, converted to an integer (`PyInteger` type) when possible. The optional second parameter is the base used while converting (16 for hex, 8 for octal) and applies only when converting strings. Converting from a complex number to an `int` is only possible using the absolute value of the complex number (`abs()`). Floating-point values are truncated, not rounded. **Syntax:** `int(x[, base])`

continues

Table A.1   **Continued**

Function	Description
	Example:
| | ```
>>> int(3.5)  # float to int
3
>>> int(5L)  # long to int
5
>>> int(abs(2.2+1.72j))  # complex to int
2
>>> int("012", 8)  # octal string to int
10
>>> int("0x1A", 16)  # hex string to int
26
``` |
| intern | This places the specified string in a **PyStringMap** of long-lived strings and returns the interned string object itself. |
| | **Syntax:** |
| | ```
intern(string)
``` |
| | **Example:** |
| | ```
>>> string1 = "a"
>>> Istring1 = intern(string1)
>>> id(string1), id(Istring1)
(7347538, 7347538)
``` |
| isinstance | Returns 1 or 0 (true or false) according to whether the instance is in fact an instance of the supplied class. |
| | **Syntax:** |
| | ```
isinstance(instance, class).
``` |
| | **Example:** |
| | ```
>>> import java
>>> hm = java.util.HashMap()
>>> isinstance(hm, java.util.HashMap)
1
>>> isinstance(hm, java.util.AbstractMap)
1
>>> isinstance(hm, java.util.Vector)
0
``` |
| len | Returns the length of a sequence or mapping type. |
| | **Syntax:** |
| | ```
len(object)
``` |

Function	Description
	Example:

```
>>> len("a string")
8
>>> len([1,2,3,4,5])
5
>>> len(range(0,100,7))
15
```

list	Accepts one argument that must be a sequence and returns a list with the same members as those in the argument.

Syntax:

```
list(sequence)
```

Example:

```
>>> list("abcdefg")
['a', 'b', 'c', 'd', 'e', 'f', 'g']
>>> list(("a", "b", "c", "d", "e", "f", "g"))
['a', 'b', 'c', 'd', 'e', 'f', 'g']
```

locals	Returns a PyStringMap containing variables defined in the locals namespace.

Syntax:

```
locals()
```

Example:

```
>>> def aFunction():
...     aVariable = "String var"
...     print locals()
...
>>> aFunction()
{'aVariable': 'String var'}
```

long	Returns the first argument, converted to a long integer (PyLong type) when possible. The optional second parameter is the base used while converting (16 for hex, 8 for octal) and applies only when converting strings. Converting from a complex number to a long is only possible using the absolute value of the complex number (abs()). Floating-point numbers are truncated, not rounded.

Syntax:

```
long(x, base)
```

continues

Table A.1 **Continued**

Function	**Description**

Example:

```
>>> long(2.7)  # float to long
2L
>>> long(abs(1.1+2.3j))  # complex to long
2L
>>> long("021", 8)  # octal string to long
17L
>>> long("0xff", 16)  # hex string to long
255L
```

map

The map function requires a function and one or more sequences as arguments. The function is called for each member of the sequence(s) with a number of parameters equal to the number of sequences supplied. If there are sequences of differing lengths, iterations continue until the largest sequence is exhausted, while shorter sequences are padded with None. What is returned is a list containing the results of each call to the function. The function can be None, and in that case, the returned list is the accumulated arguments generated from iteration through the sequence(s).

Syntax:

```
map(function, sequence[, sequence, ...])
```

Example:

```
>>> map(None, range(6), ["a", "b", "c"])
[(0, 'a'), (1, 'b'), (2, 'c'), (3, None), (4, None),
(5, None)]
>>> def pad(string):
...     return string.rjust(10)
...
>>> map(pad, ["a", "b", "c", "d"])
['         a', '         b', '         c', '
d']
```

max

Returns the largest member of specified sequence. The argument must be a sequence.

Syntax:

```
max(sequence)
```

Function	**Description**
	Example:
| | ```
>>> max(1,2,3,4,5,6,7,8,9)
9
>>> T = ("strings", "are", "compared",
"lexigraphically")
>>> max(T)
'strings'
``` |
| min | Returns the smallest member of the specified sequence. The argument must be a sequence. |
| | **Syntax:** |
| | ```
min(sequence)
``` |
| | **Example:** |
| | ```
>>> min(1,2,3,4,5)
1
>>> T = "min returns the smallest char of a string"
>>> min(T)
' '
``` |
| oct | Returns the octal representation of an integer as a string. |
| | **Syntax:** |
| | ```
oct(number)
``` |
| | **Example:** |
| | ```
>>> oct(8)
'010'
>>> oct(7)
'07'
``` |
| open | Requires a platform-specific file path and name, then opens this designated file and returns the associated file object. The optional mode parameter specifies whether the file is to be opened for reading, writing, appending, or a combination of those. The mode also specifies if the file is binary. Jython requires binary mode be specified to read and write binary data—this is different from CPython. If no mode argument is provided, non-binary, read mode is assumed. Possible values for mode are as follows:

r = reading

w = writing

a = appending |

continues
```

Table A.1 **Continued**

Function	Description
	+ = Appended to r, w, or a to designate reading plus writing, or reading plus appending.
	b = binary mode.
	The optional third parameter to the open function designates buffering. the third parameter is currently ignored in Jython.
	Syntax:
	`open(filename[, mode[, buffering]])`
	Example:
	``` >>> # open file in current directory for reading >>> # plus writing. >>> fo = open("config.cfg", "r+") >>> >>> # Open file for binary reading >>> fo = open("c:\soot\baf\Baf.class", "rb") ```
ord	Returns the integer value of a character. This function is the opposite of chr(integer). For character c, chr(ord(c))==c.
	Syntax:
	`ord(character)`
	Example:
	``` >>> ord('w') 119 >>> ord('X') 88 >>> ord(u'\uC350') 50000 ```
pow	Returns x**y. If z is provided, it returns x**y % z.
	Syntax:
	`pow(x, y[, z])`
	Example:
	``` >>> pow(3, 3) 27 >>> pow(3, 3, 2) 1 ```

Function	Description
range	Returns a list of integers built based on the start, stop, and step parameters. All arguments must be integers (PyInteger or PyLong). Counting starts at the designated start number, or 0. Counting continues to, but not including, the designated stop integer. If the optional step argument is provided, it is used as the increment number.

Syntax:

```
range([start,] stop [, step])
```

Example:

```
>>> range(4)
[0, 1, 2, 3]
>>> range(3, 6)
[3, 4, 5]
>>> range(2, 10, 2)
[2, 4, 6, 8]
```

raw_input	Reads a string from standard input with the trailing newline removed.

Syntax:

```
raw_input([prompt])
```

Example:

```
>>> name = raw_input("Enter your name: ")
Enter your name: Bilbo Baggins
>>> print name
Bilbo Baggins
```

reduce	Reduces a list of values to one value. The two required arguments are a function and a sequence. The third, optional argument is an initial value. The function provided must have two parameters. The reduction happens by applying the function to the first two sequence members, or the initial value and first sequence member if an initial value is supplied. The function is next applied to the results of this first operation and the next sequence member. This cycle continues until the sequence is exhausted and a single value is returned.

continues

Table A.1 **Continued**

Function	Description
	Syntax: reduce(function, sequence[, initial]) **Example:** ```\n>>> def add(x, y):\n... return x + y\n...\n>>> reduce(add, [5,4,3,2,1])\n15\n>>> def stripspaces(x, y):\n... return x.strip() + y.strip()\n...\n>>> reduce(stripspaces, "A string with spaces")\n'Astringwithspaces'\n```
reload	Reloads a specified module. **Syntax:** reload(module) **Example:** ```\n>>> import math\n>>> # If the math module changed- reload it.\n>>> reload(math)\n<jclass org.python.modules.math at 1401745>\n```
repr	Returns a string that represents the specified object. **Syntax:** repr(object) **Example:** ```\n>>> repr(123)\n'123'\n>>> repr(type)\n'<java function type at 4737674>'\n>>> repr("A string")\n"'A string'"\n```
round	Returns a floating-point number representing the numeric argument. If the optional argument for the number of significant digits to round to is absent, the number is rounded to 0 decimal places. Otherwise, the number is rounded to the specified number of significant digits from the decimal point. Negative ndigits numbers mean left of the decimal,

Function	Description

Description

positive means right of the decimal. The `ndigits` argument must be an integral number in Jython, which slightly differs from CPython's acceptance of anything convertible to an integer.

Syntax:

```
round(number[, ndigits])
```

Example:

```
>>> round(1.23434, 3L)
1.234
>>> round(23.2124)
23.0
>>> round(2)
2.0
```

setattr

Sets an object's attribute to a value. The three required arguments are the object, the attribute name as a string, and the value. In Jython, you can set arbitrary attributes on Jython objects, but not on Java objects. This means using `setattr` to set a previously absent attribute works for Jython objects, but a `TypeError` is raised for Java objects.

Syntax:

```
setattr(object, name, value)
```

Example:

```
>>> class split:
...     def __init__(self, token):
...         self.token = token
...
>>> s = split(":")
>>> vars(s)
{'token': ':'}
>>> setattr(s, 'count', 0)
>>> setattr(s, 'token', ",")
>>> vars(s)
{'token': ',', 'count': 0}
>>>
>>> # Java objects are different for
arbitraryattributes>>>
 # Note that javax.midi is an optional package- you
may need to download it
>>> # for this example to work.
>>> from javax.sound.midi import VoiceStatus
>>> v = VoiceStatus()
>>> v.channel
```

continues

Table A.1   **Continued**

Function	Description
| | ```
0
>>> setattr(v, "channel", 3)
>>> v.channel  # "channel" already exists- this works
3
>>> v.channel
3
>>> v.arbitraryVar = 6  # "arbitraryVar doesn't exist
Traceback (innermost last):
  File "<console>", line 1, in ?
TypeError: can't set arbitrary attribute in java
instance: arbitraryVar
``` |
| slice | The slice function is a synonym for sequence slice syntax. The slice object returned from this function can replace traditional slice notation. |

Syntax:

```
slice([start,] stop[, step])
```

Example:

```
>>> L = ["s", "o", "r", "c", "q", "a", "p", "j"]
>>> sliceobj = slice(7, 0, -2)
>>> L[sliceobj]
['j', 'a', 'c', 'o']
```

Function	Description
str	Returns a string representation of an object.

Syntax:

```
str(object)
```

Example:

```
>>> str(1)  # int to string
'1'
>>> str(4L)  # long to string
'4'
>>> str(2.2+1.3j)
'(2.2+1.3j)'
>>> from java.util import Vector
>>> str(Vector)
'java.util.Vector'
>>> v = Vector()
>>> str(v)
'[]'
>>> v.add(type)  # put a function in the vector
1
```
```

Function	Description
	`>>> str(v)` `'[<java function type at 5229978>]'`

tuple	Accepts one argument that must be a sequence and returns a `tuple` with the same members as those in the argument.
	
	Syntax:
	
	`tuple(sequence)`
	
	Example:
	
	`>>> tuple([1,2,3,4,5])  # list to tuple`
	`(1, 2, 3, 4, 5)`
	`>>> tuple("This is a test")  # string to tuple`
	`('T', 'h', 'i', 's', ' ', 'i', 's', ' ', 'a', ' ',`
	`'t', 'e', 's', 't')`

type	Returns an object's type—usually the name of the class in the `org.python.core` package that represents objects of that type.
	
	Syntax:
	
	`type(object)`
	
	Example:
	
	`>>> type("a string")`
	`<jclass org.python.core.PyString at 1923370>`

unichr	This does the same as `chr`. These two methods, `chr` and `unichr`, exist for compatibility with CPython. **Syntax:** `unichr(i)` **Example:** *See* `chr`
unicode	This creates a new `PyString` object using the specified encoding. Available encodings reside in Jython's Lib directory within the encodings folder. The optional `errors` argument can be either `strict`, `ignore`, or `replace`. **Syntax:** `unicode(string [, encoding[, errors]])`

continues

Table A.1   **Continued**

Function	Description
	Example:

```
>>> unicode("Abél", "utf_8", "replace")
u'Ab\uFFFDl'
```

Function	Description
vars	If an object is specified, vars returns a dictionary of names bound within that object. The object must have an internal __dict__ attribute. If no object is specified, vars does the same as locals().

Syntax:

```
vars([object])
```

Example:

```
>>> class aClass:
...     def __init__(self):
...         attrib1 = "An instance variable"
...         attrib2 = "Another instance variable"
...
>>> vars(aClass)
{'__init__': <function __init__ at 634037>,
'__module__': '__main__', '__doc__': None}
>>> vars()
{'aClass': <class __main__.aClass at 7033304>,
'__name__': '__main__', '__doc__': None}
```

Function	Description
xrange	The xrange function does the same as the range function. The difference is that the xrange function returns an xrange object that generates numbers when needed as opposed to generating the entire list at once. This is beneficial for extremely large ranges.

Syntax:

```
xrange([start,] stop [, step])
```

Example:

See range

Function	Description
zip	Returns a list of tuples of a length equal to the shortest sequence supplied as an argument. The tuples contain all sequence items with the same index, and each tuple has a length equal to the number of sequences supplied.

Syntax:

```
zip(seq1 [, seq2 [...]])
```

Example:

```
>>> zip([1,2,3,4,5,6,7], "abcdefg")
[(1, 'a'), (2, 'b'), (3, 'c'), (4, 'd'), (5, 'e'), (6,
'f'), (7, 'g')]
>>> zip(range(5), range(5,-1,-1))
[(0, 5), (1, 4), (2, 3), (3, 2), (4, 1)]
```

Table A.2 **Jython Statements Quick Reference**

Statement	Description
assert	The assert statement tests whether an expression is true and raises an exception if it is not true. If two expressions are supplied, they are treated as an OR so if either is true, and exception is not raised. Setting __debug__=0, and possibly the -0 command–line switch in future releases, disables asserts.

Syntax:

```
"assert" expression [, expression]
```

Example:

```
>>>a=21
>>>assert a<10
Traceback (innermost last):
  File "<console>", line 1, in ?
AssertionError:
```

break	The break statement terminates execution of an enclosing loop and continues execution after the loop block. This means it does skip the else block if it exists.

Syntax:

```
"break"
```

Example:

```
>>>for x in (1,2,3,4):
...     if x==3:
...            break
...     print x
...
1
2
>>>
```

continues

Table A.2   **Continued**

Statement	Description

class	Designates the start of a class definition.
	
	Syntax:
	
	`"class" name[(base-class-name(s))]:`
	
	Example:
	
	``
	>>>class test: # no base class
	... pass # place holder
	...
	>>>t = test() # Calls class to create an instance
	``

continue	The `continue` statement halts execution of the current loop block and starts the enclosing loop again at its next iteration.
	
	Syntax:
	
	`"continue"`
	
	Example:
	
	``
	>>>for x in (1,2,3,4):
	... if x==3:
	... continue
	... print x
	...
	1
	2
	4
	>>>
	``

def	Designates the start of a function or method definition.
	
	Syntax:
	
	``
	"def" name([parameters]):
	    code-block
	``
	
	Example:
	
	``
	>>> def caseless_srch_n_replace(string, srch, rplc):
	... return string.lower().replace(srch, rplc)
	...
	>>> S = "Some UseLess text"
	>>> caseless_srch_n_replace(S, "useless", "useful")
	'some useful text'
	``

del	The `del` statement removes a variable from the namespace in which del was called.

Statement	Description

	Syntax:
	
	`"del" identifier`
	
	Example:
	
	`>>>a="foo"`
	`>>>print a`
	`foo`
	`>>>del a`
	`>>>print a`
	`Traceback (innermost last):`
	`  File "<console>", line 1, in ?`
	`NameError: a`

exec	Executes a string, open file object, or a code object supplied as the first expression following the `exec` statement. The second and third expressions are optional and represent the `PyDictionary` or `PyStringMapping` objects to use as the global and local namespaces. If only globals is supplied, `locals` defaults to it. If neither namespace is supplied, the current namespaces are used.
	
	Syntax:
	
	`"exec" expression ["in" expression ["," expression]]`
	
	Example:
	
	`>>>exec("print 'The exec method is used to print this'")`
	`The exec method is used to print this`

for	The `for` statement is a `loop` structure that repeats an associated block of code for each member of a sequence or until a break statement occurs. Therefore, the expression provided must evaluate to a sequence. There is an implicit name binding of each sequence value to the variable(s) specified after the `for` statement. Execution of the optional `else` clause occurs after the full sequence has expired (meaning it is not executed if a `break` statement appeared in the `loop` block).
	
	Syntax:
	
	`"for" variable "in" expression":"`
	`    code-block`
	`["else:"]`
	`    code-block`

continues

Table A.2 **Continued**

Statement	Description

Example:

```
>>> for x in (1, 2, 3):
...     print x, "in first code-block"
... else:
...     print "In second code-block"
...
1 in first code-block
2 in first code-block
3 in first code-block
In second code-block
```

global
Explicitly designates that the designated name be referenced from the `globals` namespace instead of `locals`.

Syntax:

```
"global" identifier ["," identifier]*
```

Example:

```
>>> var = 10
>>> def test():
...     global var
...     print var   # try and print the global
identifier 'var'
...     var = 20    # assign to 'var' in local
namespace
...
>>> test()
10
```

if
The `if` statement designates conditionally executed blocks of code. Code blocks can be defined for `if`, `elif`, and `else` statements. Only the first approved code block executes as determined by the trueness of its expressions. The code block executed is the first block whose expression evaluates to true, or the `else` block if all other expressions evaluate to false.

Syntax:

```
"if" expression:
    code-block
"elif" expression:
    code-block
"else":
    code-block
```

Table A.2 **Continued**

Statement	Description

Example:

```
>>>a, b = 0, 1
>>>if a==b:
...     print "variable a equals variable b"
...elif a>b:
...     print "variable a is greater than b"
...else:
...     print "variable a is less than b"
...
variable a is less than b
```

import   Imports the specified Jython package, Jython module, Java package, or Java class. This creates a name binding within the namespace import was called. You can optionally change the name imports are bound to with an **as** modifier.

Syntax:

```
import module-name
```

OR

```
from module-name import names
```

OR

```
import module-name as new-name
```

Example:

```
>>>import sys
>>>from java import util
>>>import os as myOS
>>>from sys import packageManager as pm
```

pass   The "do nothing" statement. This statement is a place-holder.

Syntax:

```
"pass"
```

Example:

```
>>> for x in (1,2,3,4):
...     pass
...
>>>def doNothing():
...     pass
```

continues

Table A.2   **Continued**

Statement	Description
print	Evaluates an expression, converts the result to a string if needed and writes the string to `sys.stdout` or whatever file-like object it is directed to with the >> syntax. A file-like object is one with a `write` method defined.

Syntax:

```
"print" [expression]
```

OR

```
"print >> " fileLikeObject, [expression]
```

Example:

```
>>> print "Hello world"
Hello world
>>> print >> myFile, "Hello world"
>>>
```

Statement	Description
raise	The `raise` statement raises an exception. It precedes three optional expressions that represent exception type, value, and traceback. The type can be the exception class, a string representing the exception class, or an instance of the exception class. The value, or second expression, is a constructor parameter for the exception class. The exception's constructor receives one argument unless the second expression evaluates to a `tuple`; in that case, the `tuple` indexes are separate arguments. If the first expression in the `raise` statement is an instance, the second, or `value` expression must be `None`. The optional third expression must be a traceback object.

Syntax:

```
"raise" [expression [, expression [, traceback]]]
```

Example:

```
>>> raise ValueError, "No value provided"
Traceback (innermost last):
  File "<console>", line 1, in ?
ValueError: no value provided
```

Statement	Description
return	Terminates execution of the method or function it is within, and returns the value of the evaluated expression it prefixes. If there is no expression, `return` returns None.

continues

Statement	Description

	Syntax:
	
	```"return" [expression]```
	
	Example:
	
	```>>> def someFunction():```
	```... return "This string is the return value"```
	```...```
	```>>> print someFunction()```
	```This string is the return value```

try/except	The try/except statement is Jython's exception-handling mechanism, similar to Java's try/catch statement. The try block of code executes until completion or until an error. If there is an error (an exception was raised), control immediately switches to searching for an appropriate except clause to handle the exception. If the try/finally syntax is used, the finally block is executed regardless of any exceptions in the try block.
	
	Syntax:
	
	```"try:" code-block```
	```"except" [expression ["," target]] ":" code-block```
	```["else:" code-block]```
	
	OR
	
	```"try:" code-block```
	```"finally:" code-block```
	
	Example:
	
	```>>> try:```
	```... 1/0```
	```... except ZeroDivisionError, e:```
	```... print "You cannot divide by zero: ", e```
	```...```
	```You cannot divide by zero: integer division or modulo```
	```>>>```
	```>>> try:```
	```... pass```
	```... finally:```
	```... print "This block always executes"```
	```...```
	```This block always executes```

while	The while statement is a loop structure that executes a block of code as long as a provided expression evaluates to true or until a break statement.

Syntax:

```
"while" expression ":"
```

Example:

```
>>> x = 10
>>> while x>0:
...     print x,
...     x -= 1
...
10 9 8 7 6 5 4 3 2 1 >>>
```

Index

Symbols

J

N

O

VOICES THAT MATTER

HOW TO CONTACT US

VISIT OUR WEB SITE

WWW.NEWRIDERS.COM

On our web site, you'll find information about our other books, authors, tables of contents, and book errata. You will also find information about book registration and how to purchase our books, both domestically and internationally.

EMAIL US

Contact us at: **nrfeedback@newriders.com**

- If you have comments or questions about this book
- To report errors that you have found in this book
- If you have a book proposal to submit or are interested in writing for New Riders
- If you are an expert in a computer topic or technology and are interested in being a technical editor who reviews manuscripts for technical accuracy

Contact us at: **nreducation@newriders.com**

- If you are an instructor from an educational institution who wants to preview New Riders books for classroom use. Email should include your name, title, school, department, address, phone number, office days/hours, text in use, and enrollment, along with your request for desk/examination copies and/or additional information.

Contact us at: **nrmedia@newriders.com**

- If you are a member of the media who is interested in reviewing copies of New Riders books. Send your name, mailing address, and email address, along with the name of the publication or web site you work for.

BULK PURCHASES/CORPORATE SALES

If you are interested in buying 10 or more copies of a title or want to set up an account for your company to purchase directly from the publisher at a substantial discount, contact us at 800-382-3419 or email your contact information to corpsales@pearsontechgroup.com. A sales representative will contact you with more information.

WRITE TO US

New Riders Publishing
201 W. 103rd St.
Indianapolis, IN 46290-1097

CALL/FAX US

Toll-free (800) 571-5840
If outside U.S. (317) 581-3500
Ask for New Riders
FAX: (317) 581-4663

New Riders

WWW.NEWRIDERS.COM

RELATED NEW RIDERS TITLES

ISBN: 0735709211
800 pages
US$49.99

MySQL

Paul DuBois

MySQL teaches you how to use the tools provided by the MySQL distribution, by covering installation, setup, daily use, security, optimization, maintenance, and troubleshooting. It also discusses important third-party tools, such as the Perl DBI and Apache/ PHP interfaces that provide access to MySQL.

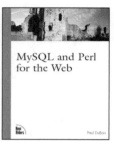

ISBN: 0735710546
500 pages
US$44.99

MySQL and Perl for the Web

Paul Dubois

Paul DuBois does it again with *MySQL and Perl for the Web*. This time, he tells you how to bring your website to life by using the powerful combination of Perl and MySQL.

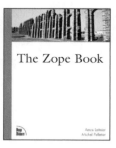

ISBN: 0735711372
400 pages
US$39.99

The Zope Book

Amos Latteier, Michel Pellatier

The much-anticipated first book on Zope from the creators themselves! This book teaches you to efficiently create and manage websites using the leading Open Source web application server.

ISBN: 0735710902
720 pages
US$49.99

Python Web Programming

Steve Holden

If you want to skip the introductory details and dive right into using Python within web-enabled applications, this is the perfect book for you! From page one, you'll begin learning how to harness the power of the Python libraries to build systems with less programming effort.

ISBN: 0735710953
464 pages
US$39.99

JSP and Tag Libraries for Web Development

Wellington Silva

This book, with its explanation of tag library technology and examples of implementation, helps to bring the capabilities of tag libraries to the arsenals of current JSP programmers.

ISBN: 0735710910
416 pages
US$34.99

Python Essential Reference, Second Edition

David Beazley

"This excellent reference concisely covers the Python 2.1 language and libraries. It is a model of what a reference should be: well-produced, tightly written, comprehensive without covering the obsolete or arcane."

—An online reviewer

Solutions from experts you know and trust.

www.informit.com

New Riders has partnered with **InformIT.com** to bring technical information to your desktop. Drawing on New Riders authors and reviewers to provide additional information on topics you're interested in, **InformIT.com** has free, in-depth information you won't find anywhere else.

- **Master the skills you need, when you need them**

- **Call on resources from some of the best minds in the industry**

- **Get answers when you need them, using InformIT's comprehensive library or live experts online**

- **Go above and beyond what you find in New Riders books, extending your knowledge**

As an **InformIT** partner, **New Riders** has shared the wisdom and knowledge of our authors with you online. Visit **InformIT.com** to see what you're missing.

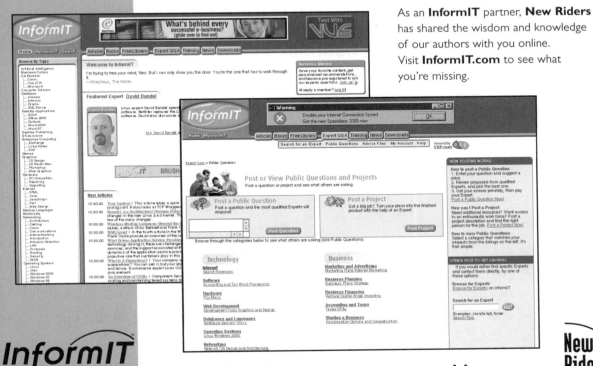

Publishing
the Voices
that Matter

OUR BOOKS

OUR AUTHORS

SUPPORT

| ::: web development | ::: graphics & design | ::: server technology | ::: certification |

NEWS/EVENTS

PRESS ROOM

EDUCATORS

ABOUT US

CONTACT US

WRITE/REVIEW

You already know that New Riders brings you the Voices that Matter.

But what does that mean? It means that New Riders brings you the

Voices that challenge your assumptions, take your talents to the next

level, or simply help you better understand the complex technical world

we're all navigating.

Visit **www.newriders.com** to find:

- ▶ Previously unpublished chapters
- ▶ Sample chapters and excerpts
- ▶ Author bios
- ▶ Contests
- ▶ Up-to-date industry event information
- ▶ Book reviews
- ▶ Special offers
- ▶ Info on how to join our User Group program
- ▶ Inspirational galleries where you can submit
  your own masterpieces
- ▶ Ways to have your Voice heard

New
Riders

WWW.NEWRIDERS.COM

Colophon

The image appearing on the cover of this book is of the Chaco ruins, the home of the Anasa (the "ancient ones") people between the mid-ninth and early twelfth centuries A.D. Located in a remote part of New Mexico, the Chaco ruins are older and larger than the famous cliff dwellings at Mesa Verde. In fact, Chaco Canyon, where the ruins are located, contains the largest collection of prehistoric ruins north of Mexico.

Today the Chaco ruins are set aside by the U.S. Government as Chaco Culture National Historical Park, which is managed by the National Park Service. The canyon may be visited by anyone willing to make a long drive down primitive roads to reach it. The State of New Mexico has proposed paving the road to make access easier, and private entrepreneurs have considered building hotels and other tourist accommodations in the area. Other people have objected that such changes will spoil the wild and remote atmosphere of the canyon. That controversy continues.

This book was written using Microsoft Word, and laid out in QuarkXPress. The fonts used for the body text are Bembo and MCPdigital. It was printed on 50# Husky Offset Smooth paper at R.R. Donnelley & Sons in Crawfordsville, Indiana. Prepress consisted of PostScript computer-to-plate technology (filmless process). The cover was printed at Moore Langen Printing in Terre Haute, Indiana, on 12pt, coated on one side.